W9-BQK-674

THE GREENWOOD COMPANION TO

Shakespeare

THE GREENWOOD COMPANION TO

Shakespeare

A COMPREHENSIVE GUIDE FOR STUDENTS

Volume I

Overviews and the History Plays

EDITED BY
JOSEPH ROSENBLUM

GREENWOOD PRESS
Westport, Connecticut • London

Library of Congress Cataloging-in-Publication Data

The Greenwood companion to Shakespeare : a comprehensive guide for students / edited by Joseph Rosenblum.
     p.   cm.
     Includes bibliographical references and index.
     ISBN 0–313–32779–3 (set : alk. paper)—ISBN 0–313–32780–7 (v. 1 : alk. paper)—
ISBN 0–313–32781–5 (v. 2 : alk. paper)—ISBN 0–313–32782–3 (v. 3 : alk. paper)—
ISBN 0–313–32788–2 (v. 4 : alk. paper) 1. Shakespeare, William, 1564–1616—Criticism and
interpretation—Handbooks, manuals, etc. 2. Shakespeare, William, 1564–1616—Examinations—
Study guides. I. Rosenblum, Joseph.
   PR2976.G739   2005
   822.3'3—dc22   2004028690

British Library Cataloguing in Publication Data is available.

Library of Congress Catalog Card Number: 2004028690
ISBN: 0–313–32779–3 (set)
     0–313–32780–7 (vol. I)
     0–313–32781–5 (vol. II)
     0–313–32782–3 (vol. III)
     0–313–32788–2 (vol. IV)

First published in 2005

Greenwood Press, 88 Post Road West, Westport, CT 06881
An imprint of Greenwood Publishing Group, Inc.
www.greenwood.com

Printed in the United States of America

The paper used in this book complies with the
Permanent Paper Standard issued by the National
Information Standards Organization (Z39.48–1984).

10 9 8 7 6 5 4 3 2 1

To Ida

Thou art the nonpareil

Contents

VOLUME I

OVERVIEWS AND THE HISTORY PLAYS

OVERVIEWS

THE HISTORY PLAYS

VOLUME II

THE COMEDIES

VOLUME III

THE TRAGEDIES

VOLUME IV

THE ROMANCES AND POETRY

THE ROMANCE PLAYS

THE SONNETS

THE LONG POEMS

Alphabetical List of Plays and Poems

The Plays

A Preface for Users

O for a Muse of fire, that would ascend
The brightest heaven of invention!

(*Henry V*, Prologue, 1–2)

In the latter half of the seventeenth century, John Dryden revised William Shakespeare's *Troilus and Cressida*. Explaining why he tampered with the text of the man he had called "divine," Dryden wrote,

> It must be allowed to the present age, that the tongue in general is so much refined since Shakespeare's time, that many of his words, and more of his phrases, are scarce intelligible. And of those which are understood, some are ungrammatical, others coarse; and his whole style is so pestered with figurative expressions, that it is as affected as it is obscure.

The twenty-first-century student of Shakespeare will likely concur with Dryden's judgment. Shakespeare is hard. Even seasoned scholars differ on subjects ranging from the meaning of individual words to the implications of entire plays. No wonder, then, if high school students, undergraduates, and general readers are sometimes puzzled as they read one of Shakespeare's works or watch one of his plays. Literally thousands of studies of Shakespeare are published each year and recorded in the annual *World Shakespeare Bibliography*, which is updated annually and printed in the *Shakespeare Quarterly*, but this thicket of scholarship often renders Shakespeare more forbidding to students rather than less.

Throughout, *The Greenwood Companion to Shakespeare: A Comprehensive Guide for Students* aims to demystify Shakespeare so that students and general readers will be encouraged to appreciate the artistry of the writing and will come to a fuller appreciation of Shakespeare's genius. Students will find here what his works mean, how they came to be, how they make meaning, and how critics and directors have interpreted them over the centuries. No reference work can include all that is known or thought about Shakespeare, but the editor, contributors, and publisher have sought to make this *Companion* the best place to begin a study of this great writer. We hope that you will find the contents both useful and enjoyable.

CONTENT AND ARRANGEMENT

The four-volume *Greenwood Companion to Shakespeare* includes seventy-seven essays offering a guide to the perplexed. All of these essays have been written expressly for this work by dedicated scholars commissioned because of their scholarship and teaching skills.

The first three volumes are devoted to the plays as follows:

- Volume I is divided into two sections: first, a series of essays about Shakespeare's age, his life, the theater of the time, the texts of his work, and the English language of his era—all of which will deepen the reader's understanding of the works; second, essays that focus on the history plays.
- Volume II explores the comedies.
- Volume III presents the tragedies.
- Volume IV begins with essays on the late plays called romances; the remainder of the volume discusses William Shakespeare's poetry, beginning with an overview of the sonnets. Thirty-one essays examine selected individual or paired sonnets, including full texts of each sonnet reviewed. Compared with the rest of Shakespeare's poetry, these sonnets are the most studied and reveal the widest range of subjects and attitudes. The other essays in this volume discuss the long narrative poems: *A Lover's Complaint*—that fascinating envoi to the sonnet cycle—immediately follows the sonnets, as it did when originally published with those poems; then, in chronological order, *Venus and Adonis*, *The Rape of Lucrece*, and *The Phoenix and Turtle*; *The Passionate Pilgrim* (in which two of Shakespeare's sonnets to the mysterious Dark Lady were first printed) has been placed last because most of the poems contained therein are not by Shakespeare.

The essays are arranged chronologically within genre. To further assist readers in finding essays on particular plays or poems, an alphabetical list of the works studied in this *Companion* follows immediately after the table of contents.

Other Features

"A Shakespeare Chronology," preceding the overview essays in volume I, shows when William Shakespeare's works were written and published and provides basic facts about his life. An annotated bibliography accompanies each essay. At the end of volume IV, an appendix offers a selected, annotated list of Web sites about William Shakespeare and his work. Following that list is a selected bibliography. A subject index and an index of key passages concludes the work.

THE ESSAYS

Forty scholars contributed essays to this *Companion*. Their writings add substantially to Shakespeare scholarship. These essays range in length from some 2,500 words for articles on particular sonnets to 26,000 words on *King Lear*. The articles dealing with the plays, subdivided into eleven sections for easy access, provide the following information to readers:

1. A scene-by-scene plot summary to help students understand what is happening on the stage/page.

2. A discussion of the play's publication history and, when relevant, its historical background context.

3. Sources for the play(s), including a discussion of controversies and recent findings.

4. A brief overview of how the play is put together in terms of structure and plotting.

5. The main characters, their actions, and their purposes within the play.

6. Devices and techniques (such as imagery) that Shakespeare used in the plays.

7. Themes and meanings of the play, citing opinions of various scholars.

8. A look at past and current critical discourse on the work to help students understand the issues that have engaged scholarly attention and to show that in many areas there is no single "correct" interpretation of these complex works. Students seeking topics to explore for their own papers may find this section especially helpful.

9. Production history, surveying the play's key theatrical and cinematic representation.

10. An explication of key passages, helping readers to understand sections of the play that are considered to be the most important.

11. An annotated bibliography for further study. This selection of sources will help students choose the most accessible works from the hundreds included in the *World Shakespeare Bibliography* or the dozens listed in bibliographical guides. The books and articles noted here include classic studies but concentrate on recent writing.

The Essays on the Sonnets and Long Poems

The essays in volume IV discuss the poems. Compared with the essays on the plays they are briefer and contain fewer sections. For the sonnets, the essays provide the following key elements:

1. The sonnet itself, from *The Oxford Shakespeare*, edited by W. J. Craig and published in 1914 by Oxford University Press.

2. A prose paraphrase to explain the content of the work under discussion.

3. A discussion that situates the poem within the sonnet cycle.

4. An exploration of devices and techniques, and themes and meanings.

5. A description of the relationship of the sonnet to Shakespeare's other works, particularly the plays.

6. An annotated bibliography.

In the essays on the long poems the reader will also find discussions of publication history and sources (treated in the overview essay on the sonnets for those poems). All of the essays on the long poems conclude with annotated bibliographies.

ISSUES IN THE SHAKESPEARE CANON

One poem that readers will not find in this volume is *A Funeral Elegy*. This 578-line poem was first printed by George Eld and published by Thomas Thorpe in 1612. Eld had printed and Thorpe had published Shakespeare's sonnets three years earlier. According to the title page, *A Funeral Elegy* was the work of "W. S." The identity of this W. S. has inspired some recent controversy. In 1989 Donald W. Foster published *Elegy by W. S.* (Newark: U of Delaware P), in which he discussed the question of attribution without reaching any conclusion. However, in the October 1996 issue of *PMLA* Foster argued that the poem was by Shakespeare. Because Foster had successfully identified the author of the "anonymous" novel *Primary Colors* (1996) as Joe Klein, Foster's view was credible enough for the editors of the revised Riverside edition of Shakespeare's works (Boston: Houghton Mifflin, 1997) to include the *Elegy*; they also included, however, something of a disclaimer by J.J.M. Tobin (pp. 1893–1895). In 2002 Foster recanted, arguing that the most likely author of the *Elegy* was John Ford.

This controversy reflects the unsettled state of the Shakespeare canon, which grows and shrinks. Brian Vickers's *Shakespeare, Co-Author* (Oxford: Oxford UP, 2002) assigns joint responsibility to five of Shakespeare's plays: *Titus Andronicus* (with George Peele), *Timon of Athens* (with Thomas Middleton), *Pericles* (with George Wilkins), and *Henry VIII* and *The Two Noble Kinsmen* (both with John Fletcher). Seeking to expand the canon, Eric Sams has argued that *Edward III* is an early work by Shakespeare (see *"Edward III": An Early Play Restored to the Canon* (New Haven: Yale UP, 1996).

On one point scholars agree: the William Shakespeare who wrote the plays and poems discussed in this companion was the son of John and Mary Shakespeare, was born in Stratford-upon-Avon in 1564, and died there fifty-two years later. Since the nineteenth century, various nonscholars have proposed dozens of alternative authors, including Francis Bacon, Queen Elizabeth, and Edward de Vere, seventeenth Earl of Oxford. Those readers curious about the authorship question may consult Samuel Schoenbaum's *Shakespeare's Lives*, new edition (Oxford: Clarendon P, 1991), section VI, which is aptly titled "Deviations." Arguments about the authorship of Shakespeare's works belong to the realm of abnormal psychology rather than literary criticism.

A Shakespeare Chronology

Note: Titles in **bold** are discussed in this four-volume set. Dates for the plays (e.g., 1593 for **Richard III** and **The Comedy of Errors**) indicate probable year of first performance.

1558   Elizabeth I becomes queen of England.

1564   William Shakespeare born (ca. April 23).

1576   The Theatre (Shoreditch), built by James Burbage, opens. The Theatre is regarded as the first true London playhouse.

1582   Shakespeare marries Anne Hathaway (ca. December 1).

1583   Shakespeare's elder daughter, Susannah, born (ca. May 23).

1585   Shakespeare's fraternal twins, Judith and Hamnet/Hamlet, born (ca. January 31).

1588   Defeat of the Spanish Armada (July 31–August 8).

1589   Shakespeare probably in London, begins writing *1 Henry VI* (published in 1623).

1590–1591   **2, 3 Henry VI** written. The former first published as *The First Part of the Contention betwixt the Two Famous Houses of York and Lancaster* (1594), the latter as *The True Tragedy of Richard Duke of York* (1595).

1592   Robert Greene attacks Shakespeare in *A Groatsworth of Witte*. This is the first printed reference to Shakespeare as dramatist.

1593   *Richard III* (first published in 1597).

   Venus and Adonis published.

   The Comedy of Errors (first published in 1623).

   Shakespeare begins writing his **sonnets**.

1594   *The Rape of Lucrece* published.

   Titus Andronicus (first published in 1594).

   The Taming of the Shrew (first published in 1623).

   The Two Gentlemen of Verona (first published in 1623).

Love's Labor's Lost (first published in 1598).

Lord Chamberlain's Men established.

1595   *King John* (first published in 1623).

Richard II (first published in 1597).

Romeo and Juliet (first published in 1597).

A Midsummer Night's Dream (first published in 1600).

1596   *The Merchant of Venice* (first published in 1600).

Hamnet/Hamlet Shakespeare dies, age 11 (ca. August 9).

1597   *1 Henry IV* (first published in 1598).

The Merry Wives of Windsor (first published in 1602).

Shakespeare purchases New Place, Stratford.

1598   *2 Henry IV* (first published in 1600).

Much Ado about Nothing (first published in 1600).

Francis Meres's *Palladis Tamia* lists a dozen plays by Shakespeare and praises him highly.

1599   The Globe Theater opens.

Henry V (first published in 1600).

Julius Caesar (first published in 1623).

The Passionate Pilgrim includes two of Shakespeare's sonnets (138, 144).

1600   *As You Like It* (first published in 1623).

Hamlet (first published in 1603).

1601   *Richard II* performed at the Globe (February 7) at urging of supporters of the Earl of Essex one day before his ill-fated rebellion.

The Phoenix and Turtle appears in Robert Chester's *Love's Martyr*.

John Shakespeare dies (ca. September 6).

1602   *Twelfth Night* (first published in 1623).

Troilus and Cressida (first published in 1609).

1603   Queen Elizabeth dies. James VI of Scotland becomes James I of England. James licenses the Lord Chamberlain's Men as the King's Men.

All's Well That Ends Well (first published in 1623).

1604   *Measure for Measure* (first published in 1623).

Othello (first published in 1622).

1605   *King Lear* (first published in 1608).

1606   *Macbeth* (first published in 1623).

1607   *Antony and Cleopatra* (first published in 1623).

Susannah Shakespeare marries John Hall (June 5).

Shakespeare's brother Edmund dies (ca. December 29).

1608   Elizabeth Hall, Shakespeare's only granddaughter, born (ca. February 18).

Shakespeare's mother dies (ca. September 7).

Coriolanus (first published in 1623).

Timon of Athens (first published in 1623).

Pericles (first published in 1609).

1609   Shakespeare's *Sonnets* published, with *A Lover's Complaint*.

Cymbeline (first published in 1623).

The King's Men begin using the Blackfriars as an indoor theater.

1610   *The Winter's Tale* (first published in 1623).

1611   *The Tempest* (first published in 1623).

1612   *Henry VIII* (with John Fletcher; first published in 1623).

1613   Globe Theater burns down during production of *Henry VIII*.

Cardenio (with John Fletcher; lost).

The Two Noble Kinsmen (with John Fletcher; first published in 1634).

1614   Second Globe opens on site of first Globe.

1616   Judith Shakespeare marries Thomas Quiney (February 10).

Shakespeare makes his will (March 25) and dies on April 23.

1619   Thomas Pavier attempts a collected (pirated) edition of Shakespeare. He publishes ten plays in quarto, some with false dates to conceal the piracy, before he is forced to abandon the project.

1623   The First Folio, the first collected edition of Shakespeare's plays, is published. It contains thirty-six plays, half of them printed for the first time.

OVERVIEWS

William Shakespeare's Age

Harold Branam

INTRODUCTION

Shakespeare's age is the latter part of the Renaissance, a period in Western culture that began during the fourteenth century in Italy. The name Renaissance (French for "rebirth") describes both a renewed interest in ancient Greek and Roman culture and a flourishing of art, literature, and learning inspired by that interest. The Renaissance was stimulated by the remains of ancient civilizations and by a growth of trade that brought Europeans into contact with each other and with peoples of other parts of the world. For example, the Venetian Marco Polo traveled back and forth to China, which traded such items as silk and gunpowder. The Europeans fought and traded with Islamic societies, which possessed advanced learning and technology and maintained libraries that had preserved some Greek and Roman manuscripts. European explorers also traveled to America and other areas previously unknown to them. The ongoing Renaissance was fueled by the Europeans' discoveries of not only new lands, peoples, and products but also new ideas and inventions—in particular, the printing press, which facilitated the dissemination of writings and ideas and led to increased literacy and learning.

The Renaissance was accompanied by a steady but sometimes dramatic decline in the monolithic hold of the Catholic Church over Western Europe. For centuries during the medieval period the Catholic Church had united Western Europeans under one fold, one vision, and one language (Latin); this unity itself contributed to the spread of Renaissance ideas. One of the most potent ideas was a growing secularism, as new products and prosperity contributed to a more comfortable earthly existence and the revival of classical humanism focused interest on this life and held up an ideal that emphasized human possibility. Shakespeare expresses this new attitude in *Hamlet* (2.2.297–307): "What a piece of work is a man, how noble in reason, how infinite in faculties, in form and moving, how express and admirable in action, how like an angel in apprehension, how like a god! The beauty of the world; the paragon of animals[.]" A rampant sense of individuality emerged that, combined with the printing press's power to spread ideas, helped cause the most dramatic decline of the Catholic Church—the Reformation, which led to Protestant religions, widespread hatred of Catholics, and religious wars. In turn, these forces, along with the establishment of vernacular languages (encouraged by printing), led to nationalism and the rise of nation-states, political power centered in monarchies, and national literatures.

The Renaissance lasted for some two to three centuries and spread gradually from Italy to France and Spain, Northern Europe, and finally England, on the European fringe. Living in England at the end of the sixteenth and the beginning of the seventeenth century, Shakespeare had the good luck to experience the Renaissance after many of its achievements, discoveries, and developments had occurred. Thus he could draw on an accumulated body of knowledge and on literary models and sources not only from the ancients but also from Italy, France, and his own countrymen. In England the theater, literary culture, and printing had also reached stages of development that prepared Shakespeare's audience to appreciate his writing and allowed his work to be seen and disseminated. Finally, Shakespeare lived immediately after the traumatic changes in state religion—back and forth from Catholic to Protestant—that racked England during the sixteenth century. Two of those changes were wrought by absolutist female monarchs: "Bloody" Mary and her half sister, Elizabeth I, who together convincingly demonstrated the power of women on the world stage.

The Renaissance, in short, was a time of change and transition, from the sacred to the secular, from communal life to individual life, from the medieval to the modern. Like the achievements of other great figures, such as Leonardo da Vinci, Michelangelo, Martin Luther, and Galileo, the work of Shakespeare both represents a high point of the Renaissance and helps to define the modern. What we are today—how we think, act, and speak—are in part due to Shakespeare. Our ideas of gender, love, integrity, and courage have been formed in part by Shakespeare, and so has our liking for wordplay and humor. Some critics have complained that Shakespeare is not modern enough—that is, more democratic, didactic, or critical of his age. Expressions of that type, however, were all dangerous if Shakespeare did not want to lose his audience or even his head. As his character Falstaff says, "The better part of valor is discretion" (*1 Henry IV*, 5.4.119–120). Still, just as this quotation and the character Falstaff himself implicitly undermine the Renaissance sense of valor, so Shakespeare provides more of a subversive critique or reality check of his age than first appears.

THE INFLUENCE OF ITALY

For Shakespeare's age, Renaissance Italy played much the same role that Hollywood has played in modern American life. It was a warm, showy, fashionable place that influenced English tastes in clothing, etiquette, personal behavior, literature, architecture, music, and politics. At the same time it was viewed as a place of immorality, violence, corruption, the center of Catholicism, and hence in Protestant eyes evil. Both sides of Renaissance Italy fascinated Shakespeare's age, as one can tell by the number of plays by Shakespeare and other English writers that are set in Italy and have characters with Italian names. The early English humanists followed the lead of Italian humanists, notably in their idea of a liberal education, and Italian models prevailed in other areas. Three Italians who stand out for their influence on Renaissance English literature and drama (as well as other areas) are Petrarch, Castiglione, and Machiavelli.

Petrarch (Francesco Petrarca, 1304–1374) was a church cleric and humanist scholar, ideologue, and poet who is sometimes credited with almost single-handedly starting the Renaissance. As a scholar, he loved searching through clerical libraries for old manuscripts containing texts from the classical Greek and Roman eras. As an ideologue, he argued that the classical authors formed a basis for reviving Italian culture along humanist lines that did not conflict with Christianity. His scholarly research and arguments stimulated the beginning of the Renaissance and influenced it throughout. But it is as a poet that Petrarch had the most direct influence on Renaissance English literature (and on literature in Italy, France, and Spain). He wrote beautiful lyric poems—*rime*, especially the sonnet (*sonnetto*, "little song")—that traced his love for an idealized lady, Laura. He thus popularized the sonnet form and started the rage for sonnet sequences that spread throughout Europe. In England this rage peaked in the 1590s, when many of the leading poets, including Shakespeare, penned sonnet sequences. By this time Petrarchan attitudes, emotions, and conceits had become clichés, and Shakespeare showed his originality and subversive nature by addressing his sonnets to a noble young man and seemingly sluttish "dark lady" rather than to a beautiful, chaste, aristocratic woman. But Shakespeare also furthered the influence of Petrarch's notion of romantic love, which he celebrated in his plays and passed on to Western culture.

Baldassare Castiglione (1478–1529), a nobleman and diplomat, could be called the Mr. Manners of his time. He wrote the highly influential book *Il cortegiano* (*The Courtier*, 1528), a manual of aristocratic thought, behavior, and achievement. Based on members of the nobility that Castiglione observed in the court of Urbino, where he served, *Il cortegiano* circulated and was translated throughout Europe. In 1561 Sir Thomas Hoby published his famous English translation, *The Courtyer*. Embraced by English society (sadly in need of refinement), the handbook epitomized the ideals of civilization. Young aristocrats formed their lives according to its teachings; Sir Philip Sidney, who came closest to achieving the ideal, is said to have carried a copy in his pocket.

The ideal courtier was a born-and-bred aristocrat and behaved accordingly. He was adept at feats of swordplay, horsemanship, chivalry, and warfare, but he did not neglect the arts: he was also a scholar, musician, dancer, and poet (though not so gross as to publish his work). A smooth conversationalist, he could swap small talk, banter, wit, and compliments with anyone. He knew how to dress and could afford the best fashions. Most of all, he knew how to treat, entertain, and romance the ladies, and he would never say an unkind or discourteous word, though he would not himself brook an insult or offense. A bit of an exhibitionist, he was on the stage of human endeavor at all times, but he performed with *sprezzatura*, a casual ease and grace that other people could only admire.

Embodying Renaissance individuality and secularism, the concept of the courtier elevated the nobility to almost godlike humanity. It also legitimated the status quo by turning the aristocracy into a superior class that ruled not by power alone but also by birthright and moral right (which became much the same). For Renaissance drama, the courtier offered a ready-made character whose heroic qualities were instantly recognizable. Shakespeare created numerous examples of the courtier, the most notable of which are perhaps Prince Hal and Hamlet. But Shakespeare also dramatizes a subversive critique of the whole concept by constantly inserting realism. In reality, the concept remained an ideal that no human could live up to. Prince Hal rebels against the concept before he finally redeems himself, and his associate Sir John Falstaff mocks the concept. Other parodies exist in the comedies; for example, drunken Sir Toby Belch and cowardly Sir Andrew Aguecheek in *Twelfth Night*.

If Castiglione's courtier was a model of human idealism, Machiavelli's prince was a model of cold, cruel human realism. A brilliant and independent thinker, Niccolò Machiavelli (1469–1527) rose from genteel poverty to political prominence in Florence, where he held several government offices and for which he traveled as an ambassador. He thus had the opportunity for firsthand observation of cutthroat Italian politics, characterized by internecine rivalries in and among the various city-states as well as regular intrusions of foreign powers. He concluded that only a strong ruler could succeed in conquering and uniting all of Italy. For his best example, he looked to the recent general of the papal armies, Cesare Borgia, son of Pope Alexander VI, but Machiavelli also drew on other authorities and examples, particularly from ancient Rome. Machiavelli set out his resulting composite portrait in *Il principe* (*The Prince*, 1513).

Although Machiavelli based his portrait on the Italian context, he expressed certain general principles with alarming force. For example, he said that it was better for a prince to be feared than loved, that a prince should not hesitate to be ruthless when necessary, that a prince did not need to keep his word, and that deception is better than morality (although the appearance of morality helps). Machiavelli's work soon gained notoriety throughout Europe, where he was sometimes dubbed Old Nick because his teachings were associated with those of the devil. Machiavelli also supplied another famous character type to the Renaissance English stage: the Machiavellian, an evil schemer and plotter, of which there are numerous examples in Shakespeare and fellow dramatists (e.g., Shakespeare's Richard III). Machiavelli also further opened the breach between appearance and reality and between hypocrisy and honesty, constant thematic conflicts in Shakespeare's work. These themes play out, for instance, in Shakespeare's great tragedy *King Lear*, which also has its share of Machiavellian characters.

LIFE OF A COURTIER

The Italian influence and life in English court society are exemplified by the courtier Henry Howard, Earl of Surrey (1517–1547). In his case, there is no doubt about the Italian influence, since Surrey is one of the earliest English translators of Petrarch's sonnets. But Surrey showed his originality by adapting the sonnet form to the English language, creating the so-called English sonnet. He is also credited with creating blank verse. Both of these verse forms use the iambic pentameter line, which seems natural to the rhythms of the English language; Surrey freed the sonnet to some extent, and blank verse entirely, from the constraints and chiming sounds of rhyme. Surrey's verse innovations thus laid the poetic groundwork for both the fashionable outburst of English sonnet sequences in the 1590s and for the greatest period of drama in history. Surrey helped make possible Marlowe's "mighty line" of unrhymed iambic pentameter and Shakespeare's great achievements in both the sonnet and blank verse.

If Surrey's poetic accomplishments are interesting, his life is even more so. Proud scion of the wealthy and influential Howard family, Surrey had a life marked by dramatic ups and downs. Surrey was the oldest son of Lord Thomas Howard, a leading nobleman during Henry VIII's reign; cousin of Catherine Howard, one of Henry's queens; and close companion of the Duke of Richmond, Henry's bastard son. These connections gave young Surrey access to Henry VIII's court, a position that had its pitfalls. Impetuous and hotheaded, he offended on several occasions and was thrown into prison for such misdemeanors as smacking another courtier and going around London at night and smashing windows. Despite these youthful indiscretions, Surrey distinguished himself in court jousts and fought bravely in various wars, even serving as Henry's commander during one campaign. His battlefield record, however, did not save him from eventually falling victim to a rival court family, the Seymours, who wrongly accused him of Catholic sympathies and treason. On Henry VIII's orders, he was executed at the age of twenty-nine. Surrey's poems were published ten years later in Tottel's famous miscellany, titled *Songs and Sonnets Written by the Right Honorable Lord Henry Howard Late Earl of Surrey and Other* (1557).

As the summary of Surrey's life illustrates, English society during Shakespeare's age was still dominated overwhelmingly by the nobility, particularly the court. It was an age of aristocracy, absolutism, and the divine right of kings. These statements are obvious facts of history, but they bear repeating, since they underlie many of the assumptions of Shakespeare's age. Except for the clergy, only members of the aristocracy were players on the national stage. The aristocracy enjoyed power and privilege, and they had quite a lot of both. In England starting with Henry VIII, even leaders of the clergy were appointed by the monarch, and often came from the aristocracy. It was pretty much expected that spirited young noblemen would indulge in such high jinks as slapping obnoxious people and smashing windows for fun. Young Prince Hal exemplifies this spirit in Shakespeare's *1 Henry IV*, where he hangs out in taverns, consorts with lowlife, and commits highway robbery.

All of these youthful high spirits were supposed to translate later into bravery on the battlefield, as they did for Surrey and for Prince Hal. Presumably, the potential for warlike exploits had been there all along, inherited with one's noble title. It was also apparent in the young nobleman's fancy dress, grooming, and personal conduct, all of which exuded pride and a hair-trigger disposition to take offense. A nobleman had to be ready at the least slight to draw his sword and defend his honor. He was often accompanied by friends or retainers who by association shared in his sense of status and were equally ready to support him. Overall, a near street-gang mentality prevailed and was fueled by past wrongs, factionalism, and family feuds, as in Shakespeare's *Romeo and Juliet*.

Such was the state of high society during Shakespeare's time—a state pretty much reflected in his plays, where the main characters are typically royalty or members of the nobility, and the others are servants and low comic characters. Shakespeare could have gotten this view of social status in drama from Aristotle's *Poetics*, but it is not likely that he did, nor did he need to. Instead, he merely reflected the class biases and realities of his time. For Shakespeare, depicting royalty and the aristocracy must have been a challenge, since he came from a much humbler middle-class background. This fact has caused a few critics to question whether he could have written the plays attributed to him or whether they were secretly written by some noble personage. The answer seems to be that his plays are works of the imagination, wherein Shakespeare relied on prevailing ideas, his reading, talks with his friends and associates, and whatever observations of the aristocracy he was able to make. His plays are also set in history or some distant place, or both, which in several ways was safer than writing about the contemporary English scene. He worked, moreover, on the premise that royalty and the aristocracy share in general human nature, which for his time was something of a subversive attitude that both broke down class assumptions and humanized his characters.

CLASSICAL PHILOSOPHICAL INFLUENCES

Although the most immediate influences on Shakespeare's age were Renaissance Italy and Europe generally, other influences go back much further. Since the Renaissance itself was a revival of interest in ancient Greek and Roman cultures, many of the ideas woven into the fabric of Renaissance thought draw on those cultures. Sometimes these ideas were acquired directly from a reading of classical authors, such as Ovid or Cicero. Sometimes the ideas were filtered down through intermediaries, often reaching the Renaissance in a simplified or eclectic form. Among the secondary sources were Renaissance humanists, who revived and disseminated the ideas of ancient Greece and Rome; other classical ideas, however, were already embedded in Christian culture, which in the New Testament and other teachings echoed ancient philosophies more than is often realized. Two of the ancient philosophies that were most influential during the Renaissance were Platonism and Stoicism.

Platonism, incorporating the dialogues of Socrates and Plato's own thinking, reached the Renaissance from several directions. Plato loomed over later Greek philosophy, including that of his student and rival Aristotle, and even over Christianity. Thinkers adopting Platonic ideas included the pagan Plotinus and the Christian St. Augustine. Plato's influence persisted through the medieval period, even though the Church Fathers after Thomas Aquinas generally preferred Aristotle. During the Renaissance the works of Plato, Plotinus, and other Platonists were published and studied in the original Greek. The Platonic Academy was revived at Florence in the fifteenth century and produced such Christian humanist philosophers as Marsilio Ficino and Pico della Mirandola. This academy especially influenced Platonic thinking in England.

The most important aspect of Plato's thought for Christianity and the Renaissance was his idealism. In *The Republic* (ca. 370 B.C.), Plato sets forth the theory that abstract Ideas or Forms are the most fundamental reality. Ideas or Forms exist in a perfect state and are not subject to the ravages of time. What we generally think of as reality—that is, material reality—is a secondary and imperfect reality, an imitation, based on the Ideas or Forms. Then, according to Plato, art is a tertiary reality created by the human imagination and based on material reality. For example, our ideal of beauty in a woman is an Idea or Form. The reality of this Idea or Form might be so strong that a man spends his whole life searching for and fantasizing about the ideal woman. But he will never find her. He might come across some beautiful women, but they will always have flaws and will eventually age and lose their beauty. He might even waste his time by photographing, drawing, or writing poems about some of these flawed women. Nothing he sees or creates will ever measure up to the ideal.

Neoplatonism ("new" Platonism) draws on Plato's theory of Ideas or Forms without necessarily accepting his hierarchy of reality. The writers of the New Testament found the theory useful for its concepts of perfection and timelessness, which are associated with spirituality and the realm of God. In the Old Testament, God behaves like a powerful and vengeful human being—in other words, like a Greek god before Plato. The New Testament, with Jesus as God made man, the perfect human being, born of the Virgin Mary, reflects the refinement in thought that Plato introduced. For example, Jesus teaches that humans must strive for spiritual perfection, that flesh and the material world must be subordinated to the spiritual, and that human integrity requires thought, word, and act to be the same.

The Renaissance absorbed Neoplatonism through both Christian and secular writers. The continuing Christian influence can be seen, for instance, in Shakespeare's agreement that human integrity requires unity of thought, word, and act. But Renaissance Neoplatonism also had a secular side, most notably in the belief that human perfection can be attained in the flesh. The ideal of the courtier shows the influence of Neoplatonism, and so does the Petrarchan idealization of the beautiful, beloved lady in poetry. In Renaissance Neoplatonism, also, art becomes not tertiary but primary, embodying and perpetuating ideals and overcoming time and mutability. This elevated notion of art informs Edmund Spenser's sonnets and his masterpiece *The Faerie Queene* (1590, 1596), dedicated to the virginal Elizabeth I, the Protestant answer to the Virgin Mary. Other English sonneteers, including Shakespeare, took up the same Neoplatonic theme: Their work captured human beauty, love, and perfection and enshrined them for all time. Sir Philip Sidney's *The Defence of Poesie* (1595) made the notion a standard argument for the value of art:

> Nature never set forth the earth in so rich tapestry as divers poets have done, neither with so pleasant rivers, fruitful trees, sweet-smelling flowers, nor whatsoever else may make the too much loved earth more lovely. Her world is brazen, the poets only deliver a golden [i.e., perfect].

Ironically, Plato had banned poets from his republic as blatant liars.

STOICISM

Stoicism also reached the Renaissance from various directions, but mainly through Christianity, the Roman Stoics, and Neostoic writers (such as Boethius and Lipsius) rather than the original Greek Stoics. The authors of the New Testament seem to have drawn from Stoic philosophy. The most fundamental tenet of Stoicism is the concept of the *logos* (usually translated as "reason" or "divine fire"), the organizing force or principle that runs through the whole universe. The *logos* shows up in John 1:1, where it is usually translated as "word": "In the beginning was the Word, and the Word was with God, and the Word was God." Another tenet of Stoicism, deriving ultimately from the *logos*, is a belief in the brotherhood of man, a concept central to Christianity. For instance, the idea shows up in Acts 17, where Paul preaches to the Epicurean and Stoic philosophers in Athens: "And he [God] made from one every nation of men." The influence of Stoicism can also be seen more generally in Christian thinking, such as in emphasizing self-control, individual responsibility, and virtue as its own reward.

The Roman Stoics were much read during the Renaissance, since Latin was the universal language and studied in school. The Roman Stoics included Seneca, Epictetus, and Marcus Aurelius, but Cicero also incorporated Stoicism into his eclectic thinking. Seneca's plays were the main classical models for Renaissance tragedy, so Stoic postures, catchwords, and ideas permeated these works. An extreme example of tragedy along Senecan lines is Shakespeare's *Titus Andronicus*, but even Hamlet's "To be, or not to be" speech debates the typically Stoic question of "the open door" (suicide). Other Shakespeare characters take "the open door," especially in the Roman tragedies (though Cleopatra gives it a distinctly Egyptian twist).

But the most common Stoic influence in Renaissance thought—and another good theme for drama—was the conflict between reason and the passions. If the universe (or nature) was ordered by reason, and man was the supreme rational creature, then living in harmony with the universe (or nature, including his own nature) meant living according to reason. If a man could live according to reason and thus in harmony with the universe, he could rise serenely above the slings and arrows of outrageous fortune. He would be in control of things rather than vice versa—at least in his own mind. His mind would be a mighty fortress that fortune could not overcome. But the passions played havoc with this scheme of things. In sonnets the passions beset reason like soldiers conquering a fort or a tempest wrecking a ship. In comedies the passions turned people into fools. And in tragedies the passions (lust, greed, ambition—there were plenty to choose from) led people to death and destruction. The passions thus were forms of madness; the solution was to control the passions and to live according to reason and nature.

Both Stoicism and Platonism enter into the Renaissance concept of the Great Chain of Being. This cosmic view, which descended from medieval times, is essentially Christian but is also a synthesis of various strands of thought. The sense of hierarchy is Platonic, while the spirit of godhood permeating creation is Stoic. The idea of man, placed at the center of the Great Chain of Being, combines elements of Platonism and Stoicism. The Great Chain of Being is filled out by God and the angels (in their various orders) above man and by animals (in their various orders), plants, and inanimate objects below man. Man can rise or fall in this hierarchy depending on whether he lives according to his nature (reason) or sinks into animal existence (driven by passions). Life for man is a cosmic stage on which he acts and is tested. Within the category of man, there is also the hierarchy of the social order from the king down to the peasant. The Great Chain of Being thus legitimates the positions of the various social classes and implies that any tampering with the chain could be disastrous. But, true to its Platonic and Stoic elements, it leaves open the possibility of spiritual striving (with potential rewards in another world). Perhaps the most famous expression of this idea of the Great Chain of Being appears in Ulysses' speech in *Troilus and Cressida*, 1.3.75–137.

ENGLISH PAST AS PROLOGUE

To Shakespeare's age, the fear that tampering with the sociopolitical order could be disastrous seemed justified by English history. In particular, the king, as the head of the whole sociopolitical order, was untouchable, even sacred, since he ruled by divine right. Although there were systems of canon, civil, and criminal law, the king still ruled with absolute authority, even (beginning with Henry VIII) dictating the state religion. Disobeying and rebelling against the king were high crimes, and traitors were punished by being beheaded, burned at the stake, or hanged, drawn, and quartered, with their remains displayed prominently—for instance, on London Bridge. The personality and character of the ruler and the question of royal succession were therefore matters of urgent concern. (A revolution that involved cutting off the king's head did occur in the middle of the seventeenth century, but it proved so disastrous that the monarchy was restored.)

For Shakespeare, recent history had brought these issues to the forefront. It all began when the aging queen, Katherine of Aragón, could not produce a male heir for Henry VIII, who started divorce proceedings against her in 1527. At that time England was still a Catholic country, so Henry VIII needed the pope's approval for the divorce. The pope, under pressure from Katherine's relatives, delayed making any decision, and the delay went on for years. Henry VIII, a huge man of enormous appetites used to getting what he wanted (including people's property), eventually would not take delay as an answer. In 1534 Henry VIII repudiated papal supremacy over the English church and thus allowed the Reformation to enter England. Thereafter began a struggle between Catholic and Protestant factions and a succession of marriages for the king, who seemed to alternate between the factions (with persecutions and executions on both sides).

When the child Edward VI became king in 1547, his Protestant supporters gained control. In 1549 the Catholic Mass was replaced by the English *Book of Common Prayer*, and ensuing Catholic revolts were put down. But in 1553 young Edward VI died and was succeeded by his sternly Catholic half sister, Mary. The Catholic Mass was restored and the execution of Protestants began, mostly by burning at the stake. Then in 1558 "Bloody" Mary died and was succeeded by her Protestant half sister, Elizabeth I. The Catholic Mass was replaced by a revised *Book of Common Prayer*. Suppressing Catholic opposition at home and supporting Protestant wars abroad (thereby stirring conflict with the pope and Catholic Spain), Elizabeth I ruled a relatively stable nation for forty-five years but never married or produced an heir. Throughout much of this time, especially toward the end, lack of a direct heir raised fears about what would happen when Elizabeth I died.

The question of royal succession was a burning issue when Shakespeare began writing in the late 1580s or early 1590s and throughout the first half of his career. The question of succession also raised other issues. What kind of personality and character would the next ruler have? Would the next ruler be Protestant or Catholic, and would there be a return to religious turmoil? Would the succession be disputed by rival contenders and factions such as had bedeviled England in the fifteenth-century Wars of the Roses (the dominant subject of Shakespeare's early English history plays)? Or would there be other kinds of disorders, leading perhaps to the breakdown of law, civil war, and foreign invasions (the subject of Shakespeare's *King John*)? How could the stability and national pride brought by Elizabeth I be celebrated and held up as an example for the next ruler? In actuality, Elizabeth I's reign included its share of personal tirades (directed at her ladies and courtiers), persecutions, and executions. By today's standards her government would be considered totalitarian: there was rigid censorship and control of speech and religion. But royal behavior was all a relative matter.

For Shakespeare, an aspiring young author but also the queen's humble subject, the question was how he could write about these royal matters without himself getting burned (literally as well as figuratively). It was risky to write about recent history, especially if it involved religion, and government censors could suppress writings they considered too controversial or subversive. The solution was to write about older history that might be relevant to the current situation. Shakespeare's age was fascinated by history and looked upon it as a subject full of examples and lessons. It also believed that there was a moral purpose in history and that events and outcomes were ordered by the providential workings of God. Among the age's favorite historical works were three that became major sources for Shakespeare: Edward Hall's *The Union of the Two Noble and Illustre Families of Lancaster and York* (1548), Raphael Holinshed's *Chronicles of England, Scotland, and Ireland* (2nd ed., 1587), and Sir Thomas North's 1579 translation of Plutarch's *Lives of the Noble Grecians and Romans*. By Shakespeare's time, the history or chronicle play, influenced by the earlier morality play, had already become an established form in English drama.

For his lessons in English history on the dangers inherent in royal succession, the horrors of civil war, and tyranny, Shakespeare went first to the Wars of the Roses (1455–1485). This civil war for the crown was fought between the houses of Lancaster (red rose) and York (white rose), descended from the fourth and fifth sons, respectively, of Edward III (1312–1377). Shakespeare dramatized the war in his first tetralogy *Henry VI, 1, 2, 3* and *Richard III*. At the end of the tetralogy he also flattered Elizabeth I by celebrating how her grandfather, Henry Tudor (from the Welsh *Tewdwr*), ended the Wars of the Roses, united the houses of Lancaster and York, and united England as Henry VII.

Later Shakespeare returned to the house of Lancaster for his second tetralogy: *Richard II*; *1* and *2 Henry IV*; and *Henry V*. Richard II, son of Edward the Black Prince, Edward III's first son (who died before his father), inherited the throne from Edward III but was self-indulgent and ineffectual. His cousin Henry Bullingbrook, son of John of Gaunt, Duke of Lancaster (fourth son of Edward III), deposed Richard II in 1399 and ruled as Henry IV. The infamous Prince Hal was Henry IV's first son and became the heroic Henry V, father of Henry VI. By the time Shakespeare wrote the second tetralogy, he seemed to care less about the legal rights to succession and more about who could unite and rule the country most successfully. His celebration of Henry V's triumphs over the French also reflects the English spirit of nationalism fed by the current conflict with Spain. That country's attempted invasion of England in 1588 resulted in a resounding defeat of the Spanish Armada, but open warfare with Spain continued throughout the last part of Elizabeth I's reign.

To the relief of most of the English, the succession of James I to the English crown in 1603 was peaceful. He was Protestant (a Presbyterian) and as James VI of Scotland, grandson of Elizabeth I's cousin James V of Scotland, he was next in line for the English throne after his mother, Mary, queen of Scots. Mary, who was Catholic, had been a dangerous rival and threat to Elizabeth I (whom Catholics considered illegitimate), but after her defeat by Protestant forces at Langside, just outside Glasgow (May 13, 1568), she sought refuge in England, where Elizabeth I kept her imprisoned for almost twenty years and finally ordered her execution in 1587. James, who had not seen his mother since he was one year old, protested her execution but otherwise did nothing to jeopardize his chances of inheriting the English

Shakespeare Reading to Queen Elizabeth I by John James Chalon. © Fine Art Photographic Library/Corbis.

throne. For her part, Elizabeth I made it known that James was her choice to succeed, and she approved his succession on her deathbed.

Although James I was never as well liked as was Elizabeth I and eventually alienated the English parliament and people with his absolutist and uncompromising nature, his reign brought some benefits. He informally united England and Scotland and in 1604 made peace with Spain. He was also a patron of learning and the arts, especially the drama. He commissioned the King James translation of the Bible (1611), for centuries the authoritative English version and a profound influence on the English language (though too late to influence Shakespeare). One of his first actions as king was to issue letters patent (royal license) making Shakespeare's acting company the King's Men, thus granting the company the king's audience and protection. Shakespeare returned the favor by drawing on Scottish history for *Macbeth*, which flattered the king by dramatizing his belief in witches and ancestral link to Banquo. Shakespeare also returned to Roman history in *Antony and Cleopatra* to dramatize the unification of the Roman Empire under young Octavius Caesar, who as Augustus inaugurated the peaceful and glorious Augustan Age of Rome and whom James I saw as his historical parallel and role model.

SHIPS, SEA POWER, AND VOYAGES

Under the Tudor monarchs, beginning with Henry VII and continuing with Henry VIII and Elizabeth I, England engaged in a shipbuilding program that made it a leading sea-going power. The sea had always been important to English life, and during the late Middle Ages a sizable English merchant fleet carried on a thriving trade with the Continent. But England was somewhat late in joining the European voyages of exploration and in developing a large navy, partly because of internal conflicts such as the Wars of the Roses and partly because the Renaissance came late to England. Growing prosperous on their trade, the Venetians and Genoese had been the first to become sea-going powers, ruling the Mediterranean. They were followed by the Portuguese and Spanish, who sailed down the coast of Africa, across the Atlantic, and finally around the world, sometimes led by Italian captains. In England the Tudor monarchs, motivated by absolutist and national pride and assisted by periods of peace, invested substantial funds to catch up. Henry VIII, in particular, was interested in building bigger ships with more firepower than any other nation's navy. Elizabeth I's able treasurer of the navy, Sir John Hawkins, made English vessels even faster and more lethal. Their investment paid off, especially during Elizabeth I's reign, in privateer looting of Spanish ships and settlements, in the defeat of the Spanish Armada, and in the assertion of English power on the high seas.

All of the ships at the time were made of wood. Since they depended on the wind for power, they were subject to becalming and being blown off course. The short trip across the English Channel could take days. Boats could run into storms, strong winds, and high waves, with no forecasts to warn them. Weather conditions in the English Channel and north Atlantic Ocean were often bad, contributing, for example, to the defeat of the Spanish Armada, which first was slowed by a slight wind off the south of England but then was scattered by a gale up the channel that wrecked many ships and blew others around the north of Scotland. The Spanish ships were bigger than most English ships, some of which were as small as 35 tons, though the English had the biggest ship, the *Triumph*, at 1,100 tons. The English ships were more maneuverable and had longer-range cannon, so they were able to stand off and fire at the Spanish.

There was no law of the sea, so pirates were a common problem. Moorish pirates off the Barbary Coast (named for the Berber inhabitants) of Morocco, Algeria, Tunisia, and Libya harassed and robbed Mediterranean trading ships, especially those of the Italians and later the Spanish. Japanese pirates frequented the straits of southeast Asia and attacked European explorers. The English, including Elizabeth I, took advantage of the lawlessness to finance privateers who sailed the Spanish Main (i.e., the coast of South America between Panama and the Orinoco River), raiding Spanish settlements and sea-lanes in the New World. The most famous English privateer was Sir Francis Drake, who in 1577 with 164 men aboard his hundred-ton *Golden Hind* and four smaller ships looted his way first down the east coast of South America, then up the west coast, and finally around the world. At an expense of only £5,000, they arrived back in England three years later with £600,000 worth of silver, gold, and jewels.

Even discounting the danger of pirates, conditions aboard ships could become quite grim. With wind and weather uncertain, crews on long voyages never knew how much food and water to stock. To keep through the long journeys, meat had to be heavily salted and still often went rancid. Fresh water sometimes ran out, and even worse, so did ale and rum. Vegetables and fruits were in short supply, if not totally lacking, so the men suffered from deficiency diseases such as scurvy. They were beset by vermin, such as fleas, lice, mice, and rats, which also spread shipboard diseases. In the crowded confines, sanitation and discipline could become problems. For offenses, floggings and other harsh punishments were meted out, and occasionally there were mutinies. Finally, there were the constant dangers of tempests, shipwrecks, and sinking, as described in Shakespeare's plays from *The Comedy of Errors* to *The Tempest*.

With all of these difficulties and dangers, it is not surprising that ancient and medieval sailors for the most part hugged the shorelines. But during the Renaissance developments in shipbuilding, navigational inventions, and improved charts and maps made distant voyages and exploration more feasible. Three-masted and even four-masted ships with more power and control and more room for crews, cargoes, and cannons were built. The cross-staff was adopted for calculating latitude, and the magnetic compass reached Europe from the Chinese via the Arabs (though the Vikings probably used lodestones). As European explorations continued, existing charts and maps were constantly updated.

The Renaissance Europeans also were highly motivated, mostly by greed, to undertake long voyages. Through trade they were able to increase the range of products available to them and improve their quality of life. The Spanish, especially, brought shiploads of silver and gold back from the New World, causing inflationary spirals in the European economy. For Europeans seeking a fresh start or escaping persecution, the New World also offered land for colonies and plantations. To work the plantations, colonists imported slaves. The Portuguese, Spanish, and French were the earliest to transport slaves to the New World, but in 1562 Sir John Hawkins became the first Englishman to enter the trade. He was soon joined by Sir Francis Drake and other English sailors, supported by English investors, including Elizabeth I.

The importance of the sea and sailing ships naturally enters into Shakespeare's work. For instance, Antonio's fortunes in *The Merchant of Venice* ride on his argosies at sea. On his way to be executed in England, Hamlet is captured by pirates and returned to Denmark. In *Twelfth Night* a shipwreck dumps the twins Viola and Sebastian separately on the shores of Illyria, where both are assisted by sea captains. Othello, a Moor who has fought on land and sea, commands Venetian reinforcements that sail to Cyprus to battle the approaching Turks, whose armada is destroyed by a tempest. Sea battles are crucial turning points in *Antony and Cleopatra*. *The Tempest*, which also starts with a storm and shipwreck, draws on travel accounts and gives a microcosm of the colonial situation, including slavery. References to the sea also enter into Shakespeare's language and are a source of metaphors, like the very title of *The Tempest*.

TOWN AND COUNTRY

The Renaissance saw further development of cities and towns that had grown up in the Middle Ages around seaports or markets. Other cities and towns went all the way back to Greek and Roman times, especially in Italy (but London, Bath, and York had also been Roman settlements). Besides offering markets, the cities and towns were centers of religion, government, learning, the arts, and crafts; as such, they stimulated the beginning and continuation of the Renaissance. But the cities and towns were not large by today's standards and remained closely tied to the country, which was their lifeline. For the most part, Italy remained a collection of city-states, each consisting of a main city with its surrounding countryside and allied towns and villages. Everywhere, most people still lived on the land or maintained their ties to it, expressing a country mentality and pursuing rural pastimes like gardening or deer hunting (Henry VIII's favorite sport).

During Shakespeare's age London experienced phenomenal growth, quadrupling in size in the sixteenth century, with an estimated population of 50,000 in 1500, 100,000 in 1560, and 200,000 in 1600. This growth extended well beyond the old medieval wall, moat, and gates, though they still remained as prominent landmarks (except where the wall had crumbled and the moat was filled in). Although only one bridge, the famous London Bridge, crossed the Thames River, growth also extended south across the Thames to the Bankside. There, beyond the city's limits and restrictive laws, flourished the district for drinking, gambling, pickpockets, prostitution, bear-baiting, and theaters (including Shakespeare's Globe). The Thames was a major thoroughfare for small boats and barges, even though it was highly polluted by garbage and sewage. The sewer system was primitive or nonexistent, consisting in some places of open ditches. One of the complaints of residents was the stench of slaughterhouses (known as shambles), although many other smells contributed to the city's rich aroma.

It is not surprising that the main royal residence was at Whitehall and the main government functions at Westminster, both located west and upriver of London. It is also not surprising that the "sweating sickness," plague, and other epidemics raged through London from time to time. When the plague struck, as it did in 1603 when James I became king, royalty and the nobility left town for the country, and the theaters closed to prevent large gatherings where contagion could spread. Though the Elizabethans knew nothing of germs, they knew that disease spread more quickly in crowded conditions. Fire was another major hazard, devastating whole sections of the city in an age when most buildings were of wood (though brick came into vogue as a building material about this time, especially among the nobility, for whom it denoted status). Among the victims of fire was the Globe Theater, which burned down in 1613 during a performance of Shakespeare's *Henry VIII*.

In addition to shipping and river traffic, London was served by four major roads leading to distant parts of England: the Great North Road, stretching all the way to Scotland; Watling Street, going northwest from London to Chester; a western road from London to Plymouth; and the Dover Road to the southeast. Watling Street, which Shakespeare likely took on his way to Stratford-upon-Avon, was an old Roman road, as were some other existing roads. Road building was not a high priority of the age, and neither was road repair. Travelers sometimes complained about holes big enough for an animal or person to fall into and break a leg or die. Practically the only means of travel were by foot or horseback. Travelers were lucky to make twenty miles during a day, so there were inns along the way to put them up at night. Farmers sold their perishable produce at nearby markets to which they drove their sheep and other livestock. Merchants could transport wool and some manufactured goods for longer distances. But travelers, farmers, and merchants all had to beware of robbers who lurked along the highways at dangerous locations. One such infamous location on the Dover Road was Gadshill, featured in Shakespeare's 1 *Henry IV*.

London, the capital and metropolis, was the only large city in all of England. The next 30 to 40 bigger towns in England had populations of only around 5,000 to 15,000 each, while the 700 to 800 other towns were no more than rural market centers with populations of fewer than 2,000. Shakespeare's Stratford-upon-Avon, about 100 miles northwest of London, was one of these small market towns. Located on a beautiful little river, Stratford was surrounded by farms and fields. To the north were the Forest of Arden and the villages of Shakespeare's ancestors, the Ardens and Shakespeares, who had lived there for generations. So Shakespeare, speaking in a Warwickshire accent, had a largely rural upbringing—a fact that can be seen in his diction, imagery, and the settings of some plays, such as *A Midsummer Night's Dream* and *As You Like It* (set mostly in the "Forest of Arden"). But his upbringing in or near the country was typical of most English people during the period.

Despite their common ties to the country, most people experienced social distinctions that were aggravated by the differences between town life and country life. Shakespeare depicts the bumbling rustic in the clown of *The Winter's Tale* and Silvius in *As You Like It*. Shakespeare probably faced the same stereotype when he first came to the city and was breaking into the theater. In Greene's *A Groatsworth of Witte, Bought with a Million of Repentance* (1592), Robert Greene, one of the so-called University Wits, described the young Shakespeare as "an upstart Crow, beautified with our feathers, . . . in his own conceit the onely Shake-scene in a country." Royalty and the nobility nonetheless built country palaces, and in some of Shakespeare's plays the upper class cavorts in the country. In these plays, the country and forest are associated with simplicity, romance, purity, and naturalness versus the scheming, posturing, and back stabbing of the city and court. And even when Shakespeare stereotypes country people, they are lovable.

DAILY LIFE

During the fourteenth and fifteenth centuries, serfdom in England came to an end, and employers began to hire workers for a wage. At the same time, outbreaks of the plague decimated the population, causing serious labor shortages. Among the results were low food prices, high wages, and untenanted land. Some farm workers whose ancestors had been serfs bought up cheap land and became, like Shakespeare's ancestors, small yeoman farmers who usually enclosed their property with hedges and stone fences. Without serfs or enough farm laborers, many large landowners also enclosed their property, including the commons (once communal land), and converted it to pasturage for growing sheep because trade in wool and woolen goods was flourishing. This process, known as enclosure, continued through the fifteenth and sixteenth centuries, driving more workers off the land. Some of these workers became beggars or vagabonds, but others found opportunities in the towns and the metropolis. A few towns, like Leeds in West Yorkshire, became centers for manufacturing wool cloth, much in demand as an English export.

During the reign of the Tudors, pressures for higher wages continued, but the lot of the laboring classes did not improve much. The Tudor governments tried to regulate the economy by setting maximum wages and prices of goods, but these controls were ineffective. As a result, periods of inflation and increases in food prices wiped out any gains in wages, so life for farm workers and artisan employees remained a struggle. Their daily life generally consisted of working, eating, and sleeping. They typically rose at dawn and worked throughout the daylight hours, then went to bed early. Their work routine was broken by three meals: breakfast, dinner before or around noon, and supper. Some employers allowed workers a nap after dinner and an afternoon snack. Workers also enjoyed breaks on the Sabbath and during the many holy days and festivals.

For other social classes during Shakespeare's age, life improved considerably. Small yeomen farmers, although following much the same daily routine as workers, became self-sufficient and sometimes mildly prosperous, able to furnish their homes comfortably and maybe to hire one or two farmhands or servants. Their lower-middle-class counterparts in town, independent artisans and merchants, like Shakespeare's father, likewise were able to own homes and to acquire the new goods and services that were available. Benefiting most from all of the building and trading was the upper middle class, whose members lived in the bigger towns or London and sometimes became so rich that they dressed in sumptuous clothes, loaned money to the aristocracy, held important political offices, and had social pretensions. While some aristocrats also invested in the prospering economy, they continued to enjoy their hereditary lands, palaces, and privileges, were waited on by servants, dressed in the latest fashions, pursued leisure pastimes, and occasionally patronized the arts.

Members of the wealthy classes dressed in fancy clothes to distinguish themselves from the working classes. Men of all classes wore the same basic garments—a shirt, hose (tights) with a codpiece, and a doublet (vest)—but for workers and artisans these were usually of wool, while for men of higher class they were made from more expensive materials, like linen or silk. Men's outerwear displayed their differences even more: for workers and artisans, a belted jerkin (jacket), sometimes knee-length; for middle-class men, a long open robe or gown, sometimes fur-trimmed (this garment still survives in academic regalia); for noblemen, a shorter robe, replaced later by a short cape. Noblemen also wore neckbands, later pleated collars, and finally enormous corrugated-looking ruffs. Among fashionable men, also, the revealing tights were first replaced by trunk hose, which puffed out around the hips and upper thighs, and then by Venetian breeches, which puffed out all the way to the knees. Almost all men had beards and wore hats. Men of the middle class and nobility first wore flat hats (still surviving in academic caps), but noblemen later switched to taller hats with a feather. Noblemen also wore a rapier (sword) that dangled beside and behind their bodies.

Women wore a kirtle (bodice and skirt) covered by a long dress. Again, in the lower classes these were of simple design and materials, but in the upper classes they became very elaborate and expensive. One elaborate device was a farthingale, a frame worn under women's dresses that ballooned and jutted out from the waist down. The dresses often had puff sleeves and a low neckline to set off jeweled necklaces. Upper-class women also wore ruffs and rabatos (wide collars), either turned up or down. Women wore caps and hoods that usually covered their hair, except some who were unmarried, though the French hood (worn in England also) fell down the back and left the front uncovered. Some aristocratic women, like Elizabeth I, had piled-up hairdos into which they wove beads and jewels. For sleeping, women, like men, tended to sacrifice beauty for warmth and comfort. Both sexes wore gowns and nightcaps.

Just as they enjoyed showing off their fancy clothes, so members of the middle class and aristocracy liked to display other signs of their wealth and status. They built new homes and palaces divided into rooms that had fireplaces and gave more privacy (though several generations of the same family, including servants, still tended to live together). They sometimes had their own beds, furnished with fresh bedclothes, while poorer people slept several to a bed on old smelly mattresses. They also had glass mirrors, carved wooden furniture, and walls decorated with wood paneling and tapestries. The wealthiest ate off of silver and gold plate and drank out of Venetian glasses, while the lower classes had to be satisfied with wooden utensils and the middle classes with pewter. Forks were not used until the very end of Shakespeare's age; instead, all social classes ate with spoons, knives, and fingers.

Generally food was plentiful, except in years when the crops failed, and the English were known for gluttony. They ate a lot of meat, bread and puddings, dairy products, and sweets. Mutton, beef, and (among the upper class) game were in plentiful supply, while along the shore there were fish and oysters. Fruits and vegetables were available in season. The drinks of choice were beer, ale, and wine (sometimes diluted with water). Sherry and sack (Falstaff's favorite beverage) were imported from Spain and the Canary Islands, while other wines came from France. Among the Englishmen famous for eating was Henry VIII, who in his later life wore a suit of armor with a fifty-four–inch waist. In Shakespeare's work, the fat tub Sir John Falstaff gives a good picture of the heavy-eating, heavy-drinking Englishman. Probably because of so much consumption of sugar and honey, many of the English had bad teeth.

Another reason for their bad teeth was the poor state of dental and medical care. In an age of no anesthetics, teeth were pulled with tongs, and barbers were the dentists. Barbers also performed surgery and other medical procedures, like setting broken bones or bleeding patients using lances or leeches; bleeding was a main cure for almost all ailments. There were trained physicians, but they tended to act more as medical advisers rather than as hands-on practitioners. These medical personnel were supplemented by herbalists (like Friar Lawrence in *Romeo and Juliet*), pharmacists, and midwives. Childbirth was an especially perilous time for both baby and mother, and infant mortality was horrendous (Shakespeare's parents lost two children before he was born, and Shakespeare's only son, Hamnet, died in childhood). Because of primitive sanitation, disease spread easily and rapidly. Besides the plague, other diseases that were rampant included measles, smallpox, tuberculosis, and venereal diseases such as syphilis. Cuts and wounds could become infected and lead to death, as they did for Sir Philip Sidney, who died a slow and agonizing death twenty-six days after being wounded on the battlefield.

The level of violence in Shakespeare's age also contributed to a short life expectancy. Besides the violence of intermittent warfare, religious persecutions, and crime, encounters on the street or in taverns could lead to arguments, fights, and death. Two of Shakespeare's friends and fellow dramatists were involved in such incidents: Christopher Marlowe was stabbed in a tavern dispute and died young, and Ben Jonson killed a man in a quarrel. Also violent were the punishments meted out for crimes: Minor offenses like being a vagabond could get one a whipping or a morning in the stocks, while those guilty of more serious crimes could get an ear cut off or suffer branding and even death. During Henry VIII's reign, 72,000 thieves and vagabonds were hanged, while Elizabeth I's reign averaged around 800 per year. Those judged guilty of murder, treason, or heresy were publicly beheaded; burned at the stake; or hanged, drawn, and quartered.

As befitting such a violent time, even the favorite games, diversions, and entertainments were mostly violent. While higher society indulged in tennis, bowling, and card and board games (like chess), and while ladies and courtiers enjoyed dancing the dignified pavane, sprightly galliard, and thrilling volta, the favorite recreation of men remained hunting and jousting. Among the lower classes, the sport of choice (though banned for its violence) was football, played without rules on fields that could be miles long. Everybody loved bearbaiting, in which a bear chained to a post fought with dogs. Some noblemen could afford to stage private bearbaitings, perhaps at home in front of a few guests, but the general public could also participate by paying admission to watch bearbaiting on the Bankside near the playhouses.

CONDITIONS OF AUTHORSHIP

It has been estimated that more than half of the English populace during Shakespeare's time could read. This estimate might seem high, but printing made reading materials available, and religious controversy spurred literacy, especially the ability to read the Bible. Parish priests ran petty or ABC schools that offered rudimentary instruction in reading, writing, and arithmetic to both boys and girls. Middle-class boys, and a few poorer ones, went on to attend grammar schools run by the church or guilds. The grammar schools offered seven or more years of instruction, concentrating on Latin and favoring rote memory and recitation. As the son of a town official, Shakespeare attended the grammar school in Stratford. Upper-class boys and girls were taught by private tutors. From the grammar schools or private tutoring, a few of the brightest boys might go on to the universities at Oxford and Cambridge or to London's Inns of Court, the law schools. By Shakespeare's time the universities, which had developed to train priests, served students with other ambitions or those merely seeking further education.

Advancements in education and literacy stimulated the production of literature, but other conditions worked against authorship as a profession. Many of the writers were aristocratic or shared aristocratic attitudes toward authorship. Among the nobility, literary accomplishments were pursued and admired, but gentlemen would not lower themselves or soil their literary works by publishing them for money. Such authors shared their writings in manuscript among friends (as Shakespeare's sonnets circulated) or read them at private parties. Their writings were sometimes published in pirated or unauthorized versions (like some of Shakespeare's works), often with corrupt texts, or published by friends, usually after the author's death (like the 1623 First Folio collection of Shakespeare's plays). These circumstances of publication, particularly in an age when spelling and punctuation were not standardized, have left some daunting textual problems.

Even authors who did not share aristocratic attitudes about publishing had trouble making money or being independent. There was no copyright, so anybody could steal and publish a writer's work or, more likely, ideas or passages from it. Even Shakespeare did not scruple about drawing liberally from his sources. Without copyright and an effective royalty system, authors usually sold manuscripts outright to publishers, but for ridiculously low prices. To survive, authors sought aristocratic patrons who would give them support, as did Shakespeare in his early career, dedicating both *Venus and Adonis* (1593) and *The Rape of Lucrece* (1594) to the rich third Earl of Southampton. Patrons had to be pleased by the work and flattered in a dedication. Finally, the government censors had to approve the work.

The only category of literature to which some of these conditions did not apply was drama in performance; in publication, it was subject to the same problems as other literary work. The companies that performed the plays owned the playhouses and ran them like a business. Since drama was popular, performances of some plays made good money, but the company had to be careful to protect its investment in scripts and reward its best authors. Again, the motivation was not to publish scripts but just the opposite: to keep them from being stolen and published, sometimes in memorized versions. Nor did the playwrights need patrons, although the company as a whole needed the protection of a powerful sponsor, since unattached or strolling players could be treated as vagabonds. The drama was still subject to censorship, but the censors could not attend every performance. Under these conditions of authorship, Shakespeare not only survived but prospered.

Annotated Bibliography

Baker, Herschel. *The Dignity of Man: Studies in the Persistence of an Idea*. Cambridge, MA: Harvard UP, 1947. Still excellent for explaining the intellectual background of the Renaissance and its links to ancient and medieval thought, this work takes up such topics as Platonism, Stoicism, humanism, and religion. It was republished in paperback by Harper Torchbooks as *The Image of Man* (1961).

Frye, Roland Mushat. *Shakespeare's Life and Times: A Pictorial Record*. Princeton: Princeton UP, 1967. This book is useful for its illustrations and brief explanations.

Raleigh, Sir Walter et al., eds. *Shakespeare's England: An Account of the Life and Manners of His Age*. 2 vols. Oxford: Clarendon P, 1916. Issued on the tercentenary of Shakespeare's death, these two volumes cover many facets of life in Shakespeare's England. Chapters include "Religion" (by the Rev. Ronald Bayne), "The Court" (by E. K. Chambers), "Education" (by Sir John Edwin Sandys); others treat the arts, the book trade, recreations, and much, much more.

Ridley, Jasper. *A Brief History of the Tudor Age*. London: Constable, 1998. Even when wandering off the subject, Ridley gives an informative and intriguing account of the details of everyday life in Shakespeare's time. The book was republished in paperback by Carroll & Graf (2002).

Rowse, A. L. *The England of Elizabeth: The Structure of Society*. New York: Macmillan, 1950. Rowse was a leading historian of Shakespeare's age. This title, together with *The Expansion of Elizabethan England* (New York: St. Martin's P, 1955) and *The Elizabethan Renaissance* (New York: Scribner, 1972), provides a panoramic portrait of England's golden age.

Smith, Lacy Baldwin. *The Horizon Book of the Elizabethan World*. New York: American Heritage, 1967. A lavishly illustrated, well-written history of the era. Includes much information about life in late-sixteenth-century England. Contains a short section on Shakespeare's theater.

Wood, Michael. *Shakespeare*. New York: Basic Books, 2003. Published to accompany the BBC television series *In Search of Shakespeare* (2003), this biography relates his life to his time and is full of interesting details, illustrations, and speculations.

William Shakespeare's Life

Joseph Rosenblum

The River Avon (which in Celtic means "river") cuts through Warwickshire. To its north lies the Forest of Arden, and along its banks rests the market town of Stratford, some hundred miles northwest of London. In the sixteenth century the journey to the capital would have required three or four days on foot, at least two days by horse. Stratford derives its name from the Roman "straet" or road that crossed or forded the Avon at this point. Michael Wood quotes John Leland's description of the town in the mid-1500s:

> The towne of Stratford stondithe apon a playne ground on the right hand of [River] Avon, as the water descendithe. It hathe 2 or 3 very lardge streets, besyde back lanes. One of the principall streets ledithe from est to west, another from southe to northe. . . . The towne is reasonably well builded of timbar. . . . The parish church is a fayre large peace of worke, and stodeth at the southe end of the towne. . . . The church is dedicated to the Trinitie. (Wood, p. 22)

In 1553 Stratford received a charter making it a royal borough.

Like the rest of England, Stratford underwent repeated shifts in its official religion in the course of the sixteenth century. Henry VIII went from being "Defender of the [Catholic] Faith," a title awarded him by the papacy for his opposition to Martin Luther, to embracing a version of Protestantism. During the reign of his short-lived son, Edward VI, England moved further along the road of religious reform, only to return to Catholicism in 1553 when Edward's half-sister Mary Tudor assumed the throne. Mary died in 1558, and under Elizabeth England once more became an officially Protestant nation, though most of Elizabeth's subjects at least initially remained loyal to the old faith.

SHAKESPEARE'S PARENTS AND HIS EARLY YEARS

John Shakespeare, who was born sometime before 1530 and died in 1601, came to Stratford from the nearby village of Snitterfield, four miles northeast of the mar-

Shakespeare's birthplace, Stratford-upon-Avon, England. Courtesy of the Library of Congress.

ket town. Here he set himself up as a glover and whitawer—a preparer of soft, white leather. William Shakespeare's acquaintance with the trade is evident in Mistress Quickly's asking of Slender in *The Merry Wives of Windsor* (1.4.20–21), "Does he not wear a great round beard, like a glover's paring-knife?" By the 1550s John was living in Henley Street, where he owned two adjacent houses that were not connected in the sixteenth century but later became so. The one to the east is called the Woolshop, for reasons to be discussed shortly. The other is known as the Birthplace. John acquired the Woolshop in 1556, and soon afterward he married Mary Arden (1540–1608), whose father owned the land in Snitterfield that Richard Shakespeare, John's father, farmed. Mary was at least ten years younger than her husband. No record of the wedding survives, but the ceremony would have been Catholic.

The family may have remained Catholic. In 1757, while retiling the Shakespeare house in Henley Street, workmen found in the rafters what became known as John Shakespeare's Spiritual Last Will and Testament. A translation of Cardinal Carlo Borromeo's "Last Will of the Soul," it was printed in the thousands, and copies were brought to England in 1580 by Edward Campion and his Catholic companions. Item I of the testament expresses the fear of being "cut off in the blossom of my sins," a phrase that Shakespeare seems to have recalled when he wrote *Hamlet*. There the Ghost laments being "Cut off even in the blossoms of my sin" (1.5.76; Holden, p. 39). The eighteenth-century Shakespeare scholar Edmond Malone initially accepted the document as genuine, then rejected it as spurious. The item has vanished, so its authenticity cannot be determined. The text certainly is genuine, but its provenance remains a matter of debate. However, the line from *Hamlet* is fascinating, and Shakespeare's plays show much sympathy for friars at a time when being a Catholic priest in England was a capital offense.

John initially prospered in Stratford. In September 1556 he was named one of the town's two tasters (that is, inspectors) of ale and bread, and five years later he became one of the two chamberlains responsible for the city's property and finances. Among his tasks in January 1563 was defacing the papist images in Holy Trinity Church. Whitewash was applied selectively and thinly; after all, another change in the religious tide was always possible.

On April 26, 1564, the local vicar, John Bretchgirdle, recorded the Anglican baptism of John Shakespeare's first son, William. Two daughters had previously died in infancy. The date of birth is not recorded, but the oft-cited day, April 23, the feast of St. George, England's patron saint, cannot be ruled out. In 1626 Shakespeare's only granddaughter, Elizabeth, married on April 22, perhaps as a tribute to her grandfather's birthday (or perhaps to avoid marrying on her grandfather's death day, which is the twenty-third).

William's birth preceded by only a few months the most severe outbreak of the bubonic plague in England since the Black Death of 1348. On July 11, 1564, the vicar wrote in his burial register, "*Hic incipit pestis*" [today the plague begins]. One-sixth of Stratford's population of some 1,200 died before the plague abated. Three doors down from the Shakespeare house in Henley Street, the Greens lost four children. The Shakespeares were spared, and in October of 1566 William got a brother, Gilbert (baptized on October 13, 1566). More siblings followed. Joan Shakespeare was baptized on April 15, 1569. Anne, born in September 1571, died at the age of seven. Behind the cemetery where she was buried runs a stream. There a girl named Katherine Hamlett drowned. The coroner examined the case, and, as the Second Gravedigger states in the play that bears the same name as the girl, "The crowner hath sate on her, and finds it Christian burial" (*Hamlet*, 5.1.4–5; Bradbrook, p. 159). Her case would become Ophelia's. Richard Shakespeare, named for his grandfather, was baptized on March 11, 1574, Edmund on May 3, 1580. Edmund would follow his older brother to London and the stage and die at the age of twenty-seven.

With so many mouths to feed, John was fortunate that business remained good. In 1565 he became an alderman, a post that entitled his children to a free education at the Stratford grammar school, and in September 1568 he was elected bailiff (mayor) of the corporation of Stratford. In 1569 he applied for a coat of arms, which for some reason was refused. The following year he was fined forty shillings for charging £20 interest on an £80 loan to a John Musshem. One source of John Shakespeare's income thus was lending money; we therefore know that he had money to lend. The sum of £20 was the annual salary of the Stratford schoolmaster. John chose not to run for re-election as bailiff. However, in September 1571 he was chosen Chief Alderman and Justice of the Peace, and deputy bailiff to his friend and Henley Street neighbor Adrian Quiney. In January 1572 the two men went to London together on Stratford corporation business. In 1575 John purchased two more houses in Stratford for £40, a sign of continuing prosperity.

SHAKESPEARE'S YOUTH

The young Shakespeare would have learned about nature from the Warwickshire countryside. He would have seen tradesmen on the town's streets and in the marketplace. He would have observed local constables like Dull and Elbow (*Measure for Measure*) and Dogberry (*Much Ado about Nothing*), especially since his father had been named a constable in 1558. William heard the local dialect and would use it in his plays, as when he writes of "caraways" (Cotswold apples; *2 Henry IV*, 5.3.3) or "breeze" (gadflies; *Troilus and Cressida*, 1.3.48; *Antony and Cleopatra*, 3.10.14). He would have heard the Bible read at church; his plays quote from and draw on the Bible more than any other source. And Shakespeare would have been exposed to theater. When John was bailiff, the Queen's Men and the Earl of Worcester's Men played in the Guild Hall, and the latter troupe returned to Stratford several times thereafter. Other companies also performed in town. Sir Thomas Lucy at Charlecote House, a bit upriver from Stratford, kept players. When Shakespeare was eleven, the Earl of Leicester hosted Queen Elizabeth at Kenilworth, a short walk from Henley Street. On Monday, July 18, 1575, the entertainment included Triton riding on a mermaid and Arion on a dolphin. In *A Midsummer Night's Dream* Oberon tells Puck,

> Once I sat upon a promontory
> And heard a mermaid on a dolphin's back
> Uttering such dulcet and harmonious breath
> That the rude sea grew civil at her song. (2.1.149–152)

Was the playwright remembering a pageant seen in his youth? At nearby Coventry, Corpus Christi plays continued to be performed through the 1570s. Based on Bible stories, these performances would include the ranting of the mad King Herod. In *Hamlet* the prince warns the players not to "tear a passion to totters [tatters], . . . it out-Herods Herod" (3.2.9–14). In 1583 Davy Jones, related by marriage to the Hathaways of Shottery, a village a mile from Stratford, led a troupe of mummers in a Whitsuntide performance. In *The Winter's Tale* Perdita says,

> Come, take your flow'rs.
> Methinks I play as I have seen them do
> In Whitsun pastorals. (4.4.132–134)

Shakespeare's formal education took place in the King's New School, a quarter of a mile from his home. He would have matriculated at the age of seven, by which time he was expected to be able to read and write English. His schoolhouse experiences recur in his plays. In *The Merry Wives of Windsor*, for example, Anne Page's little boy, who is named William, is examined by the schoolmaster Evans (4.1). Mrs. Page concludes, "He is a better scholar than I thought he was." His teacher concurs, "He is a good sprag [lively] memory" (4.1.80–82).

William Shakespeare's sprag memory of his Warwickshire is everywhere apparent in his works. Christopher Sly in *The Taming of the Shrew* takes the last name of Stephen Sly of Stratford. Sly in the play supposedly lives at Burton-on-the-Heath, a village about sixteen miles from Shakespeare's birthplace; Shakespeare's aunt and uncle Edmund and Joan Lambert lived there. Sly refers to "Marian Hacket, the fat ale-wife of Wincot" (Induction, 2.21–22). In the early 1590s Robert Hacket was living at Wincot, four miles from Stratford.

Classes at the King's New School, Stratford's grammar school, began at 6:00 A.M. in the summer, 7:00 A.M. in winter, and continued to 5:30 P.M., with respites for breakfast and lunch. From the age of seven onward, William would have been drilled in Latin. William Lily's *A Shorter Introduction to Grammar* was a basic text.

From drills in this book young William in *The Merry Wives of Windsor* repeats the Latin articles. Benedict's interjection "ah, ha, he" (*Much Ado about Nothing*, 4.1.22) comes from this text, and Sir Toby Belch quotes "*deliculo surgere*" from Lily's proverb, "*Deliculo surgere saluberrimum est*"—to rise at dawn is most healthful (*Twelfth Night*, 2.3.2–3). Leonard Culmann's *Sententiae Pueriles* (mottoes for youth) was another popular school text. According to C. G. Smith in *Shakespeare's Proverb Lore* (Cambridge, MA: Harvard UP, 1968) and G. V. Manitto in "Shakespeare and Culmann's *Sententiae Pueriles*" (*Notes and Queries* 230 [1985]: 30–31), Shakespeare quotes this work some 200 times in his plays. Holofernes in *Love's Labor's Lost* is fond of Baptista Spagnuoli, known as Mantuanus, a poet read in the schools. Students would have read and performed the Roman playwrights Terence, Plautus, and Seneca and would have studied the major Latin poets, including Virgil and Ovid. The latter was Shakespeare's favorite poet. In *Titus Andronicus* Lavinia uses Ovid's *Metamorphoses* to explain what has happened to her (4.1). The choice is apt, since Shakespeare derived her rape and mutilation from Ovid's tale of Tereus and Philomel. The boy in that scene says that his mother gave him that book. Did Shakespeare's mother do likewise?

Under the floorboards in the Woolshop bits of wool have been found. As a glover, John was not supposed to deal in wool, but much of his prosperity seems to have rested on his trading illegally in this commodity. His son knew a lot about the business. In *The Winter's Tale* the Clown enters calculating, "Let me see: every 'leven wether tods, every tod yields pound and odd shilling; fifteen hundred shorn, what comes the wool to?" (4.3.32–34). In the mid-sixteenth century a tod of wool (twenty-eight pounds) cost exactly twenty-one shillings—pound and odd shilling. The sheep-shearing festival in *The Winter's Tale* (4.4) would have been a familiar sight to the young William accompanying his father on his wool-gathering expeditions.

In October 1576 the Privy Council acted to curtail the illegal trade in wool, and John's fortunes then rapidly declined. In 1578 he was exempted from paying the weekly four-pence tax for poor relief. In that year he sold twenty acres of land that had been part of Mary's dowry. In the spring of 1579 he mortgaged Arden property at Wilmcote for £40 and never was able to repay the loan. That October he sold two houses and a hundred acres of land for the desperate price of £4. He stopped attending meetings of the aldermen; in 1586 he was dismissed from office for nonattendance. In 1592 he was cited for not attending Anglican communion and claimed that he stayed away for fear of being arrested for debt. Does this account attest to his poverty? Or was this excuse masking his Catholic sympathies?

According to Nicholas Rowe, Shakespeare's first true biographer, William had to leave school early to help his father in the latter's declining business. Shakespeare probably was about fifteen at the time, when he would have left school anyway. His activities thereafter remain a mystery. In the seventeenth century, John Aubrey claimed that Shakespeare worked for a time as a schoolmaster in the country. In his 1581 will Alexander Houghton of Lancashire mentions a musician/actor William Shakeshafte. Shakespeare's last schoolmaster, John Cottam, had ties to Houghton, and both Cottam and Houghton were Catholic. Thomas Cottam, John's brother, was a colleague of Edward Campion and was executed on December 1, 1581, for his faith. Thomas could have supplied John with his Spiritual Last Will and Testament. Shakespeare's grandfather Richard is sometimes named as Shakeshafte, but the name is common in Lancashire. Did a Catholic Shakespeare go two hundred miles north of Stratford for safety and employment? The Houghtons were friendly with the Stanleys, again Catholic. Ferdinando Stanley, Lord Strange, the son of the fourth Earl of Derby, was patron of an acting troupe that performed at least two of Shakespeare's early plays and formed the core of the Lord Chamberlain's Men, Shakespeare's company. Did the Houghtons and Stanleys provide Shakespeare's entry into the London theater world?

MARRIAGE AND FAMILY

Wherever Shakespeare was in the late 1570s, he must have been back in Stratford by the summer of 1582 because in August of that year Anne Hathaway became pregnant with his child. She was eight or nine years older than he. Sonnet 145 may be addressed to her; the concluding couplet seems to pun on her name:

> Those lips that Love's own hand did make
> Breath'd forth the sound that said "I hate"
> To me that languish'd for her sake;
> But when she saw my woeful state, . . .
> "'I hate' from hate away she threw,
> And sav'd my life, saying 'not you.'"

This sonnet is written in iambic tetrameter rather than pentameter and uses simpler diction than the sonnets surrounding it, suggesting that it is an early composition. On November 27, 1582, Shakespeare applied for a special license to marry "Anne Whately" of Temple Grafton. The license itself bears the name of Anne Hathaway: "Whately" is most likely a clerical error. The wedding probably occurred on December 1, since Advent began that year on December 2, and no marriages would have been allowed until the week after Epiphany. By mid-January, Anne's pregnancy would have been embarrassingly apparent. If the wedding occurred at Temple Grafton, perhaps the location was chosen because the vicar, John Frith, was noted in a 1586 government report as "an old priest and Unsound in religion," that is, a Catholic or having Catholic tendencies (Wood, p. 85). The newlyweds' first child, Susannah, was baptized on May 26, 1583, in an Anglican rite in Stratford, and on February 2, 1585, their twins, Judith and Hamnet/Hamlet were baptized. The children were named for Judith and Hamnet/Hamlet Sadler, Catholic friends of the family.

The only documented evidence of Shakespeare's first twenty-four years are of his baptism, marriage, the baptism of his children, and a lawsuit for the recovery of the mortgaged property at Wilmcote. No records survive from the Stratford grammar school for his years there. The Shakeshafte of Houghton's will may or may not be the future playwright. The period between the birth of the twins and the first record of Shakespeare's success in London is referred to as the "lost years." Perhaps he helped his father in the gloving business. Perhaps he was articled to a lawyer as a clerk. And how did he get to London? In 1587 the Queen's Men toured Oxfordshire. At the town of Thame one of the troupe's actors, William Knell, was killed in a brawl with another member of the company. When the players reached Stratford, they were a man short. This company would produce *The Troublesome Reigne of King John* (published in 1591), *The Taming of a Shrew* (published in 1594), and

The True Tragedy of Richard Duke of Yorke (published in 1595). The first two are closely related to Shakespeare's plays, and the third is a corrupt version ("Bad Quarto") of Shakespeare's *3 Henry VI*. Did the Queen's Men leave Stratford with a young man of literary ability? In *The Winter's Tale* the old shepherd observes, "I would there were no age between ten and three-and-twenty, or that youth would sleep out the rest; for there is nothing in the between but getting wenches with child, wronging the ancientry, stealing, fighting" (3.3.59–62). Between those ages Shakespeare certainly had gotten a wench with child. Legend claims that he poached deer from Sir Thomas Lucy. That tale must be false because Lucy kept no deer. But Lucy did have rabbits. The story goes that Lucy had William beaten and jailed for stealing game. In retaliation, William penned so vitriolic a ballad about Lucy that William had to leave Stratford. Justice Shallow in *The Merry Wives of Windsor* has a coat of arms with luces or pikes, just like Sir Thomas. "Luce" and "louse" were pronounced identically in Shakespeare's day, and Justice Shallow may be a satiric portrait of Shakespeare's old neighbor. Might young Shakespeare have been guilty of stealing and wronging the ancientry? And did he, at the age of twenty-three in 1587, begin a new life? Lucy actively pursued Catholics. Did Shakespeare head to London to escape Lucy's clutches?

SHAKESPEARE IN LONDON

There is no question that sometime in the late 1580s or early 1590s Shakespeare did go to the capital, then a city of some 200,000, the largest in Europe. London was still a walled city in 1590, with seven gates that are recalled in place-names: Bishopgate, Moorgate, Cripplegate, Aldersgate, Newgate, Ludgate, and Aldgate. Shakespeare came to London at an auspicious time, the dawn of the golden age of English drama. In 1567 the prosperous grocer John Brayne had built the first theater, the Red Lion, at Whitechapel, which was outside the city walls and so in the "liberties," that is, areas not subject to the London council and its Puritanical aversion to plays and playhouses. Muriel C. Bradbrook quotes a 1597 memorandum from the Lord Mayor of London to the Privy Council in which he condemns theaters as "the ordinary places for vagrant persons, masterless men, thieves, horse-stealers, whoremongers, cozeners, coney-catchers, contrivers of treason and other idle and dangerous persons to meet together" (Bradbrook, p. 32). In 1576 Brayne and his brother-in-law James Burbage erected another playhouse in the liberty of Halliwell (Holywell), Shoreditch, about a mile north of the city wall. They called this building the Theatre. James Burbage, like Snug in *A Midsummer Night's Dream*, was a carpenter turned actor. The next year the Curtain arose 200 yards south of the Theatre at Moorfields. Shakespeare would use both venues. A mile south of London Bridge stood a playhouse at Newington Butts. Built by Jerome Savage, it was in use by 1580. In 1587 Philip Henslowe opened yet another theater, the Rose, on the site of an old rose garden at Southwark, on the south side of the River Thames and again outside the jurisdiction of the city council.

The Rose became the home of Christopher Marlowe's plays. Here Thomas Kyd staged his immensely popular revenge drama *The Spanish Tragedy* (ca. 1587) and perhaps an early version of *Hamlet*. At the Rose audiences first saw Shakespeare's *Titus Andronicus* and the *Henry VI* trilogy, played by Lord Strange's Men. The Rose held 600 people in the yard, where standing room cost a penny, and another 1,400 in the three tiers of galleries. Despite its large capacity, spectators were close enough to the stage to create a sense of intimacy with the actors.

The various acting companies, all under the protection of patrons (as required by law), consisted of eight to twelve shareholder-performers who split the profits and hired additional actors as needed for five to ten shillings a week. An actor's livelihood was as precarious in the sixteenth century as it is in the twenty-first. Throughout Shakespeare's life, companies rose and fell. Even the Lord Chamberlain's Men, the most successful of the troupes, fell on hard times in the late 1590s. The companies needed plays, lots of plays. They performed six days a week, with a different work being produced each afternoon. The Lord Admiral's Men put on fifteen different works in twenty-seven days, some thirty plays in a season. Of these, half would be new. Actors had to be quick studies, playwrights quick composers. One way to churn out plays quickly was through collaboration. Of eighty-nine plays mentioned in Henslowe's diary, fifty-five were joint productions. Of course, in a sense every play is a joint production, since texts are altered, often drastically, in rehearsal and in response to audience reaction. Shakespeare averaged two plays a year during his career, creating forty. This pace is astonishing considering the length and complexity of many of his works, most of which he wrote by himself; and one must recall that for most of his life in the theater he was acting as well as writing. While he was prolific, others were even more so. John Chettle worked on forty-eight plays. Between 1598 and 1605 Thomas Dekker had a hand in forty-four pieces. Most of the major playwrights had attended Oxford or Cambridge and so were known as the University Wits. Kyd and Shakespeare were the two major exceptions.

According to John Aubrey, in the early 1590s Shakespeare was living in Shoreditch, near the Theatre and the Curtain, an area noted for its taverns and brothels. By 1596 records show that he had taken up residence in St. Helen's parish, Bishopgate, about a mile from the Theatre. This was a prosperous part of town but close to Eastcheap, immortalized in the *Henry IV* plays as the haunt of Sir John Falstaff. It was also near the Jewish quarter, where a musical Venetian family named Bassano lived. The name seems to be the source for the character Bassanio in *The Merchant of Venice*, which famously includes a Venetian Jew. Emilia Bassano Lanier has been proposed by A. L. Rowse and Michael Wood, as well as others, as the Dark Lady of Shakespeare's later sonnets (sonnets 127–152). Like Jessica in *The Merchant*, Emilia married a gentile. Like Imogen in *Cymbeline*, she had a mole under her neck (Wood, p. 200).

INFLUENCES

Shakespeare learned from the leading dramatists of the early 1590s. From Marlowe he took blank verse and soul-searching soliloquies. The villainous blackamoor Aaron in Shakespeare's early revenge tragedy *Titus Andronicus* (ca. 1591) derives from Marlowe's Barabas in *The Jew of Malta*, and the title character of that play resembles the vengeful Hieronymo from Kyd's *Spanish Tragedy*. Shakespeare also was reading not only his beloved Ovid and the Romans but also works like Raphael Holinshed's *Chronicles of England, Scotland, and Ireland* (1577; 2nd ed. 1587), a key source for Shakespeare's history plays, for the tragedies *King Lear* and *Macbeth*, and for the late romance *Cymbeline*. Shakespeare supplemented Holinshed with other historical accounts, including Edward Hall's *The Union of the Noble and Illustre Families of Lan-*

caster and York (1548) and John Stow's *Chronicles* and *Annales* (1565). From Sir Philip Sidney's *Arcadia* (1590–1593) he took the Gloucester subplot of *King Lear*.

Nor did he ignore contemporary events. In *1 Henry VI* (ca. 1592) he depicts the heroism of Lord Talbot, who also has the title of Lord Strange of Blackmere (4.7.65), perhaps a compliment to the contemporary Lord Strange, whose company produced the play. The work includes a fictional siege of Rouen. The French were besieging the city in 1591, and the Earl of Essex was trying unsuccessfully to relieve the town in aid of Henry of Navarre. Ferdinand, king of Navarre, is a character in *Love's Labor's Lost* (ca. 1594), which includes the names of other actual French nobles of the period, and the embassy of the princess of France to Navarre in the play derives from a 1578 visit to Henry of Navarre by his estranged wife, Marguerite de Valois.

Performed on March 3, 1592, Shakespeare's "harey the vj," as Henslowe's diary refers to it, earned £3.16s.8d., more than any other performance that season. The work was staged another fourteen times before the theaters closed on June 19. Based on Henslowe's accounting one may calculate that 16,344 people watched the play that season from the galleries, and many more stood on the ground to see it. In *Pierce Penilesse His Supplication to the Divell* (September 1592) Thomas Nashe wrote,

> How it would have joyed brave Talbot (the terror of the French) to think that after he had lain two hundred years in his tomb, he should triumph again on the stage, and have his bones new embalmed with the tears of ten thousand spectators at least. (Wood, pp. 142–144)

On the heels of this success, the almost twenty-eight-year-old playwright suffered a severe setback. In Sonnet 66 Shakespeare writes of "art made tongue-tied by authority" (l. 9). In late June 1592, after a riot at the Rose on June 11, authorities ordered London's theaters closed until Michaelmas (September 29). By then, an outbreak of bubonic plague had begun; it would keep the theaters dark for twenty months, with only two brief exceptions in the winters of 1592–1593 and 1593–1594. To earn a living, actors had to tour, and some companies would not survive the long absence from London. Shakespeare looked for another source of income.

Another blow soon followed. On September 20, 1592, Henry Chettle entered in the Stationers' Register, the list of works officially licensed for publication in that age of censorship, Robert Greene's *A Groatsworth of Witte, Bought with a Million of Repentance*. Robert Greene was an Elizabethan author who composed this work as he was dying of syphilis. It includes the first clear reference to Shakespeare as a London dramatist, and the reference is not complimentary. "[T]here is an upstart Crow, beautified with our feathers, that with his *Tygers hart wrapt in a Players hyde*, supposes he is as well able to bombast out a blanke verse as the best of you: and being an absolute *Johannes fac totum* [Jack of all trades], is in his own conceit the onely Shake-scene in a country" (in Honan, p. 159).

The phrase about the tiger's heart comes from *3 Henry VI*, 1.4.137, where the Duke of York shouts at Queen Margaret, "O tiger's heart wrapp'd in a woman's hide." In *2 Henry VI* Margaret says of Gloucester, "his feathers are but borrowed, / For he's disposed as the hateful raven" (3.1.75–76). In a sense Greene's lines are flattering. The plays were not yet in print, so Greene must have attended performances, and the lines stuck with him. That the reference is to Shakespeare, and that Shakespeare knew it, is evidenced by Polonius's observation on Hamlet's letter to Ophelia. Hamlet writes, "the most beautified Ophelia," and Polonius says, "That's an ill phrase, a vile phrase, 'beautified' is a vile phrase" (*Hamlet*, 2.2.111–113). Park Honan suggests that Shakespeare may also be referring to Greene's slur in Sonnet 112, when the poet writes, "For what care I who calls me well or ill, / So you o'ergreen my bad, my good allow" (ll. 3–4; Honan, p. 161).

In December 1592 Chettle dissociated himself from Greene's pamphlet. In *Kind-Harts Dreame* Chettle claimed that Shakespeare was a fine actor and "my selfe have seene hiss demeanor no lesse civill than he excellent in the qualitie he professes. Besides, divers of worship have reported his uprightness of dealing, which argues his honesty, and his facetious grace in writting, that aprooves his Art" (in Honan, p. 162). Honan (162) suggests that "divers of worship" may have pressured Chettle to issue that retraction, and perhaps among those influential people was Henry Wriothesley, third Earl of Southampton, a leading Catholic nobleman.

THE EARLY PLAYS AND POEMS

On December 28, 1594, *The Comedy of Errors* was staged at Gray's Inn, Holborn, one of the Inns of Court where lawyers trained. Law students were among the greatest patrons of drama. One of the members of Gray's Inn was Southampton. Shakespeare's play is based on Plautus's *Menaechmi*, though Shakespeare refers to the Phoenix (a London tavern) and the Porpentine, a Bankside inn. Shakespeare also doubles the number of twins in the original. As the father of twins, he shows an interest in this *lusus naturae*. In *Twelfth Night* Viola and Sebastian are fraternal twins but also identical. It is difficult to date *The Comedy of Errors* precisely, so the work could have been performed before the theaters closed in 1592. Alternatively, it could have been written while the theaters were closed, in anticipation of their reopening.

Certainly Shakespeare was not idle during those twenty months. In addition to probably writing one or more plays, he composed two long narrative, erotic poems (epyllions), *Venus and Adonis* (1593) and *The Rape of Lucrece* (1594), both dedicated to Southampton. Southampton's confessor, the poet Robert Southwell, was a distant cousin of Shakespeare.

Ovid depicted Venus and Adonis as lovers. Shakespeare presents an older, sexually experienced woman trying to seduce a young, prim lad who prefers hunting to lovemaking. Does the poem reflect the relationship between the twenty-six-year-old Anne Hathaway and the eighteen-year-old William Shakespeare? Elsewhere in his plays he shows women wooing men and going to bed with them to secure marriage. Titania wants Bottom and Helena pursues Demetrius in *A Midsummer Night's Dream*. In *The Two Gentlemen of Verona*, Julia disguises herself as a man to go after her beloved Proteus; and Silvia, more adept in the ways of love than Valentine, dictates a love letter to him and then has him deliver it to himself. Both *All's Well That Ends Well* and *Measure for Measure* invoke the bed trick to get men to marry. In contrast, in *The Merry Wives of Windsor* William Fenton and Anne Page elope to cement a love match opposed by Anne's parents. The first names of these lovers may be significant.

Venus and Adonis was immensely popular, going through at least six editions by the end of the decade and ten by 1617. *Lucrece* was less successful but still was reprinted five times before Shakespeare's death. Both poems were printed by Richard Field, a Stratford native who had settled in London. Field may have been a schoolmate of Shakespeare. Whereas the dedication to *Venus and Adonis* seems to

Portrait of William Shakespeare. Courtesy of the Library of Congress.

address a stranger, that of *Lucrece* is more familiar: "The warrant I have of your Honourable disposition, not the worth of my untutored Lines makes it assured of acceptance. What I have done is yours, what I have to do is yours, being part in all I have, devoted yours." The sentiment seems similar to that expressed in Shakespeare's sonnets addressed to the fair youth.

By 1594 Shakespeare probably had begun writing sonnets to Southampton, the most likely candidate for the role of the fair youth of those verses (sonnets 1–126). Sonnets 127–152 are addressed to a Dark Lady with whom the fair youth has an affair. In the dedication to *The Unfortunate Traveller* (1594), Thomas Nashe describes Southampton, perhaps with wicked wit, as "A dere lover and cherisher . . . as well of the lovers of Poets, as of Poets themselves." In 1594 an Oxford undergraduate, Henry Willobie, published *Willobie His Avisa*, in which an "old player," W. S., discusses love with H. W. The initials invite speculation. Though the sonnets were not published until 1609, Francis Meres refers to them in his 1598 *Palladis Tamia: Wit's Treasury*, and versions of sonnets 138 and 144 appeared in *The Passionate Pilgrim* (1599). Even earlier, Michael Drayton may have copied a line from Sonnet 2 in *Shepheards Garland* (1593; see Honan, p. 182), though the borrowing could have gone the other way.

One version of the sonnets' genesis is that Southampton's mother, eager to have her son wed, engaged Shakespeare to further this plan. Southampton was at the time a ward of the state, and William Cecil, Lord Burghley, wanted Southampton to marry his granddaughter, Elizabeth Vere, daughter of the Earl of Oxford. Southampton refused and so faced a ruinous fine of £5,000. The first seventeen sonnets encourage the fair youth to marry. But with sonnet 18, the one beginning famously, "Shall I compare thee to a summer's day?" the tone shifts, and by Sonnet 20 the young man is "the master mistress of my passion." Sonnets were in vogue in the early 1590s, a trend inspired by the publication of Sir Philip Sidney's *Astrophil and Stella* (1591). William Herbert is another candidate for the fair youth, though he was born in 1580, so the sonnets would have to date from later in the 1590s. Or the sonnets may have been literary exercises mocking the fashion of the moment. Whereas traditionally the sonnet is addressed by a man to a beautiful, aloof woman of high station, Shakespeare writes 126 of them to a beautiful young man of high station, and another 26 to a woman who is not beautiful by Renaissance standards and who is certainly not aloof to the poet or to others. The Romantic poet William Wordsworth wrote that in the sonnets "Shakespeare unlocked his heart" ("Scorn Not the Sonnet," l. 3). To which Robert Browning replied, "Did Shakespeare? If so, the less Shakespeare he!" ("House," l. 40). Browning means that as the consummate artist Shakespeare transmuted any personal experience. Artifice cannot be equated with autobiography.

PLAY PRODUCTION, 1594–1596

By the time the playhouses reopened in 1594 the theatrical landscape had changed. The Earl of Sussex had died on December 14, 1593, Lord Strange on April 16, 1594. In addition to the deaths of these two patrons of the drama, Lord Pembroke's Men had disbanded. Two new companies now emerged, the Lord Admiral's Men, based at the Rose, and the Lord Chamberlain's Men at the Theatre. Shakespeare became a shareholder in the latter troupe, perhaps in exchange for agreeing to write two plays a year. His recent poetic activity renders subsequent plays more lyrical, sometimes even including sonnets, such as the prologue to *Romeo and Juliet* and the sonnet the two lovers in that play compose in 1.5.93–106. The serious and comic aspects of love portrayed in the sonnets appear in *Romeo and Juliet* and its sequel, *A Midsummer Night's Dream*. Berowne in *Love's Labor's Lost* loves a woman who is "black as ebony" (4.3.243). The introspection of the sonnets also finds echoes in the plays that follow. Richard III's soliloquies reveal what such speeches had shown since the medieval mystery and morality plays: they inform the audience of what the character is like and what he has already decided to do. In *Richard II* (ca. 1597), *Hamlet* (ca. 1601), and *Twelfth Night* (ca. 1601–1602), to cite but three examples, soliloquies show people thinking, discovering for themselves who they are and what they want. Rhetoric yields to poetry; characters become dynamic rather than static.

The plays that Shakespeare wrote for the Lord Chamberlain's Men enjoyed great popularity: for example, *1 Henry IV*, first published in 1598, went through seven editions before 1623. This play introduced the world to one of Shakespeare's most endearing and enduring figures, Sir John Falstaff. Legend claims that Queen Elizabeth was so taken with him that she asked for a play showing Falstaff in love, and to satisfy this request Shakespeare quickly composed *The Merry Wives of Windsor* (ca. 1597). The title page to the 1602 quarto edition of that play states that it "hath bene diuers times Acted . . . Both before her Maiestie, and else-where."

William Brooke, the 7th Lord Cobham, or perhaps his son, was less pleased with the *Henry IV* plays because Shakespeare had originally named Falstaff Sir John Oldcastle, Brooke's Protestant martyr ancestor (though in youth Oldcastle had been quite wild). William Brooke had succeeded Shakespeare's patron, Henry Carey, Lord Hunsdon, as Lord Chamberlain (August 1596–March 1597), so his opinion mattered. In the epilogue to *2 Henry IV* Shakespeare offered an apology, promising that in the next play "Falstaff shall die of a sweat, unless already 'a be killed with your hard opinions; for Oldcastle died a martyr, and this is not the man" (ll. 30–32). Shakespeare again offended Brooke in *The Merry Wives of Windsor* by having Master Ford assume the name of Brooke when he disguises himself in conversation with Falstaff, so that name was changed to Broome.

The success of Shakespeare's plays contributed to the prosperity of the shareholders of the Lord Chamberlain's Men, including their leading writer. By 1596 Shakespeare may have been earning as much as £200 a year, the equivalent of about £100,000 in 2004. In that year he secured a coat of arms for his father (and thus himself). The crest bears a silver spear tipped with gold, and the motto is *Non sans droit* (not without right). Shakespeare's friend and rival Ben Jonson mocked this phrase in *Every Man out of His Humour* as "Not without mustard." The heralds described Shakespeare's grandfather Robert Arden as "esquire" and "armiger" (entitled to bear a coat of arms). In *The Merry Wives of Windsor* Shakespeare himself makes light of his ancestry, having the not very bright Slender declare that his uncle, Justice Shallow, "writes himself *Armigero* in any bill, warrant, quittance, or obligation. *Armigero*" (1.1.9–11).

PERSONAL EVENTS

In the midst of Shakespeare's prosperity, misfortune struck. In August 1596 Hamnet/Hamlet Shakespeare died at the age of eleven and was buried at Holy Trinity Church. The child's living monument would be one of Shakespeare's greatest plays, forever linking the names of father and son. In 1597 Shakespeare's wife and children finally left Henley Street and the in-laws (with whom they had been living for nearly fifteen years!) for Chapel Street, where Shakespeare bought the second best house in Stratford, New Place. The bill of sale lists the price as £60, but it probably cost twice that sum. The Underhills had paid £110 for the house in 1567, and it was then described as being in a state of "great ruine and decay" (Holden, p. 169). The house had been built by Hugh Clopton, a local man who had prospered in London and had risen to become Lord Mayor of that city. The three-story house boasted ten fireplaces, two gardens, two barns, and an orchard. It had a frontage of sixty feet and a depth of seventy. William Underhill, who sold the house to Shakespeare, was murdered by his son Fulke (hanged in 1599 for the crime) shortly before the Shakespeares moved in. In 1759 the Reverend Francis Gastrell tore down the house to protest the tax levied on it. Shakespeare planted apples and roses on his new property. Park Honan notes that Shakespeare refers to apples some thirty times in his plays, and to roses over a hundred (239). In his barns in 1598 Shakespeare had eighty bushels of grain at a time of shortages in Stratford. In *Macbeth* 2.3, among those whom the porter thinks are entering hell is a speculator in grain.

Late in 1598 Richard Quiney, a Stratford alderman, wrote to Shakespeare the only letter known to be addressed to the playwright. Quiney sought a loan of £30, which Shakespeare seems to have provided. Quiney's third son, Richard, would marry Shakespeare's younger daughter, Judith. Also in 1598 Francis Meres published *Palladis Tamia*, which includes kind comments about contemporary authors. Meres praises Shakespeare's *Venus and Adonis*, *The Rape of Lucrece*, and his "sugared Sonnets." Meres adds, "As *Plautus* and *Seneca* are accounted the best for Comedy and Tragedy among the Latins, so *Shakespeare* among ye English is the most excellent in both kinds for the stage" (in Honan, p. 264). There follows a list of a dozen plays. Perhaps Shakespeare read Meres's panegyric and transferred it to the players who visit Elsinore in *Hamlet*. Polonius praises their versatility by saying, "Seneca cannot be too heavy, nor Plautus too light" (2.2.400–401).

THE BUSINESS OF THEATER

While Meres attests to Shakespeare's reputation in the late 1590s, his company was facing hard times. In 1597 James Burbage had fitted out a large room in the old Blackfriars priory near St. Paul's Cathedral for indoor performances, where admission would cost at least sixpence, compared to a penny for standing room at the Theatre. But residents of the area, including the Lord Chamberlain, patron of Burbage's and Shakespeare's company, petitioned against an adult theater in the neighborhood, and the Privy Council sided with the petitioners. At the same time, the Lord Chamberlain's Men were in danger of losing the Theatre as well. Giles Allen, the owner of the land on which the playhouse stood, refused to renew the lease that was about to expire, hoping to secure the building and charge for its use. The Lord Chamberlain's Men abandoned their former home to play at the Swan, which had recently opened at Paris (that is, Paradise) Garden, Bankside, and the Curtain. E. Guilpin's 1598 *Skialethia* contains the lines, "But see yonder, / One like the unfrequented Theatre / Walks in dark silence and vast solitude" (Bradbrook, p. 138). It may be that low revenues prompted the Lord Chamberlain's Men to sell the rights to publish *Richard III*, *Richard II*, *1 Henry IV*, and *Love's Labor's Lost* at this time to earn a bit of money from the publishers.

THE GLOBE THEATRE

Seeking a new venue, in December 1598 Richard and Cuthbert Burbage took a thirty-one-year lease on land in St. Saviour's parish near the Rose theater south of the Thames across from St. Paul's Cathedral. Late that month the Burbages and their friends dismantled the Theatre, transported the timbers across the river, and built a new playhouse, the Globe. This new playhouse, a multi-sided polygon about a hundred feet in diameter and roofed with thatch, held about 3,000 people in the pit and three galleries. While the galleries and stage were protected from the elements, the pit, where the groundlings stood, was open to the sky, the only source of light in these outdoor theaters. The Burbages paid half the construction costs and held half the shares of the company. Five "housekeepers" each bought a 10 percent interest. All five belonged to the Lord Chamberlain's Men, and one of these five was Shakespeare. Another was the comic star William Kempe. When he left the company shortly afterward, his 10 percent was acquired by the four remaining householders, giving each of them a 12.5 percent share.

On days when a play would be performed, a flag would fly over the theater, showing Hercules holding the globe and bearing the motto *Totus mundus agit histrionem*: All the world's a stage. Shakespeare lived near the Globe for a time, then moved north of the river near his fellow players John Heminge and Henry Condell. These men resided in the parish of St. Mary, Aldermanbury, near St. Paul's.

In the autumn of 1599 Thomas Platter, a physician from Basle, visited London. He wrote that on September 21 he and some friends crossed the Thames and "In the straw-thatched house we saw the Tragedy of the first Emperor Julius Caesar, very pleasantly performed" (in Honan, p. 271). Shakespeare's *Julius Caesar*, based on Plutarch's *Lives*, may have been the first play staged at the Globe. Another candidate for that honor is *Henry V*, which concludes the second tetralogy begun with *Richard II*. The play's prologue to act 5 anticipates the triumphant return of the Earl of Essex from Ireland, where he had gone in late March of 1599 to put down the rebellion led by the Earl of Tyrone. Essex returned in late September after concluding a hasty, unauthorized truce, hardly comparable to Henry V's astonishing and overwhelming victory at Agincourt to which the Chorus likens Essex's hoped for success. The Globe was open by May 1599, so *Henry V* may have inaugurated the "wooden O" (*Henry V*, Prologue to act 1, line 13), that is, the Globe, in those heady days when much was still expected of Essex.

The new theater soon faced stiff competition from child actors. In late 1599 the Children of Paul's, from St. Paul's grammar school, staged John Marston's *Antonio and Mellida* and its sequel, *Antonio's Revenge*. The children's companies performed indoors to audiences limited to the genteel, who could afford the higher prices being charged. In 1600 Richard Burbage leased the Blackfriars to Henry Evans, who had managed the Children of St. Paul's and now introduced a second boys' troupe, the Children of the Chapel, for whom Ben Jonson wrote. In *Hamlet*, composed around 1600, Shakespeare refers to the threat posed by the young actors. Hamlet wonders why an adult company is touring, since it would make more money staying in the city. Rosencrantz replies that the actors are being driven into the provinces by "an aery [nest] of children, little eyases [young hawks], that cry out on the top of question, and are most tyrannically clapp'd for't. These are now the fashion, and so berattle the common stages—so they call them—that many wearing rapiers are afraid of goose-quills and dare scarce come thither" (2.2.338–344). Hamlet asks, "Do the boys carry it away?" Rosencrantz responds, "Ay, that they do, my lord—Hercules and his load, too" (2.2.360–361), an obvious reference to the Globe, with its emblematic flag. In 1600 the Lord Chamberlain's Men again released several plays for publication, perhaps a sign that they needed money.

Contributing to the boys' companies' success in this War of the Theaters (pitting adult companies against the children) was the Poets' War, in which Marston and Thomas Dekker satirized Ben Jonson in pieces staged by the Children of St. Paul's, and Jonson responded in kind with works for the Children of the Chapel. The one thing all three writers agreed upon was that the public theaters like the Globe were simpleminded and pandered to the masses.

Shakespeare responded to such claims with *Hamlet*. Perhaps Marston's *Antonio's Revenge* prompted Shakespeare to write a revenge play of his own. The Lord Chamberlain's Men apparently owned an earlier version of *Hamlet*, perhaps by Thomas Kyd, whose *Spanish Tragedy* also served as a model, as did *Titus Andronicus*. In 1599 the Lord Admiral's Men staged *Agamemnon* and *Orestes Furies* based on Aeschylus's *Oresteia*. The graveyard scene in *Hamlet* (5.1) draws on *Orestes Furies*, and the relationship between Hamlet and Horatio resembles that of Orestes and Pylades. As a man suffering from melancholy, Hamlet resembles Ben Jonson's humor characters in *Every Man in His Humor* (1598) and *Every Man out of His Humor* (1599). Shakespeare acted in the former; the latter was staged at the Globe. Of course, nothing can explain the genius of *Hamlet*, which ranges from the playwright's objection to actors' extemporizing to the Renaissance humanist celebration of human abilities, from Polonius's sententiousness and Hamlet's wit at the old courtier's expense to mystery, murder, and a recognition of mortality.

Hamlet proved to be another hit. The First Quarto (1603) of the play claims that it was acted at Cambridge and Oxford. Off the coast of Sierra Leone on September 5, 1607, the crew of the British ship the *Dragon* put on the work, and the play was soon translated into German. Shakespeare supposedly played the Ghost of Old Hamlet, while Richard Burbage assumed the title role. Without that versatile actor, Shakespeare could not have created such demanding parts.

Shakespeare followed *Hamlet* with *Troilus and Cressida*. The Trojan War was being mined by other dramatists, and in 1599 Philip Henslowe of the Rose paid Chettle and Thomas Dekker for a "Troyelles and Cresseda." Shakespeare's debunking of Homer's heroes is in keeping with his beloved Ovid's treatment of them in the *Metamorphoses*, Books 12 and 13, as well as with the satires of the children's companies. Fighting on the continent and in Ireland provided a contemporary backdrop for this cynical treatment of love and war.

In 1601 the Lord Chamberlain's Men were swept up in palace politics. The Earl of Essex's failure in Ireland had led to his estrangement from the queen, who withdrew his monopoly on the importation of sweet wines like the sack and canary that fueled Falstaff. Facing financial and political ruin, Essex adopted a desperate stratagem. On Thursday, February 5, 1601, his supporters asked Shakespeare's company to perform *Richard II* on Saturday. They hoped that this play, which depicts the deposition of a legitimate but ineffectual ruler by a young, efficient nobleman, would encourage Londoners to support the rebellion Essex launched the following day. The coup failed; Essex was sentenced to death. On February 18 the queen questioned one of the Lord Chamberlain's Men about their production. Augustine

Phillips explained that the company had refused to stage *Richard II*, claiming that the play was old and would not be worth staging, until Essex promised to add forty shillings to the day's proceeds. It was just business. Phillips may have exaggerated the play's unpopularity. In August 1601 Queen Elizabeth told the antiquarian William Lambarde that "this tragedy was played forty times in open streets and houses" (in Wood, p. 237). The same crew that performed *Hamlet* off the African coast subsequently staged *Richard II*.

Still, the queen apparently accepted Phillips's excuse. With her keen sense of irony, she summoned the Lord Chamberlain's Men to perform for her on the eve of Essex's execution, just as he had arranged for them to perform on the eve of his rebellion. Interestingly, at his trial Essex had said, "I am indifferent how I speed. I owe God a death." He seems to be quoting Prince Hal's words to Falstaff in *1 Henry IV*, "Why, thou owest God a death" (5.1.126).

SHAKESPEAREAN THEATER IN KING JAMES'S REIGN

Two years after Essex's execution (February 25, 1601), Queen Elizabeth died (March 24, 1603). She had patronized the theater and for a time had even sponsored a troupe of her own. Her successor, James I of England (who was also James VI of Scotland) would prove even more supportive. On May 17, 1603, he issued letters patent converting the Lord Chamberlain's Men into the King's Men. This translation had no immediate effect on public response to the company since the theaters were closed because of the plague and would not reopen until April 9, 1604. James did allow his players £30 to help them survive. More important, he paid them £150 for fifteen performances at court while the theaters were dark. In the next decade the King's Men would entertain the king some 140 times, 187 times by 1616. In contrast, Elizabeth had invited the Lord Chamberlain's Men to court only about three times a year. James also paid the actors twice what the queen had granted.

On December 26, 1604, the King's Men presented *Measure for Measure* at the royal banqueting room at Whitehall. Though nominally set in Vienna, it represents the Jacobean sexual underworld of the Globe's Bankside. Duke Vincentio is modeled on James. He loves his subjects, but from a distance. The duke's ability to see through hypocrisy is intended as a compliment to the new king. In November 1604 *Othello* had been presented at court. Nearly a decade earlier, in the aftermath of the execution of Dr. Lopez, the queen's Portuguese-Jewish physician (on trumped-up charges of plotting to poison her) Shakespeare had written *The Merchant of Venice*, with what strikes many viewers and readers as a sympathetic treatment of its Jewish protagonist. Now, as the government considered expelling blacks from the country, Shakespeare portrayed a noble, dignified Moor.

By 1604 Shakespeare was living in St. Olave's parish, at the northeast corner of Mugwell (Monkwell) and Silver streets, in a house owned by the French Huguenot Christopher Mountjoy. As the name Silver Street suggests, jewelers lived here. Mountjoy created "tires," elaborate jeweled headdresses, and numbered James's wife, Queen Anne, among his customers. His was a large, L-shaped house, with two gables and a frontage on sixty-three feet. Shakespeare's friendship with the Mountjoys may date from the 1590s; they may have helped him with his French scenes in *Henry V*. In that play the French herald is named Mountjoy. While living with them, Shakespeare was asked by Christopher's wife, Marie, to persuade one of their apprentices, Stephen Belott, to wed the Mountjoy daughter, also named Marie (or Mary). In *The Two Gentlemen of Verona* the duke of Milan asks Proteus to persuade his daughter, Silvia, to marry Thurio; life here imitated art. Shakespeare sped better than his character; Silvia rejects Thurio for Valentine, but Mary and Stephen wed. However, in 1612 Belott sued his father-in-law for failing to pay the dowry he had promised. Shakespeare was summoned to testify, but he claimed that he had no memory of what had been promised or paid. Another witness at the trial was George Wilkins, with whom Stephen and Mary lived after they married. In 1608 Wilkins published *The Painfull Adventures of Pericles, Prince of Tyre*, perhaps a source for, perhaps based on, Shakespeare's romance *Pericles*. Wilkins may have had a hand in that play.

On August 27, 1605, when James I visited Oxford, three students dressed as sibyls hailed him as a descendant of Banquo. During his stay at the university the king attended various debates, including one on the subject of whether the imagination can produce real effects. On November 5 of that year the Catholic Guy Fawkes intended to blow up parliament as the king was addressing that body in the presence of the entire royal family. The plot had been infiltrated by government informers and was foiled, its leaders tried and executed. On May 3, 1606, Father Henry Garnett, a Jesuit, was hanged, drawn, and quartered. At his trial he had justified equivocation to avoid incrimination.

In August of 1606 Christian IV of Denmark came to England to visit his sister, Queen Anne. This was the first visit to England by a foreign head of state since the reign of Henry VIII. Among the entertainments arranged for the Danish king were three plays; *Macbeth* may have been one of these. It treats Banquo, James's ancestor, more kindly than does Holinshed's *Chronicles*, in which he conspires with Macbeth to kill Duncan. In Shakespeare's version, Banquo is innocent of that crime. The play shows the powerful real effects of the imagination on both Macbeths; indeed, Lady Macbeth's imagination drives her to madness and death. In 2.3 the Porter imagines that he is admitting into hell "an equivocator, that could swear in both the scales against either scale, who committed treason enough for God's sake, yet could not equivocate to heaven. O, come in, equivocator" (2.3.8–11). Three witches play important roles in this work. James was fascinated with witches and had written a book on the subject (*Daemonology*, 1597). In 4.1 the witches show Macbeth that Banquo's descendants will rule "to th' crack of doom" (4.1.117). James had resumed the practice of touching victims of scrofula, known as the "King's Evil" because the royal touch supposedly cured the disease. In 4.3.141–145 a doctor informs Malcolm and Macduff that King Edward the Confessor is going to perform this rite. *Macbeth* was thus likely to appeal to James, and in addition to all these noted features it is quite short; James liked his plays brief.

On December 26, 1606, *King Lear* was performed at court. The play shows the danger of dividing a kingdom; James was seeking to unite Scotland and England under one parliament as it was now joined by one monarch. Richard Burbage played Lear, Robert Armin the Fool. Armin had replaced William Kempe as the company's leading comic actor, and for him Shakespeare created parts that are more reflective than those he wrote for Kempe. Shakespeare's plays were always conceived with his troupe in mind. For example, the presence in the company of a short, dark boy and a tall, fair one in the mid-1590s explains the physical traits of the short, dark Hermia and tall, fair Helena in *A Midsummer Night's Dream*. Kempe's comic skills are evident in Launce (*Two Gentlemen of Verona*) and Bottom (*A Midsummer Night's Dream*), whereas Armin's skills are exploited in Feste (*Twelfth Night*) and the Fool in *Lear*.

In his final great tragedies Shakespeare returned to the Roman theme. *Antony and Cleopatra* (ca. 1607) deals with a subject that had been popular in the 1590s. The Countess of Pembroke had written a "Tragedie of Antonie" (1591), and Samuel Daniel had produced a *Tragedy of Cleopatra* (1594). Shakespeare had visited Wilton, the home of the Countess of Pembroke, where he could have seen her manuscript drama. *Coriolanus* (ca. 1608) is set in the early republic. Both plays draw heavily on Plutarch's *Lives*, so useful for *Julius Caesar*. *Coriolanus* is set against a backdrop of food shortages in Rome similar to those afflicting the English midlands in 1607. The plebeians' dissatisfaction with their rulers reflects growing popular resentment against James I, and the aristocrats' disdain for the populace and their representatives is not unlike James's attitude toward his parliamentary critics, whom he called "Tribunes of the people, whose mouths could not be stopped" (in Honan, p. 346). *Timon of Athens* from this same period also derives from Plutarch, though Shakespeare's old antagonist Robert Greene also mentions Timon in *The Royal Exchange* (1590). The dialogue in *Timon* between the Poet and the Painter may be an in-joke referring to Shakespeare and Burbage, who was a skilled artist.

On June 5, 1607, Shakespeare's older daughter, Susannah, married the physician John Hall. They settled in what is now known as Hall's Croft, Stratford, a fine house. Eight months later, on February 21, 1608, Susannah's daughter, Elizabeth, was christened. Elizabeth would be the playwright's only granddaughter, and she would die childless. Shakespeare and Hall appear to have gotten along well. The next year, on September 9, 1608, Mary Arden, Shakespeare's mother, was buried at Holy Trinity Church.

Shakespeare's sonnets were finally published in 1609. In that year the King's Men were at last able to begin using the Blackfriar's Theatre. They had recovered the lease on August 8, 1608, but the theaters were again closed because of the plague from July 1608 until November 1609. Shakespeare lost some seven years of his dramatic career to theater closings between 1592 and 1611. With access to this indoor playhouse, the King's Men now played at the Globe from May to September and used Blackfriars for the rest of the year. The Blackfriars was smaller than the Globe, being forty-six feet wide and sixty-six feet long. It had two galleries and held a total of about 700 people, compared with the Globe's 3,000. But the Blackfriars was six times more expensive than the Globe; the cheapest seats cost sixpence rather than a penny. Wood quotes a contemporary observer who said that the King's Men earned £1,000 more in a winter than they had at the Globe (Wood, p. 312). Blackfriars attracted crowds despite its higher prices. According to a petition drawn up by those living in the neighborhood, "[I]nhabitants cannot come to their houses, nor bring in their necessary provisions of beer, wood, coal or hay, nor the tradesmen or shopkeepers utter their wares, nor the passenger go to the common water stairs without danger of their lives and limbs" every winter afternoon (Wood, p. 312).

SHAKESPEARE'S FINAL WORK

In the period from 1609 through 1611 Shakespeare wrote his four late romances, *Pericles*, *Cymbeline*, *The Winter's Tale*, and his valedictory *The Tempest*, though after that play he collaborated on three other works: *Henry VIII*, the lost *Cardenio*, and *The Two Noble Kinsmen*. The astrologer Simon Forman noted in his diary that he saw *The Winter's Tale* at the Globe on May 15, 1611. The play was performed at court that November. It is based on Robert Greene's *Pandosto* (1588) and includes Shakespeare's most famous stage direction: "Exit pursued by a bear" (3.3.58). The sheep-shearing festival in Bohemia recalls similar occasions in the area around Stratford. The precocious boy Mamillius who dies may be a tribute to Hamnet Shakespeare. On stage the boy-actor who had that part returns to play Perdita, the long-lost daughter who is found. Perhaps the playwright was still harping on his son.

The Tempest was also played at court in November 1611. This romance draws on Virgil's *Aeneid* and refers to Michel de Montaigne's essay "Of Cannibals" (translated into English by John Florio in 1603) and to Ovid. But its primary inspiration seems to have been the wreck of the *Sea Adventure* in the "still-vex'd Bermoothes" (*The Tempest*, 1.2.229) on its way to Jamestown. The ship was lost on July 24, 1609, and the crew presumed to have drowned. Then, on May 23, 1610, the entire crew arrived in Virginia. Bermuda had been reputed to be inhabited by demons; indeed, it was known as the Isle of Devils. The crew of the *Sea Adventure* instead found an island paradise. Shakespeare read one or more of the several reports written about this event and turned the marvelous into the magical.

It is hard not to see this play as Shakespeare's farewell to his art. After staging a wedding masque for his daughter and her fiancé, Prospero, the consummate conjurer of stage illusion, tells them,

> Our revels now are ended. These our actors
> (As I foretold you) were all spirits, and
> Are melted into air, into thin air,
> And like the baseless fabric of this vision,
> The cloud-capp'd tow'rs, the gorgeous palaces,
> The solemn temples, the great globe itself,
> Yea all which it inherit, shall dissolve,
> And like this insubstantial pageant faded
> Leave not a wrack behind. We are such stuff
> As dreams are made on; and our little life
> Is rounded with a sleep. (4.1.148–158)

And in the last words of the last play Shakespeare would write by himself he has Prospero turn to his audience and say, "As you from crimes would pardon'd be, / Let your indulgence set me free" (Epilogue, l. 20); these words are followed by the simple stage direction, "Exit."

John Fletcher and Francis Beaumont were by now the leading playwrights for the King's Men. With Fletcher, Shakespeare wrote his last history play, *Henry VIII* (ca. 1613), though some see the work as written totally by Shakespeare himself. When performed at the Blackfriars, Katherine of Aragón's trial scene was staged exactly where it had taken place on June 21, 1529. The work offers a nostalgic look back at the reign of James's predecessor as Archbishop Cranmer at the end of the play prophesies over the baby Elizabeth, "In her days every man shall eat in safety / Under his own vine that he plants, and sing / The merry songs of peace to all his neighbors" (5.4.33–35). Cranmer also predicts greatness for her successor: "Where ever the bright sun of heaven shall shine, / His honor and the greatness of his name / Shall be, and make new nations" (5.4.50–52), a reference to the founding of Jamestown (1607), the first permanent English colony in the New World. Shakespeare certainly collaborated with Fletcher on *Cardenio* (ca. 1612), which dramatizes an episode from Miguel de Cervantes' *Don Quixote* (1605), and on *The Two Noble Kinsmen* (ca. 1613), based on Geoffrey Chaucer's *The Knight's Tale*.

On June 29, 1613, *Henry VIII* literally brought the house down when wadding from the cannon used in act 1 scene 4 ignited the Globe's thatched roof. In a letter, Sir Henry Wotton wrote that the theater burned to the ground in less than an hour. "This was the fatal period of that virtuous fabric; wherein yet nothing did perish but wood and straw, and a few forsaken cloaks; only one man had his breeches set on fire, that would perhaps have broiled him, if he had not by the benefit of a provident wit put it out with bottle ale" (in *The Riverside Shakespeare*, 2nd ed., ed. G. Blakemore Evans with J.J.M. Tobin [Boston: Houghton Mifflin, 1997], 1022).

The King's Men immediately began rebuilding the Globe, at a cost of £1,400. The shareholders bore the responsibility for this expense. Shakespeare may have decided to sell his share at this time, since he was not a shareholder when he died in 1616. However, he did buy the Blackfriars Gatehouse in 1613, paying £140 for the residence, which he leased out. According to Nicholas Rowe, the playwright spent his final years in Stratford. But in November 1614 he was in London: Thomas Greene, Stratford's town clerk, went to see him there to enlist his support against an attempt to enclose open lands in Old Stratford, some of which Shakespeare owned. Shakespeare had been promised compensation for his property, which may be the reason he remained neutral in the dispute.

In February 1616 Judith Shakespeare married Thomas Quiney, who sold wine and tobacco. Because the marriage took place during Lent, the couple was excommunicated. A month after the marriage, Quiney was summoned before Stratford's ecclesiastical court and charged with fornication with Margaret Wheeler, who had died giving birth to his child. Quiney was fined five shillings. Judith gave birth to three sons. The first, named Shakespeare, died in infancy in May 1617. Richard (b. 1618) and Thomas (b. 1620) both died in 1639.

Shakespeare was not pleased with Judith's match. He had drawn up a will in January, but in March he changed it. He left Judith a "silver and gilt bowl." The rest of his silver went to Susannah's daughter, Elizabeth. Judith was to receive £150 (£100 as a marriage portion and the balance if she renounced her claim to the cottage in Chapel Lane). She would receive another £150 in three years. Almost everything else went to Susannah. His wife received the "second best bed," which may have been a piece of furniture that she brought with her when they married. Shakespeare did not want his property to fall into the hands of Hathaways or Quineys. To his sister Joan Hart, living in Henley Street, he gave £20, and each of her three sons received £5. Among other small bequests is the provision, "to my fellows John Heminge, Richard Burbage and Henry Condell xxvi s.[hillings] to buy them [memorial]

Shakespeare's memorial, Stratford-upon-Avon, England. Completed in 1879, this building burned in 1926. The Swan Theatre now occupies this site. Courtesy of the Library of Congress.

rings." He left the same sum to Anthony Nash of Stratford, whose son Thomas would marry Shakespeare's only granddaughter, Elizabeth Hall, in 1626. John Hall was named executor.

Shakespeare died on April 23, 1616, probably of typhoid, and was buried in Holy Trinity Church. According to the seventeenth-century Gloucestershire clergyman Richard Davies, "William Shakespeare died a papist" (Wood, p. 340). As scene 5.1 in *Hamlet* shows, burial space was reused; Ophelia is being interred where the court jester Yorick had lain, and Yorick's remains, including his skull, are being evicted. Shakespeare apparently did not want to suffer posthumous exhumation and so presumably composed the epitaph marking his grave in Holy Trinity Church:

> GOOD FREND FOR JESUS SAKE FORBEARE,
> TO DIGG THE DUST ENCLOASED HEARE:
> BLESTE BE YE MAN YT [THAT] SPARES THES STONES,
> AND CURST BE HE YT MOVES MY BONES. (Honan, p. 403)

A bust by Gheerart Janssen was set up in the wall of the north chancel.

Shakespeare's fellow actors Heminge and Condell erected his other monument. In 1622 they engaged Isaac Jaggard and Edward Blount to print *Mr. William Shakespeares Comedies, Histories, & Tragedies*. This large volume, a folio costing £1, appeared in November 1623. It printed thirty-six of Shakespeare's plays, eighteen of them for the first time. The work included tributes by Heminge and Condell, Ben Jonson, and others. But Shakespeare had penned his own perfect epigraph—and epitaph—in Sonnet 55:

> Not marble nor the gilded monuments
> Of princes shall outlive this pow'rful rhyme,
> But you shall shine more bright in these contents
> Than unswept stone, besmear'd with sluttish time.
>
>   *   *   *
>
> 'Gainst death and all-oblivious enmity
> Shall you pace forth; your praise shall still find room,
> Even in the eyes of all posterity
> That wear this world out to the ending doom.
>   So till the judgment that yourself arise,
>   You live in this, and dwell in lovers' eyes.

Annotated Bibliography

Bradbrook, M. C. *Shakespeare: The Poet in His World.* New York: Columbia UP, 1978. The first section of this study, "The World He Found," highlights the influences on Shakespeare of his native Warwickshire and his reading. "The World He Made" shifts to London to explore the theatrical tradition he inherited and adapted. "The World and the Dream" looks at Shakespeare's last plays and his final years.

Burgess, Anthony. *Shakespeare.* New York: Knopf, 1970. A lovely book, with forty-three color plates and many others in black-and-white. Burgess's sprightly style makes this a highly readable account. He indulges in occasional speculations, most of which he identifies as such, but they are so delightful that one forgives these novelistic interludes, such as his vision of the premier of *Hamlet.*

Chambers, Edmund Kerchever. *William Shakespeare: A Study of Facts and Problems.* 2 vols. Oxford: Clarendon P, 1930. This scholarly work presents and evaluates the facts and legends surrounding Shakespeare. Chambers eschews speculation. Chambers wrote about the Elizabethan theater, and most of the first volume deals with that world and the texts of Shakespeare's plays. The second volume reproduces in typescript, and sometimes in facsimile, the records of Shakespeare's life, contemporary allusions, and later accounts.

Holden, Anthony. *William Shakespeare: An Illustrated Biography.* Boston: Little, Brown, 2002. An abridged and sumptuously illustrated version of Holden's 1999 biography. Both versions are an attempt to present an accessible and reasonably accurate life of the playwright. Holden plays up Shakespeare's Catholic connections.

Honan, Park. *Shakespeare: A Life.* Oxford: Oxford UP, 1998. The best biography. Honan places Shakespeare within his world and soberly evaluates conflicting accounts. An outstanding work of synthesis and originality.

Schoenbaum, Samuel. *Shakespeare's Lives.* New ed. New York: Oxford UP, 1991. Surveys the biographical accounts of Shakespeare from the Gheerart Janssen monument erected in Holy Trinity Church, Stratford, shortly after Shakespeare's death through A L. Rowse's *Discovering Shakespeare* (1989). Here one learns how various authors and ages saw Shakespeare, and from these accounts a picture of the playwright emerges.

———. *William Shakespeare: A Documentary Life.* New York: Oxford UP, 1975. Presents more than 200 facsimiles of documents relating to Shakespeare's life, from his baptismal record to his will. The text commenting on and linking these materials constitutes a good biography.

Wood, Michael. *In Search of Shakespeare.* London: BBC, 2003. The companion volume to the BBC production. The book is lovely and well-written, but it should be accompanied by a saltshaker. Wood tends to present as fact much that is only speculation, and readers are not always warned. For example, Wood maintains that Emilia Lanier is the Dark Lady of the sonnets and that William Herbert, Earl of Pembroke, is the fair youth. Neither contention can be proved. The illustrations are superb. Like Holden he emphasizes Shakespeare's Catholic connections.

William Shakespeare's Theater

Robert F. Willson Jr.

The term "Shakespeare's theater" should be understood to comprise the following elements: the physical acting place, which could have been an open, public playhouse, a closed theater building, inn yard, and so forth; acting companies; audiences; and the range and style of plays performed. These elements are described and evaluated here to give the student of Shakespeare's theater a fuller understanding of both the constraints and the conventions under which the playwright worked. It is hoped that the reader will gain greater respect for Shakespeare's accomplishments as a dramatist in an age when theater was king.

Shakespeare inherited a theatrical tradition that had its roots in the Middle Ages and early Tudor England (1485–1550). Vagabond singers and actors traveled throughout medieval England, performing at various locations, such as inns and taverns, for guests who had just finished their evening meals. Most of their plays were interludes, fairly short revues that featured singing, juggling, and declaiming of improvised speeches. Many of these actors probably gained experience by performing in morality plays that were produced during religious holidays. One of the best known and most popular morality plays was *Everyman* (1485?), in which the allegorical hero is summoned by Death and told he can take along anyone willing to accompany him on his journey. In the end, he must face his own death alone. In what is generally regarded as Shakespeare's first comedy, *The Comedy of Errors*, the condemned Egeon seems to re-enact Everyman's unsuccessful quest for someone to help him during his final hours. Certainly Shakespeare's play also has classical antecedents, and Egeon does not die in the end. But the influence of *Everyman* is nonetheless evident.

Another important medieval drama is *Mankind*, in which a good and a bad angel struggle for the soul of an individual. This device appears in Christopher Marlowe's *Dr. Faustus* (1589?) and underlies some of Shakespeare's greatest works. *Othello* can be seen as the battle for the title character's allegiance between the demonic Iago and saintly Desdemona. Macbeth is torn initially between his conscience and Lady Macbeth's urgings. Similarly, King Lear must choose between the faithful Cordelia and lying Goneril and Regan. In these Shakespearean tragedies the protagonists yield to their evil tempters, with dire results. Prince Hal's relationship with Falstaff can be seen in a similar light, with Falstaff acting as Vice trying to lure the prince to evil ways.

Mystery plays of this same period retold biblical stories in dramatic form. While Shakespeare and his fellow dramatists most certainly knew the Bible from other sources, they drew also on the medieval dramatic tradition. Prince Hal in the two parts of *Henry IV* can be understood as the prodigal son. One way of looking at *Othello* is to consider it as a retelling of the story of the Fall, with Iago as the serpent, Othello and Desdemona as types of Adam and Eve.

Not only the stories but also the staging of medieval dramas would carry over into the Elizabethan age. Mystery plays were performed on wagons outdoors. Stages were thus bare, and the actors relied on natural light. Interludes would be acted in the great halls of manors, where artificial light was available from candles, but, again, sets were virtually nonexistent. The same conditions prevailed in Shakespeare's day, whether for the public outdoor stages, such as the Globe, or the indoor theaters that catered to the gentry, such as the Blackfriars Theatre, or at court.

During the early Tudor period, acting companies began to be influenced by classical drama, especially works from the Roman stage. Young boys performed dramas based on these sources in their public and private schools; one of the most popular was *Ralph Roister Doister* (1534–1541), written by a schoolmaster named Nicholas Udall. The hero is a braggart soldier who seeks to woo a widow by using outrageous language and behavior; he is foiled in the end by clever servants who easily puncture his pomposity. An exaggerated battle of the sexes, in which Ralph meets his match, highlights the comedy's finale. The plot owes a debt to the Roman playwright Plautus, whose *Miles Gloriosus* provided the model for the braggart soldier. Other features of the comedy, such as its use of mistaken identity and disguise, became conventions of much Elizabethan comedy, especially the work of Shakespeare's friend and colleague Ben Jonson.

Two additional Tudor dramas deserve mention because they influenced later works by Shakespeare and his theatrical contemporaries. Thomas Preston's *Cambises* (1569) introduced the dual-plot device in which a subplot involving comic characters mirrors and serves as a counterpoint to the main plot concerning the rise and fall of the hero Cambises, king of Persia. Characters named Huf, Ruf, and Snuff people the slapstick world of the subplot; they come from wildly popular native interludes. The Cambises tale owes its origins to the medieval tales in which heroes leaped onto the wheel of fortune, only to be thrown down as a result of blind, lustful behavior. Although highly melodramatic and embarrassingly naive, *Cambises* was widely known and loved by audiences across England; its appeal did not go unnoticed by later playwrights in search of a surefire formula for their creations.

The second important Tudor drama was written by two law students, Thomas Sackville and Thomas Norton, for a Christmas performance at the Inner Temple, one of the Inns of Court. These "inns," or schools, were located in London and comprised a prestigious legal training center for young men seeking a profession in an institution other than the church. Law students also constituted a significant segment of the audience that regularly attended public playhouses after 1576. Sackville and Norton's play *Gorboduc* (1561–1562) recounts the fall of an English king who unwisely divided the realm between his two sons; when the younger son kills his older brother and is in turn killed by his own mother, the people rise up to unseat and murder both king and queen. Civil war follows these acts, the lesson of the tragedy being that the ruler's blind decision, which initially may have appeared evenhanded, leads to the land's desolation and the people's suffering. One can see in this primitive piece the plot outline of Shakespeare's *King Lear*, and *Gorboduc* is often cited as an important source for that play, which combines history and tragedy. *Gorboduc* also relies heavily on the conventions of classical tragedy, especially in its use of long, highly rhetorical speeches and the medieval "fall of princes" theme. Sackville and Norton were praised for attempting to translate Latin hexameter verse into an early version of blank verse, the main poetic form for Elizabethan drama that was later to be perfected by Christopher Marlowe.

Traveling troupes of actors performing plays like *Cambises* and *Gorboduc* had no regular audiences or permanent playing space during the early Tudor period. Their membership was also unstable, as actors who were poorly paid or hired only for particular performances left the companies. One advantage of the traveling troupes, however, was "protection" provided by prominent Tudor lords and earls who allowed certain groups of actors to perform for them on special occasions and in return gave them the right to use the lord or earl's title and authority. The court of Elizabeth followed this practice, and one of the early companies was in fact called the Queen's Men. While this privilege did not give the actors much in the way of salary, the protectors provided costumes or "liveries" and a shield against arbitrary arrest by local officials who regarded actors as vagrants.

THEATERS AND PLAYHOUSES OF SHAKESPEARE'S AGE

Not until 1576 did public players have a permanent home in the suburbs of London; there, in a section called Shoreditch, actor and carpenter James Burbage built the Theatre, which became the model for other playhouses erected during Shakespeare's career. No blueprint or description of the structure survives, but from accounts and drawings of other playhouses, scholars have conjectured that it was polygonal or round in shape and was constructed from timbers and plaster, with a brick foundation and thatch or tile roof. The wooden platform stage jutted out into the yard, or "pit," and measured approximately forty feet across; there were probably two or three levels of galleries, where people sat on benches to watch the performances. "Groundlings" stood in the pit, where they found themselves in close proximity to the actors. According to records from other theaters, audience members standing in the pit paid one penny, gallery patrons paid two pennies, and "lords" were offered special rooms in the gallery section closest to the stage for six pennies. It was also apparently possible for patrons willing to pay three pennies to sit on the stage. Behind the stage was the "tiring room" (from "attiring," meaning to dress, that is, change costumes), which featured two doors on either side of the stage through which the actors entered or exited.

On the second level, just above the stage, was the balcony, where Shakespeare could place soldiers attempting to hold off a siege of their city (see *Henry V*, for example) or the fair Juliet excitedly discovering her lover Romeo in the garden below. Above the balcony was a roof-like cover supported by two pillars; called "the heavens," it protected the actors from rain and could be used to lower gods and goddesses into the characters' world. Near the front of the stage or platform was a trapdoor, known as "hell," which could be used for several purposes: as a grave (see

Hamlet), a hiding place for spirits and witches and so forth. Resting on top of the heavens were huts housing men who provided special effects that might include thunder for storms (see *King Lear*) or "chairs" in which Roman deities sat as they were lowered to the stage (see *Cymbeline*). On a platform near the huts, musicians were seated or stood; it was from this spot that the trumpet was sounded to signal the commencement of the play. Although evidence from contemporary playhouse records shows that the acting companies relied heavily on props, costumes, and other special effects, there is no evidence that the Theatre or other public playhouses used scenery in their productions. While costumes such as Roman togas or sultans' robes were sometimes used, the actors for the most part wore contemporary doublets and hose or gowns. There was little effort to achieve historical accuracy in costumes, in large part because audiences did not expect or require it. The bare stage, nonetheless, became the "world" on which audiences saw kings and queens, beggars and thieves interact, making profound and mundane observations about life and death. If, as Shakespeare, claimed, "All the world's a stage" (*As You Like It*, 2.7.139), then the chief aim of his plays was to mirror the actions of human beings as they performed between "the heavens" and "hell" at the Theatre.

There were other playhouses in the "suburbs," that is, beyond the walls of London. They were erected there because the city fathers of London, fearful of the threat to peace and health posed by actors and audiences, sought to control the conditions of public playing. During this period, the London council was controlled by Puritans, who opposed playing, gaming, and bearbaiting because of religious and public safety concerns. Actors were often arrested as transients or vagrants, and the playhouses themselves were closed whenever outbreaks of the bubonic plague occurred. In contrast, Elizabeth's court sought to protect the acting companies so they could be available for performances at court on special state occasions. In effect, the court allowed the acting companies to perform in public playhouses in order to make a living, though many of the companies did not prosper during the 1580s and 1590s, and their members were frequently mired in poverty.

SHAKESPEARE IN LONDON

The Theatre managed to survive through hard times, and the fortunes of the companies that performed there were sufficient to allow them continued existence. It is widely believed that one of those companies, the Earl of Pembroke's Men, was Shakespeare's first home in London. How he came to be there is unknown, but one theory is that he joined the troupe when they were performing in Stratford during one of their tours of the provinces. When the playhouses were closed down because of a rising death toll from the plague (usually in July and August), acting groups often toured the countryside, where they performed at inns and public houses. Perhaps, the story goes, one of the company's actors left or died and its members were in need of a substitute to finish their run. Given Shakespeare's talents as an actor and writer, he would have proved an invaluable addition, especially if he was ready to leave his village for the big city. There is no proof to support this theory, but it is known that Shakespeare's family had ties with the Earl of Pembroke, who may have lent his support to the fledgling playwright.

However he arrived in London, we know with some certainty that he was performing there as an actor by the early 1590s, since his name appears on lists of actors in plays by such figures as Ben Jonson. It is also speculated that he may have apprenticed as a kind of play doctor, writing scenes to rejuvenate old plays that continued in the company's repertoire. Evidence that this practice was commonplace can be found in Philip Henslowe's *Diary*, a highly valued, accurate account book kept by the manager of Christopher Marlowe's company, the Lord Admiral's Men. By 1592, when Robert Greene famously attacked Shakespeare as "an upstart crow," the man from Stratford had made a name for himself as a major new theatrical talent. Shakespeare prospered under the tutelage of the Burbages, especially James's two sons, Cuthbert and Richard, whose acting talents probably inspired Shakespeare to write certain heroic parts for them. Richard in particular would become a famous tragedian and shareholder with Shakespeare and others in the Lord Chamberlain's Men, the company that was incorporated in 1594.

In the early days of Elizabethan theater, the most popular plays were written by a group called the University Wits. These were young men who had attended universities with curriculums designed primarily to train students for the church or the law. Lacking either the desire or the influence to enter these professions, the wits instead used their educations in classical literature, especially Roman drama, to make a living writing plays for popular consumption. Thomas Kyd's *The Spanish Tragedy* (1587) introduced a style of play—the revenge tragedy—that proved to be very successful and strongly influenced other playwrights, such as Shakespeare. Based on conventions employed by the Roman playwright Seneca (his *Ten Tragedies* was translated into English and published in 1581), *The Spanish Tragedy* depicts the machinations of its mad hero Hieronimo as he seeks revenge for the murder of his son Horatio by the cruel and ambitious Don Balthazar. The action is initiated by a character named Revenge, whose ghostly companion Don Andrea has been killed in battle by Balthazar and has witnessed the wooing of his beloved Belimperia by his murderer. Hieronimo's plan for revenge involves a final-scene play-within-the-play in which the villain is murdered, along with Belimperia and others, after which the avenger Hieronimo commits suicide.

The Senecan conventions, which Shakespeare relied on in such tragedies as *Titus Andronicus* and *Hamlet*, include a ghost directing the action; a scheming Machiavellian villain; a suffering, distracted heroine; a disturbed avenger; a play-within-the-play; multiple murders; and the five-act structure. It is important to remember, however, that the University Wits attempted to appeal to popular taste; this led them to modify or distort Senecan conventions for spectacular effect. For instance, Seneca's tragedies were recited rather than performed by a company of players. This form of presentation required that murders or battles be reported by a messenger, who to be sure described the events in graphic detail. It was believed that such gory episodes should or could not be performed because the audience would be too distracted to appreciate the moral message taught by the actions of flawed men and women. As a result of modifications in the Senecan formula, Kyd, who depicted violence in lurid terms, was able to adapt an academic form of drama into a popular genre that had wide appeal and was widely copied.

CHRISTOPHER MARLOWE

Christopher Marlowe was responsible for adapting for the popular stage both the "fall of princes" genre and the chronicle history play. He was also instrumental in perfecting blank verse (that is, unrhymed verse of ten syllables with five alternating stresses) and standardizing its use for soliloquies (that is, long, character-revealing speeches delivered by an actor alone on the stage). Of all the University Wits, he was probably the most successful playwright and the group's most colorful, controversial member. It is fair to say that Marlowe was the chief creator of the style of theater that Shakespeare directly inherited and ultimately perfected. Among Marlowe's popular and acclaimed works were *Dr. Faustus*; *Tamburlaine 1, 2*; *The Jew of Malta*; and *Edward II*. These are without doubt exceptional works that demonstrate how to convert academic drama into popular entertainment. Probably the most popular of his melodramas was *Tamburlaine* (1587–1588), the tale of a Scythian shepherd who defeats European kings and threatens to establish dynastic rule unrestrained by morality or mercy. Although he ultimately dies, he never really loses power in the way that ambitious men from the "fall of princes" dramas do; Marlowe delights in shaping a figure who is both larger than life and devoted to exposing what Marlowe (or his hero) regarded as the hypocrisy of Christian church and state. His hero also delivers bombastic speeches like the following, in which the poet-playwright exhibits his mastery of blank verse:

> Nature that fram'd us of four elements,
> Warring within our breasts for regiment,
> Doth teach us all to have aspiring minds. . . .
> Wills us to wear ourselves and never rest,
> Until we reach the ripest fruit of all,
> That perfect bliss and sole felicity,
> The sweet fruition of an earthly crown. (*1 Tamburlaine*, 2.7.18–29)

It is no mistake that we encounter echoes here of Shakespearean soliloquies by such characters as Richard III or Hamlet; Marlowe's "mighty line" (because of the regularly stressed or masculine line endings) became the template for future dramatists working in the British theater.

As noted earlier, in *Dr. Faustus* Marlowe created a tragedy relying heavily on the conventions of morality plays (for example, good and bad angels compete for the hero's soul; Faustus is tempted by earthly desires and rejects spiritual authority) and following the dual-plot structure of such earlier works as *Cambises* and *Gorboduc*. The hero is a scholar who strives for God-like intelligence, aided by the "magic" powers of the devil-like Mephistophilis; while originally motivated by a wish to achieve constructive goals, Faustus loses sight of his noble ends and becomes a trickster and self-indulgent tool. Though he attempts to repent before death, his prayers fail to reach heaven; as the play ends, we hear his screams from "hell" (the trapdoor) as devils tear him apart. A comic subplot involving Faustus's pupil Wagner parallels the adventures of Faustus and serves as a commentary on them. There can be little doubt that Shakespearean antiheroes, such as Richard III and Macbeth, were meant to recall Faustus in their blind ambition that leads to their fall.

Marlowe's *The Jew of Malta* (1588?) depicts the life of another antihero, the Machiavellian villain Barabas. Such villains became popular on the Elizabethan stage largely because of the success of Marlowe's play. Dramatists relied on a caricature of the Italian political theorist, best known for his primer *The Prince* (1513), in which he outlined methods recommended for any leader seeking to seize and hold power. The pamphlet was soundly condemned by the church, primarily because its approach was amoral and naturalistic; for example, Machiavelli argues that a prince should appear to be virtuous even though in his personal life he may not be so. Marlowe relies heavily not on the book itself for the creation of his villain-hero, however, but on a popular caricature of a figure who practices the Florentine writer's ideas. He also taps into the Christian audience's prejudice against Jews and usurers or moneylenders. Barabas emerges mainly as an "overreacher," a term coined by critic Harry Levin to describe all of Marlowe's heroes, men whose ambition or desires push them to exceed the boundaries of society, where they momentarily flourish, then fall. Though Barabas manages to expose the hypocrisies of his Christian enemies and to outwit them, he is finally betrayed by the Turkish allies he had intended to ambush and kill. He dies when one of the Turks springs a trapdoor on the stage's second level, causing Barbabas to fall into a boiling cauldron below. Unlike Faustus, he expires cursing his opponents and complaining only that he was unable to carry out all of his Machiavellian schemes. It may well be that Shakespeare had this caricature in mind when he wrote *The Merchant of Venice*, a dark comedy in which the usurer Shylock plots against the life of the Christian merchant Antonio.

It is more certain that Shakespeare had Marlowe's *Edward II* (1591–1592) in mind when he composed *Richard II*, as well as other English history plays. Relying on the same source that Shakespeare would also mine—Raphael Holinshed's *Chronicles*—Marlowe dramatizes the rule of the fourteenth-century king whose realm suffered greatly because of his weakness and willfulness. When Edward falls under the control of his court favorite, Gaveston (their relationship may in fact have been a homosexual one), the barons rise up to save England, the church, and the king's neglected queen. But when their leader, Mortimer, is revealed to be a Machiavellian who makes the queen his mistress, the audience's sympathies shift again in favor of the imprisoned, now-defiant monarch. Marlowe's chief purpose apparently was, as Shakespeare's became, to show that competing forces influenced rulers in pursuit of their personal ambitions or lusts and resulted in the utterly neglected welfare of the state. Only characters like the loyal counselor Kent (*King Lear*) and Edward's young son emerge as potential caretakers of mother England, especially after we witness the cruel, drawn-out murder of fallen Edward by the hired assassin Lightborn (the anglicized name of Lucifer). Marlowe's main accomplishment in *Edward II* is his skillful compression and alteration of chronicle events to create a dramatic, though somewhat episodic, whole that also relies on techniques from the "fall of princes" and revenge plays. Shakespeare proved to be an attentive student whose career took off soon after Marlowe's sudden death in 1593.

OTHER INFLUENCES ON SHAKESPEARE

While Marlowe was certainly Shakespeare's mentor in tragedy and history, several early Elizabethan dramatists and University Wits wrote comedies that would serve as models for his creations. For plays like *The Comedy of Errors* and *The Taming of the Shrew*, which rely heavily on mistaken identity and disguise for their effect, he no doubt turned to George Gascoigne's *The Supposes* (1566) as a model. Translated from the Italian poet Ariosto's *I Suppositi*, the comedy features a plot in which young lovers must overcome obstacles posed by parents in order to wed.

They are aided in their struggle by comic servants who rely on disguises to outwit their "enemies"; these clever fellows, as well as blustering father and naive heroine, are stock characters based on caricatures invented by the Roman playwright Plautus. Wordplay and puns are the staple of the comedy's witty dialogue, which features lengthy exchanges between characters who pretend to intelligence that they do not possess. False learning, servants pretending to be masters, young lovers speaking florid poetry—these are the elements that Shakespeare would perfect in his more sophisticated, better written comedies.

John Lyly's *Endymion* (1588?) gave inspiration to Shakespeare's more romantic and courtly comedies, such as *A Midsummer Night's Dream* and *As You Like It.* Set in the court of the goddess Cynthia, the main plot of Lyly's play concerns the hero Endymion's renunciation of his love for Tellus, goddess of Earth, for the more inspiring love of his ruler and heavenly goddess, Cynthia. Mirroring this main plot is the comic subplot in which the braggart soldier Sir Thopas woos but fails to win the old enchantress Dipsas. *Endymion* explores several conventions of romance: dreams that border on nightmares, fountains as oracles, a metamorphosis or sudden transformation, magic spells, and singing and dancing. Lyly gave life to these conventions by employing a style of prose he called Euphuism (after a character in his novel *Euphues, the Anatomy of Wit,* 1578); his dialogue is marked by parallel constructions, antitheses, alliteration, and numerous puns. His comic masterpiece is also said to be allegorical, the various characters supposedly representing real court figures and their affairs. For example, Queen Elizabeth and the Earl of Leicester are said to stand for Cynthia and Endymion, respectively. Little evidence, however, supports the claims of allegorical interpretation.

Shakespeare could have read the story of Endymion and Cynthia in Ovid's *Metamorphoses,* a collection of tales about famous lovers by the first century A.D. Roman poet that was translated into English by Arthur Golding in 1567. The collection yielded the story of Pyramus and Thisbe, which Shakespeare used as the burlesque play within *A Midsummer Night's Dream,* but he also mined Ovid for characters and themes featured in other plays and in the sonnets. If Seneca was the major Roman source for conventions of Elizabethan tragedy, then Ovid and the Roman playwrights Plautus and Terence were the main sources of material for Elizabethan comedy. Although Shakespeare could read Latin and perhaps a little Greek, which he learned at his Stratford grammar school, he did not necessarily need these languages to understand the Roman writers; these sources were available in English or had been reworked in the plays of his immediate predecessors. When Marlowe died suddenly in 1593, Shakespeare assumed the mantle of leading dramatist for the public theater, where he had already achieved remarkable success in comedy, tragedy, and history.

THE THEATER BUSINESS

Along with artistic success came success in business. In 1594, Shakespeare and a small group of his fellows formed a corporation under the protection of the Lord Chamberlain; they were thereafter known as the Lord Chamberlain's Men. Their rivals, the Lord Admiral's Men, suffered greatly from the loss of their chief playwright, Marlowe, but the two companies continued to compete for the Elizabethan entertainment market during the Virgin Queen's reign. The structure of these companies should be described in detail to convey a better understanding of the practice of acting in public playhouses. The board of directors consisted of eleven or twelve "sharers," or shareholders, who divided both the costs and profits because they made equal investments in the company. We know that Shakespeare was one of these directors since his name appears with others in the legal document that established the corporation. The sharers were also the main actors and generally took on major roles in the plays. "Hired men" were engaged for a specific fee to perform in individual productions, but they were not regarded as regular members of the troupe. Apprentices, perhaps six or seven in number, were attached to particular sharers, from whom they learned their craft according to the prevailing culture of masters and apprentices. They served from the time they were ten or eleven years old until they were twenty-one, at which birthday they might move on to other companies or serve as hired men. Boys played the female roles because women were not allowed to perform on the stage in England during this time, though they could do so across the Channel in France. Not until 1660, at the commencement of Charles II's reign, was the ban lifted. It is hard to imagine a young boy playing Juliet or Cleopatra or Lady Macbeth convincingly, but apparently Shakespeare's audience accepted the convention without question or complaint.

To learn their lines, actors were given "rolls" containing their parts and cues; only the prompter or bookkeeper—so called because he kept the book of the play (we might call him stage manager today)—had a copy, called the "promptbook," of the entire work. In the second scene of *A Midsummer Night's Dream* Shakespeare gives a realistic picture of the stage manager, and director, Peter Quince handing out these rolls. Only Quince has a complete script. One may even imagine Shakespeare's actors complaining about the parts they have just been assigned, with one of the older boys seeking to graduate from a woman's role to something he thinks more becoming his virility. Given the doubling (playing two or more parts) that was common in Shakespeare's day, one can also imagine an actor seeking, like Bottom, to be given more stage time by taking on multiple parts.

The use of rolls rather than complete scripts was an attempt to control piracy, a practice that was commonplace primarily because there were no copyright laws to prevent it. A hired man with the text of the play could take it to a printer, pay a certain fee, and begin to sell copies in the bookstalls outside St. Paul's Cathedral. However, one must recall that every word of the script had to be handwritten, so making a complete copy of a play for each actor would have been both expensive and time-consuming. No promptbooks or handwritten manuscripts of any of Shakespeare's plays have survived, though we do have three pages in his hand from *The Booke of Sir Thomas More*, an unproduced work that Shakespeare was asked to try to save; but promptbooks of plays by other dramatists are extant, and they suggest that stage directions, notes, and so forth, were commonly scribbled in the margins of the pages and lines of dialogue were cut in the course of rehearsal. When the company decided to publish a play, the printed text was apparently based upon the playwright's "foul papers," or the handwritten manuscript from which the promptbook was copied. It is important to remember that the acting company, not the individual writer, controlled publication of plays by Shakespeare and others; profits from sales were divided, as were performance revenues, by the company's shareholders.

When they were published, the plays appeared in two formats, called quartos and folios. The quarto format was reserved for the printing of individual plays; eigh-

teen of Shakespeare's plays appeared this way during his lifetime. Because we know
the dates of these publications (printers were required to publish their intention to
print books and pamphlets in a record book called the Stationers' Register), we can
determine roughly when the plays were written and performed. The quarto derives
its name from the Latin for "four," the number of leaves the paper formed when
folded. Each leaf is the equivalent of two pages, that is, the front and back of the
leaf. These were normally sold after a play had lost its popularity on the stage and
may have been an attempt to revive interest in the piece. Multiple quartos might
appear for particularly popular plays, but whatever the number any profit from the
sales was returned to the company.

In 1623, seven years after Shakespeare's death, two of his acting fellows published
a folio edition containing the playwright's "complete" works. *Pericles*, later attributed to Shakespeare, did not appear in the First Folio, nor did Shakespeare's collaborations with John Fletcher, *Cardenio* and *The Two Noble Kinsmen*. *Edward III*,
which many scholars believe is at least partly Shakespeare's, also was omitted. Folios were larger than quartos, the format of choice for collected works, such as en-
cyclopedias and, dictionaries. The First Folio is a valuable source for scholars
because eighteen of Shakespeare's plays were published there for the first time; it
also contains versions of already published plays that are variants, and dedications
from fellow playwrights like Ben Jonson. Three additional Shakespeare folios were
published in the seventeenth century, but all were based on the 1623 edition.

ACTING AND PERFORMANCES

Performances were continuous on the Elizabethan stage, with no breaks for
scene changes (there was no scenery or curtain). Actors were required to double in
dramas with a large number of characters: a performer playing a messenger in an
early scene might later appear as duke or ambassador arriving at court for some
state occasion. In *A Midsummer Night's Dream* Theseus, Duke of Athens, and his
bride Hippolyta, erstwhile queen of the Amazons, are never on stage when Oberon
and Titania, king and queen of the fairies, appear. Often in modern productions
the roles of Theseus and Oberon are doubled, as are those of Hippolyta and Titania, and the same may have been done in Shakespeare's day.

Shakespeare's plays were written for a particular company and its particular actors. Arranging entrances and exits to allow doubling was an important concern.
Shakespeare also had to take into account the abilities of his cast. His first great
comic actor was William Kempe, who played Bottom (*A Midsummer Night's
Dream*), Launce (*The Two Gentlemen of Verona*), and Dogberry (*Much Ado about
Nothing*). Humor in these early comedies is broad and often relies on malapropisms
and misprision. In 1599 Kempe left the Lord Chamberlain's Men and was replaced
by Robert Armin, who created such roles as Touchstone (*As You Like It*), Feste
(*Twelfth Night*), and the Fool in *King Lear*. Armin's talent lay in more subtle humor,
seen in these later works, and he seems to have had a better voice, which Shakespeare used in writing songs for him.

Even the physical appearance of his actors influenced Shakespeare's text. In the
mid-1590s the Lord Chamberlain's Men included two apprentices, one tall and fair,
the other short and dark. The roles of Helena and Hermia in *A Midsummer Night's
Dream* were created with this distinction in mind. So there are references to "fair

Helena," and in 3.2 the two "women" spar over their physical traits. Hermia main-tains that Helena has won Lysander's love by pointing out how tall she (Helena) is, and Lysander mocks Hermia's low stature. These same boys may have been around some five years later for *As You Like It*. Rosalind there is "more than common tall" (1.3.115), so "she" disguises herself as a man, while Celia retains her woman's guise. All this cross-dressing—and cross–cross-dressing—upset Puritans (see Philip Stubbes's *The Anatomy of Abuses*, 1583) and has fascinated feminist critics.

Entrances and exits were made from doors on either side of the stage; actors changed costumes in the tiring room just beyond those doors. Stairs led to the sec-ond level, allowing an actor to move easily and unobserved from one playing level to the other. In *Richard II*, for example, Richard confronts his challenger Bulling-brook as the king stands at the parapet of Flint Castle; when he "descends" to meet his opponent—and immediately capitulate to him—we witness not only his phys-ical descent but also his fall from power. When major characters stood alone on the stage and delivered speeches exploring their states of mind or plans of action, they spoke soliloquies, a convention that Shakespeare perfected in *Hamlet*. Asides were also accepted illusions in which a character commented only to the audience his or her reaction to something said or done by other characters, who are pre-sumed not to overhear the remarks. For example, when Claudius tries to convince Hamlet that he is like a son to him, the hero's witty and sarcastic aside is "A little more than kin and less than kind" (1.2.65).

Shakespeare also relied heavily on stock characters in his dramas. Some of them, such as the father of a headstrong daughter (see *The Taming of the Shrew* and *Romeo and Juliet*) or the braggart soldier (for example, Don Armado in *Love's Labor's Lost* and Falstaff in the *Henry IV* plays) came from the Roman playwrights Plautus and Terence. He also wrote parts for Machiavellians; clever servants; lovelorn shepherds; and loyal, wise counselors, such as Kent in *King Lear*. Many of his creations were beloved by his audiences, and those audiences apparently encouraged him to bring these characters to the stage in more than one play. Battling lovers, for example, were a staple of such comedies as *The Taming of the Shrew* and *Much Ado about Nothing*, where their initial dislike for one another is gradually overcome as they realize that despite their cynicism about love, they too can fall victims to Cupid's arrow. Falstaff and his comic look-alikes (Sir Toby Belch in *Twelfth Night* and Dog-berry in *Much Ado about Nothing*) were so popular that Shakespeare had to make sure the actors didn't create a-textual business (i.e., actions or ad-libs not provided by the dramatist) intended to give them more stage time—and bigger laughs. Ham-let's advice to the players in *Hamlet* sounds very much like a playwright's plea to his performers: "And let those that play your clowns speak no more than is set down for them, for there be of them that will themselves laugh to set on some quantity of barren spectators to laugh too, though in the mean time some necessary ques-tion of the play be then to be consider'd. That's villainous, and shows a most piti-ful ambition in the fool that uses it" (3.2.38–45). One almost expects Hamlet to add, Kempe (or Armin), are you listening? Legend has it in fact that Queen Elizabeth so enjoyed the clowning of Falstaff that she asked Shakespeare to bring him back to life (his death is reported near the beginning of *Henry V*) to star in *The Merry Wives of Windsor*. While there is no sound evidence to support this theory, it does indi-cate just how popular and well-known certain characters—and actors—were in the Lord Chamberlain's company. Certainly Shakespeare liked him enough to write a sequel to *1 Henry IV* as a vehicle for capitalizing on Falstaff's popularity and even promised to bring him back in *Henry V*. Exactly why Shakespeare changed his mind for this latter play is unclear, but it may be because Kempe left the Lord Chamberlain's Men at that time. Or, if Burbage played Falstaff in the two parts of *Henry IV*, he was needed now for the title role.

The Lord Chamberlain's Men prospered at the Theatre during their residence there, primarily because of the success of the company's chief playwright. While others wrote plays and topical scenes to resurrect old plays for the company, Shakespeare's works represented the staple of their repertoire. Plays were performed in rotation, with the actors rehearsing a new or revived play while performing another. This practice placed a heavy burden on the dramatist to come up with new material to feed the entertainment appetites of public-playhouse audiences. (Consider the comparable demand of today's television audiences for ground-breaking sitcoms and so-called reality programs.) Although the standard genres of comedy, tragedy, and history continued to draw audiences, Shakespeare crafted such variations on these themes as slapstick comedy, romantic comedy, and tragicomedy; revenge tragedy, "fall of princes" tragedy, and romantic tragedy; chronicle history and more contemporary history—although it was illegal to present reigning monarchs on the stage. His skill at modifying and improvising the standard forms of drama and his poetic talent and gift for characterization (celebrated by Harold Bloom in *Shakespeare: The Invention of the Human* [New York: Riverhead Books, 1998]) no doubt account for his recognition as an artistic genius.

THE GLOBE PLAYHOUSE

Both the site and building for the representation of Shakespeare's genius changed in 1599. A dispute with their landlord drove the Burbages to tear down the Theatre late in 1598; rent concerns and a desire to move closer to recently constructed theaters led to this drastic decision. Using the timbers from the Theatre, the company's members moved to a section of the London suburbs called Bankside in the district of Southwark. Located on the south bank of the Thames, near London Bridge, Southwark had become home to such other playhouses as the Rose, the Fortune, and the Swan. This area was also home to bearbaiting arenas, houses of prostitution, and cockfighting pits—a center for pleasure seekers that was railed against by preachers and city fathers alike but that lay outside their jurisdiction. Despite many obstacles, the company managed to erect its new playhouse in 1599; for fourteen years thereafter the first Globe was the destination of choice for many Londoners in search of stimulating, often distinguished dramatic entertainment.

The Globe and other playhouses were named after well-known inns in England, as was evidenced by the sign depicting Hercules with the globe on his shoulders that hung outside Shakespeare's new home. Many playgoers ferried across the Thames to attend after they were alerted to a performance by the hoisting of a flag. Because there are no surviving blueprints and only primitive drawings of the building, we have no sure idea of its size and features. Scholars have surmised, however, that it was probably modeled on the Theatre. Excavations and X rays indicate that the Globe was about 74 feet in diameter, was a 24-sided polygon, and could accommodate 2,000 to 3,000 occupants. The stage of the Fortune, another Elizabethan theater, measured 43 feet in width and some 27 feet in depth. The Globe's

The "De Witt sketch" of the interior of the Swan Theatre. Reproduced from William Winter, *Shakespeare's England* (New York and London: Macmillan and Co., 1893).

stage probably had similar dimensions, which also correspond to a Golden Section. Although sets were nonexistent or minimal, the reconstructed Globe Theatre near the site of the original reveals the ornate painting and gilding that Shakespeare's audiences would have seen. When Hamlet speaks to Rosencrantz and Guildenstern of "this most excellent canopy, the air, look you, this brave o'erhanging firmament,

The Globe Theatre, or more likely a mislabeled Rose Theatre, from a 1616 engraving by Cornelius Visscher. Reproduced from William Winter, *Shakespeare's England* (New York and London: Macmillan and Co., 1893).

this majestical roof fretted with golden fire" (2.2.299–301), he is speaking not only metaphorically; he was in fact describing the painted roof over their heads.

Pickpockets and prostitutes often mixed with honest citizens in order to ply their trades. Orange vendors (who were often willing to sell more than oranges; Nell Gwynn, one of Charles II's mistresses, had been an orange girl at the theater) circulated among the spectators, who enjoyed nuts (which supposedly warded off the plague) so much that excavations revealed a thick layer of shells at the base of the Globe. Whether the first Shakespearean play acted there was *Julius Caesar* or *Henry V* is a question for continuing debate, but there is no question that several of the playwright's finest dramas—*Hamlet, Twelfth Night, Othello, Antony and Cleopatra*—sent appreciative audiences flocking to the company's renowned "wooden O" (*Henry V*, Prologue to Act 1, l. 13) during its existence (1599–1613). The Globe burned down in 1613 during a performance of *Henry VIII* when a spark from a cannon housed in the heavens set the thatched roof on fire; though no one was killed or seriously injured, the company suddenly found itself without a venue in which to perform. A scant one year later the second Globe was built, a remarkable feat that attests to the determination and significant resources of the King's Men (which became the company's name after Elizabeth died in 1603 and was succeeded by James I, formerly James VI of Scotland). The second Globe stood until 1644, when it was torn down by the followers of Oliver Cromwell.

ACTING COMPANIES, 1590s–EARLY 1600s

Competition between the two major companies—the Lord Chamberlain's (later King's) Men and the Lord Admiral's Men—was stiff, but for a period in the late 1590s into the early 1600s a small number of children's troupes were allowed to perform within the city's limits in indoor playhouses housing 600 to 700 citizens. The Children of St. Paul's, the Children of the Queen's Revels, and the Children of Blackfriars featured mainly satiric comedies, most of which were written by Ben Jonson, George Chapman, and John Marston. Because they were not regarded as professional players, the boys' productions were not required to be censored by the Master of the Revels, who strictly oversaw the repertory of the adult companies. As a result, Jonson and the others were able to write comedies that mocked the manners both of citizens and of court figures. As a result of the boys' acting talents and the topical humor of their plays, many members of the adult companies' audiences flocked to see these daring productions; this shift resulted in a so-called War of the Theatres (also called the *Poetomachia*, Greek for war of the poets) between the children and adult companies. Rosencrantz (*Hamlet*, 1601) complains that the "little eyases"—a pun on the name for young hawks and "asses"—are winning over audiences even from "Hercules and his load" (2.2.339, 361), an obvious reference to the Globe. But the war, if in fact it was ever very heated, was essentially over by 1605 or 1606 because the fare of the children's companies went out of fashion. No doubt another reason for the decline and fall was the aggressive stance of James I's court after Scottish characters were made fun of in a comedy by Jonson, Chapman, and Marston called *Eastward Ho!* After that, the children's companies were no longer free from the attention and scrutiny of the Master of the Revels.

The demise of the boys' troupes proved to be another boon to Shakespeare's company. Owned by the Burbages, the Blackfriars Theatre (located within the city, in the Blackfriars district) was returned to them in 1608, which in effect officially sanctioned the right of adult companies to perform in London proper. Previously, the city's authorities had refused to let Shakespeare's company use the space. Though smaller than the Globe, the Blackfriars provided a place where the plays could be acted inside during the cold, dreary winter months; it also gave the King's Men access to a more sophisticated audience of courtiers and gentlemen. The company's revenues and reputation were greatly enhanced after this move, which without doubt had the strong support of their monarch and sponsor. Even though evidence indicates Shakespeare wrote plays to be performed in both venues, it appears that he tended to rely more heavily on the material of romance for plays written between 1608 and 1613. Plays modeled on romances were popular with the educated audiences attending Blackfriars.

AUDIENCES

While audiences reflecting many socioeconomic levels attended plays at the Globe and Blackfriars, kings and queens were never in attendance. Elizabeth and James requested the players' presence at court when the monarchs were in the mood for dramatic entertainment or wanted to entertain foreign potentates and dignitaries. As the monarch's servants, the players, besides performing, were also often required to serve food and drink, answer questions, and attend to the myriad needs of their masters. Plays written for special occasions like weddings or baptisms (called "occasional" plays), such as some scholars have suggested *A Midsummer Night's Dream* and *Twelfth Night* were, featured themes and characters linked to these events and were intended as elaborate compliments to monarchs and their courtiers. A clear condition of the court's protection of the actors was the requirement that they come when called; although rewards were bestowed on the actors for their responsiveness, they were expected to make their livings from receipts of public-playhouse productions.

OTHER VENUES

The Inns of Court, which were the English law schools, were sometimes sites of productions by Shakespeare's company. The actors performed at one end of the banquet halls, relying as they did in the other venues on limited costumes and props and no scenery. The comedy *Twelfth Night* was performed at the Middle Temple Hall in February 1602 to the delight of the law students assembled there. Law students formed an important segment of Shakespeare's audience throughout his career, a fact that is confirmed by complaints from contemporary law professors whose students failed to show up for their afternoon lectures. No doubt these truants were challenged by the complex legal issues and dramatic courtroom scenes in such plays as *The Merchant of Venice* and *Measure for Measure*; perhaps they also laughed at the satire directed at lawyers and their language in such plays as *Hamlet* and *2 Henry IV*.

Regardless of venue, Shakespeare and other playwrights and actors were subject to harsh laws passed by parliament and the London city fathers. In 1572, for instance, an act "for the punishment of Vacabondes" (that is, vagabonds, vagrants) was instituted. Its main purpose was to require actors to form repertory companies and to seek the protection of nobles or magistrates; those who failed to acquire this protection could be arrested and jailed. The happy consequence of this law, however, was the emergence of professional adult companies with permanent homes and devoted audiences. In 1606 parliament passed another act, "to Restraine Abuses of Players," imposing a ten-pound fine on those actors who took God's or Christ's name in vain. While that doesn't sound like too harsh a penalty today, ten pounds in Shakespeare's time was a sizable sum. (In the 1560s the schoolmaster at Stratford's grammar school received an annual salary of twenty pounds.) As a result of this law, the names of pagan gods like Apollo and Iris tend to appear more frequently in plays written and performed after this date. *King Lear* (first published in 1608) is often cited as one interesting example. Another is *Othello*, first performed before this law was enacted. The first quarto of the play (1622) used a manuscript, whether the promptbook, a transcript of the author's foul papers, or some other text, that reflected the early performances. Thus, in 1.1.4, Iago's first word is "'Sblood." This word is of course a shortened form of God's, that is, Christ's, blood and so would have risked a fine after 1606. The Folio version of the play, reflecting a text revised after the law was passed, omits this and other such profanities. Companies were likewise restricted by public health and disturbance regulations, which meant that the government could close the theaters during months when the bubonic plague raged or when riots took place for any reason.

Shakespeare gave the theater its greatest works, but these works would have been impossible without the reciprocal gifts of the Elizabethan stage. Its flexibility allowed him, for example, to locate the first act of *Othello* in Venice and the rest of the play in Cyprus, a change of venue that is not only symbolic but also crucial to the play's development. He used its upper story and its discovery place in back of the stage to good purpose, but these spaces also allowed Juliet's balcony scene with Romeo and the revealing of Hermione at the end of *The Winter's Tale*. Shakespeare gave his actors the loftiest measures ever molded by the pen of man, but he could do so because he knew they could speak those lines as he intended them. Without Richard Burbage, there likely would not have been a Hamlet. Without gifted apprentices there would have been no Juliet or Rosalind. Without William Kempe would Shakespeare have created Bottom? In the absence of manuscript evidence, we will never know to what extent Shakespeare's company participated in the turning of his foul papers into the plays we read and see today. Theater was and still is a collaboration between playwright and actors (and audiences).

Shakespeare's genius lay not in inventing new stories but in recasting old ones. Hence, the literary tradition he inherited from the classical and medieval worlds was crucial to his dramaturgy. Without mystery and morality plays, without *Ralph Roister Doister* and *Gorboduc*, which are hardly ever seen or even read any longer, Shakespeare's plays, performed and read daily around the world, would be different and no doubt lesser works. Shakespeare reshaped the English stage, but only because the English stage helped to shape him.

Annotated Bibliography

Beckerman, Bernard. *Shakespeare at the Globe, 1599–1609*. New York: Macmillan, 1962. The author discusses staging requirements at the Globe. He considers the repertory, dramaturgy, stage design, and acting style, among other issues. He challenges the idea of an inner stage, arguing that sight lines and other factors work against it. Beckerman emphasizes dramatic illusion as a key to successful performance and believes that the inner form of each play dictated the style of its staging.

Bentley, G. E. *The Jacobean and Caroline Stage*. 7 vols. London: Clarendon P, 1941–1968. The definitive source for records and contemporary accounts of the stage from 1616 to 1642. Each volume treats a different topic. Volume 1 deals with acting companies. Volume 2 discusses actors; volumes 3–5, plays and playwrights. Volume 6 explores private, public, and court theaters. Volume 7 includes appendices to volume 6 and an index to the set. The detail can be overwhelming, but Bentley takes special care to explain the significance of material found in the public records.

Chambers, E. K. *The Elizabethan Stage*. 4 vols. London: Clarendon P, 1923. The companion to Bentley's study, Chambers's work is authoritative and exhaustively thorough. Volume 1 collects material related to the court and its control of the stage. Volume 2 treats the companies, actors, and playhouses. The third volume looks at staging, plays, and playwrights, and the fourth treats anonymous plays and masques and includes appendixes and indexes. Though dated in some ways, it is a reliable source for anyone seeking information about drama performed during Elizabeth's reign.

Cook, Ann Jennalie. *The Privileged Playgoers of Shakespeare's London, 1576–1642*. Princeton: Princeton UP, 1981. Opposing the notion that Shakespeare's public-theater spectators came from all social strata, Cook argues that Shakespeare's audience was made up almost exclusively of citizens from the upper class. She maintains that only they had the time and money to attend plays. Using historical and cultural evidence, she points out that the privileged classes were intimately involved with plays through the educational system. An analysis of the plays' content reveals that themes and characters of great interest to the upper classes are regularly featured.

Foakes, R. A. *Illustrations of the English Stage, 1580–1642*. Stanford, CA: Stanford UP, 1985. Offers 124 reproductions of theaters, stages, and performances for the period covered. Foakes includes useful commentary for seventy-nine of the pictures, interpreting the visual evidence. Fun to look at, informative to read.

Gurr, Andrew. *The Shakespearean Stage: 1574–1642*. 3rd ed. Cambridge: Cambridge UP, 1992. In clear, readable prose, Gurr provides valuable information about the genesis of acting companies, their makeup, repertories, playhouses, acting styles, and audiences. He relies heavily on the work of E. K. Chambers and G. E. Bentley (cited above), but he also uses information gathered from more recent studies of the companies and playhouses. His discussions of ordinances and statutes that affected the companies' livelihoods are especially interesting.

Howard, Jean E. *Shakespeare's Art of Orchestration*. Urbana: U of Illinois P, 1984. Howard believes that Shakespeare sought to elicit specific responses from his audience by using such theatrical devices as counterpoint, silence, placement of the actors, and orchestration of their movements. Silences might be used to signal the close of some action, for example, and dumb shows could create tension.

Styan, J. L. *Shakespeare's Stagecraft*. Cambridge: Cambridge UP, 1969. Styan offers a pragmatic approach to staging. He discusses acting conventions, their use on the physical stage, the grouping of actors, and their varying styles of delivery. Even though the text of a play gives the actor guidelines about how to perform the speeches, Shakespeare also allowed for improvisation. In discussing comedies like *Twelfth Night* and *A Midsummer Night's Dream*, Styan shows how certain techniques of voice and movement might be used for different effects.

Weimann, Robert. *Shakespeare and the Popular Tradition in the Theater*. Ed. Robert Schwartz. Baltimore: Johns Hopkins UP, 1978. Emphasizing the role of theater in society, Weimann argues that Shakespeare's plays appropriated elements of the popular tradition inherited from the Middle Ages. Weimann sees Shakespeare's works as coloring the nature of his society. Values are presented in a way that makes them appealing. Important for placing the plays in their cultural context.

William Shakespeare's Texts

Roze Hentschell

INTRODUCTION

We often look to the content of Shakespeare's plays to offer us clues as to how he perceived the world around him and, indeed, his own work. In *As You Like It*, for example, Duke Senior's melancholic courtier, Jaques, famously utters what we regard to be a favorite sentiment of Shakespeare:

> All the world's a stage,
> And all the men and women merely players;
> They have their exits and their entrances,
> And one man in his time plays many parts. (2.7.139–142)

Throughout his career Shakespeare displays an intense preoccupation with the theatricality of the world in which he lived. He exploits the performative nature of men and women with astonishingly inventive results. Disguising and dissembling, acting and improvising are all crucial functions in his plays. It is unimaginable that the richness of Viola in *Twelfth Night* or Rosalind in *As You Like It* could be displayed without the clever use of their male disguises. Richard III is fascinating in his very ability to "seem a saint, when most I play the devil" (1.3.337). In *King Lear*, Edgar and Kent are able to hide their identities convincingly with a change of garment, beard style, or way of speaking. While Shakespeare expresses a keen interest in how the dramatic mode is found in everyday life, he also recognizes the affective power of theater and playmaking. Shakespeare shows us how we incorporate the theatrical enterprise into our everyday lives. Hamlet tests the Ghost's story that Claudius killed his father by having the actors visiting Elsinore "[p]lay something like the murther of my father" because "guilty creatures sitting at a play / Have by the very cunning of the scene / Been strook so to the soul, that presently / They have proclaim'd their malefactions" (2.2.595, 589–592). In *1 Henry IV*, Hal decides to "practice an answer" by role-playing with Falstaff before he confronts his father (2.4.375). King Lear stages a mock trial to "[a]rraign" his absent daughters since he has no other recourse for justice (3.6.46). Theater, Shakespeare suggests, constitutes real life just as it reflects it. Indeed, it is difficult to think of a play that does not comment on the notion that the world of plots and acting is the very world in which we live.

Yet for all this concern with theatricality, the moments in his plays where we gain insight into the material realities of actual performances in Shakespeare's time and the actors' relationship to the script on which their performance is based are relatively rare. Shakespeare gives us little to go on when we try to discover his own attitudes toward the writing of plays or the process he went through. If the plays themselves give us few clues, even rarer is the existence of Shakespeare's actual scripts. While 18 manuscripts by Shakespeare's contemporary playwrights have survived (out of probably 3,000 plays written), with the exception of the manuscript of *Sir Thomas More*, which has three pages of text that are disputably in Shakespeare's handwriting, no original text by Shakespeare exists (Long, in Kastan, p. 414). Nor do we have much conclusive evidence regarding the extent to which Shakespeare was involved in the printing of his own plays. Despite the careful and tireless work of literary critics, historians, and bibliographers, what we do know about Shakespeare's texts must remain at least somewhat speculative. Yet print is the primary medium through which Shakespeare has been handed down from his time to the present, and performances are of course based on those printed texts. It is therefore necessary to understand the various modes of textual production of Renaissance authors in order to gain a more complete understanding of the Shakespeare we have inherited. What follows, then, is an effort to show the possible journey of a Shakespearean play from manuscript to publication, from stage to page.

TEXTS FOR PERFORMANCE

Shakespeare wrote an average of two plays a year throughout his career. Some of these plays may have been written at the request of a theater company, while others probably were drafted without outside prompting. What is clear, though, is that whatever script the playwright would initially come up with would undergo change (sometimes drastic) before the work was performed for an audience. The first draft of a play, written in the author's own hand, is known as the author's *foul papers*—so called because it may have been messy and marked up with marginal and interlinear additions and with lines crossed out. Once a dramatist completed work on a play, he would sell the manuscript to a theater company. Most playwrights peddled their play, selling it to whichever theater company would have it, usually for a set fee of five to ten pounds. If the playwright was popular and in demand, however, he may have had an established relationship with a particular theater company for which he wrote exclusively. These "attached men" were contracted for a specific length of time and earned a salary. Shakespeare's case is unique in that he wrote almost exclusively for the Lord Chamberlain's Men (later called the King's Men), acted in their performances, and was a major shareholder in the company. Thus, he benefited directly from the sale of his own plays in more than one way. Undoubtedly, some men (and they were virtually all men) barely eked out a living selling their scripts. However, there is considerable evidence that suggests the profession of the playwright could be quite lucrative. Playwrights made more money than other literary professionals of the time, and some, such as Thomas Dekker and

Anthony Munday, even supplemented their income by writing prose or verse satire or commissioned civic pageants. Although scripts were not necessarily considered to be a lofty literary art, the potential profit to be made by them lured scores of authors to try their hand at playwriting.

Once an author sold his manuscript, it no longer belonged to him but became the property of the members of the theater company, who could do with it whatever they pleased. Most playwrights would not have been able to exert any control over their text once it was purchased, especially if the playwright was not attached to a particular company. After the purchase of the script, either the author himself or a company scribe would make a copy of the original manuscript and submit this *fair copy* to the theater company. This transcription was undoubtedly slow going and, of course, subject to human error. Nevertheless, this text was then further marked up by a member of the company who made revisions in order to have the play work more clearly as a text for performance. Stage directions, cues, and other revisions may have been added at this point of the process. While this text was almost certainly "cleaner" than the original foul papers, it no doubt contained errors or inconsistencies, especially if the copy was not made by the author himself. A company scribe would then revise the fair copy manuscript into another version, which was known as the *playbook*. The playbook would probably have supplemented or clarified any stage directions that existed in the earlier manuscripts, cleaned up inconsistencies in the text, indicated the inclusion of special effects, and made any amendments demanded by the office of the Master of the Revels (see below). The fair copy and the playbook were usually the only complete versions of the play; the playbook would replace the characters' names with the names of the actors who were to perform the roles and would serve as the promptbook.

Because complete texts were expensive and time-consuming to produce, rather than having a full version of the play, each actor would have his individual part or parts (as many actors played more than one role in any given performance) written out for him (Elizabethan and Jacobean actors were always male). These individual texts, called *sides*, had cues for entrances and exits, a few lines of the speech preceding or following the actors' lines, and were often written on scrolls of paper. We see a wonderful and rare example of players interacting with their script in *A Midsummer Night's Dream*. The Athenian laborers—who desire to perform a play at the nuptial celebration of Theseus and Hippolyta—show an example, however bumbling, of how parts may have been assigned to various actors in Shakespeare's time. Peter Quince, serving as a sort of director, has "the scroll of every man's name" who is "to play in our enterlude" (1.2.4, 5–6). He then gives the actors their "parts" and requests that they "con [learn] them by tomorrow night" before they meet to "rehearse" (1.2.100–101, 103). Actors were thus required to memorize their written parts on their own before they gathered for a group rehearsal.

During rehearsal, it is very likely that further emendations, suggested by either members of the theater company or the actors themselves, would have been made to the script in order to make it more appropriate for performance. When the Athenian workers meet again to rehearse in the forest, for example, Bottom the weaver asserts that "there are things in this comedy of Pyramus and Thisbe that will never please. First, Pyramus must draw a sword to kill himself; which the ladies cannot abide" (3.1.9–12). Bottom's fear that the women of the court will be alarmed and distressed by Pyramus's suicide compels him to request Peter Quince to

> [w]rite me a prologue, and let the prologue seem to say we will do no harm with our
> swords, and that Pyramus is not kill'd indeed; and for the more better assurance, tell
> them that I Pyramus am not Pyramus, but Bottom the weaver. This will put them out
> of fear. (3.1.17–22)

Despite Bottom's humorous sense that his audience cannot discern between fiction
and reality, his call for a prologue reveals that scripts could be, and often were, revised for performance, and actors may have been the instigators of such changes.
Quince agrees to write "such a prologue" (3.1.23) for the occasion of the Duke's
marriage celebration, just as playwrights or actors in Shakespeare's time may have
added or deleted lines or whole speeches. As Roslyn Knutson argues, "as in-house
dramatist, [Shakespeare] presumably also provided routine services such as pro-
logues and epilogues for occasional performances, revisions for changes in venue
or company personnel, and emendations to avoid censorship or facilitate a revival"
(48). Of course, not all requests by actors for change could be accommodated. Bottom refuses Snout the tinker's absurd and amusing request for "another prologue"
to assert that Snug the joiner is not actually a lion (3.1.34) but suggests further modification to the script.

Significantly, the lines we see the laborers rehearse in act 3 are not the same
speeches we hear them perform in act 5, indicating that there have been further revisions. This, too, was common practice. In Shakespeare's time, the plays did not
have, as Stephen Greenblatt articulates, a "static perfection," an authentic completion, but rather were "creatively, inexhaustibly unfinished" (67). In *Hamlet*, the
prince asks the first player if his traveling acting troupe can play "The Murther of
Gonzago" (2.2.537–538) with changes that Hamlet himself will include: "You could
for need study a speech of some dozen or sixteen lines, which I would set down
and insert in't, could you not?" (2.2.540–543). Hamlet changes one play, "The Murther of Gonzago," into another, "The Mouse-trap" (3.2.237) through the inclusion
of new text, thus acting as reviser in order to "catch the conscience of the King"
(2.2.605).

Scholars have posited that Shakespeare most likely had a hand in the revision of
his own texts. This is entirely plausible given that he was not only the chief playwright of the Lord Chamberlain's Men (and later the King's Men), but also an actor
and shareholder in the company and no doubt was present at the theater much of
the time. He would have attended rehearsals (even, presumably, when he was not
performing in the plays) and would have seen what needed to be amended for the
stage. That is not to say that he was the only one to revise the texts, but that he may
have been significantly involved in versions of the written manuscript beyond the
foul papers. This does not mean, however, that he was aiming for a final and complete draft of the play. Greenblatt indicates that "there is no sign that Shakespeare
sought through such revision to bring each of his plays to its 'perfect,' 'final' form.
On the contrary, many of the revisions seem to indicate that the scripts remained
open texts, that the playwright and his company expected to add, cut, and rewrite
as the occasion demanded" (67).

One of the demands for textual change came from the office of the Master of the
Revels. Individual plays during Shakespeare's time were authorized by this official,
who monitored the theater and worked under the office of the Lord Chamberlain.
This post, created under Henry VIII in 1545, made up the department of the royal

household that oversaw entertainments. The Master of the Revels hired theatrical companies to perform at court, selected the plays, and provided them with scenery and costumes. As the Master of the Revels had the authority of censorship, he also monitored the content of the plays. In *Hamlet*, for example, before the members of the court begin watching the play within the play, Claudius asks Hamlet, "Have you heard the argument? is there no offense in't?" (3.2.232–233), in effect asking him if he has performed the role of Master of the Revels adequately. In *A Midsummer Night's Dream*, Philostrate performs the role of Master of the Revels to Theseus's court, offering "a brief" of the possible entertainment for the nuptial celebration (5.1.42). After Theseus rejects several choices, he decides that "we will hear" the play put on by what Philostrate calls the "[h]ard-handed men," Quince and the rest of the laborers (5.1.76, 72). As Master of the Revels, Philostrate unsuccessfully attempts to intercede, claiming that this play is not fit for the eyes of the court, not because it is offensive, but because the writing is so bad and the actors' abilities are "[e]xtremely stretch'd" (5.1.80). "[M]y noble lord," Philostrate entreats, "[i]t is not for you" (5.1.76–77).

The authority of the Master of the Revels reached far beyond court performances in Shakespeare's time, as he governed and controlled all theatrical productions, including those of the public theaters. He collected fees from the theater companies and inspected the content of the plays prior to performance. The Master's commission gave him the power to demand that theater companies rehearse their new plays for him. But if a play was being scrutinized for the sake of authorization rather than court performance, more often than not the Master would not attend a rehearsal; instead the theater company would prepare clean copies of the plays—most likely the playbook. If a play was deemed offensive, the theater company would be forced to revise it. "Offensive" material might have included the following categories, according to Gerard Bentley:

1. Critical comments on the policies or conduct of the government
2. Unfavorable presentations of *friendly* foreign powers or their sovereigns, great nobles, or subjects
3. Comments on religious controversy
4. Profanity (after 1606)
5. Personal satire of *influential* people (Bentley, p. 167)

Foul language or profanity was especially closely monitored. In 1606, parliament passed "An Act to Restrain Abuses of Players." Actors were forbidden to "jestingly or profanely speak or use the holy name of God or of Christ Jesus, or of the Holy Ghost or of the Trinity, which are not to be spoken but with fear and reverence." For each "offence by him or them committed," the actor or actors would have to pay a fine of ten pounds, even though the profanity may already have been put down in the text. Revivals of plays originally produced prior to 1606 were required to be revised to abide by this law. If a play passed muster, the Master of the Revels would grant a license for performances, which would be attached to the play's manuscript.

Just as it is important to recognize that plays were malleable entities, susceptible to revision by any number of individuals, so is it crucial to see that the process of initially writing a play was also entirely collaborative. The popularity of the public theater demanded a steady stream of new material, and multiple authors could put out new plays more quickly than an individual. Much of the time playwrights worked together; sometimes as many as four would be working on the same play. According to Gerard Bentley, "It would be reasonable to guess that as many as half of the plays by professional dramatists in the period incorporated the writing at some date of more than one man" (199). Authors might be given an advance of a pound if the members of a theater company liked a plot and wanted to see it finished. Playwrights would each take a part of a plot that had been outlined, sometimes by the theater company itself, and fill in the script quickly and efficiently. The most frequent method of collaboration seems to have been to parcel up and compose individual acts. Sometimes authors would fill in pieces of a play. For instance, a dramatist might add a prologue or epilogue for a special performance. Playwrights also might have been hired to "mend" or "alter" plays, either to revise them before performance or to supplement them for revival. Some of the best-known playwrights of the times—such and Francis Beaumont, John Fletcher, Thomas Middleton, Thomas Dekker, and Ben Jonson—were frequent collaborators.

Shakespeare seems to have collaborated less often than did his contemporary playwrights. This may be due in part to his status as an attached playwright for the Lord Chamberlain's and King's Men. He simply may not have had the financial need to write in the piecemeal fashion of so many of his colleagues. But it would be wrong to suggest that Shakespeare never collaborated or that his texts do not show evidence of other authors' hands. Quite the contrary, scholars have argued, based on careful textual analysis, that several of his texts were co-authored. Shakespeare appears to have collaborated with other authors in writing *Titus Andronicus*, *Timon of Athens*, *Pericles*, and *Henry VIII*, while *The Two Noble Kinsmen* and a lost play, *Cardenio*, are known to have been co-authored with John Fletcher. Even in the case of Shakespeare's best-known solo efforts, we can never be too sure that he wrote all of the play himself. In the case of *Macbeth*, for example, which was probably written in 1606, several lines spoken by the weird sisters were certainly written by another prolific playwright, Thomas Middleton. The songs in act 3, scene 5 of the play show up in Middleton's play, *The Witch*, performed sometime around 1616. In Shakespeare's Folio of 1623 (see below), the only printed source for *Macbeth*, only the first words of the song are printed, while the song is printed in full in *The Witch*. Evidence suggests that this scene was added after 1616, and most scholars agree that the language is more characteristic of Middleton than of Shakespeare.

As much as scholars desire to get a sense of what Shakespeare actually wrote, the collaborative nature of dramatic works makes it especially difficult to assign "authority" to a particular text. The multiple steps involved in the textual process demonstrate above all that a text is a fluid thing, one susceptible to error and open to revision. As Russ McDonald points out,

> The scribe who copied out the parts for the actors, for example, may have misunderstood the author's penmanship and thus introduced errors. An actor may have found a particular line difficult to deliver and requested a change—or simply made the change for himself. Actors frequently misremember or alter lines, and sometimes these erroneous versions become a permanent part of the play text. The prompter, or "book-keeper," needing more time to get an actor on stage, may have contributed a

line or two himself to stall the action until the required character could appear. If the play were running overtime in rehearsal, the author or perhaps the book-keeper might have made cuts. (195)

Of course, all of these scenarios are speculative; even so, they are all plausible and demonstrate the vulnerabilities of textual purity. With so many hands contributing at so many points in the process, and in the absence of a copy of a manuscript in Shakespeare's hand, there is almost no way that we can definitively identify his original text.

PRINTED TEXTS

A common assumption among scholars is that once Shakespeare wrote and sold his plays, he did not have much interest in what happened to them. Approximately half (eighteen) of Shakespeare's plays were printed in his lifetime, but there is no conclusive evidence that he oversaw the printing of his own texts, or even that he was interested in doing so. Had Shakespeare wanted to give input about the way in which the plays were printed, he did not necessarily have a legal position from which to do so, as the script was no longer the property of the playwright once he sold it to the theater company. As we have seen, the company itself could make whatever changes it deemed necessary for performance and printing. Changes in the author's original script reflected in the printed texts—revisions, interpolations, and extractions of scenes or parts of scenes—were likewise immune to the author's possible disapproval. But no evidence suggests that Shakespeare did disapprove of such revisions, and most likely he would have accepted the changes as part of the process of playwriting.

Shakespeare did, however, seem to have a personal investment in overseeing the printing of his two narrative poems, *Venus and Adonis* (1593) and *The Rape of Lucrece* (1594); in their printed format, each of these poems is preceded by the author's signed dedicatory epistle to the Earl of Southampton. Shakespeare calls *Venus and Adonis* the "first heire of my invention," indicating that it was his first published literary work. In the typically humble fashion of dedications, Shakespeare refers to *The Rape of Lucrece* as merely "this Pamphlet." While perhaps he belittles his poem, he still draws attention to its status as something to be printed and read. Although Shakespeare had certainly begun writing plays by this point, he (and indeed his culture) seemed to think of them in a separate category from poems. Writing poems was a more lofty enterprise; they were able to flatter their dedicatees and immortalize their subjects. "Not marble nor the gilded monuments / Of princes shall outlive this pow'rful rhyme," Shakespeare argues in Sonnet 55, precisely because poetry is intended to be read in a way that drama was not (1–2).

While his poems were prepared for the print market, Shakespeare, as most scholars would agree, wrote his plays for performance rather than publication. What Shakespeare wrote, then, were scripts to be acted rather than books to be read. Nevertheless, Shakespeare's plays did find their way to print, allowing for a phenomenon that neither he nor anyone else could have predicted. As David Scott Kastan has argued, the plays "quickly escaped his control, surfacing as books to be read and allowing Shakespeare to 'live' no less vitally in print than he does in the theater" (*Shakespeare*, p. 9). So, while it is crucial to understand that "Shakespeare's text," that is, the primary medium in which he wrote, was the play's manuscript, it is important not to underestimate the life of plays once they became texts to be read. Indeed, Shakespeare has been handed down for many generations as an author in print. We buy and read the plays in book form and have been doing so since his time.

Although we tend to focus on the popularity of Shakespeare's plays in performance, they were also reasonably popular in print form. Eighteen of his plays were printed before his death, and of those several were reprinted, sometimes more than once. An especially popular play, *1 Henry IV* appeared in print six times before Shakespeare's death, making it the most often printed play by any playwright up to 1616. During Shakespeare's lifetime, more editions of his plays were printed than of any other dramatist's work during the same period. The popularity of his plays perhaps belies the fact that in Shakespeare's age printed plays had not yet established themselves as a surefire marketable commodity. In 1630, for example, booksellers sold twenty times more religious books than playbooks (Kastan, *Shakespeare*, p. 22). Of the eighteen Shakespearean plays published, only ten saw a reprinting. At best, for the publishers, plays were a relatively inexpensive business venture—they were cheap to procure (the publisher probably paid about two pounds for a play) and cheap to produce. But they nevertheless were a financial risk because a play-reading public had not yet firmly established itself, and these publications were never a "major source of revenue" (Knutson, p. 65). Other books were likely to sell more widely in this period. By 1636, for example, Shakespeare's poem *Venus and Adonis* had been printed sixteen times, significantly more than his most popular plays. Kastan reminds us of the commercial risk of printing plays and the relative rarity of this enterprise: "Publishers did regularly assume the risk of printing plays (though between 1590 and 1615, on average only about ten were published a year). This, at a time when plays were being staged in record number. Probably less than one-fifth of the plays produced saw a printing press" (*Shakespeare*, p. 23).

If a play fell out of favor with the audience and was no longer profitable for the company, it would be taken out of the troupe's repertory and might have been sold to a printer. Plays may have also been sold in order to render the theater companies solvent for one reason or another. For example, the construction of the new Globe Theater in 1599 would likely have created substantial debt to Shakespeare's company; four of his plays were published in 1600, likely in an effort to raise funds. While theater companies may have sold their scripts to publishers to be printed in times of financial distress or when they were not making money in performance, there may have been another motive for printing the texts: advertising. As Knutson has argued, licensed theater companies "saw not only the stage but also the bookshop as a venue for advertising their special status" (71). For example, the Admiral's Men, a licensed theater company in Shakespeare's time, registered an unusual number of their plays in 1600–1601 with the company's name attached. It is possible that the opening of their new playhouse, the Fortune, prompted them to promote their company and their repertory. After a particularly intense outbreak of the plague closed the theaters in 1593, there was an increase in registered plays, presumably as a means to draw audiences back to the playhouses. The market in printed texts must therefore be seen as connected to and part of the market for performed scripts.

If a publisher wanted to get a play printed, he needed to have the text approved by a church or state official. Up until 1606, clerics from the Court of High Commission (under the authority of the Archbishop of Canterbury and the Bishop of London) were responsible for censoring and licensing scripts and all other texts for publication and printing. In this year, the Master of the Revels took over the job, thus further expanding the jurisdiction of his office. When it came to censorship of offensive material, the same rules that applied to plays in performance applied to plays in print. A famous example of such censorship is the case of *Richard II*. In this play, the king is murdered on stage after he has been deposed. The murder of a monarch would presumably be upsetting to the Master of the Revels. And yet, the scene of the murder was allowed to remain while the deposition of the king was censored. The first three printed versions of this play (beginning in 1597) omit the scene in which Richard abdicates, while the next three printed editions include it. Richard Dutton suggests that

> the most compelling explanation of this is that the scene specifically shows Richard's abdication being sanctioned by Parliament, suggesting that parliamentary authority might outweigh that of the monarch. . . . In the context of 1597, with no agreed successor to Elizabeth and no agreed mechanism for finding one, this was highly contentious . . . the censor's attention seems to be on immediately provocative matters rather than on *potentially* subversive sub-texts in the play as a whole. (8)

It is not clear whether it was the Master of the Revels who cut the abdication scene for performance or the press censor who cut the lines for printing. But we do know that matters represented on stage that might have provoked reaction about an analogous contemporary political situation had to be excised.

Once the censors gave the authorization for a play's publication, it would then need to be licensed, for a fee of sixpence, by a warden of the Stationers' Company. Incorporated in 1557, this English guild of booksellers, publishers, and printers monitored the industry. The warden of the Stationers' Company would see that the play had been authorized by the proper authority and then give it his own signature, indicating that the play had been licensed for printing. The publisher would then most likely enter the play's title in the Stationers' Register. Although, as Blayney emphasizes, nearly one-third of the books published in Shakespeare's time were not registered, entrance into the register could protect the play from piracy, as there was a written record of its existence. Registration would have, not surprisingly, required an additional fee of fourpence. The warden was not required to find out where the text that he was being given came from (that is, who the author was or how the text came into the seller's hands), but he was obliged to withhold a license from a text that had been previously registered with another stationer. While from our perspective it may seem to be a violation of intellectual property rights that an author's plays could be stolen and sold to a publisher, this was in fact a perfectly legal—however unethical—act. Only books that were previously registered with one stationer and then published again were subject to legal action by the Stationers' Company.

The term "stationers" refers generally to various aspects of the book publishing industry and can mean publisher, printer, or bookseller alone or in any combination of the three (and derives from the fact that these people have stations, or shops,

unlike itinerant vendors). A publisher was the individual who had bought the manuscript copy and paid for the printing, while the printer was responsible for the
manufacture of the book and the one who owned the printing press. In the early
modern period there was no particular word for what we would call the publisher;
this person would sometimes also be called the printer. As Peter Blayney explains,
"they generally used the word *print* in the sense of 'cause to be printed.' The for-
mulaic heading 'The Printer to the Reader' was therefore commonly used by publishers who were not strictly printers at all" (391). Most plays, though, were
published by booksellers. On the 1599 title page of *Romeo and Juliet*, for example,
we see that it was "printed by Thomas Creede, for Cuthbert Burby, and . . . to be
sold at his shop neare the Exchange." Here Burby is clearly the publisher and bookseller (it is at "his shop" where the book will be sold), while Thomas Creede was
employed by Burby to print the book.

Once a text was approved by the Master of the Revels, licensed, and (most often)
registered, it was taken to a printer (also sometimes the publisher) who owned the
typesetting equipment to be used in manufacturing the book. There were three
main formats for printed texts in Shakespeare's time: *Folio*, *Quarto*, and *Octavo*,
which referred to the size of the sheet upon which the text was to be printed. The
printer would have begun with a sheet of paper approximately 18 × 14 inches. For
a folio, the sheet would have been folded once in half and printed on both sides,
thus making two leaves (four pages) approximately 9 × 14 inches. Folios were expensive bound books and were usually reserved for texts of some importance, usually political or religious in nature. Quartos were a much more common form of
printing and were the primary format for plays. These texts were generally unbound
and were about the size of a modern-day comic book. To make a quarto, the sheet
would have been folded twice, making four leaves (eight pages). The sheet for oc-
tavos would have been folded yet again, constructing eight leaves or sixteen pages.
The publisher, bookseller, or printer (sometimes in collaboration with each other)
would take into account the nature of the book to be printed as well as readership
and then decide on the format, type size and design, paper quality, and number of
copies. All of Shakespeare's plays printed in his lifetime appeared as quartos.

When a text was to be printed, it would be set up in the print shop by a *comp-
ositor*, or typesetter. Compositors were crucial figures in this process, since they
read the manuscript and committed its words to type. They also attempted to nor-
malize spelling, punctuation, and capitalization. As George Walton Williams has
pointed out, "in that process, however, they tended to reveal their own individual
idiosyncratic standards, and it is often possible, by a close study of printed texts of
the early period, to discover the particular typographical habits and spelling preferences of the compositor(s) who set up specific texts" (54). While typesetters certainly did proofread their work, their concern was primarily "typographical, not
literary" (Williams, p. 59). They would read to make sure letters were not backward
or upside-down. Thus, they had to mind their p's and q's. More prominent books
would have received greater attention from a *corrector* of the press who would read
for content. If a particular line did not make sense, he would offer correction, possibly without consulting the manuscript. If corrections were in order, he would
amend a particular line, stop the press, and have it corrected in the type. However,
because paper and time were valuable, those sheets already printed with an error
probably would still be used, so the same edition might offer different readings, de-

pending on which *state* one consults. (*State* refers to variants within a single edition.) The Shakespeare First Folio exists in so many different states that one would be hard pressed to find two copies that are identical throughout.

Plays printed in quarto format would sell for about sixpence (and wholesale for fourpence), about the price of a cheap prose pamphlet or the most expensive seat for a performance at the Globe (or the cheapest seat at the Blackfriars theater). Booksellers would not necessarily sell all the copies themselves but would wholesale copies to other booksellers. Usually quartos would have a first printing of about 800 copies—that was all the publisher would most likely expect to sell, given that plays were not necessarily a marketable commodity. In order to break even, the bookseller would normally have to sell 60 percent of a play's first edition (Blayney, pp. 389–390). Generally, publishers would see a profit only if 500 copies were sold and, after that, the profit would be modest and usually slow in coming. Although some publishers obviously believed that printing and selling plays could possibly benefit them financially, it is likely that "no fortunes were made through publication" (Kastan, *Shakespeare*, p. 23).

Eighteen of Shakespeare's plays were printed in quarto form, many more than once, indicating a particular play's popularity. Some plays were reprinted, however, possibly because the publisher or someone else found there to be so many errors that a corrected version needed to be printed. These error-filled texts, so-called "bad" quartos, are thought to be the result of an unscrupulous printing of a manuscript. A famous example of the textual variations between early quartos occurs in *Hamlet*. The first quarto of this play, Q1, printed in 1603, is approximately half the length of the version with which we are now familiar and is significantly different in textual detail. For example, the first line of the play's most famous soliloquy, "To be or not to be, that is the question" (3.1.55), appears in Q1 as "To be, or not to be, I there's the point." A "corrected" version of the play appeared in print in 1604 (Q2), promising that it was "Newly imprinted and enlarged to almost as much again as it was, according to the true and perfect Coppie." This suggests that Q1 was possibly a pirated printing of the play; the King's Men, upset at the inferiority of the First Quarto, trumped it with their own version.

Many scholars discuss how such a text as Q1 would come to be published in the first place. Some scholars, working from W. W. Greg's early-twentieth-century theory, have argued that Q1 and several of the other "bad quartos" were memorial reconstructions, that is, inferior—and often much shorter—versions of the plays that were memorized, possibly by an actor or audience member, transcribed by a recorder, and then illicitly printed. These texts are not thought to have any relationship to the author's manuscript. They may have been legitimately published to supply the company with a playbook that had been lost; or they might have been stolen, perhaps by an actor, and taken to printers. Another possible theory, one that has gained currency in recent years, is that these texts are not corrupt at all, but rather plays that might have been early editions of performance texts, which were later revised either by the author or members of the company. In this scenario, the quartos are not "bad," just different. They went through the proper channels of authorization before they were printed, just as the later editions did. They may seem to be inferior to our ears since they differ in language from the First Folio texts, upon which most of our editions are based. But to Shakespeare's audience, they may have been perfectly suitable, even preferable. However these versions came to be—whether they are pirated texts mangled by the faulty memories of greedy actors or early drafts of Shakespeare's plays—they support the notion that there is no one authentic version of the play when there are multiple printed editions. The claim of authenticity of the second quarto of *Hamlet*—based on the statement on the title page that it is printed "according to the true and perfect Coppie" of the script—has to be read with some skepticism. Given the collaborative nature of the text, and the multiple processes that it underwent, it is unlikely that any copy could be either "true" or "perfect."

New scholarship has brought to light the fact that Shakespeare was much more interested in the printing of his texts than we have been led to believe. Lukas Erne, in particular, has astutely argued that while legal copyright did not exist in England until 1709, an author certainly would have had a sense of "moral rights to his work. In fact, the *idea* of copyright as the right of the author was very much present in Shakespeare's time, though it was not anchored in the law until the eighteenth century" (8). Further, Erne claims that "the assumption of Shakespeare's indifference to the publication of his plays is a myth" (26). In the late sixteenth century, a time of enormous outpouring of printed books and an increasing number of what we would consider to be "literary" texts—including dramatic scripts—plays "stopped having a public existence that was confined to the stage" (14). The increase in literacy among commoners contributed to the widening of readership. During Shakespeare's involvement with the stage, printed plays made up a fraction (about 3 percent) of printed texts altogether—including books of history, law, theology, official documents, ballads, and others. However, in the 1590s, the time when Shakespeare was making a reputation for himself, there was a vast increase in the numbers of copies of plays printed—in 1594 alone approximately 20,000 copies of plays were printed. This suggests that we cannot assume plays were popular only in their stage incarnation (Erne, p. 16). Some of the printed texts we have were probably expanded for print and were not necessarily meant to be performed as published. Orgel asserts that "the text, then, was not the play, and all plays would have been cut for performance" (21). The second quarto and the Folio versions of *Hamlet*, for example, are seen as simply not performable because of their length. In this view the first quarto is not "bad" or "corrupt," it is just not as literary as we would like it to be. That does not mean, however, it could not be staged successfully. On the contrary, the much shorter Q1 may seem more suitable for performance than either Q2 or the Folio.

Eight of Shakespeare's early plays were printed over a period of four years (1594–1598), suggesting the increasing popularity of the dramatist in print during the 1590s. It would be reasonable to assume that Shakespeare's popularity is what sold the plays, except for the significant fact that none of the title pages of the plays bear the author's name. It was not until 1598, with the publication of the first extant quarto of *Love's Labor's Lost*, that Shakespeare's name was attached to one of his plays. What accounts for the plays' popularity in the 1590s, and thus for their appearance in print, was not the fact that Shakespeare wrote them, but rather that they were popular plays in performance. The vast majority of the title pages of Shakespeare's plays—even those bearing his name—"advertise the authority of the text as theatrical rather than authorial, by insisting that it is published 'As it was Plaide'" by one of various theater companies (Kastan, *Shakespeare*, p. 31). To a modern readership, it is almost unimaginable that individual authors would not be bothered with attaching their names to works they created. Authors today insist on identifying themselves to demonstrate that they are the producers of the ideas in a given work. In fact, in the age of celebrity, a well-known author (or director, in the case of film) is often the very selling point of a work, regardless of the quality of the piece. In the early modern period, such notions of celebrity authorship were not necessarily operative. But the practice of selling a work based upon the fame of its author began to take shape in the late sixteenth and early seventeenth centuries. This shift may be due in no small part to Shakespeare's increasing popularity over the course of his career and even after he died.

After Shakespeare's death John Heminge and Henry Condell, along with Richard Burbage, were the remaining original shareholders in Shakespeare's theater company. After Burbage's death in 1619, Heminge and Condell were left to pursue the publication of Shakespeare's collected plays in the large text that would become immortalized as the First Folio. Published in 1623, seven years after Shakespeare's death, this text, large and expensive in format, contains thirty-six of Shakespeare's plays and is divided into three categories: comedies, histories, and tragedies (the category of romance—which includes *The Tempest*, *Cymbeline*, *Pericles*, and *The Winter's Tale*—was later constructed by more modern editors). The Folio also divides most of the plays into five acts. Nearly half of Shakespeare's plays appeared in print for the first time in this collection. Most of the plays that had already been published in quarto are presented in the Folio in revised form. Since these earlier quartos were owned by the publishers who had registered and printed them, the compilers of the First Folio needed to secure the rights to them in order to include the texts. The printers most likely relied on a number of different sources as their base text when printing the Folio. They possibly used Shakespeare's own manuscripts (the foul papers), transcripts of the manuscripts (the fair copy or the book of the play or both), or printed quartos—or a combination of all the sources.

A glorious volume, the First Folio includes the famous engraving of the balding Shakespeare by Martin Droeshout, a dedication to the earls of Pembroke and Montgomery, and five commendatory poems by others, including one to the reader by Ben Jonson. Although the front matter celebrates the gifts of Shakespeare, the Folio was only partially compiled as a commemoration to him. It was mainly a moneymaking enterprise; the Folio's address to the readers "is primarily concerned with encouraging readers to buy the book" (Brooks, p. 11). It is possible that Heminge and Condell, who sold the collection to the publishers (who then owned the book), were hoping to renew interest in Shakespeare's plays and thereby draw the public to the theater to see revivals. The editors seem to capitalize on Shakespeare's fame by advertising in the text that the plays that lie within the pages were written "as [Shakespeare] conceived them." But the printers, William Jaggard and his son Isaac, and the publishers, Edward Blount, John Smethwicke, and William Apsely, were those who stood to make a profit on the enterprise. Selling the Folio for one pound bound, or fifteen shillings unbound, they hoped to turn a profit on the sale of 800 copies. It took Isaac Jaggard (his father had died by this point) and the rest almost ten years to sell out the first printing, suggesting that the sales were disappointingly sluggish. But this may not have been the case; selling 800 copies of such a large and expensive book would naturally have taken a long time. The fact that the Jaggards

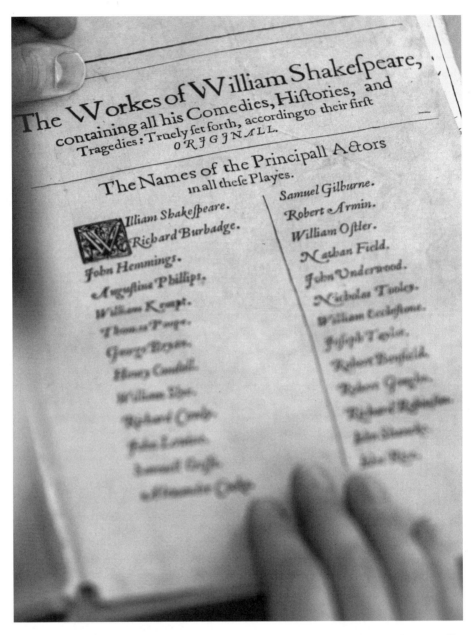

In October 2004, this previously unknown 1623 edition of William Shakespeare's First Folio, described as the most important work in the English language, sold at auction in London for about $311,500, which was far higher than early estimates. © Getty Images.

took the project on at all may be surprising, given that "the commitment of resources and the impossibility of any quick profits would make it an unattractive venture for any but the most ambitious publishers" (Kastan, *Shakespeare*, p. 60).

Although the printing of a large book of collected plays was not assuredly marketable (Ben Jonson's 1616 *Workes*, the only other folio then extant to contain dramatic texts, contained only nine plays along with masques, epigrams, and other poems), we do know that William Jaggard had previous experience with printing Shakespeare. In 1619 Jaggard had collaborated with the publisher and bookseller

Thomas Pavier to put out a collection of several of Shakespeare's plays and was successful in publishing them as separately paginated texts, despite the probable efforts of the King's Men or someone else to halt the project. Since Pavier did not hold copyright to several of the plays, he substituted false dates for them. For example, *King Lear* and *Henry V* are dated 1608; *The Merchant of Venice* is dated 1600. However, all of these texts (and seven more) were printed on the same stock of paper and from the same type. Despite the variations in dating, bibliographical scholars have concluded that they were printed together in 1619. Four years before the publication of the First Folio, then, Jaggard had a sense that Shakespeare's plays were "vendible," and he committed time and resources, and brought other publishers on board, to assist in bringing the First Folio to light.

All thirty-six plays in the First Folio have remained firmly in the canon of Shakespeare's texts. Four more not included are worth noting: *Pericles* appeared in print in 1609, but was not included in the Folio. The play, composed by Shakespeare with another playwright, most likely George Wilkins, may not have been included because the editors could not find a "corrected" text or because they could not secure the rights previously held by another publisher. It was, however, included in Pavier and Jaggard's 1619 collection of plays, and then included in the Folio of 1664. *The Two Noble Kinsmen*, performed around 1613, was a collaboration with John Fletcher. It was printed in quarto in 1634 and then included in the second folio edition of Fletcher's works. The title page, however, attributes the play to both authors, and textual investigation has secured the play as at least partially by Shakespeare. *Cardenio*, a lost play, was also co-authored with Fletcher and produced in 1612–1613. Although the play was entered into the Stationers' Register in 1653, it was never published, and the manuscript has apparently been lost. Shakespeare possibly contributed some lines to *Sir Thomas More*, a play that was never produced or printed. Part of the manuscript for this text, found in the British Library in the mid-nineteenth century, may be in Shakespeare's own handwriting ("Hand D"), which would make it the only surviving text to have that distinction. *Edward III* (ca. 1589–1595; published in 1596) probably is also at least partly by Shakespeare.

Nine years after the First Folio was published, the Second Folio (1632) appeared. In September of 1642 English theaters closed under a parliamentary ordinance that commanded the suppression of stage plays. The Puritans' disdain for theater and their oversight of printed texts contributed to the dip in the printing of plays. In 1663–1664, however, after the restoration of the monarchy in 1660 and the reopening of the theaters, the Third Folio was published as a reprint of the Second. But the second issue of this text also included seven plays not previously assigned to Shakespeare in the First or Second Folios. Of these plays, only *Pericles* has been added to the Shakespeare canon. Many scholars reject the rest—considered "apocrypha"—as not being properly Shakespeare's. Finally, the Fourth Folio of 1685 (a reprint of the Third with the seven added plays) rounded off a century of Shakespeare in print. Plays, regarded as marginal texts in the late sixteenth century, had become important textual contributions a hundred years later. The language that we use to discuss the body of Shakespeare's work, "canon" and "apocrypha," terms borrowed from the establishment of biblical scripture, shows how far he had come. Shakespeare has been handed down to us not as an actor or businessman, but as an icon.

CONCLUSION

The collaborative nature of playwriting, the various stages of revision, the printing process that was largely out of the playwright's hands, the work of subsequent editors: these all disrupt the romantic image of Shakespeare the genius, Shakespeare the solitary playwright, who conjured plays out of thin air and presented them finished and pure to an eager theater company that then passed them down to us, fully intact in their perfect original form. But what we have lost in letting go of this idealized image of Shakespeare we have gained in a deeper understanding of the complex nature of the process of writing and printing plays. Our modern notion of an author who controls his or her text is just that—a recent formulation that the author is the owner of his text and should be in charge of its fate. The enormous body of Shakespearean textual scholarship that followed the publication of the Folio, and that has persisted to our own time, suggests the intensely involved nature of textual production. As Stephen Greenblatt has written,

> The indefatigable labors of generations of bibliographers, antiquaries, and textual scholars have recovered an extraordinary fund about the personnel, finances, organizational structure, and material practices of Elizabethan and Jacobean printing houses, including the names and idiosyncrasies of particular compositors who calculated the page length, set the type, and printed the sheets of the folio. The impressive scholarship has for the most part intensified the respect for the seriousness with which the folio was prepared and printed, and where the folio is defective, it has provided plausible readings from the quartos or proposed emendations to approximate what Shakespeare is likely to have written. But it has not succeeded, despite all its heroic efforts, in transforming the folio, or any other text, into an unobstructed, clear window into Shakespeare's mind. (71)

The notion of a "master text," therefore, must remain an elusive dream, one that will remain perpetually out of reach. The persistent practice of trying to reconstruct such a master text, to determine and locate an authentic and authoritative original, only points further to the indeterminacy of the texts. The ongoing process of editing and all of the complex work that it entails continually reveals to us multiple and multiplying versions of "Shakespeare's texts."

Annotated Bibliography

Bentley, Gerald Eades. *The Profession of the Dramatist in Shakespeare's Time, 1590–1642*. Princeton: Princeton UP, 1971. This seminal work gives an overview of the playwright as professional, including discussions of collaboration, regulation, revision, and publication in Shakespeare and his contemporaries.

Blayney, Peter W. M. "The Publication of Playbooks." In *A New History of Early English Drama*. Ed. John D. Cox and David Scott Kastan. New York: Columbia UP, 1997. 383–422. Blayney's rich and well-researched essay attempts to debunk several of the ingrained myths regarding the publication and printing of plays in Shakespeare's time. He details "what had to happen both before and after a playbook was actually printed," including discussions of authorization, licensing, printing, and selling.

Brooks, Douglas A. *From Playhouse to Printing House: Drama and Authorship in Early Modern England*. Cambridge: Cambridge UP, 2000. Brooks's book is a study of how Shakespeare and his contemporaries made the often-difficult transition of turning theatrical drama into printed texts. Discussing how the printing of texts transformed the notion of authorship, Brooks details the way in which reputations were made and broken by the process of bringing a text to print.

Dutton, Richard. *Licensing, Censorship, and Authorship in Early Modern England*. Hampshire, Eng.: Palgrave, 2000. This book is a discussion of the regulation and censorship of early modern drama. While Dutton focuses primarily on the licensing and censorship of staged performance, in chapter 5, "Shakespeare: The Birth of the Author," he discusses the relationship of Shakespeare's scripts to his printed works in the context of licensing issues.

Erne, Lukas. *Shakespeare as Literary Dramatist*. Cambridge: Cambridge UP, 2003. Erne offers the argument that Shakespeare may have been much more interested in and involved with the printing of his plays than critics have heretofore believed. He carefully studies early printed quartos to suggest that Shakespeare had his print readership in mind when he wrote them. Building on the work of Stephen Orgel, he argues that Shakespeare, along with other writers of the period, abridged plays that were too long for performance for the stage.

Greenblatt, Stephen. "The Dream of the Master Text." In *The Norton Shakespeare*. Ed. Stephen Greenblatt. New York: W. W. Norton, 1997. 60–76. In this essay, part of the general introduction to *The Norton Shakespeare*, the author takes careful steps to show that any attempt to recover an authentic "master text" must remain a "dream." To demonstrate this, he focuses on the collaborative nature of playwriting and the complex process of printing in Shakespeare's time.

Kastan, David Scott, ed. *A Companion to Shakespeare*. Malden, MA: Blackwell, 1999. This guide to Shakespeare includes detailed discussions of his biography, the social context in which he worked, his sources for the plays and poems, his rhetoric, and the details surrounding the theater and the profession of the playwright. For textual concerns, the section entitled "Printing" is very useful. Essays included in this section cover the following topics: Shakespeare in print in the sixteenth and seventeenth centuries (Thomas L. Berger and Jesse M. Lander), manuscripts (William B. Long), licensing and censorship (Cyndia Susan Clegg), the craft of printing (Laurie E. Maguire), and the London book trade (Mark Bland).

————. *Shakespeare and the Book*. Cambridge: Cambridge UP, 2001. The author presents the multiple ways in which Shakespeare's work has been textually presented to readers for generations, including Shakespeare's own. By attending to the material object—the book—by which readers gain access to Shakespeare's plays, Kastan outlines how the tractability of the book contributes to Shakespeare's own resiliency.

Knutson, Roslyn. *Playing Companies and Commerce in Shakespeare's Time*. Cambridge: Cambridge UP, 2001. This book investigates the commercial connection among the theater companies of the early modern period. Rather than regarding the theater companies as intense rivals of one another, Knutson shows that their mutual cooperation helped the theater industry flourish. Of particular interest to textual scholars is chapter 3, "Playwrights, Repertories, the Book Trade, and Company Commerce," in which she discusses printed plays not only as the afterlife of performed scripts, but also as potential advertisements for theater companies.

McDonald, Russ. *The Bedford Companion to Shakespeare: An Introduction with Documents*. 2nd ed. Boston and New York: Bedford/St. Martin's, 2001. The chapter, "What Is Your Text?" offers a comprehensive overview of the textual journey, "from pen to press" of a Shakespearean play. In addition to explaining the material conditions of printing and publishing, McDonald emphasizes the textual instability of the plays.

Orgel, Stephen. *The Authentic Shakespeare and Other Problems of the Early Modern Stage*. New York: Routledge, 2002. This collection of previously published essays is indispensable for studies of textual scholarship. In particular "What Is a Text?" "What Is an Editor?" and "The Authentic Shakespeare" are useful in their careful attention to textual detail to assert that there can never be such a thing as an "authentic" text and that all textual versions of the plays are as much the work of editors as anyone else. In "Acting Scripts, Performing Texts," Orgel makes a case that performances in Shakespeare's time might have used shorter, or at least different, scripts than those that appear in print.

Williams, George Walton. *The Craft of Printing and the Publication of Shakespeare's Works*. Cranbury, NJ: Associated University Presses, 1985. This book is an overview of the invention of the printing press and the process of printing in early modern Europe. Williams also discusses in detail printing in England as well as the printing and publishing of Shakespeare's quartos and folios.

William Shakespeare's Language

Barry B. Adams

The language that Shakespeare heard spoken around him as a child in rural Warwickshire would be, for most practical purposes, readily understood by a child living in America in the twenty-first century. To be sure, that child might notice some differences in pronunciation as well as some odd grammatical constructions and would hear a few unfamiliar words. But whatever puzzlement such differences might cause would be relatively insignificant. Language learners in the twenty-first century would be able to get along well enough in conversation with their counterparts of 450 years ago, guessing their meanings from context when unable to comprehend them directly. Children living 450 years or so before Shakespeare's own time, however, would have heard and spoken a language that the young Shakespeare would have understood only with great difficulty; it would be nearly incomprehensible to a modern speaker of English. The language in question is in each case English—but English as it was spoken at different stages in history. The historical development of natural languages is a slow process but not always uniformly gradual, as is indicated by the difference between the English of the early twelfth century (that is, about 450 years before Shakespeare's birth) and that of the early twenty-first century relative to the English of the mid-sixteenth century.

The English language extends considerably further back in time than the twelfth century. Insofar as its origins can be discerned at all, they belong to the fifth century, when large numbers of several Germanic tribes, including most notably the Angles, Saxons, and Jutes, crossed the English channel to seize and occupy most of what is now England—a name derived from the first of these tribes. These conquering settlers from the European mainland spoke a variety of Germanic, one of the major branches of Indo-European or Proto-Indo-European, a prehistoric language now recognized as the common ancestor of most of the hundreds of distinct languages or major dialects spoken over the past 4,000 years in Europe and the Asian subcontinent. These include Greek and Latin along with the direct descendants of Latin (principally Italian, Spanish, French, Portuguese, and Romanian). It also includes the Celtic family of languages, which were spoken by the inhabitants of the island to which the Germanic invaders came in the fifth century. By the time of Shakespeare's birth in 1564, the English language had been in existence for more than a thousand years.

It is conventional to divide that thousand-year period into three chronological segments: Old English ("OE," from about 450 to about 1150), Middle English ("ME," from about 1150 to about 1475), and Early Modern English ("EModE," from about 1475 to Shakespeare's birth and 100 or 150 years beyond). The stage of English designated Modern English or Present-day English ("PrE") is usually dated either from 1650 or from 1700, though occasionally from 1800. The labels are a product of modern scholarship and largely a matter of convenience rather than an exact representation of linguistic or other cultural realities. Nevertheless they do serve to underscore the fact that Shakespeare's English, like our own, is "Modern" (albeit "Early") whereas the English spoken for the thousand years before Shakespeare's time, whether "Old" or "Middle," was significantly different. It is hardly surprising that these diachronic periods become progressively shorter. Whereas Old English lasted for more than 600 years and Middle English for 400 years, Early Modern English lasted for only 200 (or at most 300) years. As we approach the present, we have access to more and more linguistic evidence (thanks in part to such technological advances as the printing press and the tape recorder) and as a result feel a need to make finer and finer distinctions. It is too soon to fix the upper boundary of Present English: experts may eventually agree on whether it began in 1650, 1700, or 1800, but no one can predict with confidence when it will end, or what the period that follows will be called.

PRONUNCIATION IN SHAKESPEARE'S TIME

Despite the underlying similarities, there are noteworthy differences between the language Shakespeare learned growing up in sixteenth-century England and our own. The differences in pronunciation are difficult to identify in the absence of phonograph or other sound recordings, but there is enough indirect evidence to support reasonably definite conclusions about this element of Early Modern English. Analysis of rhyming practices in verse compositions sometimes reveals that the pronunciations of certain words have changed since the sixteenth century. Shakespeare's Sonnet 2, for example, rhymes *field* with *held*, *herd* with *beard*, *created* with *defeated*, *doting* with *nothing*, *passest* with *least*, *past* with *waste*, and *eye* with *alchemy*. The evidence from rhymes applies for the most part to vowel sounds and typically reveals an identity or close similarity of two sounds without indicating the precise nature or quality of those sounds. Consequently, we may feel confident that in Shakespeare's English the vowel sounds of *field* and *held* were the same without being able to determine whether the sound in question resembled more closely the /i/ heard in PrE pronunciation of the first of these words or the /e/ in the PrE pronunciation of the second.

Another limitation of the evidence from rhymes is the existence of so-called "eye rhymes," in which a poet relies on spelling rather than pronunciation to create the repetition that underlies the artistic patterning of elements. This evidence in turn is compromised to some extent by the fact that standards of spelling that obtained in Shakespeare's time were much less firmly established than those in place today. Shakespeare's spelling of his own family name is inconsistent, appearing on various official documents as "Shaksper," "Shakspere," and "Shakspeare." Moreover, printers exercised liberty in their treatment of the written or printed copy they set in type, modifying the spellings of some words to make them fit within the margins of the books they were composing. This common practice is obscured by the fact that all modern editions of Shakespeare's works apart from those prepared for specialized scholarly purposes regularize the spellings of the original texts to conform to contemporary standards.

Similarly, modern productions of Shakespeare's plays invariably employ one or another form of PrE pronunciation. While some performers of early music count it a virtue to use original instruments, playing Mozart's piano sonatas on a five-octave fortepiano rather than a Steinway grand, there is no comparable tradition when it comes to the performance of early dramatic works. John Barton, former director of the Royal Shakespeare Company, provides a taste of what a phonologically authentic performance might sound like in a brief videotaped rendition of a passage from *Henry V* (see "Language and Character," the first segment in the series *Playing Shakespeare*, produced by the BBC-TV in 1984). A more extended sampling of Elizabethan English may be found in Professor Helge Kökeritz's audio recordings of selected passages from the plays and sonnets, prepared to illustrate the results of his research into Shakespeare's pronunciation. In his rendering of what is probably the most famous passage in English literature, Hamlet's "To be or not to be" soliloquy (*Hamlet* 3.1.55ff.), "be" is closer to PrE "bay" than to "bee"; the word "fortune," pronounced like the PrE sequence "for" + "tune," lacks a medial "ch" sound; "opposing" is spoken as if spelled "opposin," without the "ing" sound at the end. (A phonetic transcription of Kökeritz's reading is included in his *Shakespeare's Pronunciation* [New Haven: Yale UP, 1953], 365.) While not all experts accept Kökeritz's phonetic analysis, there is general agreement that the differences between Shakespeare's pronunciation and our own are perceptible but not very great. They certainly do not raise an insurmountable barrier to comprehension.

In reconstructing the sounds of Elizabethan English, Kökeritz relied partly on evidence from rhymes; partly on wordplay, which sometimes reveals pronunciations that are no longer current; but also on the descriptions and advice in linguistic treatises published in Shakespeare's own day. The very existence of these works testifies to a self-conscious interest in language. This interest was fed by a powerful nationalistic sentiment prevalent at the time, a sentiment manifested dramatically in the stirring adventures of such celebrities as Sir Francis Drake and Sir Walter Raleigh and in the English victory over the invading Spanish Armada in 1588, when Shakespeare was in his early twenties. English nationalism of the time was also fed by the Protestant Reformation, which a generation before Shakespeare's birth had led to the formal establishment of the Church of England as an institution distinct from, and in some (though not all) respects strongly antipathetic to, the Church of Rome (that is, Roman Catholicism), which had dominated European culture for the previous thousand years. But English nationalism and insularity (both literal and figurative) were not entirely incompatible with incipient globalization. Although there is no evidence that Shakespeare himself ever traveled outside his native land, many of his contemporaries did. As a result, a number of dictionaries and textbooks published during this period were designed to offer practical instruction for English speakers wishing to learn German, French, Spanish, or Italian. Other such works that shed light on the state of the language during the EModE period were aimed at the large population of Englishmen intent on acquiring firsthand knowledge of classical Greek and Roman literature, widely regarded as the hallmark of an educated person.

ARCHAIC WORDS

Many of the most interesting and significant differences between Shakespeare's English and our own, including differences in pronunciation and grammar, are best examined at the level of the word. Among the words in Shakespeare's dramatic and poetic writings are those that are completely unfamiliar to speakers of PrE. Some of these designate objects no longer found in our culture. Fundamental changes in military technology, for example, make such words as "caliver" (a kind of musket) and "gorget" (a piece of body armor) meaningless to most contemporary speakers. And even though the vocabulary of a learned profession like the law is highly conservative, much Elizabethan legal terminology is unfamiliar to a modern lawyer. Two recent contributions to the Athlone Shakespeare Dictionary Series, one of them devoted to Shakespeare's military language and the other to his legal language, run to more than 400 pages each. Not all the entries in these reference works treat words that are completely unfamiliar to a modern reader, but the large number of entries testifies to the extent of Shakespeare's specialized and in some instances technical vocabulary.

A more interesting class of Shakespearean words consists of those that strike a modern speaker or reader as manifestly archaic. These include words like *orgulous* (proud), *eke* (also), *dole* (sorrow), and *bodkin* (pin) but also more common words, like *thou* and *thee*, the subjective (or nominative) and objective (or accusative) cases, respectively, of the second-person singular pronoun—both of which have been replaced in PrE by the undifferentiated *you*. Shakespeare's *ye*, which is part of the same set of second-person inflectional forms in EModE, has also been replaced by *you*. At one time it was reserved for the nominative plural, but in Shakespeare and many other writers of his time it is used as a singular as well as a plural accusative. Furthermore, a simple statement of Shakespeare's practice is made more difficult by the fact that he frequently makes use of the all-purpose second-person *you*, just as we do today, and he does so at times in the same passage in which he employs a more traditional and (to us) archaic form of the same word. An example of this appears in Prospero's speech near the end of *The Tempest* in which he formally releases from service the diminutive creatures he has employed in his magic. In the course of nine lines (5.1.33–41), *ye* appears three times and *you* twice.

The difference between *thou / thee* and *you* in Shakespeare resembles the distinction between *tu* and *vous* in French or *du* and *Sie* in German. In these languages, the choice of second-person pronoun is affected by a subtle sense of social propriety based in large part on the degree of familiarity that exists between the speaker (grammatically the "first person") and the person being addressed (the "second person"). In a comically satiric passage from *Twelfth Night*, Sir Toby Belch makes use of this social distinction in urging the hapless Sir Andrew Aguecheek to provoke an opponent by employing an inappropriately familiar form of address: "Go, write it [the challenge] in a martial hand. . . . If thou thous't him some thrice, it shall not be amiss" (3.2.42–46). Although *thou* in this situation is clearly insulting, it does not always produce this effect. There are many places in the works of Shakespeare and his contemporaries where this form of the pronoun conveys the sense of af-

Sale of a Shakespeare text at Sotheby's. © Polak Mathew/Corbis Sygma.

fectionate familiarity rather than inferiority. Its social connotation is not constant or fixed but determined by its position in a system of active contrast. Where the pronoun *you* is the norm in a particular stretch of dialogue, as is the case in this passage from *Twelfth Night*, the appearance of the "marked" form *thou* carries special weight (Quirk, in Salmon and Burness, pp. 7–9).

Another set of manifestly archaic words is represented by *dost* and *doth*, each of them a form of the verb *do* with specific grammatical meaning. The first of these is inflected to indicate a second-person singular subject ("How dost thou, Guildenstern?" [*Hamlet*, 2.2.224–225]), the other a third-person singular subject ("The lady doth protest too much, methinks" [*Hamlet*, 3.2.230]). These forms have been replaced in PrE by *do* and *does*, respectively. As with *thou*, *thee*, *ye*, and *you*, Shakespeare uses both the forms that were going out of fashion in the late sixteenth and early seventeenth centuries as well as, and sometimes alongside, the forms that were displacing them. With respect to the verb system, the *-st* and *-th* inflectional endings inherited from ME were being supplanted by a system in which the second-person–singular inflection was identical with the first-person singular ("I do," "you do") and in which the third-person singular was designated by the *-s* inflection ("he / she / it does"). Once again we sometimes find Shakespeare making use of both systems in the same passage, as in Edmund's gnomic observation on the ways of the world in the society of *King Lear*, "The younger rises when the old doth fall" (3.3.25); or Graziano's rhetorical question in *The Merchant of Venice* designed to capture a universal truth about desire and its fulfillment, "who riseth from a feast / With that keen appetite that he sits down?" (2.6.8–9).

It is possible to distinguish between archaisms like *doth* and *dost*, which English speakers around 1600 probably felt to be only slightly old-fashioned, and the extreme archaizing represented by the speech of the medieval poet Gower, who appears as the Chorus figure in *Pericles*, the first of Shakespeare's "late romances," which date from the last six or seven years of his career. His introduction to the third act is marked by archaic grammatical features like the obsolete prefix *-y* that marks "yslacked" (line 1) as a past participle or the obsolete plural "eyne" (line 5) for "eyes." These features are common in the poetry of Shakespeare's contemporary Edmund Spenser, who deliberately cultivated a poetic archaism. But the archaism of Gower's speech is also a matter of vocabulary: his "rout" (line 1; "crowd"), "drouth" (line 8; "dryness"), "attent" (line 11; "attentive"), and "eche" (line 13; for "eke," that is, "supplement") would no doubt have sounded almost as affectedly old-fashioned to Shakespeare's audience as they do to us. Similar archaizing of the grammatical sort is found in Armado's "tofore been sain" (for "previously said") in *Love's Labor's Lost*, 3.1.82, and in the pleonastic repetition of "did" in Quince's prologue to the inset play of "Pyramus and Thisby" in *A Midsummer Night's Dream*:

> This grizzly beast, which Lion hight by name,
> The trusty Thisby, coming first by night,
> Did scare away, or rather did affright;
> And as she fled, her mantle she did fall,
> Which Lion vile with bloody mouth did stain. (5.1.139–143)

"Did" and other forms of the verb *do* are atypical inasmuch as they may function as auxiliaries as well as main verbs. The auxiliary *do*, as in "I do believe you," serves to emphasize or intensify the sense of the main verb. In PrE, it also plays an important grammatical role in interrogative sentences, such as "Do I believe you?" This grammatical construction was just coming into use in Shakespeare's time, when the more commonly used interrogative construction consisted in reversing the order of subject and verb: "Believe I you?" The same state of affairs existed with respect to negations, where constructions like "I believe you not" were in the process of being replaced by "I do not believe you." Then as now *do* could also function as a main verb with its own lexical sense of "perform" or "execute," as in "I do it every day," but its auxiliary use is much more frequent. Such frequently used words are less susceptible to change over time, which is why we encounter so many more instances of archaisms like *dost* and *doth* than *riseth*.

Two other auxiliary verbs of high frequency, in Shakespeare's day and our own, are *be* and *have*, whose obsolete forms (*art, wert, wast; hast, hath, hadst*) have become paradigmatic archaisms, frequently employed in playful parody of the antique. Their status derives in part from their frequent occurrence in the Bible, or more precisely the Authorized Version, commonly known as the King James Bible. Published in 1611, as Shakespeare was approaching the end of his active career as a dramatist, this enormously influential work deliberately preserves forms and expressions that were felt at the time to be at least tinged with an archaic flavor, which then as now was deemed to be appropriate if not mandatory in a sacred text. It is partly for this reason that the King James Bible uses *-(e)th* exclusively in present third-person–singular verb inflections, whereas Shakespeare uses both this and the more modern *-s* ending. It is thus something of an accident of history that the English Bible (and by extension English religious language generally) sometimes sounds Shakespearean, just as Shakespeare can sound biblical to a modern reader. (This same conservative impulse in religious texts explains the use of Gothic typeface in the 1611 printing of the King James Bible, at a time when most books were printed in the roman typeface you are looking at right now.)

Troublesome Words from Shakespeare's Time

It frequently happens that either the more archaic or the more modern meaning of words makes reasonably good sense in the dramatic contexts in which they occur. An unwary PrE reader is likely to accept the more modern meaning uncritically and in the process miss an important nuance. Among the many such "false friends" from the works of Shakespeare and his contemporaries are the following:

- *advertise* (v.): instruct, inform, notify, sometimes privately or even surreptitiously.
- *apparent* (adj.): manifest, obvious (rather than the opposite of real or actual)
- *brave* (adj.): splendid (as well as courageous)
- *competitor* (n.): partner, associate (as well as rival, a word that can also mean partner)
- *complete* (adj.): accomplished, as in a complete gentleman (as well as finished)
- *effeminate* (adj.): compassionate (as well as unmanly)
- *excrement* (n.): outgrowth of any bodily material (specifically hair in *Love's Labor's Lost*, 5.1.104), not just fecal matter
- *fame* (n.): report, account (as well as illustrious reputation)
- *free* (adj.) innocent, generous, noble (as well as unconstrained)
- *glance* (n.): innuendo, hint (as well as ricochet or look quickly)
- *hint* (n.): occasion or opportunity (rather than suggestion)
- *honest* (adj.): sexually pure (as well as truthful)
- *idle* (adj.): foolish or trivial (as well as inactive)
- *infer* (v.): report (as well as derive by reasoning)
- *lewd* (adj.): worthless, vile (as well as lustful)
- *luxury* (n.): lust, lechery, or lasciviousness (rather than extreme material comfort)
- *only* (adj.): habitual or typical (as well as outstanding or exclusive)
- *portly* (adj.): majestic or dignified (not a euphemism for fat)
- *pregnant* (adj.): likely or evident (rather than with child, although this sense is found in other EModE texts)
- *present* (v.): represent (Dogberry's "you, constable, are to present the Prince's own person" [*Much Ado about Nothing*, 3.3.74–75], which looks like one of his characteristic verbal blunders, may be only an archaism)

In addition to words that are unfamiliar or manifestly archaic, there are a fair number of familiar words whose meanings have changed since the time of Shakespeare. Some of these have narrowed their semantic coverage. In EModE the noun *meat*, for example, was applied to food of any kind, not just the flesh of animals, and the noun *deer* designated animals of any kind other than human. Similarly the verb *starve* usually signified dying (or, when used transitively, killing) regardless of the manner or means. Turning to more abstract words, we find in EModE *success* meaning "outcome" or "result," whether good or bad; *doom* designating a decision or judgment of any kind, not just one that is ominous or disastrous; *accident* applied to any event or happening, not merely one regarded as unfortunate; and *lust* referring to desire or pleasure generally, not just the sort that is considered improper or the kind that is associated specifically with sexual activity. By contrast, in some instances the meaning of a particular word has broadened to cover a wider semantic range than it did in Shakespeare's time. Thus the word *luxury* and *luxurious*, in Shakespeare as in EModE generally, had a specifically sexual application, while *go* meant not simply to travel from one's present location but to do so by walking, as is suggested by Trinculo's "Nor go neither" as a retort to Stephano's "We'll not run" (*Tempest*, 3.2.18–19). The primary meaning of the adverb *still* in Shakespeare is "always" or "constantly," as in Claudius's commendation of Polonius, "Thou still hast been the father of good news" (*Hamlet*, 2.2.42). However, it can also refer more narrowly to an action continuing from the past up to the present, as in Speed's complaint against Launce, the punning clownish servant in *The Two Gentlemen of Verona*, "your old vice still: mistake the word" (3.1.284), which is its primary meaning today. The two Shakespearean senses are close but not identical.

MULTIPLE MEANINGS OF SHAKESPEARE'S WORDS

Shakespeare at times invites or even requires his readers to hold two or more meanings in mind at the same time. Hector's "keep Helen still" (*Troilus and Cressida*, 2.2.191), for example, straddles the two senses of the adverb "still." He is advising his fellow

Trojans not to return Helen to the Greeks at present, but the stronger, more absolute sense of the adverb in effect extends that advice into the indefinite future, implying that she should never be returned. A similar ambiguity surrounds the word "success" in one of Macbeth's most famous soliloquies. Contemplating the prospect of killing King Duncan, Macbeth considers whether or not this deed "Could trammel up the consequence, and catch / With his surcease, success" (*Macbeth*, 1.7.3–4). The speaker's "success" has first of all its ordinary, PrE meaning of "favorable outcome," which in this instance refers to Macbeth's becoming king of Scotland. But it also functions as a synonym for "consequence" in the previous line and covers results of any kind whatever. Thus Macbeth is thinking not only about the pragmatics of political ambition and murder but also, more philosophically, about the realization that events have an afterlife. He recognizes that, as much as we might wish to do so, we can never totally isolate an action so as to keep it separate, dis-

- *rash* (adj.): sudden (rather than impulsive)
- *rather* (adv.): sooner (as well as more properly or on the contrary)
- *reduce* (v.): bring back or restore (rather than make smaller)
- *sad* (adj.): serious, solemn (as well as morose)
- *science* (n.): knowledge or learning (not just that associated with the physical or natural sciences)
- *silly* (adj.): helpless (as well as foolish)
- *slut* (n.): an ungracious and slovenly woman (not necessarily one who is sexually loose)
- *still* (adv.): always (as well as nevertheless)
- *suggestion* (n.): temptation or prompting toward evil (as well as insinuation)
- *supervisor* (n.): observer (rather than one who manages others)
- *virtue* (n.): power (as well as moral goodness; *Love's Labor's Lost*, 5.2.348–349 plays on the two senses)

tinct, and to that extent manageable. Much of the thematic development of *Macbeth* consists in the protagonist's vain attempt to do just that even though he recognizes he cannot.

Like many other writers of the Early Modern English period, Shakespeare was especially fond of what is variously designated as the pun or quibble, a literary device that requires the reader or listener to oscillate between two (or more) meanings of a word. These various meanings all make sense in context, though one definition is usually primary or dominant while the other requires a kind of mental stretching that produces what is known as "bistable illusion," a phenomenon exemplified by the graphic figure that resembles either a rabbit or a duck (or a vase or two faces in profile) depending on how the observer looks at it. (See Richard A. Lanham, *A Handlist of Rhetorical Terms*, 2nd ed. [Berkeley: U of California P, 1991], 127.) Verbal oscillation, or focusing and refocusing of attention on one and then another meaning of a word, is ordinarily very rapid. This oscillation is so rapid, in fact, as to amount to simultaneous apprehension, as with the Early Modern English speaker who heard Macbeth speak of catching "success." Even though we now require knowledge about the semantic change the word has undergone over time to appreciate the complexity of its meaning in this context, such was not the case for Shakespeare's contemporaries. Still, their perception of the two (or more) relevant meanings of the word was not literally simultaneous but rather the result of extremely rapid oscillation from one to the other.

Shakespearean punning involves not merely individual words that are capable of more than one meaning but also different words that are brought into close proximity. Thus, Lady Macbeth's offer to "gild the faces of the grooms" with blood to make the murder "seem their guilt" (*Macbeth*, 2.2.53–54) brings together two homonyms that are unrelated etymologically, semantically, or grammatically. On closer inspection, however, it is possible to see that in this passage they are subtly linked by their common reference to the shedding of Duncan's blood. The reference to gilding—the covering of the surface of an object with a layer of gold—suggests concealment. Lady Macbeth proposes to hide her husband's guilt by an act designed to transfer it from him to others, and to do so by means of an action that resembles that of a worker skilled in metals. A more obvious word for the physical action in question is "smear," and a lesser writer might have used it. But Shakespeare characteristically preferred a combination of words that required a rapid, no doubt largely subliminal, oscillation between realms of experience that are ordinarily unconnected.

The use of "gilt" might also recall Macbeth's comment earlier when he argues with his wife against killing Duncan: "I have bought / Golden opinions from all sorts of people" (1.7.32–33). By killing Duncan, Macbeth trades true golden opinion for its image, for baser metal merely gilded. Gilding thus connects with other imagery in the play about false appearances, such as that of clothing. Angus describes Macbeth's kingship as fitting him badly, "like a giant's robe / Upon a dwarfish thief" (5.2.21–22). One may think of the disguise Macbeth's opponents use when they hide behind the boughs of trees hewn from Birnam Wood, or indeed the witches' words that mask their true meaning behind what may be deemed gilded promises. For example, "none of woman born / Shall harm Macbeth" (4.1.80–81). Macduff, who kills Macbeth, was not "born" naturally but delivered by Caesarian section.

Dr. Samuel Johnson, the most eminent man of letters in eighteenth-century England and an editor of Shakespeare's plays, objected to the punning involved in "gilt"/"guilt." Johnson prized clarity and definitiveness over ambiguity and playfulness. Johnson remarked, "A quibble [pun] was to him [Shakespeare] the fatal Cleopatra for which he lost the world and was content to lose it" (*Samuel Johnson on Shakespeare*, ed. W. K. Wimsatt Jr. [New York: Hill and Wang, 1960], 36). This comment indicates a significant shift in sensibility between Shakespeare's age and Johnson's, as well as between Johnson's age and the present, which again appreciates Shakespeare's verbal agility.

Such punning also reflects the Renaissance's recognition of the slipperiness of language. In the Middle Ages, words and things were believed to be divinely linked. For example, the Italian word for man, "omo," was supposedly derived from the two eyes (the o's) and the nose (m) of a person's face. Shakespeare's Richard II, a medieval monarch, believes in the reality of words: "Is not the king's name twenty thousand names? / Arm, arm, my name!" (3.2.85–86). Richard's successful antagonist, Bullingbrook, recognizes that words are just counters, subject to whatever meaning people assign them. Brutus is another Shakespearean character who trusts in the reality of language, especially his own. In justifying the killing of Caesar, he likens the Roman leader, whom he concedes is still faultless, to a serpent in the shell (*Julius Caesar*, 2.1.34) and so must be killed before becoming dangerous. Later, Brutus famously likens his army to a ship that must take advantage of a favorable tide if it is to reach its destination (4.3.218–224). Brutus therefore overrules the better advice of Cassius to take up defensive positions and wait for their enemies to attack. The second analogy proves false, as Brutus's defeat proves, and the first analogy probably is false as well. Punning suggests that the meaning of words is unstable and hence suspect. Many of the best speeches in Shakespeare's plays are delivered by misguided or misleading characters.

A third major type of change of meaning over time involves transfer from one semantic domain to another. Such transfer is akin to what students of rhetorical and poetical language treat under the heading of metaphor. In light of Shakespeare's extraordinary facility with metaphor and other types of figurative language, it is frequently difficult or even impossible to determine whether a given word in a given passage represents his personal imaginative extension of that word beyond its literal sense or an instance of a natural development of his medium—that is, of EModE itself.

Demonstrations of Shakespeare's verbal inventiveness are based in part on his so-called neologisms, or words first recorded in his works and therefore possibly coined or invented by him. The evidence for such inventiveness is derived primarily from the *Oxford English Dictionary*, the monumental historical dictionary compiled between 1879 and 1933, which in its most recent printed version fills twenty large volumes. The *OED* is the premier exemplar not only of a historical dictionary but also of a citation dictionary—one that prints actual occurrences of words in context to illustrate or substantiate its definitions. Given Shakespeare's status as national poet and playwright *par excellence*, it is understandable that his works received particularly close scrutiny by readers and editors who produced the *OED*, and that scrutiny is in part responsible for some of the first occurrences attributed to him. Since the completion of the *OED*, scholars have found instances of alleged Shakespearean neologisms in earlier texts, but such antedating is only one reason to treat with caution attempts to quantify Shakespeare's verbal inventiveness. Another is the practice of mixing senses or meanings of words with the words themselves in compiling statistics about an author's usage. In some lists such innovation counts as a new word while in others it is considered a metaphorical or figurative extension of an existing sense of the word in question. Furthermore, instances of what is known as conversion or functional shift, in which a word that appears in one passage as a particular part of speech (such as a noun) appears in another as a different part of speech (such as a verb) with no change of form, are sometimes cited as examples of Shakespeare's exceptional verbal inventiveness, but in fact English from earliest times has made heavy use of this grammatical versatility in ordinary discourse.

The fact remains, however, that some words that we think of as part of the general vocabulary of English made their first appearance (or at least their as yet first recorded appearance) in Shakespeare's works. Among these are *assassination*, *fretful*, *laughable*, *duteous*, *dwindle*, *domineer*, and *amazement*. But it is also a fact that many of Shakespeare's inventions did not catch on. His *reverb* was rejected in favor of *reverberate*, while his *attask* (take to task) and *subduement* (conquest) were simply rejected. It is also a fact that many additions to the English vocabulary appear for the first time in the works of one or another of Shakespeare's contemporaries. Whether Shakespeare was measurably more or less creative or inventive in this respect than other writers or speakers of the time is difficult to say.

The notion of creativity or inventiveness may be extended to include what are commonly called borrowings. Such reaching out to foreign languages for words to enrich the native English stock of vocabulary items was fairly common practice in the sixteenth century, but it was also a matter of lively dispute. On the one hand, there were those who felt that the English language was deficient and should be augmented by importing words from more prestigious languages like Latin and Greek, with only minimal changes to make them look or sound English. On the other hand, there were those who felt that such borrowings were not only unnecessary but even an affront to English national pride. For many of these critics, patriotism required adopting an Anglo-Saxon word in favor of a Latinate one whenever possible. One well-known expression of this preference is found in a mildly satirical passage by Thomas Wilson, author of an influential manual *The Art of Rhetoric*, published in 1553. To call attention to terms he denigrated variously as "oversea" (that is, foreign) or "inkhorn" (that is, pretentiously learned), Wilson concocted a letter supposedly written by a clergyman seeking ecclesiastical appointment. The letter is deliberately clogged with Latinisms that Wilson expected his readers to find ridiculous.

Many of the words in this letter, like *adepted*, *accersited*, and *obtestate*, seem basically foreign. Someone who knew Latin could make reasonably good sense of them when examined in context, but there is no disputing that they were not and are not part of the English word stock. Many other words in Wilson's letter, however, now appear quite ordinary, apart from a few details of their spelling, and have become extremely useful if not actually indispensable. These include *affabilitie*, *ingenious*, and *capacity*. That a professional man of letters like Wilson could not appreciate the potential of these words is puzzling but instructive.

The difficulty of predicting which new words will survive and which will not is illustrated in a less pleasant satirical passage from a play by Ben Jonson, one of Shakespeare's most accomplished and admired contemporaries and one of the most learned. By way of ridiculing a rival playwright, Jonson invents a scene in which his rival is administered a pill that forces him to vomit a string of disconnected words. As each word drops into a basin, one or another character repeats it by way of confirmation: *retrograde, reciprocal, incubus, glibbery, lubrical, defunct, magnificate, spurious, snotteries, chilblained, clumsie, inflate, turgidous, ventosity, oblatrant, furibund, fatuate, strenuous, conscious, damp, prorumped, clutcht,* and *obstupefact* (*The Poetaster*, 5.1). As with the diction of Wilson's mock letter, some of these words that Jonson found so objectionable have become staple items of PrE vocabulary while others still strike a twenty-first-century reader as silly or grotesque, or both.

Shakespeare himself did not engage actively in this linguistic culture war. To be sure, he gives a fairly extended sample of ridiculous diction in the speech of the "fantastical Spaniard" Don Adriano de Armado and the schoolmaster Holofernes in *Love's Labor's Lost*:

> *Armado*: Sir, it is the King's most sweet pleasure and affection to congratulate the Princess at her pavilion in the posteriors of this day, which the rude multitude call the afternoon.
>
> *Holofernes*: The posterior of the day, most generous sir, is liable, congruent, and measurable for the afternoon. The word is well cull'd, chose [well chosen], sweet, and apt, I do assure you, sir, I do assure. (5.1.87–94)

Part of the humor for a modern audience comes from the fact that the noun *posterior* in PrE is usually applied to the human buttocks. Because Shakespeare uses the word only in this and a similar passage elsewhere this same play it is difficult to say if this incongruity contributed to the satire of the passage, in which both speakers are ridiculed for their pedantry rather than the social impropriety of their diction. The same applies to Armado's use of the word "excrement" for the hair of his mustache (*Love's Labor's Lost*, 5.1.104). More typical of Shakespeare's linguistic alertness is the Duchess of York's plea in *Richard II* that her son receive a plain English "pardon" rather than a French "pardon" (5.3.130), which would be understood as an idiomatic way of expressing a polite refusal, roughly equivalent to PrE "pardon me, but. . . ." With the help of his creation Hamlet, Shakespeare also mocks the high-flown, "aureate" (gilded) diction of the courtier Osric's description of Laertes:

> Sir, his definement suffers no perdition in you, though I know to divide him inventorially would dozy th' arithmetic of memory, and yet but yaw neither in respect of his quick sail; but in the verity of extolment, I take him to be a soul of great article, and his infusion of such dearth and rareness as, to make true diction of him, his semblable is his mirror, and who else would trace him, his umbrage, nothing more. (*Hamlet*, 5.2.112–120)

Shakespeare sometimes puts similar words into the mouths of characters like Ulysses in *Troilus and Cressida*, who is not an object of satire, or at least the same sort of satire. His deservedly famous speech on degree (1.3.75–137) merits close study not only for its diction but also for a number of noteworthy grammatical constructions that help to flesh out the difference between EModE and PrE. This passage is remarkable, first of all, for the kind of Latinate diction so admired of Holofernes. The most obscure word of this type is "insisture" (line 87), a nonce word known only from this single occurrence. The *OED* records (without endorsement) several attempts to guess its meaning, which is only vaguely suggested by its occurrence in the series of grammatically parallel terms: "degree, priority, place, / Institure, course, proportion, season, form, / Office, and custom" (1.3.86–88). The meaning of the verb "deracinate" (line 99), which is first recorded in an earlier play by Shakespeare and may be safely regarded as a genuine Shakespearean invention, is also suggested by its place in a series of grammatically parallel items but more by its fairly transparent etymological source in the Latin *radix* (root) by way of the French *racine*, yielding the sense of uproot or eradicate. The noun "neglection" (line 127) appears for the first time in Shakespeare, who elsewhere uses the synonymous *negligence* (14 times) and *neglect* (10 times), both of which have survived into PrE as *neglection* has not. The underlying verb *neglect* is attested only from 1529. The noun "oppugnancy" (opposition) in line 111 occurs nowhere else in Shakespeare. Its appearance in this passage from *Troilus and Cressida* is the earliest *OED* citation, although the adjectival *oppugnant* (related to PrE *repugnant*) is older and the verb *oppugn* even older than the adjective. Shakespeare may be said to have invented this noun as well as "neglection," but given the prior existence of closely related words built on the same stems, these inventions are less impressive than his coining words like *deracinate*.

Ulysses' "instances" (line 77) and "specialty" (line 78) are not conspicuously Latinate but do retain elements of meaning from their Latin origins that have been mostly lost in their PrE derivatives. The first is closer to "causes" than "occurrences" or "examples," though elsewhere in Shakespeare it carries these more modern meanings. The second is the only example of this word in Shakespeare, but the plural *specialties* appears in two other passages, both times with more obviously technical meanings. The *OED* helpfully defines the singular as it appears in this passage as "Special or particular character or quality; a special feature or characteristic" and records only one earlier occurrence in this sense, from 1575. Some modern linguistic authorities refer this use of the word to a more narrowly technical sense also recognized by the *OED*. The abstract noun "imbecility" (line 114) appears nowhere else in Shakespeare, nor do any of its morphological relatives, such as "imbecile." Its use in this passage accords with the *OED*'s conclusion that the word's reference to general, unspecified feebleness antedates its application to a specifically mental deficiency, which is first attested in 1624, eight years after Shakespeare's death. The adjective "dividable" (line 105), which elsewhere in Shakespeare and in EModE usually means what it means today, "capable of being divided," here means "that which has been divided." Although this more passive sense of the word is unique to this passage, there are several analogous verbal adjectives in Shakespeare that can mislead a modern reader. Thus "wish'd" in *Measure for Measure*, 5.1.79, can be taken as equivalent either to "I wished" or "I was wished" (that is, "you wished that I . . ."). Adjectives ending in *-able* sometimes run counter to what they should mean logically in a similar way, like "med'cinable" in Ulysses' speech (line 91), which means "that which serves as a medicine" rather than "that which is capable of being medicated."

Another deceptive word from Ulysses' speech is the adjective "mere" (line 111), which signifies totality or absoluteness rather than, as in PrE, minimality. Gertrude's characterization of Hamlet's behavior as "mere madness" (*Hamlet*, 5.1.284) carries the same signification. Conversely, Hamlet's "bare bodkin" (*Hamlet*, 3.1.75), which modern readers are inclined to understand as a reference to a naked weapon such as a knife or sword, is a good deal less threatening, "bare" being equivalent to PrE "mere" and "bodkin" designating a pin. The point of Hamlet's phrase, then, is that it is possible to kill oneself with the most insignificant of instruments.

The word "degree," which is repeated often enough by Ulysses to become the generally accepted shorthand label for his entire speech, is a slightly disguised Latinism. It is derived from the Latin noun *gradus*, meaning "step" or "rung," which is also (and more transparently) the etymological root of the English *grade*, *gradual*, and *graduate*. Ulysses (as well as Shakespeare) glances at the word's Latin origins when he characterizes this degree as a "ladder" (line 102) and its "neglection"—that is, the disregard of the intertwined principles of gradualism, order, harmony, and hierarchy that it symbolizes—as the cause of a series of backward steps or paces (related keywords repeated in lines 128, 130, 131, 132) that the Greeks have taken. According to Ulysses, this backwardness keeps Troy from falling and enables it to remain "on foot" (line 135). The idea of steps and stepping is further reinforced by the patterned repetitions in lines 119–122 ("power / . . . will, will . . . appetite") and lines 130–131 ("By him one step below, he by the next, / That next by him beneath"). The rhetorical figuration itself evokes the idea of vertical stepping that is at the conceptual core of these passages.

One of the grammatical features of EModE, found with some frequency in the works of Shakespeare, is the double negative. According to the rules of logic, or at least logic that is grounded in mathematics, one negative cancels the force of another in the same clause, and as a result two negatives make a positive. Thus, to say "I don't have none" is, logically speaking, equivalent to saying "I do have some." In the earlier stages of English, however, such constructions were perceived as emphasizing the intended meaning rather than canceling it out. When Celia tells Rosalind, "You know my father hath no child but I, nor none is like to have" (*As You*

Like It, 1.2.17–18), we understand her "nor none" as equivalent to "and none." King Claudius deploys a double negative to similar effect when he takes issue with Polonius's explanations of Hamlet's peculiar behavior: "Love? his affections do not that way tend, / Nor what he spake, though it lack'd form a little, / Was not like madness" (*Hamlet*, 3.1.162–164). The principle of emphasis was even extended to encompass quadruple negation, as in Viola's statement about her heart: "And that no woman has, nor never none / Shall mistress be of it, save I alone" (*Twelfth Night*, 3.1.159–160). The modern view according to which such multiple negation is regarded as "bad grammar" became the prevalent one in the course of the eighteenth century, when certain rules of correctness were promulgated by prescriptive grammarians, who took it as their task not to describe the actual practice of speakers and writers but to determine by the use of logic or other means what was right and what was wrong. This general attitude as well as certain specific condemnations still colors our reaction to Shakespeare's double comparatives and superlatives. Antony's reference to the wound Brutus inflicted on Caesar as "the most unkindest cut of all" (*Julius Caesar*, 3.2.183), for example, achieves a heightened emphasis at the expense of what strikes modern speakers of English as illiterate redundancy.

Another usage condemned by some of these prescriptivists is the grammatical conversion or functional shift described above in connection with Shakespeare's lexical inventiveness. Current examples are the words *impact* and *host*, which some usage authorities insist should be employed only as nouns and never as verbs. These authorities would require sentences like "A impacted B" to be rewritten as "A had an impact on B," and "I agree to host the party" as "I agree to serve as the party's host." Prescriptivists tend to be highly selective in their judgments, ignoring many cases of functional shift like *table*, *run*, and *hit*, all of which are used extensively by all speakers, including the purest of linguistic purists, as both nouns and verbs, with no sense of impropriety. The language has always freely allowed such functional shifting, particularly during the ME period, when French influence was at its height.

Even if Shakespeare and the Elizabethans seem at times bolder or more daring in this regard, they are not doing anything fundamentally different from what native speakers have always done and continue to do. For instance, "vizarded" in Ulysses' speech on degree (line 83), which is based on the noun *vizard* (mask), strikes us as a particularly colorful or poetic transformation of a noun into a verb (or rather, strictly speaking, into a past participle, which is actually as much adjective as verb), but it was fairly common in the late sixteenth century. Ulysses' "Exampled" (line 132), another past-participial construction based on a noun, is also fairly common in EModE, with more than one sense. In fact, it is possible to distinguish four distinct meanings of the verb in addition to the past-participial sense exemplified in Ulysses' speech (Crystal and Crystal, p. 157). Less semantically complex is Ulysses' "spher'd" (line 90), a past participle obviously based on the noun *sphere*. It is here yoked with "enthron'd," a form that illustrates an alternative device for deriving verbs from other parts of speech, by attaching the prefix *en-*, as in *enable, envision, ennoble, enrich, enroll, ensure*, and so forth. The stricter type of conversion, without prefix or other morphological change, occurs with unusual frequency in Shakespeare's *Antony and Cleopatra*. Cleopatra detects strategic flattery in Caesar's behavior, which she encapsulates in a shrewd comment to her attendants, "He words me, girls, he words me" (5.2.191). A few lines later she anticipates being defeated and taken to Rome, where, she says, "I shall see / Some squeaking

Cleopatra boy my greatness / I' th' posture of a whore" (5.2.219–221). The word *boy* in this context alludes to the Elizabethan theatrical practice of having all female roles played by young male actors; its use as a verb rather than a noun is based on the common linguistic feature of functional shift. Another such shift, less striking but in some ways more complex, comes in Antony's warning about being "window'd in great Rome" (4.14.72), a compressed way of describing a situation in which someone is positioned in a window of a house or other building and observing a scene outside that structure, although in another dramatic or narrative situation it might be equivalent to "framed," with the observed rather than the observer positioned in a window. The competing possibilities illustrate the overriding importance of context.

Prescriptivist objections to the grammatical phenomenon of functional shift, unlike their objection to the double negative, are based not on logic but on etymology broadly conceived. As with their objection to the split infinitive (another grammatical phenomenon common in Shakespeare and first condemned in the later seventeenth century), the tacit assumption is that the linguistic principles underlying English are the same as those found in languages like Latin and French, from which English had borrowed some of its vocabulary. Where actual speech deviated from those principles, this difference was assumed to be a sign of carelessness. The force of this commitment to etymological evidence is even more pervasive in the realm of lexical semantics. Where there was dispute about the meanings of English words, an appeal to origins—especially when that origin was a prestigious classical language such as Latin—was decisive. For some students of language, this view of origins was based on philosophical beliefs about the very nature of language and its relation to reality. In a remarkable but far from typical piece of etymologizing, one of Shakespeare's characters asserts that *mulier*, the Latin word for woman, is derived from the words *mollis aer* (tender air; *Cymbeline*, 5.5.446–448). But Shakespeare's etymologizing is by and large more subtle and indirect, deployed for artistic resonances rather than serious philosophical argumentation. Those resonances include forms of wordplay, as in Ulysses' artful reiteration of words and senses of words related to the Latin *gradus*, or more fancifully with the associations of the proper name Romeo and the city of Rome as well as the verb *roam* (characteristic of a pilgrim, which is how Romeo is dressed at Capulet's masked ball where he first meets Juliet), not to mention the fish *roe*, which Mercutio introduces by way of commenting on his friend's lovesick appearance. In response to Benvolio's "Here comes Romeo, here comes Romeo," he says, "Without his roe, like a dried herring: O flesh, flesh, how art thou fishified!" (*Romeo and Juliet*, 2.4.36–38).

All languages change over time. It is impossible to predict precisely how they will change or how fast, but the fact of change is beyond dispute. Prescriptive grammarians of the eighteenth century were well aware of this principle but sought to stop or at least to limit the changes they perceived in English. One of their favorite ways of describing this effort was to speak of "fixing" the language—not in the modern sense of mending or repairing something that was broken but rather of pinning something down and thereby rendering it immobile, which amounts to preventing change. This latter sense, which is the dominant one in EModE generally and the only one in Shakespeare's works, is conveniently illustrated in the word "fixture," which some modern editors substitute for "fixure" in Ulysses' speech on degree (line 101). The prescriptivists failed in their attempt, of course, but it is possible that Shakespeare's prestige may have inadvertently produced a certain amount of fixing by slowing the rate of natural change. Thus the fact that EModE is much closer to PrE than to ME may be explained in part by the continuing and all pervasive presence of Shakespeare's plays and poems in the cultures of English-speaking people. The distinguished twentieth-century American critic John Crowe Ransom presented a version of such a hypothesis in an important discussion of what he called the "latinical elements" in Shakespeare, particularly those doublets whereby Shakespeare glosses a Latinate word with an English equivalent, as in the phrases "enthron'd and spher'd" and "rend and deracinate" from Ulysses' speech on degree (lines 90 and 99) ("On Shakespeare's Language," *The Sewanee Review* 55 [1947]: 181–198). Even if this hypothesis were to become generally accepted, it is by no means clear that it could be applied to aspects of language beyond those "latinical" items found in the English lexicon. Nevertheless, the possibility offers an intriguing question for speculation as well as an opportunity for further research.

Annotated Bibliography

Abbott, E. A. *A Shakespearian Grammar: An Attempt to Illustrate Some of the Differences between Elizabethan and Modern English.* 3rd ed. New York: Dover, 1966 [1870]. Still valuable, though superseded to some extent by Blake's *Grammar.*

Barber, Charles. *Early Modern English.* Edinburgh: Edinburgh UP, 1997. A substantially revised version of Barber's book with the same title published by André Deutsch in 1976. An authoritative and accessible account of the entire period, without disproportionate attention to Shakespeare.

Blake, N. F. *Shakespeare's Language: An Introduction.* New York: St. Martin's P, 1983. A linguistically sophisticated but accessible treatment of grammar (morphology and syntax) as well as vocabulary. Blake's *A Grammar of Shakespeare's Language* (Houndmills: Palgrave, 2002) covers the same ground in greater detail.

Crystal, David, and Ben Crystal. *Shakespeare's Words: A Glossary and Language Companion.* London: Penguin, 2002. The best Shakespeare glossary now available (though not as comprehensive as Schmidt's *Shakespeare-Lexicon*), with a generous selection of encyclopedic as well as lexical information.

Görlach, Manfred. *Introduction to Early Modern English.* Cambridge: Cambridge UP, 1991. A rich collection of original sources, scrupulously transcribed, coupled with a sophisticated linguistic analysis, but the arrangement of materials makes it extremely difficult to use.

Quirk, Randolph. "Shakespeare and the English Language." In Salmon and Burness, 3–21. Rpt. from *The Linguist and the English Language* (London: Edward Arnold, 1974); originally published in *A New Companion to Shakespeare Studies*, ed. Kenneth Muir and S. Schoenbaum (Cambridge: Cambridge UP, 1971). Provides an excellent orientation to broad theoretical issues as well as those related directly to Shakespeare.

Salmon, Vivian, and Edwina Burness, eds. *A Reader in the Language of Shakespearean Drama.* Amsterdam: John Benjamins, 1987. A collection of previously published articles and essays, some of them narrowly technical, covering a wide range of topics but deliberately excluding phonetics and stylistics.

Schmidt, Alexander. *Shakespeare-Lexicon and Quotation Dictionary: A Complete Dictionary of all the English Words, Phrases, and Constructions in the Works of the Poet.* 3rd ed., rev. and enl. by Gregor Sarrazin. 2 vols. New York: Dover, 1971 [1902]. Still valuable though superseded in some respects by Crystal and Crystal's *Shakespeare's Words.*

Spevack, Marvin. *The Harvard Concordance to Shakespeare.* Cambridge, MA: Harvard UP, 1973. An indispensable reference tool for word-based studies of Shakespeare. A reduced but fully autonomous redaction of Spevack's 9-volume *Complete and Systematic Concordance to the Works of William Shakespeare*, published by Georg Olms (New York) between 1968 and 1980.

———. "Shakespeare's Language." In *William Shakespeare: His World, His Work, His Influence.* Ed. John F. Andrews. 3 vols. New York: Scribner's, 1985. 2: 343–361. Treats orthography,

punctuation, phonology, vocabulary, morphology, taxonomy, and syntax in explicitly la-
belled sections. The section on vocabulary is especially good. Very full bibliography.

Williams, Joseph M. *Origins of the English Language: A Social and Linguistic History*. New York:
The Free P, 1975. A topical rather than a narrative account of the history of the language,
with stimulating questions and projects but only incidental treatment of Shakespeare.

THE HISTORY
PLAYS

Henry VI, Parts 1, 2, and 3

John D. Cox

PLOT SUMMARY

Henry VI, Part 1

1.1. The play begins with a state ceremony: the funeral of King Henry V. As nobles in the funeral party praise the dead king and lament his loss, angry verbal sparring breaks out between Humphrey, Duke of Gloucester (brother to Henry V and Lord Protector while King Henry VI was still a legal minor), and Henry Beaufort, Bishop of Winchester. Arriving messengers further disrupt the ceremony, announcing numerous English military reverses in France, the crowning of the Dauphin Charles as the French king, and the capture of Lord Talbot by the French. Winchester ominously determines in soliloquy to kidnap the king and run the kingdom.

1.2. Meantime, in France, Charles the Bastard introduces Joan La Pucelle, "a holy maid" (1.2.51), to the court of King Charles. Though Reignier pretends to be the king at their first meeting, Joan recognizes Charles at once, and he quickly becomes so infatuated with her that his nobles make bawdy jokes about the two of them. She urges the French to continue the battle of Orleans and promises, "This night the siege assuredly I'll raise" (1.2.130).

1.3. Back in England, the conflict between Gloucester and Winchester breaks into open fighting between their followers, finally quelled by the Lord Mayor of London.

1.4–6. In France, Lord Talbot returns to the English camp, having been released in an exchange of prisoners. He is shocked when a French sharpshooter kills the Earl of Salisbury, and when Joan, whom he recognizes as a witch, easily defends herself against him and recaptures Orleans. Act 1 ends with the French celebrating their victory, and Charles's predicting that Joan "shall be France's saint" (1.6.29).

2.1–2. Led by Talbot, the English retake Orleans, and the unready French leap over the walls "in their shirts" (stage direction after 2.1.38). Some surmise that Charles and Joan have been paying attention to each other rather than the city's defense.

2.3. The Countess of Auvergne invites Talbot to visit her and attempts to capture him by locking the door of her castle, but he escapes the trap by producing a company of soldiers he had hidden for just such a purpose.

2.4. Back in London, the Duke of Somerset and the Earl of Suffolk quarrel as young law students in the garden of the Inns of Court, each plucking a rose (red and white, respectively) to signify his faction. Thus Shakespeare invents a myth for the beginning of the English civil wars known as the Wars of the Roses because the York symbol was the white rose and the Lancaster emblem was the red rose.

2.5. Richard Plantagenet visits his uncle, Edmund Mortimer, imprisoned by Henry V as the declared heir of Richard II, whom Henry IV had deposed. Plantagenet discovers that he, in turn, is Mortimer's heir, and he determines to regain his title as Duke of York.

3.1. The quarrel between Gloucester and Winchester breaks into open brawling between their serving-men in the presence of King Henry, until the Earl of Warwick compels an uneasy truce. Warwick petitions the king to install Plantagenet as Duke of York, and the king agrees, though Somerset quietly deplores the decision.

3.2. Disguised as peasants, Joan and the French infiltrate Rouen, capturing it by surprise. While Sir John Falstaff flees to save his life, Talbot leads a counterattack that retakes the city.

3.3. Joan successfully persuades Burgundy to abandon the English side and then comments cynically on Burgundy's spinelessness.

3.4. King Henry VI, who has come to France, promotes Talbot to the earldom of Shrewsbury, as another quarrel breaks out between Vernon and Bassett, each wearing a different colored rose.

4.1. King Henry VI is crowned in Paris, and Talbot disgraces Falstaff publicly for his cowardice at Rouen. Gloucester reads a defiant letter from Burgundy, whom the king orders Talbot to attack. Vernon and Bassett quarrel openly before the king, drawing Somerset and York into their wrangling. Henry dons a red rose, though claiming to incline to neither faction. He appoints York regent in France and orders Somerset to support him. In soliloquy, Exeter deplores "This jarring discord of nobility" (4.1.188) and the king's immaturity.

4.2–4. Besieging Bordeaux, Talbot is caught between the city and a relieving French army. Though informed of Talbot's dilemma, neither York nor Somerset comes to his aid, each hoping to make the other look bad. Sir William Lucy comments that "The fraud of England, not the force of France" (4.4.36) has doomed Talbot.

4.5–6. Though fighting heroically to the end, both Talbot and his young son John are killed. In response to Lucy's honorific recital of Talbot's many titles, Joan mocks Talbot cynically as "stinking and fly-blown" (4.7.76).

5.1. Gloucester informs King Henry about negotiations for the king's marriage to the Earl of Armagnac's daughter. Winchester, now promoted from bishop to cardinal, introduces ambassadors from Armagnac. He declares his determination to defeat Gloucester.

5.2. Charles announces that the Parisians are revolting against the English. A scout arrives to say that the English army is preparing for battle.

5.3. Joan summons fiends, but they hang their heads, silently refusing to help her, and York captures her easily. Suffolk captures Margaret of Anjou, daughter of the impoverished Reignier, and becomes infatuated with her. He determines to retain her as his mistress, since he is already married, and persuade the king to marry her, so Suffolk can continue the liaison. He negotiates with Reignier to accept the French provinces of Maine and Anjou in exchange for Margaret.

5.4. Condemned to die as a witch, Joan repudiates the shepherd who claims to be her father. When her captors reject her assertions of inspired virginity, she attempts to avoid being burned alive by claiming to be pregnant by Alanson and Reignier. Cardinal Beaufort announces a peace treaty with the French, whose terms Charles initially rejects, only to relent when Alanson assures him quietly that he can break the treaty "when your pleasure serves" (5.4.164).

5.5. King Henry declares that, because of Suffolk's description of Margaret, he is determined to marry her. The English nobles protest indignantly, but Suffolk emphasizes her father's titles as king of Naples and Jerusalem. Henry stubbornly persists in his infatuation, ordering Suffolk to fetch Margaret immediately and to levy a tax for his expenses. Suffolk exults to himself: "Margaret shall now be Queen and rule the King; / But I will rule both her, the King, and realm" (5.5.108).

Henry VI, Part 2

1.1. The play begins with a state ceremony: the formal reception into England of Queen Margaret by her new husband, King Henry VI. Reading the marriage terms aloud, Humphrey, Duke of Gloucester, suddenly breaks off, because they are so humiliating for England, but Henry promotes Suffolk from earl to duke in reward for arranging the marriage. The nobles quarrel: Cardinal Beaufort scolds Gloucester for condemning the marriage, and York scolds Suffolk for arranging it. Gloucester departs in a rage, and Beaufort follows, determining to curb Gloucester's power. The Duke of York soliloquizes on his ambition, recognizing the need to be patient but resolving to "claim the crown, / For that's the golden mark I seek to hit" (1.1.242–243).

1.2. The Duchess of Gloucester urges her husband to "reach at the glorious gold," that is, the crown of England (1.2.11), but he scolds her for her presumptuousness. Her priest, Sir John Hume, reports on his consultation with a witch and a conjurer on the duchess's behalf, but in soliloquy Hume divulges that he is a paid informer for Beaufort and Suffolk.

1.3. The queen and Suffolk intercept petitioners to Gloucester, including one Peter, who petitions against Thomas Horner, his master, for asserting that York is the rightful heir to the throne. To Suffolk, Margaret complains about Gloucester's influence, Henry's meekness, and the Duchess of Gloucester's ambition. Another quarrel among the nobles over who should be regent in France results in a verbal assault on Gloucester, whose wife the queen strikes when the duchess fails to pick up a fan the queen dropped. Horner is brought before the king but denies that he claimed York should be king, and York repudiates him. Following Gloucester's advice, the king appoints Somerset as regent in France and orders a trial by combat between Peter and Horner.

1.4. A conjurer procured by Hume raises a spirit that prophesies in riddles, but the ritual is interrupted by York, who thus catches the Duchess of Gloucester in the illicit act of consulting spirits. The duchess is arrested, but York reads the prophecies she obtained. Though York dismisses them as unintelligible, they foretell the deposing of Henry VI and the deaths of the dukes of Suffolk and Somerset.

2.1. Henry's nobles and Queen Margaret argue angrily while hawking, though the king urges the queen to desist, "For blessed are the peacemakers on earth" (2.1.34). The king asks a man who claims to have been born blind to recount his miraculous healing, "That we for thee may glorify the Lord" (2.1.73), but Gloucester proves the man is an imposter. The Duke of Buckingham reports that the Duchess of Gloucester has been caught conjuring.

2.2. Salisbury and his son Warwick hear York's claim to the throne and kneel together to acknowledge his right. York predicts that "the good Duke Humphrey" (2.2.74), that is, the Duke of Gloucester and uncle to Henry VI, will be destroyed.

2.3. The king banishes the Duchess of Gloucester for her conjuring and orders Gloucester to surrender his staff of office as Lord Protector. Peter and Horner fight in a trial by combat, and when Peter prevails, King Henry infers that Horner was guilty of treason.

2.4. Dressed as a penitent, the Duchess of Gloucester departs for the Isle of Man, her place of banishment. She warns her husband of treachery, but he is sure no harm can come to him so long as he is "loyal, true, and crimeless" (2.4.63). Within ten lines Gloucester is summoned to the king's parliament at Bury; thus Gloucester's security is shown to be mistaken.

3.1. In the king's council, the nobles complain about Gloucester; Somerset announces the loss of France; and Suffolk arrests Gloucester for treason when he arrives. He protests his innocence, but all except Henry condemn him, and the king hopes Gloucester can clear himself as he is delivered to prison in Cardinal Beaufort's charge. Heartsick, Henry quits the council, and Margaret urges that Gloucester "be quickly rid the world" (3.1.233), to which Suffolk, Beaufort, and York assent. When a post announces an uprising in Ireland, York sarcastically suggests that Somerset be sent to quell it, since he has just lost France, but the other nobles urge York to go, and in soliloquy he describes his reason for accepting the appointment: he will gain an army thereby, and he will use Jack Cade to stir up unrest in England as supposed claimant to Mortimer's inheritance, giving York a pretext for returning from Ireland with an army behind him.

3.2. Two hired murderers report to Suffolk that they have dispatched Gloucester. When the king summons Gloucester to be tried by his peers, Suffolk goes to fetch him but reports that he is dead, whereupon the king swoons. Recovering, he blames Suffolk for Gloucester's death, but Margaret scolds him for this suspicion. Warwick reports that the commons are angry because they suspect Beaufort in Gloucester's death. Seeing Gloucester's corpse thrust forth on a bed, Warwick says that he appears to have been strangled and blames Suffolk, who rejects the charge, supported by the queen, while the king speaks piously about just quarrels. Suffolk and Warwick draw their swords against each other just as Salisbury announces that the commons have risen in support of Gloucester and are demanding Suffolk's execution. Henry banishes Suffolk, despite the queen's objections. Margaret and Suffolk bid each other farewell, and a messenger announces that Beaufort is dying.

3.3. The king visits the cardinal, who raves in guilty delirium as he expires.

4.1. Having been captured by a privateer while en route to exile, Suffolk is assigned to Walter Whitmore for ransom or execution. Though he behaves haughtily, Suffolk is frightened of Walter, since the spirit raised by Hume had prophesied that Suffolk would die "by water," that is, "Walter" (4.1.35), as he in fact does, when Walter wearies of his arrogance.

4.2–3. Jack Cade leads a mob on its way to London. He orders a clerk hanged for being literate and not only rejects Sir Humphrey Stafford's challenge but also overpowers the knight and his brother and kills them, donning Sir Humphrey's armor as a trophy.

4.4. Cradling Suffolk's severed head, the queen addresses it lovingly, while the king prepares to flee from London as Cade's mob approaches, but Lord Saye (whom Cade hates for his part in Margaret's marriage settlement) decides to remain and hide.

4.5–8. Once in London, Cade orders that he be called "Lord Mortimer" (4.6.6), commands that the Inns of Court and parliament be destroyed, and declares that "henceforward all things shall be in common" (4.7.18–19). Lord Saye is captured and killed at Cade's order, despite eloquently defending himself. Clifford and Buckingham confront the mob, which inclines now to them, now to Cade, depending on who spoke last. Seeing their fickleness, Cade flees.

4.9. Bemoaning his inheritance of the kingship at nine months of age, Henry is cheered by news that Cade has fled and the rebellion is over but dismayed by news that York has landed with an army from Ireland, though he urges Buckingham not to be "too rough" with York, "For he is fierce and cannot brook hard language" (4.9.44–45). Famished and exhausted, Cade takes refuge in the garden of Alexander Iden, in Kent. Iden finds him, they fight, and Iden kills Cade.

5.1. Hiding his ambition, York dissembles, declaring that his reason for returning from Ireland is merely to remove Somerset. Iden presents Cade's severed head to the king, who knights him for his deed. Seeing Somerset at court, York openly defies Henry for the first time, declaring himself more fit than Henry to be king. York is joined by his sons and armed followers; Henry, by Clifford and his son, also with an armed following. In response to the Cliffords' declaration of loyalty to Henry, York summons Warwick and Salisbury with more soldiers, and Salisbury declares his allegiance to York. Henry asks Salisbury about his oath of loyalty to the king, but Salisbury declares it was a sinful oath. York's son, Richard, threatens young Clifford, who insults Richard as "foul stigmatic" (5.1.215).

5.2. In the first battle of St. Albans, York kills old Clifford, whose son swears to avenge his father's death on the whole house of York. Richard kills Somerset near Castle Inn, fulfilling the prophecy of the spirit raised by Hume that Somerset should "shun castles" (1.4.35).

5.3. York reports that Henry has fled to London to convene parliament, and Warwick urges immediate pursuit.

Henry VI, Part 3

1.1. The play begins with the triumphant Yorkists in parliament, having broken in by force while still bloody from their recent victory. Richard displays the severed head of Somerset, which York addresses mockingly. York enthrones himself just as King Henry enters, and a debate rages as to who should rightly reign. Henry eventually admits that "my title's weak" (1.1.134) and compromises by taking a mutual oath with York that Henry will be allowed to reign, but his son will be disinherited in favor of York. Queen Margaret is outraged when she hears of this oath, pointing out that Henry has put his own life at risk by means of it, and she declares herself divorced from his table and his bed.

1.2. Back in Yorkshire, York's son, Richard, argues that the oath York took "is of no moment" (1.2.22) and successfully persuades his father to seek the crown and Henry's death.

1.3. Margaret attacks York at Wakefield, where Clifford captures York's youngest son, Rutland, a schoolboy, while he is trying to escape, and murders him.

1.4. Margaret captures York himself and taunts him with the death of Rutland, compelling his exclamation that she has a "tiger's heart wrapped in a woman's hide" (1.4.137). She joins others in stabbing him to death.

2.1. Near England's border with Wales, York's sons, Richard and Edward, see a vision of three suns, and Edward decides to take the sun for his personal emblem. A messenger tells them that Rutland and York died at Wakefield, for which Richard swears vengeance. They are joined by the Earl of Warwick, who reports that he lost King Henry, whom he had had in custody, when Margaret defeated Warwick at the second battle of St. Albans, and that Henry and Margaret have gone together to London to persuade parliament to reverse the compromise Henry made with York.

2.2. Henry arrives with Margaret at York, where the Duke of York's severed head is displayed, and exclaims guiltily about having broken his oath, but Clifford chides him for disloyalty to his family and urges him to assist Margaret by leaving the battlefield. When Edward arrives and demands Henry's obeisance, Margaret and Clifford refuse.

2.3–6. Fighting breaks out at Towton, where the Lancastrians at first prevail. Henry, withdrawn from the battle, fantasizes about the happy, ordered lives of shepherds, till his reverie is interrupted by two lamenting commoners, one of whom has unknowingly killed his own father in the battle; the other, his own son. Margaret and Prince Edward urge the king to flee, and Clifford, dying with an arrow in his neck, blames York's rebellion on Henry's weakness. Edward, Richard, and George find Clifford's body and mock it. To celebrate the victory at Towton, Edward promotes his brothers: Richard, to Duke of Gloucester; George, to Duke of Clarence. Warwick declares his intention to arrange a marriage for Edward with Lady Bona of France, and Edward acknowledges his dependence on Warwick.

3.1. Two forest keepers with crossbows capture King Henry on the English side of the border with Scotland, declaring that they owe him no allegiance now that Edward has deposed him.

3.2. Lady Grey petitions King Edward for the return of her dead husband's lands, and he is so taken with her beauty and manner that he not only restores her lands but asks her to marry him, while his brothers mock him bawdily behind his back. Richard of Gloucester soliloquizes hatefully about Edward's way with women and his own frustrated ambition and misshapen ugliness. He determines to pursue the crown ruthlessly but slyly.

3.3. In France, King Lewis responds noncommittally to Margaret's request for assistance, and when Warwick arrives with a proposal from King Edward for the hand of Lady Bona, Lewis's sister, Lewis readily agrees. A post suddenly arrives with news that Edward has married Lady Grey, however, and Warwick is so infuriated at being thus undercut that he switches his allegiance to the Lancastrians, whom Lewis promises at last to assist. Warwick pledges his eldest daughter as wife to Prince Edward of Lancaster and swears to depose the Yorkist King Edward.

4.1. Richard of Gloucester and George of Clarence object to Edward's marriage, but Edward willfully rejects their criticism. A post arrives from France with news of Warwick's defection to Lancaster, prompting Clarence's defection as well, though Gloucester quietly determines to remain with Edward for reasons of his own.

4.2. Warwick, once again in England, promises to marry his second daughter to Clarence.

4.3. In a sudden night assault, Warwick captures King Edward and commits him for safekeeping to the Archbishop of York, Warwick's brother. Warwick plans to free Henry and return him to the throne.

4.4. When Queen Elizabeth, now pregnant, hears the news of Edward's capture, she determines to seek sanctuary.

4.5. Gloucester releases King Edward from captivity on the archbishop's estate.

4.6. After Warwick frees King Henry from captivity in London, Henry declares Warwick lord protector and prophesies that young Henry Tudor, Earl of Richmond, will restore England's fortunes.

4.7. King Edward and Gloucester demand and gain access to the city of York, and Edward proclaims himself king. He recaptures Henry in London and orders him imprisoned in the Tower.

5.1. King Edward arrives before the walls of Coventry, where Warwick is encamped. Oxford and Montague join Warwick, but Clarence throws away the red rose of Lancaster to join his brothers Gloucester and Edward.

5.2–3. In the ensuing battle near Barnet, Warwick is killed, and Edward and Gloucester lead the victorious Yorkists in pursuit of Margaret.

5.4–5. Queen Margaret cheers her flagging troops bravely, but in the battle of Tewkesbury she and her son Prince Edward are captured, and King Edward, Gloucester, and Clarence stab the prince to death in front of her. Gloucester departs suddenly for the Tower of London.

5.6. Henry is surprised by Gloucester's ominous arrival at the Tower and calls him a devil, prophesying that he will cause much suffering, but Gloucester cuts him off with a dagger blow. He affirms Henry's prophecies and determines to destroy his brothers: "I am myself alone" (5.6.83).

5.7. King Edward celebrates the birth of his son, but as Gloucester kisses the baby, he compares himself quietly to Judas. Margaret is to be exiled to France, and King Edward looks forward to "lasting joy" (5.7.46).

PUBLICATION HISTORY

Three separate allusions to the *Henry VI* plays date from 1592: one in Philip Henslowe's account book to "harey the vi" performed in March at the Rose Theatre (*Henslowe's Diary*, ed. R. A. Foakes and R. T. Rickert [Cambridge: Cambridge UP, 1961], p. 16), another in Thomas Nashe's *Pierce Penniless* to "brave Talbot" dying on the stage (*The Works of Thomas Nashe*, ed. R. B. McKerrow, 6 vols. [Oxford: Clarendon P, 1958], 1.212), and the third an adaptation of York's line in *3 Henry VI* referring to Queen Margaret's having "a woman's heart wrapped in a tiger's hide." This allusion was made by Robert Greene, an aspiring playwright, who accused an unnamed rival of being an "upstart crow . . . with his tiger's heart wrapped in a player's hide," who is "in his own conceit the only Shake-scene in a country"

(*Greene's Groatsworth of Wit*, ed. D. Allen Carroll [Binghamton: State U of New York P, 1994], pp. 84–85). Greene undoubtedly alludes to Shakespeare, thus identifying him as the author of these plays about English history. Greene's is also the first mention of any play by Shakespeare.

Versions of *2* and *3 Henry VI* were published in single-play editions in 1594 and 1595, respectively, but these editions differ substantially from the texts of the *Henry VI* plays that appeared in the 1623 First Folio—the first collection of Shakespeare's work—and *1 Henry VI* was published for the first time in the First Folio. Not only are the single-play editions much shorter than their Folio counterparts, but their titles are also different. A long-accepted theory to account for the earlier versions of *2* and *3 Henry VI* is that they were reconstructed from memory by actors who had performed the plays at the Rose Theatre and then used the truncated texts for touring performance away from London, publishing them without authorization from the playing company that owned them and thus increasing the illegitimate income they generated. This theory has been recently discredited. Laurie Maguire showed the weakness of "memorial reconstruction" as an explanation for such texts in *Shakespearean Suspect Texts: The "Bad" Quartos and Their Contexts* (Cambridge: Cambridge UP, 1996), and Peter Blayney showed the economic implausibility of the argument in his essay, "The Publication of Playbooks," in John D. Cox and David Scott Kastan, eds., *A New History of Early English Drama* (New York: Columbia UP, 1997, pp. 383–422). Lukas Erne argues that at least some of the shorter texts were acting editions, in contrast to the "literary" versions preserved in the Folio (*Shakespeare as Literary Dramatist* [Cambridge: Cambridge UP, 2003]).

Editors have favored the Folio texts of *2* and *3 Henry VI*, if only because they are substantially longer (by about one-third) than the versions printed earlier. In the case of *3 Henry VI*, however, the stage directions of the earlier play (called *The true Tragedie of Richard Duke of Yorke*) are fuller and more graphic, so editors have customarily added them to the Folio text. Only *The true Tragedie* specifies, for example, that the opposing parties in the first scene have either red or white roses "in their hats" (depending on their dynastic affiliation), that "three suns appear in the air" to Edward and his brothers after the battle of Wakefield, and that Clifford enters at the battle of Towton "with an arrow in his neck."

A common explanation for Shakespeare's turning to English history as the subject of plays in the late 1580s and early 1590s is that he was taking advantage of curiosity about the English past that had been stimulated by national euphoria following the defeat of the Spanish Armada in 1588. It is puzzling, however, that Shakespeare would depict such dispiriting events as those in the *Henry VI* plays in a time of national celebration and self-confidence. One possible explanation for his doing so helps to account for Shakespeare's later English history plays as well: a common feature of all his history plays from the 1590s is their concern with the transition of power from one monarch to another. This is true even of *Henry V*, which treats the most heroic and successful of all Shakespeare's kings, for Henry V has a guilty conscience about the way his father gained the throne (*Henry V*, 4.1.289–305), and the closing Chorus offers a pointed reminder that Henry V was disastrously succeeded by his son—the subject of Shakespeare's first history plays, as the Chorus remarks: "Which oft our stage hath shown" (*Henry V*, Epilogue.13).

Shakespeare's consistent focus on royal succession is arguably topical, because the transition of power is not only the greatest inherent challenge to stability in a monarchy but was certainly the weakest feature of the only monarchy Shakespeare had known firsthand when he wrote these plays: that of Queen Elizabeth I (1558–1603). Despite her skill in governing, she remained unmarried and therefore without an heir, thereby creating anxiety and frustration in her people, her parliament, and her royal council. Both Elizabeth and her older sister, Mary, had inherited the throne under even less stable circumstances than those in the 1590s, and their brother, Edward, had succeeded to the throne as a child. The sequence of four monarchs (Henry VIII, Edward VI, Mary, and Elizabeth) over the course of eleven years at mid-century (1547–1558) was still well within living memory in the early 1590s. Political upheaval and uncertainty had been pervasive then, and no one had been sure that the civil tumult of the fifteenth century (depicted in the *Henry VI* plays) would not return. Moreover, with factionalism rife at Elizabeth's court in the 1590s, courtiers were positioning themselves for competitive advantage in anticipation of the old queen's death.

In such an atmosphere, even if Shakespeare were satisfying curiosity about the English past, the *Henry VI* plays' depiction of England's steady decline into deadly squabbling and eventual civil war makes sense as a result of thoughtful reflection about the situation late in Elizabeth's reign. The early Elizabethan tragedy *Gorboduc* (1562) boldly used political analogy to admonish the young queen morally about the danger of having no successor, and Shakespeare seems to have done something similar in his English history plays some thirty years later. The difference is that they have less to do with moral admonition than with political analysis. Both series of Shakespeare's English history plays begin with the reign of a monarch who succeeded as a child: Henry VI at the age of nine months, and Richard II at nine years. "Woe to that land that's govern'd by a child!" exclaims an anonymous citizen in *Richard III* (2.3.11), the play immediately following *3 Henry VI* in historical sequence. The sentiment itself is biblical (see *Ecclesiastes* 10:16), but Shakespeare focuses on the political consequences of such an unfortunate transition of power: the increasing influence of caretakers ("lord protectors") who were reluctant to surrender their power when the child kings came of age, producing explosive conflicts between rival court factions, civil war, and the violent deposing of one king by another. The *Henry VI* plays' consistent focus on the steady degeneration of public confidence and on Henry VI as a good man but a weak and inept king is an incisive analysis of how secular power actually functions in a monarchy.

In addition to the *Henry VI* plays' general interest in the dynamics of monarchical power, scholars have found more specific links between the early history plays and their immediate historical context. Shakespeare's reductive interpretation of Joan la Pucelle (Joan of Arc) in *1 Henry VI* surprises most first-time readers of the play, but it is entirely consistent with the antipapal attitude and suspicion of the French that characterized English sentiment in the early 1590s. England had expeditionary forces in France in 1589–1592 to assist in opposing the influence of the Spanish King Philip II, and scholars have pointed out that the military ventures Shakespeare stages in *1 Henry VI* are more like contemporary campaigns in France than the fifteenth-century war described by Raphael Holinshed in his *Chronicles* (1587).

Despite Joan's hypocrisy and seemingly demonic inspiration in *1 Henry VI*, she is a bold and vital character and a courageous leader, and some interpreters have seen startling resemblances between her and Elizabeth I. It is certainly true that in contrast to Shakespeare's other English history plays, the *Henry VI* plays feature assertive and powerful female characters: Joan in the first play and Margaret in the next two. Margaret is, in fact, the only character who appears in all four plays of the first series of linked plays (*1 Henry VI* to *Richard III*), and she is the only character who appears in all four plays of either series. In addition to bold leadership, both she and Joan are marked by unusual rhetorical skill in public speaking, an ability for which Queen Elizabeth was also widely famous.

SOURCES FOR THE PLAYS

Shakespeare's principal source for all three of the *Henry VI* plays was Raphael Holinshed's *Chronicles*, though the playwright used other chronicles and literary sources on occasion. Duke Humphrey's disproof of a supposedly miraculous healing in *2 Henry VI*, for example, is borrowed from John Foxe's *Acts and Monuments of the English Church* (1583). Shakespeare's cynical interpretation of Joan of Arc in *1 Henry VI* was conventional. Richard Hardin has shown that Shakespeare took his view of Joan from Holinshed and other English chroniclers who manifest Protestant skepticism about the Virgin Mary (whom Joan claims as her inspiration in *1 Henry VI*, 1.2.74–86) and about other saints and miracles that were revered by adherents of traditional faith ("Chronicles and Mythmaking in Shakespeare's Joan of Arc," *Shakespeare Survey* 42 [1990]: 25–35).

Now and then in the *Henry VI* plays, Shakespeare's version of events is also anticipated by *A Mirror for Magistrates* (1559), a compendium of moralistic versified monologues by various prominent people from the past. Whether Shakespeare actually consulted the *Mirror* or not, it includes monologues by Henry VI, Edward IV, the Duke of York, the Duke of Suffolk, Jack Cade, and others in the *Henry VI* plays. Long before Holinshed, the *Mirror* reported that Henry VI died at the hands of Richard of Gloucester.

In addition to consulting sources of historical information, Shakespeare also absorbed the influence of other writers, especially writers of drama. Chief among these for the *Henry VI* plays are the Roman playwright Seneca, Shakespeare's contemporary Christopher Marlowe, and various forms of medieval religious drama. Seneca's reputation had risen steadily throughout the second half of the sixteenth century, in keeping with the innovative English admiration for classical Latin literature and Roman centralized power. Seneca was admired for his Stoic morality, his style, and his drama, all of which left discernible traces in the *Henry VI* plays. Shakespeare may have drawn on Seneca's *Medea* in both *2 Henry VI* (5.2.57–60) and *3 Henry VI* (1.4.127–155), though the stories he alludes to are also recounted by Ovid in *The Metamorphoses*, one of Shakespeare's favorite sources for classical mythology. (He includes a line untranslated from Ovid's *Heroides* in *3 Henry VI*, 1.3.48.) Vengeance, violence, inexorable fate, prophecies, omens, and premonitions are all features of Senecan tragedy that make their way into the *Henry VI* plays, but Seneca's influence may be most direct in Shakespeare's frequent use of rhetorical declamation, such as Joan's appeal to Burgundy in *1 Henry VI*, 33.44–77, York's soliloquy on his ambition in *2 Henry VI*, 1.1.214–259, and Margaret's oration to her troops in *3 Henry VI*, 5.4.1–38. Shakespeare's major difference from Seneca in these flights of elocution is that Shakespeare integrates them into the action, making them function as part of the story rather than bracketing them, like an operatic aria, as set-piece examples of the playwright's and performer's skill.

Though Shakespeare was thoroughly original in his choice and treatment of English history as dramatic subject matter, he was influenced by his contemporary, Christopher Marlowe, in other ways. Marlowe had invented the two-part play in *Tamburlaine* (1587 and 1588, respectively), and some scholars believe that Shakespeare started with a two-play conception for *Henry VI*, adding what is now 1 *Henry VI* later as a "prequel" and *Richard III* as a conclusion to a four-part series (see "Critical Controversies," below).

Shakespeare and Marlowe were both indebted to medieval drama for the kind of character that Shakespeare creates in Richard, Duke of Gloucester (the future Richard III). Marlowe's counterpart is Barabas, the Jew of Malta, in a play whose prologue is spoken by "Machevil," a caricature of Machiavelli, the Italian political theorist whom the Elizabethans loved to hate. Shakespeare may allude to this prologue in Richard's determination to "set the murtherous Machevil to school" (*3 Henry VI*, 3.2.193), but he did not need Marlowe to inspire his conception of Richard, because he had ample precedent in the so-called Vice of the morality play. Richard's gleeful hypocrisy, his direct address to the audience, his cunning trickery, theatricality, and heartless cruelty, all derive from the Vice, as Bernard Spivack showed in *Shakespeare and the Allegory of Evil* (New York: Columbia UP, 1958, pp. 386–407). Even Richard's chilling line "I am myself alone" has a specific precedent in Ulpian Fulwell's *Like Will to Like*, when the Vice, Nichol Newfangle, chortles to himself: "I am left alone, / Myself here to solace" (567–568). Though it originated in the 1560s, Fulwell's play was still being performed on the Elizabethan commercial stage as late as 1600.

STRUCTURE AND PLOTTING

The first serious attempt to understand the *Henry VI* plays critically was by E.M.W. Tillyard in *Shakespeare's History Plays*. Tillyard argued that they should be interpreted as a unit with *Richard III*—and ultimately with the four plays from *Richard II* to *Henry V*—because all these plays together construe a particular stretch of English history as guided by providence. The outcome of the divine plan is the Tudor regime, initiated by Henry VII at the end of *Richard III*, and the troubles of Henry VI (depicted in the *Henry VI* plays) fit this plan as God's punishment of England for Henry IV's deposing of Richard II (depicted in *Richard II*). This way of understanding English history Tillyard called "the Tudor myth," and he claimed that Shakespeare found it in Edward Hall's *Chronicle* (1548). In this view, the structure of the plays reveals the plan of God in English history, though Tillyard could not explain why Shakespeare wrote the second half of the story before the first half, and the theory has trouble accommodating the heroically successful Henry V.

This way of understanding the structure of the *Henry VI* plays was eventually abandoned for several reasons (see "Critical Controversies," below), leaving unanswered the question of what structure the plays have, if not one that reveals a Tudor providence. David Scott Kastan responded by pointing to the conception of history that seems to be embodied in all of Shakespeare's history plays. Far from being a providential conception, Kastan argued, this view of history is decidedly secular. The only plays about history on the English stage before Shakespeare were the religious mystery plays, which staged selected events from the history of the world based on God's decisive actions in them: the Creation, the fall of Adam and Eve,

Cain's murder of Abel, God's preservation of Noah, and so forth. Dramatic sacred history was marked, in other words, by God's unambiguous intervention in events and by discontinuity between events, because what matters in sacred history is not how events relate to each other but how each event relates to God. Shakespeare's focus on secular history, Kastan argued, required not only a shift from one kind of subject matter to another; it required the invention of a new dramatic form.

Kastan pointed out that all of Shakespeare's English history plays are marked by two distinctive formal features: insistent open-endedness and a thematic emphasis on time (the second of these features is discussed in "Themes and Meanings," below). Both features enact a secular sense of history as events embedded in continuous time rather than as events directed providentially by the hand of God. The past weighs heavily on the present in the first scene of *1 Henry VI*, for example, which begins with the burial of a king. While we are told that this king was heroic and will be much missed, we are not told how he died, why he was fighting in France, or what lies behind the quarreling between rival courtiers. An ambitious bishop ends the first scene by determining to seize the king and rule the realm, but we are not told that the king is an infant, so it is hard to understand how one might seize a king, or why the king is not ruling the realm himself. The play begins as if it were a "slice of time," in Kastan's phrase, rather than the true beginning of an independent story. It ends, moreover, in the same way. Suffolk captures Margaret only three scenes before the play ends, and he formulates a bizarre plan in the play's closing lines: he will propose marriage between Henry and Margaret (despite the serious political disadvantages to England in such a marriage), because he wishes to enjoy Margaret as his mistress, and he can foresee doing so only if she is married to Henry. Will this intricate plan succeed? Will Henry be weak enough to fall for it? Will other courtiers permit it? What will be the consequence if it succeeds? The play raises all these questions as it ends, but it does not answer them.

The *Henry VI* plays have always been overshadowed by the English history plays that Shakespeare wrote later (the sequence from *Richard II* to *Henry V*), and there is no question that Shakespeare improved in skill in this genre as the decade of the 1590s progressed. Characterization in the later plays is more vivid; their poetry more powerful; their thematic coherence richer and more thought provoking; their portrayal of political behavior more thoughtful and incisive. This is not to say, however, that they are different in kind from the *Henry VI* plays. On the contrary, early in his career Shakespeare invented a compelling structure for dramatic analysis of real political behavior in a monarchy, and he did not abandon it in the ensuing years; he simply got better at doing it.

MAIN CHARACTERS

Henry VI and Gloucester (Richard, Duke of Gloucester)

The two characters in the *Henry VI* plays who have received the most critical attention are King Henry himself and his nemesis, Richard, Duke of Gloucester. This critical interest reflects the emphasis of the plays themselves. Henry and Richard are balanced opposites in the pattern of the four plays from *1 Henry VI* to *Richard III*. "It is quite possible to find a good man who would not make a good prince," observes Erasmus, "but there can be no good prince who is not also a good man" (quoted by Edward Berry, p. 50n.), and the two halves of this sentence nicely summarize the difference between Henry and Richard. Henry is pious, gentle, and idealistic, but he is a weak and inept king; Richard is blasphemous, cruel, pragmatic to a fault, and a ruthless tyrant. Henry appears in the first three of the four plays, and Richard appears in the last three. Richard kills Henry, and Henry prophesies the successful reign of the providential deliverer who kills Richard at the end of *Richard III* (*3 Henry VI*, 4.6.68–76).

Examining the schematic contrast between these two figures is useful in understanding how Shakespeare created character in these early plays. Still strongly influenced by allegorical personification in the morality plays, he draws human beings more as types than as psychological portraits. Henry's weakness, for example, is simply a given; it does not result from correlating behavior with motive, self-perception, and biographical circumstances. Henry appears for the first time (briefly) in the third act of *1 Henry VI*; and in each of the last two acts, he commits major follies by failing to see the dire political consequences of his actions. He arbitrarily decides to don a red rose (4.1.152) rather than putting on both a red and a white one or refusing to wear either; moreover, he becomes foolishly infatuated with Margaret (5.5.1–9), based only on Suffolk's report of her beauty. More serious is his failure to defend Duke Humphrey in *2 Henry VI*, when Humphrey's enemies are determined to destroy him. Henry has a strong claim to the throne, since he inherited it legitimately from his father, but he quails in the face of York's accusation that Henry's grandfather obtained the throne through rebellion (*3 Henry VI*, 1.1.134), even though York's father had rebelled against the crown in his own turn, and York's claim was arguably no stronger than Henry's. The king's impotence reaches its nadir when Clifford urges Henry to leave the battle of Towton in order to increase Margaret's chances of success (*3 Henry VI*, 2.2.73–74) and then tells the king to "be still" (3.2.122). Henry does not reply. All this says that Henry is a type of the weak king.

Confusingly, however, Henry is also a type of the Pious King, a reputation deriving from a tradition that very nearly canonized the historical Henry VI. Both his successors of the same name (Henry VII and Henry VIII) led a popular movement that revered Henry VI as a saint after his death, and his official canonization by the pope was prevented only by the disruption of the Reformation. Shakespeare's character seems to allude to this tradition in *3 Henry VI*, 4.8.38–46, and Henry's prophecy of Henry VII's succession (*3 Henry VI*, 4.6.68–76) not only flatters the first of the Tudor kings but also attests to Henry VI's saintliness. Perhaps the best explanation for this unusual mix of qualities in Henry is, again, that these plays emphasize political analysis rather than providential undertaking. The conjunction of holiness and political ineptitude renders the character politically disastrous as a king, no matter how good he is as an individual, and this conjunction in Henry suggests that Shakespeare's political analysis in the *Henry VI* plays turns on character. History, in effect, consists of crucial decisions by individual characters in regard to acquiring and maintaining political power.

Richard of Gloucester is different, not only because he is the opposite of Henry VI but also because Shakespeare does something more with Richard than make him a type of the Evil Man. Evil he undoubtedly is, and his derivation from the morality play Vice is as certain as Henry's derivation from a saint. But Shakespeare hints that Richard's character may be at least in part a product of the way society has treated him, and that hint gives him more psychological depth than any other character in the *Henry VI* plays. In *3 Henry VI*, where he addresses his situation and his future in a long soliloquy (3.2.124–195), Richard suggests that he has been socially constructed. This remarkable speech immediately follows Edward's flirtation with Lady Elizabeth Grey, which prompts Richard's jealous lament about Edward's ease with women, in contrast to Richard's hopelessness. "[L]ove foreswore me in my mother's womb" (3.2.153), he complains, citing his shrunken arm, the hump on his back, and his disproportioned legs. Recognizing that "this earth affords no joy to me" (3.2.165) except acquiring and exercising power, he determines to aim for ultimate power—the crown. His audacious ambition is thus linked to sexual frustration and social rejection. Since society has cruelly mistreated him, he is determined to respond in a ruthless drive to dominate those who have rejected him.

If this were all Shakespeare did with Richard's character, he would be almost pitiable, and there is no question that his credible motive for hating the world makes him the most complex character in the *Henry VI* plays. But from Richard's first appearance in *2 Henry VI*, we see something else as well: a suggestion that his misshapen body is merely an outward expression of his inner depravity. "Foul stigmatic," young Clifford calls him, suggesting that Richard's deformity is a mark set on him by God—like the mark of Cain in the Bible—and Margaret repeats and interprets the term in *3 Henry VI*: "foul misshapen stigmatic / Mark'd by the destinies to be avoided" (2.2.136–137). All of this points to traditional characterization by type and helps to prevent such a cruel interpretation of physical deformity from being merely arbitrary. It is linked so closely to Richard's Vice-like qualities as to identify him predominantly as a type of the Evil Man; the play's prodigies, prophecies, and supernatural events reinforce Richard's deformity as a moral emblem.

Margaret

Though Margaret has received much less attention than Henry and Richard, she is only slightly less remarkable a character than Richard. She is the only character who appears in all three *Henry VI* plays and *Richard III*, and she has some of the dual quality that Richard has: both a type and a motivated human being. As a type, she is a shrew or "domineering female," in David Bevington's phrase (*Shakespeare Studies* 2 [1966]: 51–58). Margaret makes up for what Henry lacks in political will and determination, reversing the received notion of the hierarchy that was supposed to order the relationship of husband and wife. Though she is not identified with hell and witches, as Joan is, Margaret is like Joan in being French, overweening, and militarily aggressive; Margaret even succeeds Joan literally in *1 Henry VI* as a character of this type, when first Joan and then Margaret are captured by English noblemen in the same scene (5.3). Like Joan too, Margaret is sexually adventurous: Joan seems to be sexually involved with King Charles, but she claims that two other French noblemen fathered her unborn child (*1 Henry VI*, 5.4.72–78), and Margaret maintains a sexual liaison with Suffolk while he is negotiating her marriage to Henry and even after her marriage. Thematically the two women are closely related in the *Henry VI* plays, though Margaret is by far the more important of the two in the total scheme.

Moreover, hints of psychological motivation appear for Margaret, whereas Joan is little more than a stereotypical witch. Margaret is the only character in the early histories who moves through a life trajectory from youth to old age, and her youth seems to be emphasized when she first appears in *1 Henry VI*, though her age is not specified; historically she was only sixteen when she married Henry. Her expressed affection for Suffolk (*2 Henry VI*, 1.3) is "the first passionate love-scene Shakespeare wrote," as Honor Matthew points out (*Character and Symbol in Shakespeare's Plays* [Cambridge: Cambridge UP, 1962, p. 18]), and though Margaret lacks Juliet's innocence in this scene, she anticipates Juliet's youthful passion. The same passion appears again, albeit grotesquely, when Margaret cradles Suffolk's severed head (*2 Henry VI*, 4.4). Suffolk appears to be Margaret's first lover, and her intense affection for him, coupled with her extreme youth, her marriage to an exasperatingly weak and vacillating king, and her being thrust into the center of England's chaotic power struggles, all help to create the outline of a credible psychological portrait, which (like Richard's) is at least understandable, if not very sympathetic. Margaret is hardly a "domineering female"; furthermore, in *3 Henry VI*, 5.5, when she holds the body of her young son, who has just been stabbed to death before her eyes by the enraged York brothers, she is sympathetic. "Passionate" describes her lament in this scene (5.5.50–67), thus linking it to Margaret's character in the first two plays. The passion she shows in grief, however, also links her to every mother who grieves for her dead child, including the archetypal grieving mother, Mary, whose lament for Christ in the extant mystery plays Margaret occasionally echoes as she holds her son's body in a secular pietà. It is easy to see that Margaret is outspoken, opinionated, overbearing, and quarrelsome, but to see her as nothing more than that is to succumb to the misogyny that shapes attitudes toward her in the plays themselves.

DEVICES AND TECHNIQUES

Anyone who is familiar with Shakespeare's mature poetic drama will recognize that, by contrast, the *Henry VI* plays are deficient. Allowance has to be made, however, for the playwright's youth and inexperience when he wrote these plays. Taken by themselves, and taken in comparison with other contemporary writing for the London stage, the *Henry VI* plays are remarkable achievements.

The stylistic influence of the Roman playwright Seneca is evident in the *Henry VI* plays and *Richard III*, as it is in *Titus Andronicus*, Shakespeare's first effort in tragedy, written at about the same time. To Senecan tragedy he owed the emphasis on prophecy, omens, vengeance, violence, declamatory rhetoric, and the near exclusion of commoners. These qualities generally distinguish the *Henry VI* plays from the later set of four history plays (*Richard II* to *Henry V*). Scholarly attention to the many declamations in the *Henry VI* plays and *Richard III* has established Shakespeare's conscious debt to Seneca where this aspect of his style is concerned. Wolfgang Clemen points out, for example, that Clifford's long speech in *3 Henry VI*, 2.2.9–42, is formally correct in the Senecan manner, as Clifford appeals to Henry to reverse the decision he made to disinherit Prince Edward ("Some Aspects of Style in the *Henry VI* Plays," in *Shakespeare's Styles*, ed. Philip Edwards et al. [Cambridge: Cambridge UP, 1980], pp. 9–24). Clifford asks rhetorical questions ("Whose hand is that the forest bear doth lick?" *3 Henry VI*, 2.2.13), appeals to proverbial examples from nature ("The smallest worm will turn, being trodden on," ibid., 2.2.17), and employs elaborately parallel phrasing in contrasting York and Henry VI:

> He, but a duke, would have his son a king,
> And raise his issue like a loving sire;
> Thou, being a king, blest with a goodly son,
> Didst yield consent to disinherit him,
> Which argued thee a most unloving father. (Ibid., 2.2.19–25)

Henry's reply makes clear that Shakespeare was aware of the heightened style in this passage and perhaps wanted to make sure his hearers were also aware of it: "Full well hath Clifford play'd the orator" (ibid., 2.2.43).

Christopher Marlowe showed Shakespeare how to put "high astounding terms," (as the Prologue to 1 *Tamburlaine* calls them) into dramatic verse on the Elizabethan stage: the rhetorical flights of Shakespeare's characters probably owe as much to Marlowe as to Seneca. Tamburlaine's "aspiring mind" prompts him to reach for "the ripest fruit of all, / That perfect bliss and sole felicity, / The sweet fruition of an earthly crown" (1 *Tamburlaine*, 2.7.20 and 27–29), and this kind of aspiration is articulated by both York (2 *Henry VI*, 1.1.236–243) and the Duchess of Gloucester, when she admonishes her husband in the following scene (1.2.5–11). Neither of these characters is much like Tamburlaine, but their overweening ambition is expressed in terms similar to his, as many of Shakespeare's contemporaries must have recognized (see David Riggs).

Shakespeare found his own voice early, however, and we can hear it in the *Henry VI* plays, apart from the influence of other stylistic models. One of the most remarkable orations in the *Henry VI* plays is Margaret's speech to her troops just before the battle of Tewkesbury (3 *Henry VI*, 5.4.1–38). The lines are organized around an extended metaphor—the Elizabethans called it a "conceit"—of a ship in a storm:

> What though the mast be now blown overboard,
> The cable broke, the holding-anchor lost,
> And half our sailors swallow'd in the flood?
> Yet lives our pilot still. (5.4.3–6)

"Our pilot" is Henry VI, leader of the Lancastrian faction, and Margaret develops the metaphor elaborately in relation to other members of her party. But the development is not merely mechanical. As Andrew Cairncross points out, the last fourteen lines of Margaret's oration (ll. 25–38) are organized in three groups of four lines each, followed by a single group of two lines (3 *Henry VI* [London: Methuen, for the Arden Shakespeare, 1964], pp. lxiv–lxv). This is the way Shakespeare organized his distinctive sonnet form, though with this difference: in Margaret's speech the lines are not grouped by rhyme but only by syntax and theme:

> And what is Edward but a ruthless sea?
> What Clarence but a quicksand of deceit?
> And Richard but a ragged fatal rock?
> All these the enemies to our poor bark.
> Say you can swim, alas, 'tis but awhile;
> Tread on the sand, why, there you quickly sink;
> Bestride the rock, the tide will wash you off,
> Or else you famish—that's a threefold death.

> This speak I, lords, to let you understand,
> If case some one of you would fly from us,
> That there's no hop'd-for mercy with the brothers
> More than with ruthless waves, with sands and rocks.
> Why, courage then! what cannot be avoided,
> 'Twere childish weakness to lament or fear. (5.4.25–38)

Actual embedded sonnets appear frequently in other early plays, such as *The Two Gentlemen of Verona* and *Romeo and Juliet,* but Shakespeare seems to have experimented with this device as early as *3 Henry VI.*

Margaret's nautical imagery appears elsewhere in *3 Henry VI* but not in the first two *Henry VI* plays, and her conceit of a beleaguered ship is appropriate to the near collapse of public order in the last play of the series. Other patterns of imagery continue through all three plays, as Caroline Spurgeon pointed out (*Shakespeare's Imagery and What It Tells Us* [Cambridge: Cambridge UP, 1935]). The Temple Garden scene in *1 Henry VI,* 2.4, for example (an episode Shakespeare invented), begins a consistent strain of garden imagery that continues into the other two *Henry VI* plays. Imagery of the slaughterhouse, in contrast, appears for the first time in *2 Henry VI* and continues into *3 Henry VI.* This imagery might be expected in plays that deal with civil war, but in *2 Henry VI* the pattern begins long before the first battle of St. Albans, in the scene where Henry laments what the English nobles are doing to Humphrey, Duke of Gloucester:

> And as the butcher takes away the calf,
> And binds the wretch, and beats it when it strays,
> Bearing it to the bloody slaughter-house,
> Even so remorseless have they borne him hence. (3.1.210–213)

Distinctive patterns of imagery suggest a cohesive imaginative conception for the three plays and reinforce Edward Berry's thematic analysis of persistent political decline (see "Themes and Meanings," below).

One of the most variously interpreted images of the *Henry VI* plays is Richard, Duke of Gloucester's remarkable description of his tortured questing in *3 Henry VI:*

> And I—like one lost in a thorny wood,
> That rents the thorns, and is rent with the thorns,
> Seeking a way, and straying from the way,
> Not knowing how to find the open air,
> But toiling desperately to find it out—
> Torment myself to catch the English crown. (3.2.174–179)

The image arguably belongs to Spurgeon's category of garden imagery, but it is one of the most arresting of the lot, because it powerfully evinces Richard's psychological state (see "Explication of Key Passages," below). "The thorny wood in which he is lost is the nightmarish world of his own monstrously distorted and protesting humanity," observes James Winny (*The Player King: A Theme of Shakespeare's Histories* [New York: Barnes and Noble, 1968], p. 29). Robert Watson reads Richard's tormented determination in light of Freud: "Such a declaration of autonomy verges on a claim to autogeny," so Richard's image is a metaphor of a Caesarean section performed by a mother-hating foetus (*Shakespeare and the Hazards of Ambition* [Cambridge, MA: Harvard UP, 1984], p. 16). John Blanpied reads the image as an allegory of writing plays, so Richard becomes a symbol of the playwright seeking the crown, "meaning the symbolic interpretation of 'England' through her past" (*Time and the Artist in Shakespeare's English Histories* [Newark: U of Delaware P, 1983], p. 72), and Joseph Candido sees the image as part of a pattern (not noticed by Spurgeon) of seeking release in the *Henry VI* plays ("Getting Loose in the *Henry VI* Plays," *Shakespeare Quarterly* 35 [1984]: 392–406). The sheer variety of these responses suggests the richness of the image itself and resembles the range of response to the more complex style of later plays, such as *Hamlet, King Lear,* and *Antony and Cleopatra*.

THEMES AND MEANINGS

In addition to constructing each of the *Henry VI* plays independently as a slice of time (Kastan, pp. 259–277), Shakespeare also made the three plays work together, not only in continuous plot lines but also in theme, and this alone is an accomplishment unmatched by any other playwright at the time. From a nation unified and victorious over its enemies at the beginning of *1 Henry VI*, we witness a steady political decline to the end of *3 Henry VI*, where the most powerful character is Richard, Duke of Gloucester, who is treacherous, ruthless, and loyal to no one: "I am myself alone." Edward Berry points out that the focus shifts from one play to the next: from a community rapidly abandoning its unifying affirmation of heroic warrior values (exemplified by Talbot) in *1 Henry VI*, to a steady erosion of justice (exemplified in Humphrey, Duke of Gloucester) in *2 Henry VI*, to ubiquitous clan feuding, civil war, hatred, and treachery, exemplified by the socially alienated Richard, Duke of Gloucester, in *3 Henry IV*.

The thematic coherence in the *Henry VI* plays is Shakespeare's most important departure from Marlowe. Though these plays may have inspired Marlowe to write *Edward II* (1592), Marlowe wrote just one play about English history and did not use his impressive talent for ironic plotting to analyze power, as did Shakespeare. Shakespeare complements the plays' structural emphasis on open-ended history with a thematic emphasis on time that runs through all the *Henry VI* plays and reappears in his later histories as well. The story they all tell is explicitly determined by time—that is, by the actions of human beings in time—not by eternity or, in other words, the decisive intervention and interaction of God in human affairs. The two characters who are most attentive to timely action in *1* and *2 Henry VI* are also the most politically astute and ruthless: the Duke of York and his son, Richard. While still a law student (before gaining his dukedom), York swears that he will vindicate his disgraced father—"Were growing time once ripened to my will" (*1 Henry VI*, 2.4.99)—and he determines to wait "till time do serve" to move against Henry, when he hears that France has been lost (*2 Henry VI*, 1.1.248). York accordingly puts a long-term plan into effect, stirring up Jack Cade to foment rebellion and returning from Ireland with an army to make a show of power at an opportune moment, as Henry Bullingbrook does in *Richard II*. While King Henry meditates poetically on a fantasy of timeless idealism (*3 Henry VI*, 2.5.21–40), York's youngest son, Richard, imitates his father in concealing his motives and planning carefully to seize "the golden time I look for" (ibid., 3.2.127). Though Richard is undoubtedly modeled on the Vice, the stakes he plays for are not anyone's eternal destiny; they are emphatically political.

Shakespeare's thematic emphasis on time complements the history plays' attention to political succession in a monarchy (see "Publication History," above) to create an astute political analysis that has no contemporary parallel. Shakespeare's political realism has sometimes been compared to Machiavelli's, but Machiavelli has very little interest in political succession, whereas Shakespeare's history plays are centrally concerned with it; Machiavelli, moreover, emphasizes the importance of fortune, rather than time, in seizing and maintaining power. Even as a young playwright at the beginning of his career, Shakespeare was dramatically inventive, bold, and original, as well as one of the most thoughtful observers and interpreters of the Elizabethan political scene.

CRITICAL CONTROVERSIES

The earliest controversy concerning the *Henry VI* plays arose in the eighteenth century, and it has still not been resolved. This is a controversy about their authorship. Did Shakespeare share their composition with other playwrights (as first proposed by Lewis Theobald in 1733), or is he their sole author (as asserted by Samuel Johnson in 1765)? Originally, this argument was largely one of aesthetics— that is, it turned on the question of whether these early plays were good enough to have been written by Shakespeare, or whether they had been contaminated, so to speak, by the writing of others.

Beginning with the magisterial work of Edmond Malone in 1790, factors other than taste have been cited by scholars in defence either of Shakespeare's sole authorship of the *Henry VI* plays or of his shared authorship, and the arguments have become increasingly complex and sophisticated. At present, scholarly opinion generally favors multiple authorship (the position first proposed by Theobald and later defended by Malone), but not everyone agrees, and opinion has remained divided since the eighteenth century. Some scholars have recently attempted to solve the controversy by writing computer programs to analyze the style of the plays, but the results have been mixed. Donald Foster, for example, used a program he called Shaxicon to establish not only that Joe Klein wrote *Primary Colors* (an accurate attribution, as it turned out) but also that Shakespeare wrote "A Funeral Elegy to Master John Peter," attributed only to "W. S." when it was published in 1612. Foster published his book *Elegy by W. S.: A Study in Attribution* with the University of Delaware Press in 1989, and "A Funeral Elegy" was included in several editions of Shakespeare published in the 1990s. Later, however, in the face of an article by G. D. Monserrat, "*A Funeral Elegy*, W.S., and Shakespeare," *Review of English Studies* 53 (2002): 186–203—and a then-forthcoming book by Brian Vickers ("*Counterfeiting*" *Shakespeare: Evidence, Authorship, and John Ford's Funerall Elegye* [Cambridge: Cambridge UP, 2002])—Foster announced on the listserv SHAKSPER that he was formally withdrawing his claim (www.shaksper.net, 13 June 2002). Foster has not addressed the authorship controversy concerning the *Henry VI* plays, but it seems unlikely that he would resolve it to everyone's satisfaction, even if he did address it; it is not yet clear that any other computer program would be more successful than Shaxicon in settling the controversy.

A second unresolved question concerns the order in which the *Henry VI* plays were written. Theories about this issue, as with the authorship debate, are based both on external evidence about the plays and on interpretation of them: for example, *2* and *3 Henry VI* were published in shorter single-play editions before the 1623 First Folio, and the title of the earlier edition of *2 Henry VI* is *The First part of the Contention betwixt the two famous Houses of Yorke and Lancaster*. Given this title and the initial publication of *1 Henry VI* in the First Folio, some scholars have argued that *2* and *3 Henry VI* were written first, and that *1 Henry VI* was written later as a "prequel" to them. This is the view taken, for example, by the editors of the *Oxford Shakespeare* in 1986, and it has been followed by Stephen Greenblatt, editor of the *Norton Shakespeare* (New York: W. W. Norton, 1997), and by Edward Burns in the Third Arden edition of *1 Henry VI* (London: Thomas Nelson for the Arden Shakespeare, 2000). Complementing external evidence for this view is the argument from internal evidence that *2* and *3 Henry VI* are more consistent with, and interdependent on, each other than *2 Henry VI* is with *1 Henry VI*. In *2 Henry VI*, for the first time, York becomes ambitious for the crown, his ominous son Richard appears, and Warwick makes political moves that earn him the sobriquet "kingmaker."

As in the controversy over authorship, these arguments are suggestive but have not decided the order of the plays' composition definitively. Elizabethan play titles are notoriously unreliable guides to the content of the works to which they are attached, and arguments from internal evidence are inevitably interpretive. York may not be explicitly ambitious for the crown in *1 Henry VI*, but he is indisputably ambitious, and his claim to the crown (as well as his dukedom) is cited in detail in both *1 Henry VI*, 2.5, and *2 Henry VI*, 2.2. Richard is the youngest of York's sons; Shakespeare made him much older than he was historically in order to include him actively in events in *2* and *3 Henry VI*. Arguably, therefore, Shakespeare omitted him from the first play because he was too young (King Henry is omitted from the first two acts of *1 Henry VI* for the same reason). Moreover, Richard's absence from *1 Henry VI* (along with that of his brothers, Edward and Clarence) is no less inconsistent with the second two plays than is his characterization in *2* and *3 Henry VI*. Richard's diabolical nature is hinted at for the first time in *3 Henry VI*, 1.1, and his treachery erupts suddenly in *3 Henry VI*, 3.2. Again, while it is true that Warwick is not a kingmaker in *1 Henry VI*, he is a powerful presence at court, staunchly representing York's case for preferment and thus anticipating his siding with York when York openly declares his opposition to Henry in *2 Henry VI*. Edward Berry's argument for thematic coherence across the three plays is just as compelling as are the internal arguments for *1 Henry VI* as a prequel, and *1 Henry VI* is no less open-ended than are the other two plays, even if it is the first play in the series. This debate, in short, would appear to be a draw.

The two critical controversies just discussed (authorship and the order of the plays' composition) are only secondarily concerned with interpretation of the *Henry VI* plays. In contrast, a third critical debate is entirely concerned with how the three plays (together with *Richard III*) should be interpreted in regard to one particular feature, namely, divine providence. Tillyard, as we noticed, initiated this line of argument with his assertion that the four plays together manifest the "Tudor myth," in that they exhibit God's punishment of England for Henry IV's overthrow of Richard II, thus setting up Henry VII's miraculous delivery of England from civil war and tyranny.

Tillyard's reading of the *Henry VI* plays was persuasive by virtue of its breadth and explanatory power, but it was eventually abandoned when critics examined it in detail. A. L. French argued that the deposition of Richard II is not a credible explanation for the political chaos of the *Henry VI* plays ("*Henry VI* and the Ghost of Richard II," *English Studies* 50 [1969], Anglo-American Supplement, xxxvii–xliii), and H. A. Kelly pointed out that Shakespeare's chronicle sources do not put forward a "Tudor myth" (*Divine Providence in the England of Shakespeare's Histories* [Cambridge, MA: Harvard UP, 1970]). Rather, Kelly showed, particular chronicles interpret history providentially in support of the particular version of history they favor (Yorkist, Lancastrian, or Tudor), but none of them offers the version that Tillyard found in Shakespeare's plays. John Wilders argued that the Tudor myth is not in Holinshed, any more than it is in Shakespeare (*The Lost Garden: A View of Shakespeare's English and Roman History Plays* [Totowa, NJ: Rowman and Littlefield, 1978]), and David Frey thought the *Henry VI* plays were designed specifically to deny "the concepts of divine justice, personal providence, and divine intervention"—just the opposite of Tillyard's view (*The First Tetralogy: Shakespeare's Scrutiny of the Tudor Myth* [The Hague: Mouton, 1976], p. 2).

Despite the skepticism that has undermined Tillyard's argument, the *Henry VI* plays and *Richard III* contain innumerable supernatural phenomena (devils, prophetic dreams, verbal prophecies that come true, oaths and broken oaths, omens, celestial signs, "prodigies," and at least one "stigmatic") that require explanation, even if they do not add up to a providential interpretation of the plays as a group. One way to account for these phenomena in the plays is by reference to what social anthropologists call "magical" thinking, which still functioned vitally in late-sixteenth-century England, when these plays were written—not only in literary influences like the Bible and Senecan tragedy but also in politics and in people's daily lives (as in fear of witchcraft and demonic possession). Magical thinking is treated quite variously in the *Henry VI* plays. Fiends actually appear on stage in the company of a witch in *1 Henry VI*, 5.3, and an accurately prophetic (albeit equivocal) "spirit" called "Asmath" (likely a misprinted anagram for "Sathan") is raised by incantation in *2 Henry VI*, 1.4, which also includes a fake miraculous healing (2.1) and a highly ambiguous trial by combat (2.3). At the same time that the plays court antipapal satire by identifying Joan of Arc as a witch, they present Richard of Gloucester quite seriously as a "prodigy" and a "stigmatic," and *3 Henry VI* includes a celestial omen (2.1) and an accurate verbal prophecy (4.6).

The puzzling combination of credulous magical thinking and skepticism in these plays reflects the Elizabethan state of mind with remarkable fidelity. The English Protestant church defined itself in contrast to the papacy, in part, by asserting that miracles had not been possible since the apostolic era: "miracles are ceased," as the Archbishop of Canterbury says (anachronistically) in *Henry V* (1.1.67; the same idea appears in *All's Well That Ends Well*, 2.3.1–6). But habits of thinking were still overwhelmingly religious, and the boundaries between the natural and the supernatural were far from being drawn with the clarity they would acquire when early modern science transformed thinking in the eighteenth century. Frequent instances of magical thinking in Shakespeare's early history plays are not, therefore, necessarily an indication that the plays affirm a transparent providential ordering of human affairs; similarly, Shakespeare's skepticism about the political process is not itself an indication of religious disbelief. Many Protestant thinkers recognized what they called "secondary causes" in history, that is, causes that bear no discernible relation to divine providence. These include the many obvious causes that operate in the *Henry VI* plays: accidents, human weakness, miscalculation, envy, aristocratic rivalry, marital incompatibility, mistiming, treachery, ambition, anger, and chance. Out of such causes rich stories can be made with no particular reflection, either way, on the issue of providential direction in human history.

PRODUCTION HISTORY

On March 3, 1592, Philip Henslowe, who managed the Rose Theatre, recorded in his diary that a new play, "Harey the vj," earned £3 16s 5d, more than any other play that season. Before the theaters were closed in June, this play—it is unclear which of the *Henry VI* plays is referenced—was repeated fourteen times. However, after their first successful production at the Rose Theatre in the early 1590s, the *Henry VI* plays were not performed again for almost a century, by which time conditions in both the theater and national politics had changed immeasurably. John Crowne's *The Miseries of Civil War* (1680–1681) adapted *2* and *3 Henry VI* for performance as a single play on the indoor stage of the Duke's Theatre in London, using painted backdrops, or "scenes," that were unknown in the open-air Elizabethan theaters. Crowne's play opened with Jack Cade's rebellion from *2 Henry VI* and included two "scenes": one with soldiers "looting and raping" at a cottage and a second with burning houses, hanged citizens, and children tossed on soldiers' pikes. The play thus left little doubt about Crowne's royalist view of civil war, which for his audience inevitably recalled the civil wars of the 1640s and the execution of Charles I, whose son, Charles II, was reigning at the time of Crowne's play.

In the early eighteenth century Colley Cibber followed Crowne's example of conflating two early history plays and initiated the enduring custom of combining *Richard III* with some part of *3 Henry VI*. Cibber's production of *Richard III* in 1700 thus opened with *3 Henry VI*, 5.6, the scene in which Richard of Gloucester murders Henry VI; this particular combination reappeared as recently as the 1990s in Ian McKellen's stage production of *Richard III*, produced as a feature film by Richard Loncraine in 1995. Another influential stage adaptation of *Richard III*, by Laurence Olivier in 1944 (followed by a film in 1955 directed by and starring Olivier), also opened with Richard's soliloquy in *3 Henry VI*, 2.3.

Beginning in the later eighteenth century, directors sought increasingly to mount productions of the *Henry VI* plays that they deemed to be closer to the historical production values of the 1590s. James Anderson directed *2 Henry VI* by itself at the Surrey Theatre for the Shakespeare tercentenary in 1864—the first time since the 1590s that one of the early histories was produced without conflating it with some other play. The outcome of this process was the first production since the 1590s of all three *Henry VI* plays independently—a production mounted by Frank Benson at Stratford in 1906. Benson excluded stage scenery entirely, made the action continuous, and required actors to double some of the roles—all departures from standard nineteenth-century staging and a movement in the direction of "authentic" Shakespearean stage conditions. Moreover, Benson updated the plays' politics to emphasize the Whig view of history. He made Joan a tragic figure in *1 Henry VI*, for example, in order to suggest that wars of wanton domination destroy innocents and reap a grim reward. While this interpretation involved a considerable departure from Shakespeare's antipapal version of Joan, it arguably maintained the spirit of the plays' original political topicality.

Since World War II, producers of the *Henry VI* plays have used one or another of all the production styles for the early history plays that were established by the early twentieth century. Barry Jackson followed Frank Benson by producing the three plays separately at the Birmingham Rep in 1951–1953 and by eliminating stage sets, emphasizing continuous action, and requiring actors to double roles. Costumes were researched for precise historical accuracy matching the time of the plays' action in the later fifteenth century, thus correcting the anachronism of Elizabethan staging that used largely contemporary costumes, no matter what the place or period. What Jackson thus gained in historical costume accuracy he sacrificed in historical theatrical accuracy, though he strove to reproduce Elizabethan production values in other respects.

In contrast to Jackson, John Barton and Peter Hall revived the Restoration custom of conflating the three *Henry VI* plays when they jointly directed *The Wars of the Roses* at Stratford in 1963—the most influential postwar production of these plays. Two plays (*Henry VI* and *Edward IV*) thus emerged from three, each focusing on a different duke of Gloucester—Humphrey and Richard, respectively—with about half the lines cut from the Folio texts of the three plays and some 1,400 new lines added by Hall. The directors, moreover, were explicit about their political motive in adapting the plays, following the example of John Crowne in 1680–1681. Hall read Jan Kott's *Shakespeare Our Contemporary* (trans. Boleslaw Taborski [Garden City, NY: Doubleday, 1964]) while *The Wars of the Roses* was in rehearsal, and he thought the production reflected Kott's bleak political outlook.

As if in reaction to Barton and Hall, Terry Hands returned to the separate-play, full-text production values of Frank Benson and Barry Jackson when the Royal Shakespeare Company next staged the *Henry VI* plays in 1977. Hands encouraged an acting style that emphasized raw emotion and visceral realism. Helen Mirren (playing Margaret) reported that after torturing and killing York in *3 Henry VI*, 1.4, she nearly always had to vomit and sometimes could hardly keep from vomiting onstage. Hands also reacted to *The Wars of the Roses* by eschewing politics entirely. "Shakespeare goes far beyond politics. Politics is a very shallow science," he said of his production (Robert Shaughnessy, *Representing Shakespeare* [New York: Harvester Wheatsheaf, 1994]). Not everyone agreed. Alan Sinfield, for example, took the Royal Shakespeare Company to task for its political conservatism, arguing that if productions did not openly object to or criticize the status quo, they implicitly endorsed it ("Royal Shakespeare: Theatre and the Making of Ideology," in *Political Shakespeare: New Essays in Cultural Materialism* [Manchester, Eng.: Manchester UP, 1985], pp. 158–181).

Two productions of the *Henry VI* plays in the 1980s seemed to respond to Sinfield's critique. In fact, Sinfield was asked to write the program notes for Adrian Noble's production with the Royal Shakespeare Company called *The Plantagenets*, which again conflated the three plays into two, called, respectively, *Henry VI* and *The Rise of Edward IV*. The revised scripts were written by Charles Wood, author of *Tumbledown* (1989), a television docudrama about the Falklands War. Noble was unapologetic about the antiwar emphasis of his production, arguing that art is inescapably political, and that people object only to those political interpretations that they find disagreeable. Equally radical was Michael Bogdanov's 1987 production of

(Foreground, top to bottom) Walker Jones as Cardinal of Winchester and Tom Nelis as King Henry with (background, left to right) Patrick Morris and Mark Kenneth Smaltz in the Joseph Papp Public Theater/New York Shakespeare Festival 1996 production of *Henry VI*, directed by Karin Coonrod. Courtesy of Photofest.

the *Henry VI* plays with the English Shakespeare Company as part of a seven-play sequence, from *Richard II* to *Richard III*, which he called *The Wars of the Roses*. Following the example of John Crowne, Bogdanov conflated *2* and *3 Henry VI*, which thus became the sixth play in the seven-play sequence. The plays' political message was evident in several ways, among them a double time scheme: the historical chronology of successive medieval kings was juxtaposed with costuming that ran from Victorian (in the early plays) to punk in the latest, thus suggesting the collapse of the British Empire into Thatcherism. This suggestion was reinforced by June Watson's performance of Queen Margaret as if she were Margaret Thatcher.

The Royal Shakespeare Company's latest staging of the *Henry VI* plays was part of an eight-play production of all of Shakespeare's history plays in regnal order, as in Bogdanov's *Wars of the Roses*. The production took two years to enact (1999–2001), with four plays staged in each of the two seasons. Different directors were responsible for different plays, with Michael Boyd directing all four of the plays in the sequence of *1 Henry VI* to *Richard III* at the Swan Theatre in 2000–2001. Boyd saw the plays more as a spiritual journey than a political statement, and he used the phrase "magical realism" to describe the production's style. Bodies of the dead were not carried or dragged off stage; they visibly rose and followed a red-robed "keeper" through an upstage aperture that may have been the mouth of hell or simply death. The dead also returned to the action as the same actors in the same costumes but with new names. Talbot and his son in *1 Henry VI* thus returned in *3 Henry VI* as the Son who has killed his Father and the Father who has killed his Son. Just two actors performed the latter scene by simply switching places at the appropriate point in the dialogue.

Most people who see the *Henry VI* plays performed will probably do so on videotape or DVD, in the production made jointly by the British Broadcasting Company (BBC) and Time-Life and directed by Jane Howell in 1983. (The only other televised version of the plays was made in 1960 as part of Peter Dews's series called *An Age of Kings*, but this version is much shorter than the BBC/Time-Life version, and it is not commercially available.) Each part of the *Henry VI* plays is a separate film in the BBC series, ranging from 185 minutes to 210 minutes in length. Characters who appear in more than one play are played by the same actors (though some actors double in several roles), and the action is always performed on the same indoor set. Reflecting the thematic collapse of civil and political order throughout the three plays, this set becomes increasingly battered and even burned as the action progresses. It bears some similarity to an elaborate playground fixture, with steps, ladders, and multiple levels for the actors to use. This effect is deliberate. Howell said she considered the behavior of the nobility in the *Henry VI* plays to be childish in its egocentricity and destructive energy, and she wanted a set that reflected that behavior symbolically. She also drew a parallel between this kind of political behavior and what she saw in England at the time she was producing the plays. Her production thus recalled Barton and Hall's *Wars of the Roses* and anticipated the politically activist stage productions by Adrian Noble and Michael Bogdanov later in the 1980s.

EXPLICATION OF KEY PASSAGES

1 Henry VI, 3.3.44–85. **"Look on thy country, . . . turn and turn again!"** Joan la Pucelle successfully appeals to the Duke of Burgundy in these lines, urging him to desist in his support of the English and return to the French fold, where, she claims, he naturally belongs. The passage is remarkable for its persuasive power in a cause that the play explicitly identifies as perverse and demonic. Only with Joan's triumphant and cynical aside, "Done like a Frenchman—turn and turn again!" (3.3.85), are we shocked back to reality from her compelling vision of the French cause. Shakespeare's ability to present situations convincingly from different angles is striking in this set piece declamation, which proves not only the smooth credibility of hypocrisy (recalling the wiliness of the Vice and anticipating the plausible power of Richard III) but also the poet's own virtuosity.

The poetic decoration of Joan's speech is formal, measured, deliberate. She uses repetition ("Look on . . . look on," 3.3.44; "See, see," 3.3.49; "Behold the wounds, the most unnatural wounds," 3.3.50), chiasmus ("Strike those that hurt, and hurt not those that help," 3.3.53), and one carefully placed simile: "As looks the mother on her lowly babe / When death doth close his tender-dying eyes" (3.3.47–48). The image of the grieving parent and the dying or dead child reappears repeatedly in the *Henry VI* plays: in *1 Henry VI* with Talbot and his son, in *2 Henry VI* with King Henry's lament for Duke Humphrey (3.1.210–222), and in *3 Henry VI* with York and Rutland, the Father who has killed his Son and the Son who has killed his Father, and finally with Margaret and Prince Edward. After appealing to Burgundy on behalf of his homeland, Joan attacks the English for their perfidy, and Burgundy immediately registers the effect of her "haughty words" that "have batt'red me like roaring cannon-shot" (3.3.78, 79). Their effect on him is inevitably their effect on us as well.

2 Henry VI, 3.1.4–41. "**Can you not see? . . . my words effectual.**" Only slightly less hypocritical than Joan's lines, Margaret's are a public attempt to manipulate King Henry into siding with her and other courtiers against Humphrey, Duke of Gloucester, who is in reality the only trustworthy supporter the king has left. Margaret begins with a series of rhetorical questions that accurately describe Gloucester's behavior (he has been withdrawn, distracted, and troubled because of his wife's recent arrest) but deliberately misconstrue his actions as arrogant, haughtily distant, and disdainful of others—a slanderous technique that follows the example of Cardinal Beaufort, Gloucester's old nemesis (1.1.147–164). She makes her point with a pithy animal analogy of the sort that John Lyly had made famous in his two-part prose fiction, *Euphues* (1578 and 1580), a style that Shakespeare later mocked in *1 Henry IV*, 2.4.397–417:

> Small curs are not regarded when they grin,
> But great men tremble when the lion roars,
> And Humphrey is no little man in England. (3.1.18–20)

Each line in this analogy is a separate clause in a compound sentence. The phrase "small curs" at the beginning of the first clause is counterpointed by "lion roars" at the end of the second, and complemented by "no little man" at the end of the third. "Grin" at the end of the first clause is similarly balanced by the alliterated "great" at the beginning of the second.

Margaret continues her slanderous attack by developing the implications of "no little man." Though Gloucester has, in fact, supported the king in unswerving loyalty, Margaret urges that Gloucester must be a threat, because he is the king's uncle, and if Gloucester is so arrogant, it is imprudent to have him so close to the throne. Again the queen makes her point proverbially, this time using a garden analogy (3.1.31–33) that ties into a sequence of garden images running through all the *Henry VI* plays, as Caroline Spurgeon pointed out in *Shakespeare's Imagery* (see "Devices and Techniques," above). Margaret concludes her appeal to Henry with a display of emotion and pretended vulnerability, claiming that she cares only for her husband and calling on other nobles present (who she knows all hate Gloucester as much as she does) to correct her "woman's fear" if she is mistaken. Unlike Joan's appeal to Burgundy, Margaret's to Henry is unavailing, because he remains convinced of Gloucester's loyalty; Margaret's rhetorical ability is, however, no less powerful than is Joan's. Margaret's deviousness matches Joan's cynicism, and though she fails to persuade her husband, she is nonetheless highly instrumental in destroying Gloucester.

3 *Henry VI*, 3.2.124–195. "Ay, Edward will . . . pluck it down." Some of the points in this remarkable soliloquy by Richard, Duke of Gloucester, are repeated in his opening soliloquy in *Richard III*, 1.1.1–40, but this one reveals more profoundly and complexly his motive for hating the world and wanting to avenge himself on it. The *3 Henry VI*, 3.2, soliloquy has sometimes, therefore, been spliced into the opening lines in productions of *Richard III* (see "Production History," above). The soliloquy immediately follows King Edward's flirtation with Lady Elizabeth Grey, concluding with Edward's asking her to marry him. Richard and his brother, George, Duke of Clarence, have witnessed the exchange between Edward and Elizabeth, commenting salaciously and cynically about it all the while. This is the background to Richard's opening sarcasm about Edward's "honorable" use of women (3.2.124) and his hateful wish (which is, in effect, a magical malediction) that Edward would be "wasted, marrow, bones, and all" (3.2.125), so that Richard could take his place.

This exclamation is the first of seven distinct stages in Richard's soliloquy, alternating between despair and manic determination and punctuated by sexual references that continually evoke Richard's deep hatred and envy of Edward's success, both political and sexual. The second stage (ll. 128–145) is a despondent admission of the odds against Richard's becoming king, because not only Edward but also Clarence, Henry, and Henry's son, Edward, all stand between Richard and the throne. (Richard will eventually be responsible directly or indirectly for the death of them all except King Edward.) Richard makes the challenge concrete by imagining himself as one who sees a place he would reach across a wide stretch of the sea, and who can do no more than scold the sea in consequence or try to empty it with a ladle (ll. 135–143). In this mood, Richard blames himself for hoping for more than he can possibly have (ll. 137, 144–145).

A brief compensatory thought occurs to him: the happiness he cannot gain through political power he will acquire through sexual conquest (3.2.146–150), but he no sooner thinks of this compensation than he plunges into even deeper despair at the thought of his misshapen body (ll. 151–164). Love cheated him while he was still in the womb, bribing nature to prevent him from sexual satisfaction by withering his arm, putting a hump on his back, and making his legs of unequal length (3.2.154–159). This reference to Richard's own unfortunate fetal experience recalls his earlier wish that Edward's "loins" would be "wasted" (3.2.125–126)—an expressed longing that the lusty Edward would experience the same blasted hopes (both politically and sexually) that Richard himself suffers. Richard's phrase "monstrous fault" (3.2.164) means literally "huge mistake," referring to his thinking that anyone would ever love him, but the phrase also means "unnatural vagina" (see John Astington, "'Fault' in Shakespeare," *Shakespeare Quarterly* 36 [1985]: 330–334), referring to any woman who would accept Richard sexually and referring back both to Richard's wish that Edward would be infertile and to what nature did to Richard in his mother's womb.

"Then" in line 165 signals a logical transition from Richard's sexual despondency to the next phase of his soliloquy: a declaration of compensatory ruthless ambition (3.2.165–171). Richard repeats "I'll make my heaven" (3.2.168; see 148), but he refers now to political power, not to sexual satisfaction. Again, however, he plunges into despair, articulating the most striking and complex image of his soliloquy (3.2.172–181), one that has been more variously interpreted than anything else Richard says (see "Devices and Techniques," above). Imagining again the "many lives" that stand in his way, Richard compares himself to someone in a "thorny wood," who tears the thorns and is torn by them as he hews his way "to find the open air" (3.2.177). So, he says, [I will]

> Torment myself to catch the English crown;
> And from that torment I will free myself,
> Or hew my way out with a bloody axe. (3.2.179–181)

The analogy powerfully evokes Richard's pain and hatred, his suffering and his determination to make others suffer in revenge for his suffering. Paradoxically, the torment he tries to escape is self-inflicted, as if he realizes that the more he tries to escape his pain by inflicting pain on others, the greater his pain will become. Shakespeare returned to a similar insight much later, when he had Macbeth recognize something like Richard's paradox, as Macbeth contemplates murdering Duncan (*Macbeth*, 1.7.1–28).

The final movement in Richard's virtuoso soliloquy is his gleeful recognition that he can, in fact, succeed in his murderous quest through misdirection and hypocrisy (3.2.182–195). Each line in this segment expresses another means or example of deliberate deception: some drawn from nature (the mermaid, the basilisk, the chameleon), some from mythology (Nestor, Ulysses, Sinon, Proteus), and, finally, one from contemporary political philosophy—"the murtherous Machevil" (3.2.193). Richard has not forgotten his torment; he has merely suppressed it. He declares he can "cry 'Content' to that which grieves my heart" (3.2.183), but he has decided on a ruthless course of action from which he will not turn back. It affords him a measure of grim satisfaction and self-confidence: "Can I do this, and cannot get a crown? / Tut, were it further off, I'll pluck it down" (3.2.194–195).

Annotated Bibliography

Berry, Edward. *Patterns of Decay: Shakespeare's Early Histories*. Charlottesville: UP of Virginia, 1975. Examines the images, symbols, themes, and the context of ideas in the *Henry VI* plays and *Richard III*.

Bullough, Geoffrey. *Narrative and Dramatic Sources of Shakespeare*. 8 vols. New York: Columbia UP, 1957–1975, 3 (1960): 23–217. The most accessible version of the chronicle histories and other sources that Shakespeare consulted for his history plays.

Cox, John D. *Shakespeare and the Dramaturgy of Power*. Princeton: Princeton UP, 1989. Sets the *Henry VI* plays against their medieval dramatic background.

Kastan, David Scott. "The Shape of Time: Form and Value in the Shakespearean History Play." *Comparative Drama* 7 (1973): 259–277. The best essay on the distinct generic qualities of Shakespeare's history plays.

Riggs, David. *Shakespeare's Heroical Histories: "Henry VI" and Its Literary Tradition*. Cambridge, MA: Harvard UP, 1971. Places the *Henry VI* plays against the background of Marlowe's *Tamburlaine* and similar plays on the Elizabethan stage.

Tillyard, E.M.W. *Shakespeare's History Plays*. London: Chatto and Windus, 1944. The first critical study of all the history plays and the most influential study for the second half of the twentieth century.

Richard III

Andrew Macdonald and Gina Macdonald

PLOT SUMMARY

1.1. As the play begins the Wars of the Roses are over, and Richard, Duke of Gloucester, who feels discontent with the calm of peace, speaks directly to his audience, making plans to play the villain and seize the throne. With wry irony he describes himself as physically misshapen, rejecting "sportive tricks" (1.1.14). He informs the audience that King Edward IV is ill and possibly dying, and six people stand between Richard and the throne. These include Edward IV's two sons (Edward, Prince of Wales, and Richard, Duke of York) and Edward IV's daughter, Elizabeth. (This play includes three Edwards, two Richards, two Elizabeths, and two Margarets, all of which can prove confusing.) Also in Richard's path stand Richard's older brother George, Duke of Clarence, and Clarence's young son (Edward Plantagenet) and daughter (Margaret Plantagenet). From the start Richard plots to eliminate these relatives in order to seize the throne.

Richard already has begun to put his plan into action, taking steps to make Edward IV distrustful of his brother Clarence's ambition (warning Edward of a prophecy "that G / Of Edward's heirs the murtherer shall be," 1.1.39–40). Fearing this vague prediction, Edward locks the Duke of Clarence (whose first name is George) in the Tower. (Of course, the "G" actually stands for "Gloucester.") Richard seems to sympathize with Clarence and blames the queen and her relatives for Clarence's arrest. As Clarence enters the Tower, the newly released Lord Hastings exits, and Richard tells the audience of his hopes for Edward's quick demise so he, Richard, will have the world "to bustle in" (1.1.152).

1.2. Richard confronts Lady Anne, the widow of Henry VI's son, Edward, Prince of Wales, who was stabbed by Richard at the battle of Tewkesbury. The confrontation takes place during the funeral procession for Edward's father, King Henry VI, also killed by Richard. In spite of Anne's curses at her husband's killer, Richard uses his rhetorical skill and daring to court her, twisting her hate into grudging acceptance of him when he presses his ring on her. He tells the grieving widow that love for her motivated his actions and hence she is to blame for the deaths of her husband and father-in-law. He even gives her his sword and bares his breast, inviting her to take her revenge. In shock from grief and morally confused by Richard's arguments, Anne accepts Richard's unconventional marriage proposal. After she leaves the stage Richard brags, "Was ever woman in this humor won?" (1.2.228). He confides that he does not intend to "keep her long" (1.2.229), for she is but a stepping-stone to the throne.

1.3. Richard next confronts Elizabeth, the Queen Mother, who sees through his stratagems and deceptions. She is accompanied by her brother, Lord Rivers, and her son, Lord Grey. Richard accuses her of plotting against his brother Clarence. Old Queen Margaret, wife of the dead Henry VI and mother of Edward, the dead Prince of Wales, also upbraids Richard, cursing him as a murderer and as a devilish "rooting hog" (1.3.227), alluding to Richard's emblem of a wild boar as well as to his destructive behavior. Most of the scene is an exchange of insults and accusations between these parties. When Sir William Catesby enters to call the group to court, Richard remains, and in a soliloquy admits his plots against them: he will claim that the queen and her party are urging the king to act against Clarence. Richard is proud of his deception, the way he can "clothe" his "naked villainy / . . . And seem a saint" when most he plays "the devil" (1.3.335–337). At the end of the scene, he engages two murderers to kill Clarence, providing them with a warrant for Clarence's execution, having already schemed to divert the blame. He warns the murderers not to be moved by pity for Clarence, who is well spoken. He intercepts the stay of execution so that his henchmen can serve the first warrant and legally execute Clarence.

1.4. Clarence, in the Tower, dreams of drowning in the sea, thrown overboard by Richard while crossing to France; in his dream, which he recounts to his keeper, he thinks about the wrongs he has committed. He then sleeps, only to awaken to Richard's hired men who, having debated their deed, determine to kill him. They allow him to speak and repent his sins committed under his brother Edward's rule before they stab him and then drown him in a vat of Malmsey wine.

2.1. In ironic contrast to the violence of the previous scene, act 2 begins with the dying King Edward, his family gathered around him, apparently achieving peace. Richard announces Clarence's death, and Edward repents of his suspicions of his brother. Because of Richard's devious misdirections, King Edward blames himself for the killing. After Edward is helped offstage, Richard again accuses the queen and her party of responsibility for Clarence's death.

2.2. The Duchess of York and Clarence's two children, Edward and Margaret Plantagenet, are joined by Queen Elizabeth in common mourning for their losses. The queen announces that the king has died. Young Prince Edward is called from Ludlow for his coronation. Buckingham, whom Richard calls his "other self" (2.1.151), agrees to separate the young prince from his family protectors.

2.3. Citizens on the street express their hopes and fears for the future of the young prince and the country. They put their trust in God's providence.

2.4. Elizabeth learns that her defenders, Lord Rivers, Lord Grey, and Sir Thomas Vaughn, have been imprisoned at Pomfret Castle by Richard. Expecting the worst from Richard, Elizabeth seeks sanctuary with her younger son, the Duke of York.

3.1. Buckingham and Richard install the young Prince Edward in the Tower of London (then a palace as well as a prison) and work to remove the young Duke of York from sanctuary to join his brother Edward, as if to await the prince's coronation. Buckingham instructs Catesby to sound out Hastings about making Richard king. Richard adds that Catesby should tell Hastings that Hastings's enemies Rivers, Grey, and Vaughn are to be executed.

3.2. Lord Stanley sends a messenger to Hastings urging him to flee Richard, but Hastings ignores the warning. Catesby arrives to execute Buckingham's commission and finds that Hastings opposes Richard's usurpation. Buckingham enters to accompany Hastings to the Tower, where Hastings is to dine. In an aside Buckingham adds that Hastings will not be leaving the Tower.

3.3. Rivers, Grey, and Vaughn are executed at Pomfret Castle.

3.4. Richard, continuing his guileful manipulation, incongruously sends for strawberries and then, having learned of Hastings's loyalty to King Edward's son, argues the need to execute Hastings immediately in order to forestall an imagined threat of witchcraft, which has supposedly shriveled Richard's arm. Hastings, like most of Richard's other victims, comes to see the evil reality too late and is led off to execution.

3.5. Richard and Buckingham, in rusty, battered armor, convince the Lord Mayor that Hastings, whose head is brought on stage, was a traitor. When the Lord Mayor leaves, Richard sends Buckingham after him to "[i]nfer the bastardy of Edward's children" (3.5.75) and, indeed, of Edward IV himself, in order to further Richard's attempt to seize the throne.

3.6. A scrivener brings the indictment against Hastings on stage, marveling at how arbitrary the so-called justice system is.

3.7. Richard and Buckingham put on a show of piety for the citizenry. Richard walks on a balcony with two clergymen, pretending to be lost in prayer, while Buckingham and Catesby, like modern political spin doctors, work the crowd, denigrating Edward's line and praising Richard. Richard acts as if he cannot tear himself from his devotions, and the citizens of London, taken in by his supposed piety, ask him to accept the crown of England. After a show of reluctance, Richard agrees, and his coronation is immediately scheduled.

4.1. The Queen Mother (Elizabeth), Anne (Duchess of Gloucester), and the Duchess of York learn that Richard has usurped the throne. All three despair of the future. Anne regrets her weakness before Richard's blandishments: "my woman's heart / Grossly grew captive to his honey words, / and prov'd the subject of my own soul's curse" (4.1.78–80).

4.2. Richard tells Buckingham that if they are to consolidate their hold on the kingship, young Edward and his brother must die. Buckingham hesitates at murdering the little princes and asks for time to consider. Richard, typically impatient, seeks out a murderer named Tyrrel and sends him to dispatch the boys. Richard tells Catesby to start rumors that Richard's wife, Anne, is dying. Richard wants to prepare the public for her death so he can marry Edward IV's daughter and so consolidate his hold on the crown. As he says, "I must be married to my brother's daughter, / Or else my kingdom stands on brittle glass" (4.2.60–61). He also arranges a marriage of Margaret, daughter of the Duke of Clarence, to a lowly nobody to neutralize her influence. When Buckingham, still averse to killing Edward IV's sons, requests Richard's promised gift of the earldom of Hereford, Richard replies, "I am not in the giving vein to-day" (4.2.116). Buckingham, who understands Richard's treacherous nature, resolves to abandon him and join Richmond (Henry Tudor, the future Henry VII).

4.3. Tyrrel reports the murder of the young princes to Richard, admitting that even the killers he hired hesitated before destroying the youth and innocence of the princes. Richard has also had Anne killed. He learns that John Morton, Bishop of Ely, and Buckingham have joined Richmond. He reacts with decisive energy, organizing his defenses.

4.4. This scene is full of weeping women as Queen Margaret (widow of King Henry VI) sees Queen Elizabeth (widow of King Edward IV) weep for her dead children as Margaret once wept for her losses; she sees retribution coming full circle. The Duchess of York weeps, too, and all curse Richard as a "hell-hound" (4.4.48), a "carnal cur" (4.4.56), "hell's black intelligencer" (4.4.71), a "bottle spider" and a "foul bunch-back'd toad" (4.4.81) whom they all wish dead, even Richard's own mother. When he enters and confirms the death of Hastings, they curse him to his face, and his mother wishes she had strangled him at birth. Richard's announcement that he has come to woo Queen Elizabeth's daughter demonstrates his unrelenting ambition; Richard even considers using the same argument he had used with Anne: he killed those dearest to her out of love for her. Richard uses all his rhetorical powers to charm a woman whose family he has destroyed. Queen Elizabeth has the good sense at the end to seem to yield to Richard's demands, only to be cursed by him after she leaves as a "Relenting fool, and shallow, changing woman" (4.4.431). She, however, outwits him, for she goes away supposedly to plead his cause to her daughter, but really to seal her daughter's engagement to Richmond.

Ratcliffe and Catesby bring word of Richmond's arrival in England with a large army. Lord Stanley, too, brings word of Richmond and all his supporters, and Richard, fearing his loyalty, makes Stanley leave his son as hostage before joining Richard's supporters on the plains of Salisbury, where the confrontation will occur. A series of messengers bring word of defectors to Richmond's cause, but Buckingham is captured.

4.5. Lord Stanley asks Sir Christopher Urswick to name the defectors to Richmond's cause and sends Richmond a secret letter of support.

5.1. The captured Buckingham repents the crimes he committed in support of Richard.

5.2. An energetic and commanding Richmond exhorts his followers in God's name to help him rid the land of Richard.

5.3. This scene contrasts Richard and his camp with Richmond and his followers. Richard, who pitches his tents in Bosworth Field, has three times as many soldiers as Richmond, but Richard still fears defectors from his ranks. He sends Catesby to remind Lord Stanley of his son's threatened death if Richard is betrayed, even as Stanley meets with Richmond, agreeing to hold back his troops from Richard's support until he can fully act to back up Richmond. Richmond prays, describing himself as God's captain. While Richard sleeps, the ghosts of Richard's victims come one by one (Prince Edward, Henry VI, Clarence, Rivers, Grey, Vaughn, the young Princes, Hastings, Lady Anne, and finally Buckingham) to damn the usurper for his murderous deeds and to praise Richmond and predict his success. Catesby calls Richard's dreams "but shadows" (5.3.215), but they leave Richard unnerved, while Richmond wakes refreshed after sweet dreams; unlike Richard, he has a clear conscience. Then both leaders address their troops before the ensuing battle. Richmond calls on "God and Saint George" (5.3.270) and explains the rightness of their cause against "God's enemy," a phrase he repeats (5.3.252, 253). Richard, the sun hidden in shadows, rejects "conscience" as a "word that cowards use" (5.3.309) and gives a rousing speech that denigrates Richmond's troops as vagabond foreigners who have come to "ravish" English daughters (5.3.337). As the battle begins, Lord Stanley holds back his forces.

5.4. Richard fights bravely in the midst of danger, seeking Richmond, who has many soldiers disguised as him to mislead the enemy. Afoot, Richard calls for a horse but dismisses the loyal Catesby when he tries to provide one.

5.5. Richmond and Richard fight, and Richard is killed. Richmond proclaims, "The day is ours" (5.5.2). Stanley delivers the crown to Richmond, declaring Richard a usurper, and Richmond generously proclaims pardon to all who will now support him as he brings together in unity the houses of Lancaster and of York and thus truly ends the Wars of the Roses by binding up the divisive wounds inflicted by Richard. The unity comes, too, from Richmond and Elizabeth ("the true succeeders of each royal house" of York and Lancaster, 5.5.30) joining in matrimony, with God's blessing. The final lines of the play look forward to a time of peace, plenty, and prosperity, in which civil war is replaced by unity. In these lines Shakespeare confirms the Tudor Myth that saw his queen, Elizabeth I of England, the direct descendent of Richmond's royal line, as part of a dynasty blessed by Heaven.

PUBLICATION HISTORY

The play was written sometime between 1592 and 1594. On the basis of internal evidence, both style and content, scholars connect *Richard III* with the *Henry VI* plays. *Richard III* is the last in Shakespeare's early series of plays exploring the collapse of feudal order in fifteenth-century England. The reference to the play in John Weever's *Epigrams* (1599), a work written two or three years before *Richard III* was published (1597), further suggests an early date, 1593 or 1594, or perhaps even earlier. The Riverside edition of Shakespeare (Boston: Houghton Mifflin, 1997) argues for 1592 as the date, not long after *3 Henry VI*, to which it is a sequel. Francis Meres in *Palladis Tamia* (1598) mentions "*Richard* the 3" as one of Shakespeare's stage works. All Elizabethan publications were supposed to be listed in the Stationers' Register; this play was registered on October 20, 1598, by Andrew Wise.

An anonymous version of *Richard III* had already appeared in London in 1597 (Q1), printed by Valentine Sims ("in Paules Church-yard, at the Signe of the Angell") for Andrew Wise. It was apparently a memorial reconstruction by actors on tour, that is, a bootlegged version written from memory, possibly without a promptbook to consult (though this last fact is in dispute). A reprint of this poor reconstruction was brought out in 1598 (Q2), this time with the name "William Shake-speare" on the title page. Reprints of this quarto recurred in 1602 (Q3), 1605 (Q4), 1612 ("As it hath been lately Acted by the Kings Maiesties seruants"—Q5), and 1622 (Q6), a sign of the play's popularity. A better version of the text was published as the ninth play in the History section of the 1623 Folio edition (F1), with additions, variations, and expansions; yet the play reappeared in the earlier quarto form in 1629 and 1634. The longer, more ornate folio version was set from Q3 or Q6 (or both), yet the quarto edition includes some scenes not in the folio; for instance, the rejection of Buckingham appears only in the second scene of the fourth act of the quarto edition.

The play purports to be a factual history of Richard III, who ruled from 1483 to 1485, though it is, in fact, a patriotic rewriting of the historical record to defend the Lancastrian line and the claim of Henry Tudor, Earl of Richmond, to the English throne. As such, it is often in accord with the historical records available to Shakespeare at the time. The real Richard III, the last of the Yorkist kings, was normal in appearance and popular with his subjects, as the records of the time show and as Josephine Tey makes clear in her modern vindication of him—the mystery novel *Daughter of Time* (1957). He fought with distinction in the Wars of the Roses on the side of the house of York, and he became protector to his thirteen-year-old nephew Edward V. However, he questioned the legitimacy of Edward as heir to the throne, and he imprisoned both Edward (son of Edward IV) and Edward's brother, Richard, Duke of York, in the Tower of London, where they were eventually murdered. The historical record leaves open the question of whether Richard or his successor actually murdered the two young princes.

The Tudor monarchies needed Richard to have been a villain to vindicate their right to the throne through the House of Lancaster. In 1485 Henry Tudor, Earl of Richmond, claimed the crown through the Lancastrian line and led an army to depose Richard. Defeated and killed at the Battle of Bosworth Field, Richard III then became an embarrassment to the line of kings that included Henry VIII and Elizabeth I. Elizabethans very much opposed regicide and saw the king as an analogical equivalent to the deity; therefore, the deposition of Richard III by a Tudor ancestor had to be defended as a just and proper act against a tyrannical monster, especially when Yorkist defenders of Richard persisted, as confirmed in *A Brief Discourse in Praise of King Richard the Third: or an Apology Against the Malicious Slanders and Accusations of his Detracting Adversaries* (1616). Thus, the political chroniclers of the time began to rewrite history to justify the Lancastrian assumption of the throne. In consequence, Shakespeare's play simply follows the propaganda pieces, or rewritten history, to match the Tudor myth: Richard as a secret villain who deceives most of the people of his time—a hunchback with his left shoulder higher than the right, a withered arm, and a cloven foot, a dissembler in league with the devil, committing foul deeds behind a hypocritical smile, malicious, wrathful, and envious. It is significant that the 1559 coronation pageant of Queen Elizabeth I purposely alluded to Richmond's reign.

The text of the play has major problems. The first quarto edition was reported and memorially contaminated, so that while authorities agree that it is an unusually good "bad quarto," it still is unreliable. Moreover, each of the five quarto editions that followed was printed in succession following the quarto that most recently preceded it, so that at each printing the text moved further away from the original and introduced more and more copy errors. Thus, the sixth quarto is the worst one of all, perpetuating the errors introduced in each of the other quartos. Then, too, the First Folio edition is also based on ambiguous authority, having been printed in part from Q3 or Q6, or both. Some sections of the Folio version were corrected from a manuscript that may have been Shakespeare's rough draft ("foul papers") or a transcript of that draft. But much of the Folio text (3.1.1–158; 5.3.48 to the end of the play) was not collated with even this manuscript. Around 190 lines printed in F1 appear nowhere else, though the authoritative Riverside edition (Boston: Houghton Mifflin, 1997) describes these as "closer to Shakespeare's actual text than any other lines in the play" (794). Variations include differences in language as well as content in scenes.

SOURCES FOR THE PLAY

The play builds on the image of Richard III established by the Lancastrian historians who wrote to justify Henry Tudor's seizing the throne. In fact, Shakespeare
must have been familiar with a number of Lancastrian/Tudor works meant to confirm the winning side's version of events. Henry VII commissioned Polydore Vergil's
Historia Anglia (1534) to establish Richard III's reputation as a villain. Vergil had as
a model Thomas More's *History of King Richard the Third* (1513), the Latin version
of which was perhaps the work of John Morton, a strong supporter of the Earl of
Richmond, later Henry VII, and a mortal enemy of Richard III. Morton has a small
role in Shakespeare's play, where he appears as the Bishop of Ely. As More's respected patron, Morton must have had some influence on his version of events, for
Morton could provide the younger man with firsthand accounts of events. More
cites contemporary testimony, often repeating the phrase "as men constantly say."
A mutilated English version of More's *History* was printed in Richard Grafton's continuation of John Hardyng's *Chronicle* (1543) and then reprinted by Edward Hall in
his *Union . . . of Lancaster and York* (1548). Historians Raphael Holinshed and John
Stow both include the detail Shakespeare uses about the bleeding corpse of Henry
VI (1.2.55–56). Richard III also is treated in the first two editions of *A Mirror for
Magistrates* (1559 and 1563). In 1579 a three-part Senecan tragedy (based on Hall's
history) appeared in Latin, *Richardus Tertius*, by Thomas Legge, Master of Caius
College, Cambridge. This work was followed in the early 1590s by an anonymous
English play entitled *True Tragedy of Richard III*, which appeared in print in 1594.
Shakespeare's familiarity with this source is confirmed by quotations borrowed
from it in *Hamlet*.

In converting a prose tale to a poetic and theatrical one, Shakespeare added a
dramatic structure based on contrasts and employing the artificiality of blank verse,
stichomythia (rhyming lines of alternating speakers), antithesis, and wordplay. He
also added minor clues to character, such as Richard's feigned refusal of the kingship followed by his clever acceptance speech. However, many details of plot and
character derive from his sources, as do many turns of phrase and concrete details
of time and place. For example, where More says, "[B]efore such great things, men's
hearts of a secret instinct of nature misgive them; as the sea without wind swells of
itself sometimes before a tempest" (*Richard III: The Great Debate*, ed. Paul Kendall
[London: Folio Society, 1965], 67), Shakespeare writes, "Before the days of change,
still is it so. / By a divine instinct men's minds mistrust / Ensuing danger; as by
proof we see / The water swell before a boist'rous storm" (2.3.41–44).

STRUCTURE AND PLOTTING

Shakespeare builds his play on the medieval pattern of the wheel of fortune, the
rise and fall of a great man as the wheel turns. In the opening scene, after his first
soliloquy describing himself on an upward progress toward the crown, Richard encounters, in effect, an emblem of the wheel turning, as Clarence enters the Tower
and, at the very same time, Hastings is freed. As the fortune of one player sinks, the
fortune of another rises, and vice versa. As the play progresses, the audience witnesses Richard's seemingly unstoppable march toward power and kingship. As he
rises ever higher on the wheel of fortune, it seems almost as if he will break the pat-

tern and continue his reign of terror ever upward and onward. Mark Rose in *Shakespearean Design* (Cambridge, MA: Belknap P of Harvard UP, 1972) notes that Shakespeare intentionally delays the turn of the wheel in Richard's case in order to achieve a strong psychological effect: the audience fears that providence no longer orders the human pattern and that Richard will get away with his damnable deeds. Thus, the turn of the wheel, what Rose calls "the delayed center" (133), does not come until 4.2. This pivotal point, the seventeenth scene, is short, just over a hundred lines, but it marks the beginning of the end for Richard.

This scene begins with the kingmaker, Buckingham, escorting the newly crowned King Richard to his throne; the men walk arm in arm. Both are at the zenith of their fortunes, but Richard is already anticipating problems; using the royal "we," he asks Buckingham whether the new king will "wear these glories for a day?" (4.2.15) or whether they will last. Fear of being deposed drives him to ask Buckingham to rid him of the young princes, but Buckingham's hesitation at accepting the murderous task spells Buckingham's doom. At his moment of triumph, he is already on his way out. While Buckingham takes a moment to consider what to do, Richard has already dismissed him, fearing his rival's own growing power and independence. Moments earlier Buckingham was the second-most powerful man in the kingdom. Now he must leave quickly in disgrace and flee for safety. In those interim moments, a mere fifty-five lines, Richard has sent for and interviewed Tyrrel, a desperate man ready to murder the child princes to fill his purse. Richard learns that the Marquess Dorset has fled to Richmond, and Richard has begun to remember and fear predictions that Richmond would be king. Thus, this short scene marks the rise and fall of Buckingham and prepares viewers for the upcoming fall of Richard. Rose calls the scene "an emblematic design, a picture of fortune's turning wheel" (134). Richard has had his way for so long that he has begun to think of himself as in control of the wheel, when, in fact, it is turning inexorably on its own, moving toward his loss of fortune, power, and life.

Other carefully structured emblematic designs provide variations on a theme or significant contrasts. For example, the scene of Clarence's death (1.4) divides into two sections. In the first, Clarence relates to the jailer his prophetic dream of Richard's striking him overboard into the English Channel, where he drowns. The dream includes an undersea vision, a memento mori image that suggests the vanity of earthly pride symbolized by the gold, pearls, and jewels scattered uselessly across the ocean floor. This vision is followed by a dream of hell and of the ghosts of those Clarence had injured. Close upon Clarence's dream comes its fulfillment: the entrance of his killers and his murder. However, the villains engage in a comic debate on conscience versus reward before killing Clarence. Together, the two parts of the scene explore the question of conscience—that of Clarence and that of his murderers. In terms of the totality of the play, this early scene provides a pattern that is confirmed and repeated at the play's end, when Richard faces the ghosts of men he murdered and thrusts conscience behind him as he leads more men to needless death. A balanced sequence also occurs at the conclusion to reinforce the idea of conscience, for Richard's damning ghosts, reminding him of his terrible deeds, turn to Richmond and bless him. Richard sleeps the restless sleep of the guilty, plagued by conscience and beset by nightmares, while Richmond sleeps the peaceful sleep of the innocent. As Richard's wheel turns downward, Richmond's fortune rises and so does England's. Ironically, the image of the wheel's turning and the sets of balanced contrasts suggest closer ties than might be intended. The young prince, the Duke of York, in parodying his uncle's gait suggests the genetic ties that link them. Furthermore, the closeness of Richard and Richmond's names and the wheel's turning upward for Richmond at the play's end, as it turned upward for Richard at the play's beginning, suggest the shared nature of human fate.

MAIN CHARACTERS

Richard III

The character of Richard, Duke of Gloucester and then King of England, is central to the play. Except for Hamlet, his role is the longest of any Shakespearean creation. If he is not on stage, he is just offstage spying and scheming. Through this historical construct, Shakespeare must make clear why so many of his real, historical contemporaries might have thought highly of Richard (that is, he must explain Richard's positive public image); yet at the same time he must confirm the Tudor image of Richard as a Machiavellian figure in the most negative sense of that term, a man who manipulated people and situations to his own devious and devilish ends. Thus, Shakespeare must deal with the facts that Richard persuaded Anne, whose father-in-law and husband were supposedly murdered by Richard, to marry him and that Queen Elizabeth, whose sons he supposedly murdered, left sanctuary and remained at court after he assumed the throne, and even allowed him to court her daughter. Shakespeare must also provide some credible explanation of how Richard could have become king in the first place, ruled well for about two years, and persuaded a large army of decent, honorable Englishmen to support him in the field. Were his supporters capable of some Orwellian form of "doublethink," denying the evidence of their senses, or were they truly convinced of his virtues? Shakespeare's solution is to depict a complex figure, one with a pious public facade behind which lurks a pure malevolency. Richard's frequent soliloquies allow the audience to see what none of the characters can discern about Richard's true nature.

This dichotomy between seeming and reality is clear from specific strategies that Richard uses to gain the crown. These strategies include masking his true intentions, confusing the issue, removing obstacles to his goal, and engaging in indirect manipulation. He cloaks his true intentions again and again, wooing Anne by telling her he killed for love of her, vowing to Rivers that he does not want the crown, asserting his wholehearted devotion to Edward IV, and convincing the Lord Mayor that Hastings was a traitor and so deserved to die. In 3.7 he makes a show of refusing the crown, later accepting it only when seemingly urged to do so by the citizenry. He lodges the young princes in the Tower, supposedly for their safety, and he asks Queen Elizabeth for young Elizabeth's hand because of love, or so he says. Richard confuses situations by instigating dissention among those who oppose him and by spreading rumors that did not exist until he began them. For instance, he convinces Hastings and Buckingham that the queen's faction is responsible for Clarence's imprisonment. Likewise, he tells Edward IV of the plot of "G," knowing Clarence will be suspected. Then, he convinces Clarence's children that Edward IV is responsible for their father's death and points out the "guilty looks" of the queen's faction to Buckingham after Clarence's murder. He also manufactures a story about Edward IV's sexual misbehavior and of the princes' illegitimacy. Another of his strategies is to remove any obstacles to his goal early on. Thus, he murders Clarence before King Edward IV dies and woos and marries Anne. He imprisons and executes (or assures the execution of) the queen's supporters—Lord Rivers, Grey, and Vaughn. He imprisons the young princes and arranges their deaths, solicits the help of Buckingham with promises of rewards, and lessens public resistance to his ascendance with claims of the illegitimacy of the princes and stories of Edward IV's licentiousness. Usually, in order to maintain his public image, he relies on indirection, wherever possible getting others to do his dirty work so he can claim ignorance of the deed. He hires murderers to take care of Clarence and the princes for him, lets the state execute Rivers, Grey, Vaughn, and Hastings for him, and gets Buckingham to convince the citizens that he should be king while avowing no interest in the crown.

Because Richard confides in his audience through soliloquies and asides and thus reveals his duality, the public saint, the private schemer, he is the most well-rounded character of this play—witty, forceful, intelligent, tricky, duplicitous, and charming, a psychologically convincing personality. In Shakespearean tragedy, malevolence will triumph for a while because of its fascination, trickiness, and power, but it eventually collapses from the weight of its own plots, bringing down many good people with it but leaving hope for the future in a good man who surveys the destruction and learns a moral lesson from it. Thus, Richard is indisputably the most interesting character in the play, much more interesting than the good Richmond. In fact, Michael Neill in "Shakespeare's Halle of Mirrors" calls him "the only lively moral positive in the play" (*Shakespeare Studies* 8 [1975]: 103). Richard is strongest at the play's beginning but declines rapidly. At the end, though we may admire his bravery, his credibility as a force that could cause so much destruction is severely undermined as we see him offering to trade his kingdom for a horse. He is no longer superhuman, but a man. Evil has collapsed of its own weight, and can be defeated.

Anne

His victims, in contrast, are stick figures. Anne, the sweet moral wife, is clearly innocent of evil and falls prey to Richard. She mourns her dead husband and father-in-law and initially seems strong as she curses Richard. However, she then unaccountably yields to Richard's forceful wooing. Her function is passive: to be used, abused, and discarded. The pattern of seeming strength followed by weakness in the face of Richard's assault is repeated in the other women in the play, strong in their hatred but overcome by his opposing presence. Through Anne's relationship with Richard, Shakespeare begins the play's investigation of the effects of evil on helpless innocence. Clarence appears on stage under arrest, for which he blames the queen and her brother. He goes to his grave believing the wrong brother (Edward IV) has had him killed. The princes hardly have time to be distinguished from one another before their piteous demise, though the younger one's infelicitous jokes about being small enough to ride like an ape on his uncle's hunched shoulders makes his death inevitable. Hastings, a decent and sympathetic character, the epitome of loyalty, believes implicitly in Richard's good public face and in his commitment to the line of succession, until the command for his execution rudely awakens him to the truth. His affair with Lady Jane Shore, the former king's mistress, makes him vulnerable to rumor and innuendo, but his gestures to make peace with the opposition are genuine, as are his firm support of Richard and his belief in his goodwill until the very end. Lord Rivers, brother to Lady Elizabeth Grey (who marries King Edward and becomes Queen Elizabeth), stands in the way of Richard's ambitions simply because he is the queen's brother, just as Lord Grey, Queen Elizabeth's younger son, and Sir Thomas Vaughn, one of Queen Elizabeth's allies, also block Richard's ambitions and thus are executed at Pomfret. They function in this play chiefly as victims who highlight Richard III's cruelty and ambition.

Buckingham

The aristocratic Buckingham, Richard's cousin, stands as Richard's right-hand man throughout his rise to power, playing the political game to eliminate the Lancaster opposition—both his enemies and Richard's—and manipulating the populace and their understanding of Richard to help propel him to the throne. Later, seeing Richard's ingratitude to those who have supported him and his fear of any whose power might be great enough to threaten him, Buckingham flees while he still has his head and properties. Even he, however, is merely Richard's cat's-paw and then his victim. Buckingham is powerful but finally two-dimensional.

Lord Stanley

Lord Stanley is bound to Richard against his will, for Richard holds his son hostage to assure Stanley's support in battle. However, once Stanley can act, he joins Richmond to topple Richard and avenge his dead relatives. He functions to create sympathy for all the parents whose children Richard has threatened and destroyed. In contrast is Catesby, the most developed of Richard's henchmen, a man who is willing to do whatever his lord requires as long as a reward is forthcoming. He is the cat, who acts with the rat (Ratcliffe), to serve the boar, that is, to do Richard's bidding. He is one of the few to remain loyal to Richard to the end, yet his loyalty on the final battlefield meets with Richard's disdain.

DEVICES AND TECHNIQUES

In order to contrast the public face of Richard with the private reality, Shakespeare has Richard indict himself through soliloquies (self-revealing monologues) and asides to the audience. That is, Shakespeare has Richard testify against himself, a dramatic technique not found in Shakespeare's sources and clearly an innovative addition to make credible the disjunction between the public and the private man. Thus, the play begins with a powerful soliloquy in which Richard tells his audience directly that he is jealous of his brother and is "determined to prove a villain" (1.1.30). Soliloquies follow thereafter at the end of the first and second scenes, and near the end of the third scene. These initial four soliloquies establish beyond a doubt Richard's evil nature and evil goals. In the second soliloquy, Richard shares with his audience his plans for taking power, while in the third he confirms his techniques and strategies in a self-congratulatory way; in the fourth, he spells out his hypocrisy: playing the saint when most he acts the devil, bragging about his "secret mischiefs" and "naked villainy" (1.3.324, 335). Once this characterization has been made, Shakespeare drops the soliloquy until the final act, after the confrontation with the ghosts but before the battle (5.3.178–207). At this point, Richard confesses that he believes he has done his work; the goal of his first soliloquy attained, he affirms, "I am a villain" (5.3.191).

Throughout the play, Richard's asides also serve as reminders of the dark reality that the soliloquies reveal and as comments on the reality that lies behind appearances. For instance, having flattered Queen Elizabeth, Richard turns to the audience to tell us what he really thinks about her, "Relenting fool, and shallow, changing woman" (4.4.431). Jaunty asides pronounced like proverbs but damning in their indifference to the fate of others reveal how much he enjoys his dastardly deeds, as when he says of the young princes, their lives soon to be cut short by murder, "So wise so young, they say do never live long" and "Short summers likely have a forward spring" (3.1.79, 94). Such confidences, in the form both of asides and of soliloquies spoken directly to the audience, shape our interpretation of his nature and explain the puzzle of how a seemingly decent king could really be so deserving of his untimely fate. Together these confidences make the audience almost co-conspirators with Richard, a psychological strategy designed to help Shakespeare's contemporaries understand the attraction Richard held for his supporters and to experience grudging admiration for a character they know they should and must condemn. Thus Shakespeare transmutes propagandistic history into art, showing the complex human dimension that informs all great tragedies.

Shakespeare also relies heavily on imagery to make his case. He replaces the conventional portrait of the good and fatherly king, God's agent on Earth, with the shocking picture of an evil, selfish ruler who, like the devil, serves only himself. Throughout the play, hellish references compare Richard to a devil in human form, and clusters of animal images debase his nature. As with the soliloquies, however, Shakespeare uses key images revelatory of Richard's inner nature mainly in the first and final acts. In 1.2 Anne curses Richard as a devil (1.2.45, 50, 73), a beast (1.2.71), a hedgehog (1.2.102), and a toad (1.2.147). Margaret in 1.3 reinforces these images, calling him a dog (1.3.215), a hog (1.3.237), a spider (1.3.241), a toad (1.3.245), and the devil (1.3.117). The toad image, which the duchess also uses in 4.4.145, emphasizes not only a repulsive lower life form but also visually captures the image of a hunchback. So too does the animal most appropriately associated with Richard, the boar of his coat of arms and of his nickname. In act 5 Richmond denounces Richard as "The wretched, bloody, and usurping boar," a "foul swine" whose traits are made repulsively clear: he "spoil'd your summer fields and fruitful vines, / Swills your warm blood like wash, and makes his trough / In your embowell'd bosoms" (5.2.7–10). These images reflect both Richard's physical and his spiritual deformities, a connection conventionally made at the time: his misshapen form indicates his misshapen spirit.

Richard is also an actor who can lay plots and "inductions dangerous" (1.1.32), who, Buckingham says, comes "upon [his] cue" (3.4.26), and who "counterfeit[s] the deep tragedian" (3.5.5). He is the playwright/director who controls other characters, as when he orchestrates the scenes with the Lord Mayor in 3.5 and 3.7. In the former scene he instructs Buckingham rather as Hamlet later advises the players at Elsinore:

> Come, cousin, canst thou quake and change thy color,
> Murther thy breath in middle of a word,

> And then again begin, and stop again,
> As if thou were distraught and mad with terror? (3.5.1–4)

Richard is also the leading actor in his self-created drama, always playing to an audience, whether that be the citizens in 3.7, the peers in 3.4, or the paying customers whom he addresses in his soliloquies.

Another recurring and significant image is that of Richard as a "shadow in the sun" (1.1.26), an image Richard himself introduces in his first soliloquy—one that he and Queen Margaret both repeat throughout act 1 and that recurs in the final act when Shakespeare describes how Richard cast his shadow over the kingdom so that the sun does not shine over his last battle (5.3.278–287). Traditionally, a king in both medieval and Renaissance hierarchies was the analogical correspondent to the sun; but Richard, as a false king, blots out the sun and instead brings darkness to the kingdom. Only a true king can cast out the shadows and restore the sun and light. For a Renaissance audience schooled in analogy, the shadow-sun image would also be tied directly to the devil-God image, with the false king corresponding to the devil, darkness, and deception and the true king corresponding to God, the sun, and the heavenly light of truth.

The contrast is heightened by the imagery associated with Richmond. In his oration to his troops, Richmond refers to Richard as "God's enemy" (5.3.252, 253) and declares that God sides with Richmond's forces. Richmond mentions God six times in that speech. Richard does not name God even once in his address to his soldiers. Whereas Richard is cursed by the ghosts of all his victims, Richmond is praised. Richard's sleep is one of restless nightmare; Richmond, in turn, enjoys "the sweetest sleep and fairest-boding dreams / That ever ent'red in a drowsy head" (5.3.227–228). Richard appeals to the baser motives of his soldiers: their prejudices against the French as Breton "scum" (5.3.317), "vagabonds, rascals, and runaways" (5.3.316) and their fear of insults to their manhood (an enemy who will ravish their wives and daughters—5.3.336–337). Richmond, in contrast, focuses his rousing cry to battle on patriotism and high ideals. Richard calls on his followers to follow him "hand in hand to hell" (5.3.313), while Richmond proclaims the fight for "God and St. George!" (5.3.270).

The contrast is also heightened by the allegorical nature of relationships. As in the morality plays of the medieval church, in which good angels and impish devils competed for the soul of Everyman, Richard competes with Richmond for the soul of England. The allegorical nature of the play is clear from the initial scene with Anne, a microcosm or scene in miniature of the overall allegory. Anne is a good woman who must choose between her own conscience and her sense of right on the one hand and, on the other, the flattery of Richard, who pits his wits and claims to love against the silent, bleeding body of Henry VI, fresh from slaughter. Richard's argument that love for Anne made him kill Henry VI and her husband seems absurd in the face of a dead man and a grieving widow, but Shakespeare makes Anne succumb to evil because she is unable to understand deception and accepts false avowals of love as genuine. Psychological realism is not the point. From a Renaissance perspective, Richard is a devious seducer, misleading both Anne and the English public, even in the face of irrefutable proof of his villainy.

Just as Anne cannot believe the depths of Richard's depravity and thus accepts him at his word, so the English public was blind to his true nature and accepted

him as king, as Anne accepted him as her husband, lord, and master, in the analogical correlatives considered natural in the period. In turn, just as Anne was but
a stepping-stone to the throne, soon to be discarded in favor of a more prestigious
and valuable alliance, so England would have been betrayed by Richard had not
Richmond come to her rescue. The parallel final scene in which Richard tries to
win Elizabeth's permission to woo her daughter, only to learn she has been affi-
anced to Richmond, marks the shift Shakespeare has hoped to make in his audience. Unlike Anne, Elizabeth understands Richard's nature and tricks him, as he
has tricked others. Her conversations with Richard are merely biding time until
Richard can be overcome.

Shakespeare also uses conventional poetic patterns of language to carry his argument. One pattern, called stichomythia, alternates single lines of dialogue between two characters, characterized by the stylized sense of a debate or a
confrontation of opposing views. Shakespeare uses this technique, for example, in
the confrontation between Anne and Richard. The following passage is typical in
its give and take:

> *Anne*: I would I knew thy heart.
>
> *Richard*: 'Tis figur'd in my tongue.
>
> *Anne*: I fear me both are false.
>
> *Richard*: Then never was man true.
>
> *Anne*: Well, well, put up your sword.
>
> *Richard*: Say then my peace is made.
>
> *Anne*: That shalt thou know hereafter.
>
> *Richard*: But shall I live in hope?
>
> *Anne*: All men, I hope, live so.
>
> *Richard*: Vouchsafe to wear this ring.
>
> *Anne*: To take is not to give. (1.2.192–202)

Another stylized verbal strategy is to give contrasting characters balanced lines of
opposed meaning:

> *Richard*: Sweet saint, for charity, be not so curst.
>
> *Anne*: Foul devil, for God's sake hence, and trouble us not. (1.2.49–50)

>   *   *   *
>
> *Richard*: Fairer than tongue can name thee, let me have
> Some patient leisure to excuse myself.
>
> *Anne*: Fouler than heart can think thee, thou canst make
> No excuse current but to hang thyself. (1.2.81–84)

Stichomythia to suggest the antagonism between characters and the battle of wits
recurs in the final scene between Queen Elizabeth and Richard (4.4.343–377), as he
struggles to bend her to his will and as she struggles to protect herself and her
daughter long enough for Richmond to assure their safety.

Still another strategy is to have Richard ask the audience rhetorical questions,
that is, questions to make them think about a situation, but not a question to which

he expects an answer. For instance, in the scene with Anne, Richard asks his audience (or perhaps simply himself) with wonder, "Was ever woman in this humor woo'd? / Was ever woman in this humor won?" (1.2.227–228).

Other recurring devices include prophecies of revenge, particularly made by the women in the play, who come to serve a function like that of Cassandra in Greek plays, foretelling doom. The prophecies are tied directly to promises of divine retribution, particularly voiced by Margaret, and to dreams. In fact, the word "dream" and its cognates appear more often in *Richard III* than they do in any other Shakespearean play. There are King Edward IV's dreams of danger, Stanley's dream of the boar razing his helm, Anne's belief that Richard dreams of butchery, Richard, Richmond, and Clarence's dreams, and Queen Margaret's calling Queen Elizabeth "A dream of what thou wast" (4.4.88) because Richard would destroy Elizabeth's happiness. Scene after scene shows Richard's victims bemoaning their fates just before their deaths, so that the audience bears witness to repeated condemnations of Richard. The women of the play, dressed in black, form tableaus of grief and mourning that remind the audience of the violated ties of kinship.

THEMES AND MEANINGS

In the history plays, Shakespeare converts literal history into "mythological" history. He must, as Hardin Craig points out in his edition of Shakespeare (Glenview, IL: Scott, Foresman, 1951, 300), support the Lancastrian line of succession and attack the opposing claims of the Yorkists as both selfish and inspired by the devil. Thus, Shakespeare, a good patriot, shows that, while the course of England's throne did not always run smooth, its more embarrassing moments were deviations from the norm, just as the devil's subversion often disrupts God's orderly and just earthly rule. Shakespeare's solution to dramatizing such highly sensitive subjects as regicide and usurpation was to balance carefully the demands of Tudor legitimacy with those of dramatic and historical credibility, to pull together elements from very different and sometimes contradictory traditions (the morality play, medieval allegory, Machiavelli, the historical pageant) to make Richard a believable figure, one who plays on the credulity not only of characters within the play but also of the audience itself so that there is justification for having believed him good (as did the doomed Hastings) and so that his hidden nature is revealed in damning fashion. The play shows that it is hard for good, innocent people to recognize evil and that it takes some subtlety to expose the reality of bad men disguised as good.

Ironically, it ill serves the Tudor cause to have Richmond easily defeat a villain. Instead, to heighten his stature and to make him worthy of the kingship, Shakespeare must restore to Richard some measure of nobility at the end of the play. Thus, though justly defeated by the noble Richmond, he fights a brave fight, wading in forcefully and honorably among his enemies in hand-to-hand combat. His famous line "my kingdom for a horse!" (5.4.6) provides a final image of the witty, daring figure who has shared his plans so intimately with the audience, a man with high ambitions and the courage to face angry women and fierce enemies. Richmond's military prowess and kingly power depend on his having a worthy foe in the final confrontation, and Shakespeare makes Richard ultimately a warrior who stays the course even when the battle turns against him.

Through Richard's relentless pursuit of the crown Shakespeare explores the question of the use or value of power, for having once attained the throne, Richard finds no pleasure in it and simply becomes the center of plots to remove him. The retribution of the power hungry reveals the emptiness of the attainment and the new fears of plots and schemes like those in which Richard himself engaged. However, the conclusion returns to the Renaissance political ideal: evil scourged, the country renewed by a just and rightful king, the return of "smooth-faced peace," smiles, and plenty as "fair prosperous days" lie ahead (5.3.33, 34). Like other of Shakespeare's history plays, *Richard III* shows the evil of civil war and the good that comes from unity. As Shakespeare writes in his next history play, *King John*, "Nought shall make us rue, / If England to itself do rest but true" (5.7.117–118).

CRITICAL CONTROVERSIES

Critical controversy centers around two key questions: the nature of Richard and the wooing of Anne. Both controversies hinge on the difficulty of mistaking the complex for the simple or of fitting Renaissance ideas into medieval frames. Modern readers expect realism, while Shakespeare's audience was more accepting of icon, metaphor, and tableau.

The nature of Richard, the type and degree of his evil, and its relevance to Shakespeare's argument has been a subject of critical controversy for a long time. Nineteenth-century critic Edward Dowden believed Richard was dominated by an internal necessity to release upon the world the force and the will that drove him (quoted in Arthur Eastman, *A Short History of Shakespearean Criticism* [New York: Random House, 1968], 147–148). In *Shakespeare Studies* (New York: Macmillan, 1927) E. E. Stoll called Richard a man turned inside out or upside down, beyond the pale (Eastman, 211). Caroline Spurgeon (*Shakespeare's Imagery and What It Tells Us* [Cambridge: Cambridge UP, 1935]) found the animal imagery indicative of the baseness of the man, while Bernard Spivack in *Shakespeare and the Allegory of Evil* (New York: Columbia UP, 1958) turned to the medieval stock figure of Vice as an older source—for the Vice figure played on human frailty and gullible honesty to confound and mislead his human victims, as do Richard and his fellow devil/vice figure Iago, of *Othello*. Bettie Anne Doebler agrees. Michael Torrey and Richard Marienstras explore the monstrous qualities of Richard, while Vance Adair provides a poststructuralist exploration of and explanation for Richard's evil. Shakespeare's difficulty in *Richard III* is to explain how a monster like the Richard of Tudor Myth could have been supported and praised by so many worthy Englishmen. Simply to make him unquestionably evil is to call into question the honesty and virtue of decent men whose children and grandchildren supported Elizabeth in Shakespeare's day. Thus, he must find a way to suggest a dichotomy between outward seeming and inner reality, between the public image and the real man. At the same time, he will lessen Richmond's success if he depicts a Richard who was easily conquered. Richard must be a worthy foe in battle, one whose fall proves Richmond's worth.

The modern controversy over Richard's wooing of Anne relates directly to this same conflict. Shakespeare places this scene early in the play to emphasize its significance. It is very short, only 193 lines, and its substance is outrageous by the standards of realism—an angry woman mourning the deaths of two saintly men, her husband and her father-in-law, persuaded by their killer to wed him, despite his misshapen body and aggressive approach. Critics have tried to explain the scene as an example of the hypnotic fascination of danger, like that governing a small, defenseless animal facing a cobra, or as a medieval tableau of evil overpowering good—the dark demon pulling down the naive and innocent angel. Yet all admit the risk that the scene will fail and the audience will find it unbelievable. The Olivier film version breaks the scene into two parts to make it a little more credible: the first, full of Anne's curses and firm resistance but with signs that her feminine side has been flattered; the second, a yielding and melting in the face of seeming passion and seeming love.

One explanation that makes sense in terms of Renaissance practice and Shakespearean rhetoric is that the wooing scene is a summary, a prefiguring of events to come. In the rest of the play Richard goes on to woo England as he has wooed Anne, with pretense, feigned emotions, and unfair stratagems. That he can take a woman in such a state and win her as his wife prepares his audience to understand how virtuous Englishmen could succumb so easily to an obviously evil man: they were seduced as Anne is seduced. The violation of her innocence is the first in a series of such episodes. Richard's weapon is language, his virtuosity in twisting the truth and constructing an image that suits his needs and those of his listeners. Anne curses him, as do Queen Margaret, Queen Elizabeth, the Duchess of York, and many others who fall victim to his ambition, but curses fail to overcome him and to counter his quest to seize the future. The wooing scene begins with Anne on a fixed course and in the role of grieving widow and daughter-in-law, spitting on Richard. However, once Richard stops the funeral procession and offers the mourner his sword to strike him down he wins control because she is incapable of murder and confused by his reversal of blame: he claims that she is responsible for her husband's death because she won Richard's heart and made him pursue her. By force of personality, he triumphs over her; as the funeral procession continues on its way, Richard reinforces his accomplishment, asking the audience, in effect, if they can really believe what they have seen. This scene past, the audience is ready to believe anything about Richard's rhetorical skill in capturing England. If he could woo and win Anne in such a humor, he is capable of anything. His coldhearted willingness to take advantage of a grieving mourner makes credible his coldhearted willingness to take advantage of a grieving nation, to play on the weaknesses and vulnerabilities of its cities, to break the rules of civilized behavior, to murder his wife and his nephews and to deserve a mother's curses.

PRODUCTION HISTORY

According to Philip Henslowe's *Diary*, which records performances at his theater, the Rose, *Richard III* was performed on December 30, 1593, but was not then noted as new. It was repeated three times in the next month. Records also show that on November 15, 1633, the play was performed by the King's Men at St. James's Palace for the queen's birthday.

George C. D. Odell's two-volume *Shakespeare from Betterton to Irving* (New York: Scribner, 1920) provides a sound historical survey of productions, beginning with Colley Cibber's most famous Shakespearean adaptation: the 1700 Drury Lane production of *Richard III*. Cibber interpolated bits and pieces from 2 *Henry VI*, *Henry V*, and *Richard II* into his version of the play, particularly the scene in which Northumberland learns of the death of Hotspur. Cibber added fourteen lines from the fourth chorus of *Henry V* to Richard's eve-of-battle soliloquy (lines most out of character for Richard) and numerous other bits and pieces that transformed Shakespeare's play into something quite different from the original. Cibber also omitted many passages, such as Clarence's dream and Margaret's curses, and, more significantly, Richard's opening soliloquy, which Cibber thought would be too fearful. He also added his own lines, in which, for example, Richard tells Anne he finds her boring and means to marry another, and a scene in which Elizabeth says farewell to her sons. Cibber's play opened with Richard's murder of King Henry VI. Richard's famous line "Off with his head; so much for Buckingham" was written by Cibber, as was the line "Richard's himself again!" In this version Richard, played by Cibber himself, was a melodramatic egomaniac, a monster, and a criminal, without the subtlety or complexity of Shakespeare's creation. Yet this version of Shakespeare's play dominated the productions for at least a hundred years. Frank Benson's 1910 film followed some of Cibber's stage traditions, including having an assertive actress play the young prince Edward, and the credits to the modern (1955) Olivier film production note an indebtedness to Cibber.

On March 12, 1821, the manager of Covent Garden produced a new version of the play, omitting the interpolations of Cibber and largely presenting Shakespeare's original, restoring characters like Queen Margaret and Clarence. Some critics of the time found Shakespeare's version inferior to Cibber's and the actor who played Richard good at bursts of anger (especially when he exposes his deformed arm to prove witchcraft done to him in 3.4) but not as controlled and diffident as he should have been. Edmund Kean, another famous nineteenth-century actor, also performed *Richard III*. He starred at Drury Lane in the late 1830s, returning to the Colly Cibber interpretation and lines to make Richard an unrelenting and deformed monster. William Hazlitt, the critic from the Romantic period, described Kean's "smooth and smiling villainy" as Richard employs "wily adulation" and humility to smooth his way with Anne (quoted in Eastman, 113–114). In 1848 Samuel Phelps brought out a production of the original play at Sadler's Wells, but the actors refused to adhere to the script and kept bringing in lines and scenes from the Cibber version. In 1877 Henry Irving finally restored the play, though severely cut, for performance at the Lyceum. In March of 1889 the ambitious Richard Mansfield played Richard at the Globe Theatre. He tried, without great success, to revive Shakespeare's version of Richard and took the production to America. In the 1890s actor Henry Irving transformed *Richard III* from a tragedy to an artistic and unrealistic study of court manners. His Richard is an amusing character who tickles his audience with humor, not with subtle and conspiratorial evil.

The character of Richard III provides an opportunity for a star actor to dominate the play and the stage. Consequently, the tension in many productions is between Richard's role as villain and the way in which he ingratiates himself with his audience, confiding in them, joking with them, bringing them to share in his plans and even, as silent witnesses, in his culpability. He is a whole being, a modern man, bustling about in his world and making things go his way, whereas the other characters are like figures in a medieval morality play in their style and manner, icons rather than real people. Through the delivery of Richard's final line, "A horse, a horse! my kingdom for a horse" (5.4.13), and through his physical bearing, intonation, and weight of utterance, lead actors have traditionally tried to capture some sense of the gutsiness and defiance of fate that can make Richard likable in spite of his disgusting deeds. According to John Russell Brown, in *Shakespeare's Plays in Performance* (London: Edward Arnold, 1966), Ian Holm at Stratford-upon-Avon in 1962 (with Peter Hall as director) played Richard as childish and peevish, sitting alone after the scene with the two religious men (in this production soldiers comically disguised) and kicking his heels. Holm emphasized Richard's enormous ego, stressing the words "I" even above the word "fear" (4.4.477). Holm's Richard simply became violent and more furious, asserting himself loudly and vocally and engaging in taxing fights, so the audience would feel that at the end a monster had been rightly stopped. In the Holm production, Richard struck Catesby a blow when he offered help, but then his voice failed at the end so that his final cry for a horse sounded both weak and mad; his death agonies were prolonged in good Elizabethan fashion: Richard performed his final writhing close to the audience, "at the center of a vast empty stage" (Brown, 213). Holm thus provided the audience only the possibilities of disgust and aversion at the end. Alec Guinness restored complexity to the role in the 1953 Stratford Festival Production in Ontario.

Brown finds traces in this play of "an earlier iconographic style of acting and stage-management" (45), and in fact such iconographic images run throughout the play. For example, just before Hastings leaves for London and the trap Richard will stage for him, Shakespeare introduces two new characters identified by costume and bearing as a pursuivant, representing the affairs of the world, and a priest, representing the affairs of heaven—their function like that of the bad and good angel of the earlier mystery plays (3.2). This iconography is also clear in most stage productions in the early scene between Richard and Anne, with Richard dressed in black, Anne in white; Richard active evil, Anne passive good; their battle fought over the coffin of Anne's saintly but dead father-in-law. Richard's gamesmanship, conniving, and downright lies are clearly manipulation, as his asides to the audience confirm; but Anne, timid and unnerved, begins with righteous indignation and quickly succumbs to his guile. The Laurence Olivier–Claire Bloom film production of this scene ends with Richard's shadow cast over Anne and her bowing down. The sets also duplicate medieval icons with figures on different levels engaged in readily identifiable patterns of behavior, even at a distance. The appearance of the ghosts to Richard just before the final battle is another such iconographical moment, with curses for Richard and blessings for Richmond; the line of dead testifiers to Richard's evil are set off against a larger-than-life king-to-be in gleaming armor, a symbol of right and sun and kingship.

A production in which Peggy Ashcroft played Margaret, entering Edward's divided court as a vindictive old woman bowed by extreme age, emphasized Margaret's compulsion to speak, no longer having the patience for silence, and the strange verbal exaggeration of her speeches—an exaggeration born of spite, anger, and helplessness. Brown describes her talking to herself, her victims, and the heavens, laughing madly and enjoying the effect of her cruel phrases.

Bill Alexander's production in 1984 with the Royal Shakespeare Company emphasized the "monstrous" qualities of Richard. In fact, Antony Sher as Richard used crutches and hopped about, his huge sleeves hanging to the floor and increasing the image of insect monstrosity. Sher brought to life the evil facet of Richard's animal nature; his gargoyle qualities of toad, spider, devil, cacodemon, and lump of foul deformity guide the performance as imagery becomes visual symbol. In contrast, says Chris Hassel in the *Shakespeare Quarterly* article "Context and Charisma,"

Christopher Ravenscroft played Richmond as "humane, thoughtful, reaching out
with love" (36 [1985]: 638). Sam Mendes' 1992 production drew on the Elizabethan
tradition of having the princes played by the same boys who played women's roles
in the play. That is, he had Annabelle Apsion play both the Duke of York and Anne;
Kate Duchene played both Prince Edward and Queen Elizabeth. Mendes also had
Margaret, played by Cherry Morris, reappear hauntingly each time one of Richard's
victims went to his death. Ian McKellen's 1995 film adaptation of Richard Eyre's
1992 stage production is set in the 1930s and, under the direction of Richard Loncraine, draws a Hitler-like Richard, a fascist who nonetheless persuades us with se-
ductive charm (Howlett, 2000).

For a modern audience, the most readily accessible production is the classic 1955
cinematic version put out by Janus films, produced and directed by Sir Laurence
Olivier, and starring Olivier himself as Richard, supported by an impressive host of
British actors also honored for their work: Sir Cedric Hardwicke, Sir Ralph Richardson, and Sir John Gielgud. A youthful Claire Bloom plays Anne, while Pamela
Brown and Stanley Baker round out the distinguished cast. The film, running 138
minutes, introduced more people to the play than the sum total of those who had
ever before seen it performed on stage. It necessarily cuts the text and rearranges
some scenes. Cinematic battle scenes, such as the climactic clash on Bosworth Field,
inevitably extend the shorthand representation of warfare that Shakespeare wrote:
a handful of actors racing back and forth across the tiny Globe apron standing in
for the clash of thousands the large screen can accommodate. Although somewhat
stylized, spare, and restrained by late-twentieth-century standards of cinematic medieval warfare—standards set by Kenneth Branagh in his film *Henry V* or Mel Gib-
son in *Braveheart*—Olivier's depiction of early combat is nonetheless persuasive and
sometimes brilliantly dramatic, capturing Shakespeare's literal and metaphorical intentions with great force. Richard's death scene, for example, has the dismounted
ruler surrounded by scores of foot soldiers, who close on him in a circle that turns
into a rugby scrum of stabbing and chopping at the fallen Richard. The wild ram-
paging boar, as in Cibber's eighteenth-century production, has been trapped and
slaughtered; Richard's emblem has been dispatched both literally and metaphorically. His crown rolls from his head only to catch in a bush and be retrieved by a
beaming Lord Stanley, who gladly places it on the new, fit-looking Richmond.

Modern viewers may find other scenes less engaging, particularly matte shots of
the landscape in color tints that show their age, a repeated motif of crowns held
above the heads of pretenders to the throne, including one oversize crown that
seems more like an advertising emblem than a representation of history, and some
interiors of court and castles that look unconvincing, located in an uncertain place
somewhere between the suggestive abstraction of a stage and the realism of a location shoot.

Limitations aside, Olivier's *Richard III* remains the definitive film adaptation of
the play, mainly because of its star's superb performance and the powerful support
provided by his outstanding fellow actors. Richard may be Olivier's best film role,
a part that allows him to push the limits but then to pull back before going over
the top. The film, for all its datedness, is still a delight to experience. Kenneth
Branagh's 2002 Sheffield Crucible Theater production, for all its modernity, is, in
contrast, a weaker production. Toby Young in "Of Kings and Witches," a *Spectator*
review of this Michael Grandage production, accuses Branagh of turning Richard

Laurence Olivier as Richard III in Olivier's 1955 film *Richard III*. Courtesy of Photofest.

into "a cold-blooded yuppie murderer" who preens amid spectacles but who "never really connects with the audience" and who hence fails at a role Shakespeare intended to be a disturbingly sympathetic face of evil (23 March 2002: 66). See John Scott Colley's *Richard's Himself Again: A Stage History of "Richard III"* (Westport, CT: Greenwood P, 1992) for more on this topic.

EXPLICATION OF KEY PASSAGES

1.1.1–41. "Now is the winter . . . here Clarence comes." Richard's opening speech reveals his character and anticipates the action that follows. Shakespeare's appreciation of its importance can be gained by imagining the play's beginning in its absence. The scene would start forty-one lines later with the entrance of Clarence and the discussion between Richard and his brother about the reasons for Clarence's imprisonment. There would be no context for the events that follow. With his bravura explication of his character and secret attitudes missing, Richard would have no means to entrap the audience, and so there would be no complicity created between Richard and his audience. We can compare Shakespeare's introduction of Hamlet in that play, a literally dark figure out of sorts with what Richard terms the nimble capering in ladies' chambers, the "merry meetings" (1.1.7) and "sportive tricks" (1.1.14) that characterize the current court. The play as we have it is as unthinkable without the opening soliloquy as *Hamlet* would be without the similar appeal to the audience's disapproval of a decadent, self-indulgent society.

While Hamlet's malaise is justified by the events that precede it, Richard blames his appearance, his physical makeup, and the reactions of others for his disposition. An Elizabethan audience would have immediately seen him as dominated, according to the physiological theory of the time, by his characteristic humor: that is, the predominance of what we might call body chemistry that determines his nature. The humor theory was taken quite literally: Richard's choler and bile would be seen as the driving forces that we might term "motive." Shakespeare thus prepares the audience for all of Richard's subsequent behavior, obviating the need for exposition of particular reasons for the twists and turns of his plotting. Richard is what he is, angry and mean-spirited. As in the case of Iago in *Othello*, parsing his motives is pretty much beside the point.

Seen from this perspective, lines such as "I, in this weak piping time of peace, / Have no delight to pass away the time, / Unless to see my shadow in the sun" (1.1.24–26) make sense. Richard chooses negativity because he is negative. He is "determined to prove a villain / And hate the idle pleasures of these days. / . . . And if King Edward be as true and just / As I am subtle, false, and treacherous" (1.1.30–37), he will lock up Clarence in the Tower. Shakespeare is now ready to launch us into the plot with little further ado.

1.2.43–263. "What do you tremble? . . . as I pass." Another key passage is the wooing of Anne. The opening soliloquy establishes Richard's nature; this scene dramatizes how others respond to Richard's negativity and, by extension, provides a psychological explanation of his seduction not only of his contemporaries but even of us, his audience. Anne's triple curses (1.2.14–16) and evocation of hated lower life forms ("wolves . . . spiders, toads, / Or any creeping venom'd thing that lives!", 1.2.19–20) change into her grudging acceptance of his ring in less than 200 lines. Richard's strategies in the face of continual insult include appeals to Anne's charity, outrageously twisted evocations of Christian doctrine (if Henry VI was "gentle, mild, and virtuous" [1.2.105], God is better off having him, and Richard is to be thanked for sending him to heaven!), and other false reasoning that turns reality on its head. Mainly, Richard is simply relentless and shameless, refusing to grant any validity to Anne's accusations and employing a lover's blandishments familiar to any student of Shakespeare's love sonnets. The lines "Was ever woman in this humor woo'd? / Was ever woman in this humor won?" (1.2.227–228) could as well be asked about the English populace and the audience itself.

1.4.2–63. "O, I have passed . . . made my dream." At the beginning of this scene Clarence describes a dream he has had, one that foreshadows his death. Clarence tells his guard that in this dream he (Clarence) had escaped from imprisonment in the Tower and was fleeing to Burgundy, where once before he and his brother Richard had taken refuge. Richard again is with him. Richard persuades Clarence to leave the safety of the cabin and walk on deck. As they converse, Richard stumbles and in falling knocks Clarence overboard. As his body sinks, Clarence sees a thousand wrecked ships and the bodies of dead men nibbled by fish, as well as the great wealth that has been lost in the ocean. Some of these gems lie in dead men's skulls or have come to rest in their hollow eye sockets. Though Clarence is drowning, the water prevents his soul from escaping his body, so that he feels he is suffocating.

In the second part of his dream, he has died and has passed over the River Styx. In Hades he meets the Earl of Warwick and Prince Edward, son of Henry VI; Clarence had killed the latter after the Battle of Tewksbury. Prince Edward calls upon the Furies to avenge his death, and fiends appear to torment Clarence.

Clarence's dream reminds the audience that he is not an innocent, though he is not the "G" whom Edward should fear. The king has been warned that someone with a name beginning with "G" will disinherit him and has interpreted this omen to point to George, Duke of Clarence. Of course, the real threat is Richard, Duke of Gloucester, who will make himself king and kill Edward's sons. In the first part of Clarence's dream, Richard's villainy appears in his betraying and then killing his brother. Clarence shortly is to be murdered through Gloucester's machinations and will be drowned in a butt of malmsey.

The second part of the dream anticipates Richard III's dream in 5.3, discussed below. In both instances the murderer's victims return to haunt them and cast a pall over them when they awake. Clarence's crimes pale when compared with his brother's, and audiences sympathize with him. He acted to help his brother Edward become king, so his motives are not as selfish as Richard's; and any victim of Richard (even the rapacious Queen Margaret, Henry VI's wife) will in this play gain the sympathy of a reader or viewer. Still, perhaps Shakespeare is trapping us through our sympathy. If we can feel sorry for someone who killed one Edward, Prince of Wales (son of Henry VI), why do we condemn another person (Richard) who is responsible for the same action in killing another Edward, Prince of Wales (son of Edward IV)? If we can like Clarence despite his crimes, maybe others can like Richard, or at least feel compassion when he faces death.

4.4.1–125. "So now prosperity . . . pierce like mine." Queen Margaret, wife of the murdered Henry VI, leads a chorus of anguished noblewomen as they curse Richard and bemoan the deaths of all the men they loved and lost to his murderous ways. In her opening lines Margaret observes that Richard's reign has reached its zenith and begins to decline as the wheel of fortune turns in its inevitable course. She has watched with pleasure as her enemies have suffered the same fate that she endured. She is preparing to leave England for France, where she will observe what happens in England. She hopes that the evils beginning to beset the reign will continue, that the play will match the "induction" or prologue (4.4.5). Queen Elizabeth, wife of the dead Edward IV and mother of the princes Richard has ordered killed in the Tower of London, and the Duchess of York, mother of Richard III, Clarence, and Edward IV, enter. When they lament their losses, Margaret at first is hardly sympathetic. These other women had been her enemies. The Duchess's children had killed and usurped hers; Queen Elizabeth had dethroned Queen Margaret.

Yet she recognizes that misery has made them equal. In parallel statements that show how well their conditions match, Margaret says to Elizabeth,

> I had an Edward [Edward, Prince of Wales, son of Henry VI], till a Richard killed him;
> I had a Harry [Henry VI], till a Richard killed him;
> Thou hadst an Edward [Edward V, son of Edward IV], till a Richard killed him;
> Thou hadst a Richard [Duke of York], till a Richard killed him. (4.4.40–43)

There is also a sense here that the world is providential, that evil is punished. She tells the Duchess, "Thy Clarence he is dead that stabb'd my Edward" (4.4.67).

Margaret goes on to name Richard's other victims: Clarence, Hastings, Rivers, Vaughn, and Rutland, all but the last killed in this play. She blames the Duchess of York for giving birth to Richard and thanks God for making Richard a scourge for his mother. Richard thrives for the moment, but in this just world his end, too, is near, and she hopes she will be alive to see it.

Elizabeth remembers Margaret's prophecy that the new queen would some day ask the old queen to help her curse Richard. Margaret also recalls that time, and she remains bitter. Since Elizabeth has usurped Margaret's throne, she should also take over Margaret's grief. This grief Margaret gladly gives to Elizabeth. Elizabeth asks Margaret, who is excellent at cursing, to help her curse Richard, but as Margaret exits she replies that Elizabeth's sorrows will teach her what to say.

This litany of the dead and the cursing of Richard anticipate Richard's dream in 5.3. They also sum up the historical events portrayed before (in the *Henry VI* plays) and during this work. They show how the wheel of fortune turns, and they look ahead to Richard's fall. By the end of this scene news arrives that Richmond has landed in England and that others have already risen in revolt against the king. As Margaret warned, "Earth gapes, hell burns, fiends roar" for Richard (4.4.75).

5.3.118–176. "Enter the Ghost of young Prince Edward . . . all his pride." This dream sequence parallels Margaret's listing of Richard's victims (4.4) and brings on stage the ghosts of all whom Richard III betrayed. Richard's crimes are brought vividly to the stage one more time here. The ghosts appear in the order in which they died. First to enter is the son of Henry VI. The ghost of the slain king comes on stage next, then Clarence, followed by Rivers, Grey, Vaughn (who were executed together and so appear together), the two princes murdered in the Tower, Hastings, Lady Anne (Richard's first wife), and Buckingham. Each ghost or group recalls to Richard the way the king killed him/them and concludes, "Despair and die!" Then the ghosts turn to Richmond, who would be sleeping on the other side of the stage, and wish him success in the forthcoming battle. The two princes pray that Richmond, the future Henry VII, will "Live and beget a happy race of kings" (5.3.152). Thus, this play that draws on the Tudor view of Richard III also blesses the Tudor line and so by implication the reigning monarch, Queen Elizabeth I.

The ghosts portray Richmond as Richard's antithesis, saint to his sinner. Henry VI calls Richmond "Virtuous and holy" (5.3.128). Clarence declares, "Good angels guard thy battle!" (5.3.138). The princes also call upon "Good angels" to protect Richmond (5.3.151), and Buckingham concludes, "God and good angels fight on Richmond's side, / And Richard falls in height of all his pride!" (5.3.175–176). The words "fall" and "pride" suggest that Richard is Satan, about to be defeated by God and His angels through the agency of Richmond.

This dream sequence absolves Richmond of usurpation. The ghosts highlight Richard's own unlawful possession of the throne. Moreover, the rightful rulers want Richmond to reign. Henry VI, venerated in England as a saint, reminds the audience that he had prophesied that Richmond would be king. (Shakespeare had mentioned this prophecy earlier, at 4.2.95–96.) Henry's rightful heir says that he fights for Richmond. So do the "wronged heirs of York," Clarence and the children of Edward IV, who favor this "offspring of the house of Lancaster" (5.3.137, 136). The Yorkist claimants renounce the throne; Richmond as Henry VII becomes the legitimate successor to Henry VI.

First, though, he must defeat Richard. In the hands of a lesser dramatist Richard might have been depicted as spiraling down to guilty despair, or perhaps as repenting. Shakespeare shows Richard as fearful after his dream. But like Satan he does not repent or give up without a fight. He is brave and energetic, still demonstrating that strong inner force that drove him to mount the throne on the bodies of those who have just appeared to him.

Annotated Bibliography

Adair, Vance. "Back to the Future: Subjectivity and Anamorphosis in *Richard III*." *Critical Survey* 9.3 (1997): 32–58. Building on poststructuralist theory, Adair links Richard's monstrous physical and psychological deformities thematically to the drama's problematic representation of history, observes the theatricality of his life performance and the paradoxical parallels between Richard and Richmond.

Andrews, Christopher. "*Richard III* on Film: The Subversion of the Viewer." *Literature/Film Quarterly* 28 (2000): 82–94. Andrews evaluates the relationship between the viewing audience and the film representations of the character of Richard III, as performed by Laurence Olivier, Ron Cooke, and Ian McKellen, noting that, despite the plethora of "Richards" in performance, in all productions there are two audiences: the duped victims of Richard's rhetoric and the viewers watching him on the screen, sympathizers who progress to accomplices and confidantes before ultimately coming to their senses along with the "circumspect" Buckingham. Andrews examines the cuts, additions, acting styles, and filmic techniques that control the dominant image of each production and concludes that the soliloquy, when spoken with direct address to the camera, is most intimate and most successful at manipulating and deceiving. Thus, film productions can capably catch the audience off guard as Shakespeare intended his theater production to do.

Brown, Stephen. "Do We Like Him Now?" *Times Literary Supplement*, no. 5166 (5 April 2002): 24–25. Brown analyzes Kenneth Branagh's performance as Richard as intelligent and complex but limited, its opening scene of a crucified Richard startling and showy, but its portrait of political morality too shallow for a play dependent on complexity. Brown would prefer some sign of an Anti-Christ in Branagh's crucified king.

Carroll, William C. "Desacralization and Succession in *Richard III*." *Deutsche Shakespeare-Gesellschaft West, Jahrbuch* 1991: 82–96. Richard blames his mother for his form and nature, but when she rejects him he must find a new explanation of who and what he is, so that his annihilation of form, kinship, and law turns back on him, and the responsibility he has tried to shift to others rests on his shoulders.

Doebler, Bettie Anne. "'Dispaire and Dye': The Ultimate Temptation of *Richard III*." *Shakespeare Studies* 7 (1974): 75–85. This essay evaluates Richard III's character in the light of the medieval dramatic allegory of the Vice figure, arguing that Shakespeare involved his audience fully in ethical and historical situations suggesting universality and yet also explored the theological dimensions of more conventional materials. According to Doebler, a reader unfamiliar with iconographical patterns like the *ars moriendi*, or deathbed scene, will miss the full complexity of Shakespeare's vision. An Elizabethan audience would have been horrified at the images of the death of the soul and would have brought more to the final scene than a modern audience lacking the traditional religious motifs of that earlier time.

Goodland, Katherine. "'Obsequious Laments': Mourning and Communal Memory in Shakespeare's *Richard III*." *Religion & the Arts* 7 (March 2003): 31–64. Goodland explores this tragic history of an England divided against herself in the context of Elizabethan tensions over mourning and burial ritual. She explores the significance of burial rituals and provides information on women's laments in medieval drama.

Helgerson, Richard. "Weeping for Jane Shore." *South Atlantic Quarterly* 98 (Summer 1999): 451–477. Helgerson discusses the origins of domestic tragedy and the significance of the adulterous relationships of the middle-class Jane Shore in Shakespeare's play. He discusses the main source for the play and Shakespeare's treatment of his feminine characters and the urban middle class.

Howlett, Kathy. "Vivid Negativity: Richard Loncraine's Richard III." In *Framing Shakespeare on Film*. Athens: Ohio UP, 2000. 128–148. Howlett argues that the fascist past in which Loncraine's film establishes Richard's story is as "stylized, self-invented, and replicated history" as Olivier's "theatrical 'medievalism'" (132). Yet, it raises the problem of representation, of fragmented recovery of the past, and even of recent history fragmenting a play and making its issues seem alien and vulnerable to misframing. In this case, the addition of Hollywood gangster styles on top of German Nazi ones makes for befuddled history as Loncraine projects Richard's end as our future.

Knights, L. C. "Richard III." In *William Shakespeare: The Histories*. London: Longmans, Green & Co., 1962. 16–26. Knights demonstrates that the structure and method of characterization of *Richard III* draws on morality play patterns but goes beyond them to explore new moral territory through ironic patterns of speech. In this play, Knights argues, vigorous language, moral insights, and artifice combine with psychological realism and a deep probing of the complex realities behind the public facade.

Marienstras, Richard. "Of a Monstrous Body." In *French Essays on Shakespeare and His Contemporaries*. Ed. Jean-Marie Maguin and Michèle Willems. Cranbury, NJ: Associated University Presses, 1995. 153–174. Marienstras studies the cultural and literary tradition of deformed monsters and the symbolic significance of Richard's deformed body in the light of Bell Alexander's 1984 production of the play, biblical imagery, and historical concepts of chaos.

Torrey, Michael. "'The Plain Devil and Dissembling Looks': Ambivalent Physiognomy and Shakespeare's *Richard III*." *English Literary Renaissance* 30.2 (Spring 2000): 123–154. Torrey focuses on Richard's physiognomy, connecting his deformity to his psychological motivation, his destruction of beauty, and his evil; and exploring the relationship between outward appearances and inward reality.

King John

Michael Egan

PLOT SUMMARY

1.1. Enter King John of England and his mother, Elinor of Aquitaine, widow of John's father, Henry II, surnamed Plantagenet. They are accompanied by the earls of Pembroke, Essex, and Salisbury. Also present, and the reason for this meeting, is Chatillion, a messenger from Philip, King of France.

John asks Chatillion what Philip wants. The answer is that John is a usurper and must resign as king in favor of Arthur, the young son of his deceased brother, Geoffrey. The implied claim is that after the death of King Richard I, Geoffrey (the next eldest son) should have succeeded but that John wrongly seized the throne. In a whispered aside, Elinor reminds John that this is true. Now that Geoffrey is dead, Chatillion continues, the crown should rightly pass to Geoffrey's son, Arthur, living in France with his mother, Constance, at King Philip's court. In addition to the crown, Philip demands that John surrender control of Ireland, the French duchies of Anjou, Touraine, and Maine, and the town of Poictiers, all part of the England's Angevin empire at the time. (The name Angevin derives from the French province of Anjou.) If he does not, France will declare war.

John gives the only possible answer: it's war, then. He sends Chatillion back to France with the promise that he and his forces will soon follow.

Now two gentlemen enter, Philip and Robert Faulconbridge, requesting the king's judgment in a dispute over their inheritance. Robert, the younger and scrawnier brother, claims that he should inherit their father's estate because Philip is illegitimate—a bastard. His illegitimacy is proved by the fact that he is taller, handsomer, and stronger: that is, nothing like Robert himself or their father. Indeed, Philip strikingly resembles none other than King Richard I, as everyone at court quickly notices. Robert testifies that years before, in his father's absence, King Richard slept with Robert's mother. On his deathbed his father had disowned Philip. (There is an interesting parallel with the "garter scenes" in *Edward III*, in which the monarch, unsuccessfully in this case, tries to seduce the wife of one of his nobles who is away at war.)

The matter is quickly resolved. Robert gets his inheritance and leaves. King John agrees that Philip is obviously his brother Richard's son and knights him on the spot as Sir Richard Plantagenet. Gratefully the new knight joins the king's entourage and immediately assumes an important position at court. At the end of the scene his mother enters and admits that Richard Cordelion (Coeur de Leon), as King Richard I was known because he once killed a lion by ripping its heart out through its mouth, really did get her pregnant. The Bastard joyfully embraces his bastardy—and his new life.

2.1. In France the town of Angiers, an English possession, is besieged by the French and the Austrians. Present are King Philip of France with his son Lewis (the Dauphin or "Dolphin," that is, heir to the French throne), young Arthur, and his mother (Constance), and Lymoges, the Duke of Austria. Lymoges wears the lion skin he took from the corpse of Richard Cordelion, for whose death he was responsible (the play is unclear just how).

Chatillion enters with the news of King John's defiant rejection of Philip's demands. He has barely finished speaking when the English army itself appears, led by John, Elinor, the Bastard, and Pembroke. Accompanying them is Blanch of Spain, daughter of John's sister and the king of Castille.

Philip restates his claim that John is a usurper and should abdicate in favor of his nephew Arthur, as well as give up the territories of Ireland, Anjou, Touraine, and Maine. John again refuses, and in the ensuing verbal sparring the two mothers, Elinor and Constance, also start insulting one another. Philip proposes to settle the matter by asking the citizens of Angiers which of the two—John or Arthur—they recognize as their king.

The monarchs summon representatives of the town to the walls but receive the canny answer from the chief spokesperson, Hubert de Burgh, that Angiers' allegiance is to the true king of England. And who is he? The one who defeats the other in battle, replies Hubert. Hostilities thus commence, but the outcome is uncertain: both sides claim victory.

The Bastard offers a solution: let France and England combine their forces against the town and settle the kingship matter afterward. The townsfolk quickly propose instead that Lewis and Blanch should marry, thus uniting England and France. John agrees because the match will avoid war and confirm his own title to the English crown. As a sweetener, he throws in the disputed French territories and 30,000 marks (a large monetary sum) as Blanch's dowry. The French accept, and the agreement is sealed when John creates Arthur Duke of Britain (Bretagne) and Earl of Richmond, giving him Angiers to rule over. The town's gates are opened and everyone adjourns to a nearby church for the wedding.

The scene ends with one of the play's most important speeches as the Bastard, alone on stage, draws the lesson. There are no moral principles in the world, he tells us, just crude self-interest, which he calls "tickling commodity" (2.1.573).

3.1. Back at the French pavilion Arthur's mother, Constance, becomes furious when she hears of Philip's betrayal. As soon as he arrives, accompanied by the English and the wedding party, she berates him as a traitor to the cause of setting Arthur on the throne of England and demands renewal of the war.

She is helped by the sudden entrance of Cardinal Pandulph, representing the pope, who has come to seek out King John. The issue is who is to be the next Archbishop of Canterbury, the most senior cleric in England. John has rejected, and continues to reject, the pope's nominee; his punishment for this defiance is excommunication. Pandulph insists that the French king, a loyal Catholic, continue his war against England and enforce the pope's will. Philip is caught in a double bind: by attacking England he breaks the peace and makes an enemy of Blanch, his new daughter-in-law; but if he refuses he'll be excommunicated. However, when his son Lewis joins with Pandulph and Constance, Philip gives in and the suspended battle immediately resumes.

3.2. England wins the day. The Bastard enters triumphantly with the head of Lymoges, Duke of Austria, killer of his father. King John follows with Arthur as his captive, whom he entrusts to Hubert de Burgh.

3.3. Now fully in control, John leaves his mother, Elinor, in France to rule his possessions there. He instructs the Bastard to return to England ahead of him and loot the Catholic monasteries and other church possessions. Finally, in what is perhaps the most powerful scene in the play, he hints strongly to Hubert (who fully understands him) that Arthur must be killed.

3.4. Back in the French camp, Constance is hysterical with anguish: she knows Arthur's fate is sealed. When she rushes out, Philip follows, fearing she may kill herself. Later we hear that she has, in fact, died, perhaps of grief.

Pandulph and Lewis are left together, and the wily cardinal finally shows his Machiavellian side. Still hoping to control the English church, he encourages Lewis to invade and conquer England. He points out that as soon as John kills Arthur (inevitable the moment French troops land) popular sympathy will turn toward Lewis, who will then easily be able to install himself as king.

4.1. In a castle in England Hubert prepares to execute John's death warrant—or at least apparently so, for it appears to have been modified. Instead of death, Hubert is going to put out Arthur's eyes with red-hot irons. It is unclear whether the change represents a modification of John's order or is a mistake on Shakespeare's part reflecting an earlier version of the play. (See "Publication History," below.) The boy is tied to a chair but appeals so movingly to Hubert's conscience that he is spared. Hubert resolves to lie to the king, telling him that Arthur is dead.

4.2. The scene opens immediately after John has had himself crowned king a second time, an odd but historically accurate move suggesting his insecurity on the throne. A further indication of his questionable claim is his willingness to mollify the assembled peers, critical of his "double coronation" (4.2.40), by offering to grant whatever requests they submit to him. There is only one, spelled out by their spokesperson Pembroke: that Prince Arthur be freed from prison.

John agrees just as Hubert arrives to tell him of the boy's supposed murder. Pale, John has to reveal to the lords that Arthur is dead, apparently of illness. No one believes him, and the angry lords, suspecting murder and muttering rebellion, depart to view the body themselves. They are no sooner gone than John hears that Lewis and the French army have landed in England and that his beloved mother, Elinor, has died.

John's grip on the situation is failing. The Bastard enters to report on his progress looting Church properties in England. He tells John that the people are possessed of wild rumors and superstitions stirred up by self-appointed seers, such as Peter the Prophet, whom he has brought with him. Confronting John, Peter predicts that before noon on the next Ascension Day (forty days after Easter Sunday, commemorating the Ascension of Christ into heaven) John will resign his crown. Furious and frightened, the king tells Hubert to imprison Peter and hang him at noon on Ascension Day. Then he dispatches the Bastard after the angry lords with a request to meet with them again.

Hubert returns with even more bizarre news: five moons have been seen in the sky that night, one whirling around the other four. John turns on Hubert and accuses him of willfully murdering Arthur. When Hubert produces the king's own signed warrant, John insists that it's still all Hubert's fault—he should have hesitated more or protested. Finally Hubert tells John the truth: Arthur lives. With joy and relief John sends Hubert to summon the lords so that he can break the good news.

4.3. The imprisoned Arthur resolves to escape. He climbs the steep walls and jumps, killing himself.

Enter the Lords, agreeing among themselves to meet with Cardinal Pandulph, at his request, two days hence at St. Edmundsbury. The Bastard arrives with the king's message, but hardly has he delivered it than they find Prince Arthur's body. The Lords immediately conclude that, as they feared, he was murdered. When Hubert arrives, only the intervention of the Bastard stops them from cutting him down as the assassin. The outraged peers storm off, determined to throw in their lot with the French invaders.

5.1. It is Ascension Day, and John has yielded up his crown to Pandulph so that he may be crowned yet again, this time by the Church itself. In return for John's act of contrition and submission, Pandulph agrees to dissuade the victorious French from continuing their invasion.

The Bastard returns with news of Arthur's death. John is crushed and now hopes only that Pandulph will succeed. But the Bastard rises to the occasion, urging John to do battle once again. Weakly John hands over the running of the war to his dead brother's illegitimate son, the only man at court willing to fight for England.

5.2. At Lewis's camp near St. Edmundsbury the English lords have gone over to the French. Pandulph enters, but despite his eloquence is unable to stop Lewis from continuing a war that seems virtually won. He is followed by the Bastard, who pours scorn and defiance upon the French. Battle is joined.

5.3. A corner of the battlefield. Sick and weakened, King John leaves for the Abbey of Swinstead close at hand.

5.4. Three English peers, Salisbury, Pembroke, and Bigot, meet on the battlefield. They are soon joined by Melune, a wounded French lord, who warns them that Lewis means to execute his English allies as soon as the war is over. Shocked, they resolve to hurry back to King John's side.

5.5. As night falls, Lewis hears the bad news: Melune is dead, the English lords have fled his camp, and the fresh supplies from France he was counting on are lost at sea.

5.6. Near Swinstead Abbey Hubert and the Bastard meet in the dark. The king, Hubert reports, has been treacherously poisoned by one of the abbey's monks and is close to death.

5.7. In the orchard at Swinstead Abbey King John dies in horrible pain. He is attended by the Bastard, the repentant lords, and his son and heir, Prince Henry. Pandulph too is at the abbey with an offer of peace from the French. As his final act of authority, the Bastard accepts, then kneels in fealty to the new king. He speaks the play's moral: England will never be defeated if it stands united against the world.

PUBLICATION HISTORY

The date of *King John*'s composition is hotly debated and bound up with the vexing question of its relationship to an anonymous but similar play, *The Troublesome Raigne of John King of England*. The only hard information we have is that *The Troublesome Play*, as it is sometimes wryly called, was published in 1591 and reprinted in 1611 and 1622; the latter two editions identified Shakespeare as the author. *The Life and Death of King John* was first published in the Folio of 1623 (F1), and its earliest recorded performance was given in Covent Garden, London, 1737.

Everything beyond this is speculation, inference, and deduction, though some of it is well founded. For instance, a document dated January 12, 1669, suggests that *King John* was among the plays performed by the King's Men at Blackfriars some time between 1608 and 1642 (cited in Irwin Smith, *Shakespeare's Blackfriars Playhouse: Its History and Its Design* [London: Owen, 1966], 503–504). It is probable that the date was after 1623. Braunmuller (pp. 79–80) finds possible echoes of *King John* in *Captain Thomas Stukely* (1595), which may derive from Peele; John Bodenham's (attributed) *Belvedere* (1600); Thomas Heywood's *2 Edward IV* (1600); and Thomas Deloney's "The Death of King John Poisoned by a Friar" (1602). But these all seem very tenuous indeed.

Many of the accepted verities about *King John*, especially the period of its composition, are currently in radical transition. For example, an established scholarly belief is that the play must have been generally known by the late 1590s because Anthony Munday's *Death of Robert, Earl of Huntingdon* (ca. 1598) apparently contains a reference to it. A dumb-show features major characters from John's reign including Hubert, described as "thou fatal keeper of poor babes" (signatures D3^v, F4). Among others, L. A. Beaurline (p. 3) and E.A.J. Honigmann (p. lxxiii note, and p. 171, claiming that in Holinshed "Arthur appears as a young soldier aged sixteen or seventeen") contend that this phrase must allude to Shakespeare's play since it uniquely portrays Prince Arthur as a boy, whereas in other versions, including the chronicles, he is a young man. But aside from the fact that a boy is not a babe, the assertion itself is not true: the second edition of Holinshed's *Chronicles* (1587), the major source for all Elizabethan accounts of King John, describes Arthur as "but a child . . . but a babe to speake of." Holinshed's first edition (1577) does not describe John's reign. Holinshed is much closer to Munday than Shakespeare and more probably where Munday found his language and portrayal.

Also in 1598 an Elizabethan cleric and schoolmaster, Francis Meres, published a book called *Palladis Tamia* in which he says that

> As Plautus and Seneca are accounted the best for comedy and tragedy among the Latins, so Shakespeare among the English is the most excellent in both kinds for the stage; for comedy, witness his *Gentlemen of Verona*, his *Errors*, his *Love Labours Lost*, his *Love Labours Won*, his *Midsummer's Night Dream*, & his *Merchant of Venice*; for tragedy, his *Richard the 2*, *Richard the 3*, *Henry the 4*, *King John*, *Titus Andronicus*, and his *Romeo and Juliet*. (Meres, p. 282. A photographic reproduction of the original may be found at http://uvic.ca/shakespeare/Library/SLTnoframes/life/meres.html.)

The *King John* referred to is invariably taken to be the one published in 1623, though there is no clear warrant for this assumption: as we've noted, Shakespeare's play never appeared in Quarto, and its earliest recorded performance dates from the eighteenth century. It is also true—though almost never perceived as a difficulty—that Meres's catalog is problematic in a number of telling ways, including that puzzling reference to *Love Labours Won*, a lost or nonexistent drama that some scholars conjecture to be *The Taming of the Shrew* or *Much Ado about Nothing* or *As You Like It* (in an early and no longer extant version). But as these guesses indicate, we really have no idea what Meres had in mind nor to which of Shakespeare's works *Love Labours Won* actually refers, if any: Meres might have simply made it up. He also gets Shakespeare's known titles slightly but significantly wrong, for example, *Love Labours Lost*, *Midsummer's Night Dream*, and so forth, and fails to mention others certainly well known by this time, including the *Henry VI* plays. These anomalies and misprisions suggest that at least some of Meres's data were not derived firsthand, and all of it thus less than reliable. (See Don Cameron Allen, ed., *Francis Meres's Treatise, "Poetrie": A Critical Edition* [Urbana: U of Illinois P, 1933], 31–50.)

Meres's most significant inaccuracy for our purposes is his recording of *Titus Andronicus* as Shakespeare's unaided work, though we now know that it was actually written collaboratively with George Peele. Meres was either unaware of this fact or Peele's death in 1596 and/or secondary role as author led to his omission. Whatever the actual sources of Meres's information, Peele's long-suspected contribution to *Titus Andronicus* has been incontrovertibly proved by Brian Vickers in a recent analysis, *Shakespeare, Co-Author: A Historical Study of Five Collaborative Plays* (Oxford: Oxford UP, 2002), pp. 148–243. Using a wide variety of textual and stylometric measures, many of them never before applied to the play, Vickers overwhelmingly demonstrates Peele's creative presence in at least four scenes: the whole of act 1 (a single scene), 2.1, 2.2, and 4.1. Common sense suggests that Peele may have contributed much more—collaboration implies discussion, planning, feedback, and even mutual editing—but nothing further has been definitely established.

The confirmation that Peele was one of Shakespeare's co-authors in the early 1590s has profound implications for our study of *King John*, because *The Troublesome Raigne* was certainly known when Meres put his catalog together. Much of this play, published three years ahead of *Titus* and seven before *Palladis Tamia*, has now also been conclusively attributed to Peele by Vickers in an extension of his earlier analysis, *"The Troublesome Raigne*, George Peele, and the Date of *King John."* But the drama's plotting, characterization, and general political orientation are so similar to Shakespeare's acknowledged play that there are really only three options available to us:

1. *King John* preceded *The Troublesome Raigne*, and its author stole Shakespeare's plot and some of his language (a position taken by an important school of critics).

2. It was Shakespeare who ruthlessly plagiarized another writer's work (a process neither excused nor sanitized by politely calling *The Troublesome Raigne* a "source play," the majority view among modern scholars).

3. In the light of Vickers's new work Peele and Shakespeare wrote *The Troublesome Raigne* together, and some time later Shakespeare revised it as *King John*.

If this last—the likeliest scenario—is the case, Meres's 1598 reference might actually be to *The Troublesome Raigne* and not to Shakespeare's acknowledged history, an observation also made by Eric Sams in *The Real Shakespeare: Retrieving the*

Early Years, 1564–1594 (New Haven: Yale UP, 1995, 147). This conclusion, however, leaves the actual composition date of *King John* wide open.

In strong support of the third option we may note that as late as 1623 everyone connected with the theater and publishing appears to have believed that Shakespeare wrote *The Troublesome Raigne* or at least was closely enough identified with it to claim possession. The play was extremely popular for more than thirty years, judging by its original title page and two subsequent editions, both of which describe Shakespeare as the author. While these attributions are not conclusive, since literary imposture was common enough, their publishers were respectable businessmen closely associated with Shakespeare and unlikely to engage in piracy. Not all uncertain attributions are forgeries. Valentine Simmes, who handled the 1611 edition ("Written by W. Sh."), also published the first three quartos of *Richard II* (1597–1598), as well as the quartos of *Richard III* (1597), *2 Henry IV* (1600), and *Much Ado about Nothing* (1600). Augustine Matthews, responsible for the 1622 text ("Written by W. Shakespeare"), later published the second (1630) quarto of *Othello* (Frank Kermode, *Riverside Shakespeare* [Boston: Houghton Mifflin, 1997], 1288, and Sams, *The Real Shakespeare*, 128, noting that there was no "demurrer from any quarter" when these editions were published under Shakespeare's name).

What seems really decisive, however, is that on November 8, 1623, Isaac Jaggard and Edward Blount, representing the syndicate preparing the first edition of Shakespeare's complete plays, registered with the Stationers' Office sixteen new titles "as are not formerly entered to other men" (Braunmuller, 19). That is to say, they legally claimed sixteen previously unpublished Shakespeare dramas with the intention of including them in F1. The revealing fact is that *King John* was not among them: that is, all those who were in a position to know, including Shakespeare's friends, professional associates, and competitors, accepted that the play had already been published by him. But in 1623 the only previously available *King John* was *The Troublesome Raigne*. A third play, John Bale's *King Johan* (1536–1539), not published until 1838, has little connection with either *King John* or *The Troublesome Raigne*. Bullough (pp. 3–4) notes that "Shakespeare can hardly have known this work." *King Johan* is remembered chiefly for its virulent anti-Catholicism—it was written and performed at the time of Henry VIII's break with Rome—and the subject matter it distantly shares with the two later plays. Without them it would be completely forgotten.

We may add that Jaggard, Blount, and their associates were exceptionally scrupulous when handling doubtful cases, excluding from the First Folio *Pericles*, *The Two Noble Kinsmen*, and the now-lost *Cardenio*. *Pericles* in particular, published under Shakespeare's name in 1609, had been registered by Blount himself the previous year (Chambers, *William Shakespeare*, 2 vols. [Oxford: Clarendon P, 1930], 1.518). They still left it out. For whatever reasons, perhaps because some or all of these plays were disproportionately collaborative, perhaps because the editors felt their texts were insufficiently accurate, the syndicate declined to claim them. Obviously the same might have done for *King John* without commercial damage to the final enterprise.

The syndicate may also have been cautious because *Timon of Athens*, *Titus Andronicus*, and *Henry VIII* were included, despite the fact that these plays are now known, and probably were then known, to have been co-written. Again the test may have been proportionality: that is, whether the editors knew or felt that Shakespeare had contributed the authorial lion's share.

We may note finally that if *King John* had been, in fact, an original play "not formerly entered to other men," there was nothing to stop its registration in 1623, that is, by entering seventeen new plays. The implicit claim that *The Troublesome Raigne* was Shakespeare's thus means that either the editors and publishers of F1 were uncharacteristically and gratuitously fraudulent, or they genuinely believed that his *King John* was, in fact, the final version of a work that he originally helped to write.

Even the best scholars have reacted to these facts with some consternation. E. K. Chambers, for example, unwilling on stylistic grounds to accept Shakespeare's part in *The Troublesome Raigne*, nonetheless observes that by 1623 both it and *King John* were "regarded as commercially identical" (*William Shakespeare*, 1.365), meaning that everyone believed Shakespeare's executors held the copyright. This inference is now generally accepted, even by those who continue to maintain, despite what it implies, that the anonymous work follows *King John*. E.A.J. Honigmann evades the issue in an ambiguous footnote claiming that "apparently" the existence of a "bad quarto" conferred copyright privileges on "derivative" plays, an assertion for which there is no evidence. (Honigmann, lxxiii note. Honigmann is either dishonest or confused, since the copyright he refers to supposedly legitimated *King John*, not *The Troublesome Raigne*, the play he argues must be the "derived . . . bad quarto.") Peter Alexander, who first suggested that *The Troublesome Raigne* might be the debtor play, reluctantly concedes in his *Shakespeare* (London: Oxford UP, 1964), pp. 170–171:

> For *King John* there is no entry of any kind in the Stationers' Register before its inclusion in the First Folio. Heminge and Condell treated the publication of *The Troublesome Raigne* as authorizing the printing of *King John*, a claim which could hardly have been maintained had *The Troublesome Raigne* been an original play by an author other than Shakespeare.

The conclusion clearly is that *The Troublesome Raigne* was believed to be Shakespeare's; this view is resisted by modern scholars only because the play's verse (if not its plot) seems so unlike what we find in *King John*. Until now, however, no one has considered the possibility that *The Troublesome Raigne* might be a collaboration between Peele and the young Shakespeare, who later rewrote it alone. Yet this hypothesis accounts not only for everything that is known about the publication and performance histories of both works but (more important) their contrasting stylistic qualities, plot similarities, and narrative contradictions. It also extends by one the list of Peele's and Shakespeare's known collaborations.

Moved principally by a reluctance to connect Shakespeare in any way with *The Troublesome Raigne*, which is poetically second-rate but excellently planned and devised, a large and powerful school maintains that the play must have been composed after *King John* by a plagiarist. This accounts neatly for the two dramas' narrative overlaps and differences, preserves the originality of Shakespeare's plotting and characterization—apparently stolen by Anonymous, who nevertheless left behind the poetry, that is, he ran off with the casket but abandoned the jewels—and, of course, absolutely rules out Shakespeare's involvement with a lesser work.

If this view is right, however, the accepted chronology of Shakespeare's plays has to be completely revised. It also blows apart Marlowe scholarship and much else in Elizabethan studies, since it would mean that *King John* was written and frequently acted before 1591 (allowing Anonymous at least half a year, and in practice much longer, to secure a copy, rewrite it, then publish his new version). If *The Troublesome Raigne* itself was actually performed, as all the evidence confirms and none refutes, we must push our dates back further still, claiming *King John* as one of Shakespeare's earliest dramas, if not his very first. But this also turns everything we know about his stylistic evolution on its head and implies, further, that it would have had to be famous enough—that is, played many times through the mid 1580s— to make the whole enterprise worth Anonymous's plagiaristic effort. The improbable scenario is that a popular, pre-Armada chronicle, *King John*, was rewritten as an even more popular but poetically inferior post-Armada play, *The Troublesome Raigne*, which had an identical plot, characters, and theme. This outrageous and inferior imitation was then published repeatedly to capitalize not on its own success but that of its predecessor.

Unsurprisingly, there is no objective support for this bizarre reasoning; in fact, quite the reverse. Nothing except critical fantasy suggests that the publication of *The Troublesome Raigne* was anything less than a legitimate business venture, while claims that it was generated merely to exploit the undemonstrated esteem of Shakespeare's *King John* imply a level of conscious deceit on the part of its writer, publisher, and printer unequivocally contradicted by everything else we know about it and those associated with its publication. Like subsequent publishers of *The Troublesome Raigne*, Sampson Clarke was well respected and his imprint perfectly normal. (Wilson, *King John*, xviii.)

All the evidence indicates, too, that while *The Troublesome Raigne* was often staged, *King John* was probably never performed during Shakespeare's lifetime. Braunmuller (p. 23) among others notes that the F1 text "shows comparatively little evidence of theatre use," a conclusion supported by the fact that the first two acts, as they are now usually designated, are confusingly headed *Actus Primus, Scæna Primus,* and *Scæna Secunda,* while "*Actus Secundus*" comprises what are evidently the first 74 lines of act 3, scene 1. Elsewhere, stage directions imperfectly relate to or follow the spoken lines referring to them, for example, drums heard before they are sounded, again suggesting a text never actually staged:

> The interruption of their churlish drums
> Cuts off more circumstance. They are at hand[.]
> *Drum beats* (2.1.76–77)

The few Elizabethan promptbooks we possess, that is, the actual scripts used in performance, clearly indicate that offstage sound effects, such as the noise of approaching troops, preceded the on-stage speeches acknowledging them. (See, for example, the manuscript B. L. Egerton 1994, reproduced in W. P. Frijlinck, ed., *The First Part of the Reign of King Richard the Second, or Thomas of Woodstock* [London: Malone Society, 1870, rpt. 1929], where "dromes" sound three or four lines before the words "how now what dromes are these" (lines 2750–2760, pp. 93–94).

Beaurline (p. 184), Honigmann (p. xxxiv), and W. W. Greg (*The Editorial Problem in Shakespeare* [Oxford: Clarendon P, 1951], 155) also note the inconsistencies and confusions in *King John*'s stage directions and speech heads. For instance,

Eleanor of Aquitaine is variously labeled *Queene Elinor, Eleanor, Queene, Elea., Elin., Eli., Qu. Mo.* (that is, Queen Mother), *Qu.,* and *Old Qu.* The French king is called *Philip King of France, France, Fra, King,* and *Lewis* (incorrectly, twice). These discrepancies, usually regularized by modern editors, would also have been quickly corrected by a stage manager. It follows then that the F1 text was never performed.

In contrast, the title page of *The Troublesome Raigne,* records performances "sundry times" by the Queen's Men, a prominent company that declined rapidly after the death in 1588 of its principal comedian, Richard Tarleton. Credible evidence associates Shakespeare with the Queen's Men and Richard Tarleton, whose jests are quoted in *Hamlet* Q1 (1603) and who may have been the original of Yorick (see Eric Sams, "Taboo or not Taboo? The Text, Dating and Authorship of *Hamlet* 1589–1623," *Hamlet Studies* 10.1–2 ([Summer–Winter 1988]: 38). Like Marlowe's *Tamburlaine* (1587–1588), *The Troublesome Raigne* was published in two parts, with an opening address to readers referring directly to that spectacularly successful drama, implying that it was a kind of English equivalent:

> You that with friendly grace of smoothed brow
> Have entertaind the *Scythian Tamburlaine,*
> And given applause unto an Infidel:
> Vouchsafe to welcome (with like curtesie)
> A warlike Christian and your countreyman. (*The Troublesome Raigne,* 1.1)

These details, together with the fact that Elizabethan plays were rarely if ever published in the year they were first acted, all point to the conclusion that *The Troublesome Raigne* was originally written and staged 1588–1590 (Robert Adger Law, "On the Date of *King John,*" *Studies in Philology* 54 [1957]: 120). It enjoyed considerable success before publication by a bankrupt company seeking to wring a few last pennies from its assets, an inference borne out by the fact that the Queen's Men sold about a dozen other plays about this time, too (E. K. Chambers, *The Elizabethan Stage,* 4 vols. [Oxford: Clarendon P, 1923], 4.382–386).

An objective look at *The Troublesome Raigne*'s style and content confirms it as one of the so-called Armada plays composed and enthusiastically received during the excitement, national fervor, and anti-Catholic sentiment sweeping England after its victory over the invading Spanish fleet in 1588. There are close similarities between the fates of Philip of Spain's fleet and Philip of France's unsuccessful invasion, while many of the play's episodes and characters are deeply hostile to Catholicism. Apart from the ruthless Cardinal Pandulph, the papal legate responsible for the resumption of war between France and England recently at peace, and who otherwise provokes all kinds of trouble, we see "faire Alice," a "fausen [wriggling] Nunne" hidden in a friar's money chest. We also hear a priest smarmily declare "*Amor vincit omnia*" when he is discovered in the closet of a second lecherous nun, and later we're shown the King perfidiously murdered by a monk enraged at his treatment of the Catholic church (*The Troublesome Raigne,* I.1266, 1249–1263, II.869–929).

An earlier *King John* is not impossible, of course, though the hypothesis raises a great number of other difficulties, many of which have never been addressed. First, where would the author of *The Troublesome Raigne* get a version of Shakespeare's unpublished fair copy so he could follow it so exactly (see Wilson, *King John*, p. xxxii)? Comparison shows that *The Troublesome Raigne* is unlikely to have been assembled from memory or notes taken during a performance or even performances—it matches *King John* too exactly in structure, overall design, speech and scenic sequence, characters (particularly the nonhistoric figures of Chatillion and the Bastard) and stage directions, which of course are not spoken. In a critical review of Honigmann's edition, Alice Walker also shrewdly observes that Essex is not addressed by name in *King John*. His coincident inclusion in *The Troublesome Raigne* therefore—assuming it to be the later play—means that Anonymous must have had Shakespeare's manuscript before him. (*Review of English Studies*, New Series, 7 [October 1956]: 421–422.)

There are also several identical or near-identical lines, many of them quite trivial. But their very triviality confirms rather than disproves the intimate connection, since few are vivid with images or striking turns of phrase one can imagine jumping off the stage to implant themselves in a hearer's memory. On the contrary, most are poetically dull, mere narrative fact, precisely the sort of functional statement a rewriter or editor working from a text would retain. Compare

> "of Ireland, Poitiers, Anjow, Torain, Maine" (*The Troublesome Raigne*, I.33–34);
>
> "To Ireland, Poictiers, Anjou, Touraine, Maine" (*King John*, 1.1.11);
>
> "Next them a Bastard of the Kings deceast" (*The Troublesome Raigne*, I.490);
>
> "With them a bastard of the king's deceas'd" (*King John*, 2.1.65);
>
> "And thirtie thousand markes of stipend coyne" (*The Troublesome Raigne*, I.842);
>
> "Full thirty thousand marks of English coin" (*King John*, 2.1.530);
>
> "Which in S. Maries Chappel presently" (*The Troublesome Raigne*, I.857);
>
> "For at Saint Mary's Chapel presently" (*King John*, 2.1.538).

As these and other examples show, if *The Troublesome Raigne* were, indeed, written later than *King John*, its author must have had a copy of Shakespeare's play at his elbow. But it is well known that complete manuscripts, in the form of promptbooks, were both rare and jealously guarded by the theater companies owning them. Actors possessed their own lines and cues, nothing more, as Shakespeare shows in *A Midsummer Night's Dream*, 3.1, when the "rude mechanicals" (3.2.9) rehearse their performance of *Pyramus and Thisbe*. No company was likely to hand over its single precious copy—especially of a smash hit—to a lesser dramatist so that he could work up an inferior version for sale under the impression that it was the original author's (one of Honigmann's wilder assertions, p. lxxiii). If Shakespeare and his associates wished to capitalize on *King John*'s popularity, why not just publish the real thing and keep the profits themselves?

It is perfectly true, as Braunmuller (p. 20) and others have pointed out, that various forms of an unpublished play could and did exist—the author's private copy (his draft version, or foul papers) and perhaps a fair copy or some form of private transcript, or a combination of all three. Yet in each of these cases the probability of its falling into the hands of a rival dramatist by theft or carelessness seems so remote we can safely discount it (though this is precisely one of the speculative claims made by Beaurline, p. 209). Certainly there is no record of such a thing actually happening (in this case or any other) and no reason to think that if it did the victim would not have loudly complained. Literary theft was as much disliked then as now. (For good discussions of hostile Elizabethan attitudes toward plagiarism, see Sams, *The Real Shakespeare*, pp. 180–181; Brian Vickers, *"Counterfeiting" Shakespeare: Evidence, Authorship, and John Ford's Funerall Elegye* [Cambridge: Cambridge UP, 2002], 87–89, and *Shakespeare, Co-Author: A Historical Study of Five Collaborative Plays*, 522–527.)

The likeliest possibility then, supported by an examination of both texts, is that *The Troublesome Raigne* was written before *King John* and that the drama published in the First Folio represents a reworking of its scenes, characters, and episodes. It is often said that Shakespeare tones down the play's anti-Catholicism, but such is not the case, as we shall see below. What he does take out are *The Troublesome Raigne*'s semicomic allegations of sexual dissoluteness in the priesthood, leaving in place far more serious charges of political meddling and influence. In so doing he fleshes out both personality and motivation, displaying a strong editorial hand at work on the earlier text.

Textual details corroborate a date no earlier than 1594 for *King John*. In *The Troublesome Raigne* the Bastard is recognized as Richard I's son because of his handsome features, but in Shakespeare's play his physique or "large composition" (1.1.88) is much more greatly emphasized. This is done especially in contrast to his brother Robert, who has legs like "riding-rods," arms like "eel-skins stuff'd," and a face as thin as "three farthings" (1.1.140–143). These descriptors are quite specific and obviously neither would nor could have been included unless Shakespeare had in mind particular individuals—in the case of the Bastard, the Chamberlain's Men's leading heroic figure, Richard Burbage, "a large man with a bluff manner," and in that of Robert Faulconbridge, John Sincklo or Sinckler, "a tall thin-faced fellow, whose comical figure Shakespeare exploits again and again, as Pinch, Holofernes, the Apothecary in *Romeo and Juliet*, Slender, Aguecheek and so on" (Wilson, *King John*, p. lii). But Shakespeare did not join the Chamberlain's Men until 1594, indeed could not have—the company was only founded in that year, when the theaters reopened following a long hiatus due to the plague.

There is another extraordinary piece of evidence, which in my estimation has never received the weight it deserves. In *King John* 3.3.59–68 Hubert is urged to kill young Arthur. But when Hubert comes to do it, the royal command has radically altered or at least softened. The assassin now carries with him a written warrant to blind his captive (4.1.37–42). This startling anomaly is completely unexplained. We never see or hear John's countermanding his original order, and later in the play he again desires Arthur's death. Everything is satisfactorily accounted for, however, if we recognize that Shakespeare was working from *The Troublesome Raigne*, that is, *King John* was written sometime after 1591, because in the earlier play the king, following Holinshed, explicitly instructs Hubert, in writing, to blind his rival, which would be sufficient to disable him as a ruler. Dramatically the blunder does not matter: the scene's interest resides wholly in Hubert's Macbeth-like conscience, his decision to spare Arthur and then lie to the king.

An additional small but significant textual pointer is the First Folio's redundant stage direction, "Enter a Sheriffe," a character who says and does nothing (1.1.44). Most modern editors, reluctant to delete but quick to add, conjecturally supply "and whispers Essex in the ear," partly by analogy with *The Troublesome Raigne* (see below) and partly because that lord then announces the arrival of the Faulconbridge

brothers requesting settlement of their inheritance dispute. Sidney Thomas, however, demonstrates that the meaningless Folio stage direction is actually what survives of a much longer sequence in *The Troublesome Raigne*, where the Sheriff of
Northamptonshire enters, "whispers in the ear" of the Earl of Salisbury (immediately sent off by King John on another mission), and then makes a longish speech
of his own describing the Faulconbridge matter (Thomas, 1986 and 1987).

It is worth observing, too, that in *King John* Essex is never on stage again. Most
modern productions thus give his part to Lord Bigot, a character absent from the
first scene but later a visible English lord. I think it more than likely that this was
Shakespeare's intention (the substitution of Bigot for Essex is, in fact, made at *King
John*, 4.3.10 stage direction; cf. *The Troublesome Raigne* II.26 s.d.) which Shakespeare
either overlooked or never got around to correcting—the manuscript from which
F1 was prepared seems not to have been a fair copy. Either way, the obvious conclusion is that *The Troublesome Raigne* must be the earlier work; little is gained by
elaborating the Sheriff's otherwise silent part and much lost in slowing down the
action. Shakespeare's changes in *King John*, cutting the Sheriff/Salisbury business
and giving a short speech to someone else, are marked improvements on the clunky
original.

Set in the context of Shakespeare's development as a whole, *King John* and especially the ambiguous figure of the Bastard date more probably from 1594–1597,
the years everyone agrees were pivotal for Shakespeare. (See, for example, Frank
Kermode, *Shakespeare's Language* [New York: Farrar, Straus, and Giroux, 2000],
13–17, and Bullough, 1962, 3.356, where he notes that "*Richard II* [written 1594–1595]
marks in fact a new beginning which embodies the growing complexity of the
dramatist's mind and art . . . and the new interpretation given to politics.")

Stylometrics (the computation and statistical analysis of writing patterns) confirms this period for *King John*. Practitioners note the play's "firm placing" after
Richard III and *Love's Labor's Lost* and its rough contemporaneity with *A Midsummer Night's Dream*, *Romeo and Juliet*, and *Richard II* (Brian Vickers, *Shakespeare,
Co-Author*, p. 56). Vickers cites a variety of numerical tests based on vocabulary and
metrical counts assigning the play to 1594–1597. Among these are tabulated
chronologies—W. Fischer and K. Wentersdorf, eds., "Shakespearean Chronology
and the Metrical Tests," *in Shakespeare-Studien: Festschrift für Heinrich Mutschmann*
(Marburg: Elwert Verlag, 1951), pp. 161–193; Macdonald P. Jackson, *Studies in Attribution: Middleton and Shakespeare* (Salzburg: Institut Für Anglistik und Ameri-
kanistik, Universität Salzburg, 1979); Ants Oras, *Pause Patterns in Elizabethan and
Jacobean Drama. An Experiment in Prosody* (Gainesvile: U of Florida P, 1960)—that
reveal high verbal and rhythmic correlations between *King John* and plays Shakespeare is known from other evidence, for example, performance and publication
dates, to have written during these years.

The four-year span 1594–1597, however, is too broad for our needs. Precisely dating *King John* requires the sharper focus of verse and phrase parallels, stylistic and
thematic affinities, and other points of contact with related work, all of which suggest that it is a close companion of *Richard II*, a play known to have been completed some time in 1595. Scholars derive this date from the fact that Samuel Daniel's
The Civil Wars was entered in the Stationers' Register on October 11, 1594, and released the following year. Unmistakable traces of Daniel's language and usages in

Shakespeare's play, such as the unusual spellings *Bullingbrooke* and *Herford*, not found elsewhere, show that *Richard II* must have been written or at least finished after 1594 but no later than 1597, when it was first published (see Robert Metcalf Smith, *Froissart and the English Chronicle Play* [New York: Columbia UP, 1915], pp. 145–154, and George Logan, "Lucan-Daniel-Shakespeare: New Light on the Relation Between *The Civil Wars* and *Richard II*," *Shakespeare Studies* 9 [1976]: 121–140). This gives 1595 for the play's completion and 1596 for its London debut: as we've seen, new dramas, especially popular ones, were rarely published while still fresh upon the stage.

But *King John* and *Richard II* clearly derive from the same creative period—even Honigmann describes them as twin plays (Honigmann, *King John*, xvii, elsewhere noting that the lion-skin, a stage property apparently introduced by Shakespeare, features also in *A Midsummer Night's Dream* [1595–1596] "and belongs to the same years" [p. 28n]). Both are written entirely in verse, omit secondary plots paralleling the main action, and feature baronial uprisings against the king.

Bullough compares the "fanciful word play" in both dramas (*Narrative and Dramatic Sources* 4.23), and indeed a number of verse and verbal echoes connect *King John* and *Richard II*. Perhaps the most striking is Pembroke's description of how young Arthur, freshly killed, will find "His little kingdom of a forced grave" (*King John*, 4.2.98). This clearly parallels Richard II when he surrenders at Flint Castle, bewailing the way he will be forced to exchange "my large kingdom for a little grave, / A little little grave, an obscure grave" (*Richard II*, 3.3.153–154).

Everything thus points to 1594–1595 for *King John*'s composition, its verse, characterization, and other formal qualities suggesting that it probably preceded *Richard II*. It is a good play but noticeably more experimental than its author's tragic handling of the deposed monarch whose fall ushered in the catastrophic Wars of the Roses. The scene in which Arthur leaps from the walls to his death, for example, is theatrically powerful but notoriously difficult to stage—the jump must be credibly fatal but not from a point so high as actually to hurt the actor—while Richard's politically suicidal descent "like glist'ring Phaëton" into the base court of Flint Castle is a moment of exalted historical tragedy (3.3.178).

King John represents an assay for Shakespeare's evolving narrative strategies following the watershed years 1592–1594. As Tillyard says (p. 233), "though the play is a wonderful affair, full of promise and new life, as a whole it is uncertain of itself," which is what we would expect of an experimental work. A sculptor might call it a *moquette*, a Renaissance painter a cartoon, a trying-out of angles and expressions. Though not Shakespeare's best work, it may be one of his most important, bridging the gap between his two tetralogies, that is, his early manner and his middle period. More specifically, it's an anticipation of *Richard II*, a theatrical trial-run resulting in a cruder and dramatically less accomplished history which, for just these reasons, may well have been set aside when it was done. I consider it very possible that the unpolished manuscript was recovered from the playwright's papers by Heminge and Condell and published unedited in F1. This would account both for *King John*'s apparent dependence on *The Troublesome Raigne* and its inconsistencies (for example, the blinding/killing of Arthur, discrepant speech heads, misplaced stage directions, and so forth) and would explain why there is no record of its ever having been performed or published with the author's blessing.

SOURCES FOR THE PLAY

Getting the relationship right between *King John* and *The Troublesome Raigne* clarifies many other contentious issues, including the ongoing debate about Shakespeare's sources. If *King John* came first, *The Troublesome Raigne* is obviously eliminated as a source—no one finds it remarkable that another dramatist would steal wholesale from Shakespeare—and is for this reason often ignored. But if *King John* was the later play, then as Braunmuller says (p. 18):

> the existence of *The Troublesome Raigne* makes nearly impossible any direct or sustained analysis of how Shakespeare handled his main historical source, Holinshed's *Chronicles*, since that "source" may have largely and already been dramatized for him. Although Shakespeare has details from Holinshed not in *The Troublesome Raigne*, his treatment of Holinshed generally parallels that in the anonymous play, and Shakespeare's "handling of his source" then becomes one dramatist's reworking of another's play rather than a dramatist's reworking of a chronicle history.

The conundrum appears unresolvable. However, if Shakespeare was at least part-author of *The Troublesome Raigne*, as I suggest, all the difficulties bedeviling the record are quickly and easily dispatched. In *King John* he revisits an earlier work, fundamentally trusting his own research but adding and/or correcting details based on his subsequent reading, theatrical experience, and analysis. Finally he strips away almost all of his co-author's contributions—especially the lesser verse and crude scenes of monastic lechery and murder—to produce a powerful new version reflecting his own political emphases and of course poetry. Though not entirely successful, the play gives him the confidence and impetus to deal with the ambiguously tragic deposition of Richard II and to create that sustained examination of heroic leadership we call the *Henriad*.

Shakespeare seized upon the following isolated reference in the cacophonous welter of Holinshed's fragmented narrative:

> The same yere [1199], Philip bastard sonne to king Richard, to whom his father had giuen the castell and honor of Coinacke, killed the vicount Limoges, in reuenge of his father's death, who was slaine (as yee haue heard) in besieging the castell of Chalus Cheuerall. (*Chronicles* 3.278)

This becomes that strikingly characteristic opening scene, where the themes of legitimacy and inheritance are exemplified and reviewed, but in the process Shakespeare invented modern humanity. Later the reference is developed into the revenge miniplot, in some ways like *Hamlet*, where a princely son, who is himself his father's revived spirit, avenges his father's unjust killing by slaying the worthless slayer.

The word "bastard" leapt from Holinshed's page for Shakespeare, and upon its associations he built the analogous structures of political justice and injustice, of John's and Arthur's competing claims to the throne, and indeed the drama's overarching exploration of the whole question of legal power and legal possession. The dangerously intelligent Cardinal Pandulph is another distinctively Shakespearean figure composed from a variety of Holinshed's hints and touches describing a series of papal delegates dispatched to England over the years.

Indeed, the bedrock of both *The Troublesome Raigne* and *King John* is Holin-shed's *Chronicles* (1587). Most of the story springs from this source, including its emphasis on English nationalism, John's struggle to retain his Angevin empire, the challenge to his legitimacy posed by Arthur, his battle with and submission to the Roman church, the treachery of his nobles and their on-again, off-again alliance with France, the almost successful invasion of England by the Dauphin, and finally John's murder and excruciating death by poison at Swinstead Abbey. Holinshed also articulates what could be called Shakespeare's political theme, the importance of unity in the face of a common foe (*The Troublesome Raigne*, II.1187–1198, *King John*, 5.7.110–118):

> The communaltie also grew into factions, some fauoring, & some cursing the king, as
> they bare affection. The cleargie was likewise at dissention, so that nothing preuailed
> but malice and spite, which brought foorth and spred abroad the fruits of disobedi-
> ence to all good lawes and orders, greatlie to the disquieting of the whole state. So
> that herein we haue a perfect view of the perplexed state of princes, chéeflie when they
> are ouerswaied with forren & prophane power, and not able to assure themselues of
> their subiects allegiance and loialtie. (Holinshed, *Chronicles*, 3.299)

Among the bizarre events Shakespeare included are the appearance of the five moons (Holinshed, 3.282), which is given symbolic resonance, and the strange story of Peter the Prophet (Holinshed, 3.311).

Evidence that Shakespeare revisited Holinshed before updating *The Troublesome Raigne* may be found in the many small touches and corrections he apparently later brought to *King John*. For instance, the earlier play contains no mention of Lewis's embassy to the English lords ahead of his military invasion (Holinshed, 3.329), though it is noted in *King John*, 4.3.15–17. Similarly, the audience learns from a dying speech by the half-French, half-English lord Melune of the Dauphin's planned treachery against these same nobles (*King John*, 5.4.10–48, following Holinshed, p. 334), whereas in *The Troublesome Raigne*, II.586–624, we're given its fictional dramatization. Likewise, in the anonymous play, following Holinshed, Arthur's supposed murder drives the English lords into alliance with the Dauphin. In the more politically nuanced *King John*, however, they join him beforehand from a sense (mistaken as it turns out) of collective safety. It is a subtler, more considered, and complex set of motivations expressing "the infection of the time" (*King John*, 5.2.20).

As part of his case for the priority of *King John* and the dependence on it of *The Troublesome Raigne*, Honigmann provides strong evidence for Shakespeare's also having consulted John Foxe's *Actes and Monuments* or *The Book of Martyrs* (1583 edition). Ironically, Honigmann successfully demonstrates only the reverse, that is, Shakespeare's subsequent amendment of *The Troublesome Raigne* story. His best ev-idence—"the case for Foxe as a source becomes watertight" (Honigmann, xx)—is a reference in *King John* to "Swinsted Abbey" as the place of John's death (Foxe, p. 256, *King John*, 5.3.8), where all other possible sources, including Holinshed and Matthew Paris, whom Holinshed cites, give "Swineshead" or (in a variant spelling) "Suenesheud."

But Honigmann is notably silent about the fact that *The Troublesome Raigne* refers to "Swinsteed Abbey" (II.876), a small but significantly different spelling with a more antique ring. *King John* also employs several other expressions and incidental references derived from Foxe that fail to appear in *The Troublesome Raigne*, some quite consequential. For example, in *The Troublesome Raigne*, following Holinshed, Peter of Pomfret's politically dangerous prophecy that the king will be forced to resign his crown before Ascension Day is announced to John's face. In *King John*, however, following *Actes and Monuments* (pp. 252–253), it is first published abroad and becomes the reason he is brought to court—a more developed and persuasive version of the story. Verbal echoes from Foxe noted by Honigmann (pp. xiii–xiv) include "yield up," and "take again" in reference to the crown (Foxe, p. 253, ii, *King John*, 5.1.1–2), the word "burst" to describe the effects of poison on the bowels (Foxe, p. 256, *King John*, 5.6.30), and "meddling," "juggling," and "revenue," in connection with the Roman church (Foxe, pp. 250, i, ii, 253, i, *King John*, 3.1.163, 169). Shakespeare worked from both Holinshed and Foxe when preparing his Author's Plot for *The Troublesome Raigne* and then later, like a good historian, checked his sources again, incorporating a few new words and details. This accounts both for the references to Foxe found in the two plays and the unique citations in *King John*.

A recent study by John Klause records a great number of parallels between the poetry of Robert Southwell (1561–1595) and Shakespeare's play (John Klause, "New Sources for Shakespeare's *King John*: The Writings of Robert Southwell," *Studies in Philology* 97 [Fall 2001]: 401–427). A Jesuit and a martyr hanged at Tyburn in February, 1595, Southwell clearly had an influence on some of Shakespeare's language in *King John*, though none of it suggests secret Catholic sympathies on the playwright's part. Finally, there is some evidence that around 1594 Shakespeare consulted the *Wakefield Chronicle*, an unpublished Latin history, the only possible place he could have discovered that Eleanor of Aquitaine died on April 1, 1204.

STRUCTURE AND PLOTTING

As so often in Shakespeare, *King John* is a drama of division and structural symmetry. Its parts, like its characters and themes, are quasidialectical complements, both of which challenge John's authority and pose the question of his legitimacy. With him stands his mother Elinor; against him, Arthur's mother, Constance; at his right hand, the illegitimate but loyal prince, Philip Faulconbridge; confronting him, the legitimate but disloyal prince, Lewis; behind him lie usurpation and the past; ahead, deposition and renewal. The sense of Hegelian conflicts unresolved is relentlessly depressing, which may account for the play's lack of popular appeal. Even the Bastard's rise, which mirrors John's sad decline, lacks climactic power because in the end he steps politely aside for Henry III. "The Bastard ought to be king," as Harold Bloom remarks, but he is instead dissolved into the play's "unused potential" (*Shakespeare: The Invention of the Human*, 56). Similarly, John's awful death carries with it no sense of salvation, though it makes national redemption possible—it is his finest and most nearly tragic moment.

The action itself is structurally divided. The first three acts concern Prince Arthur—the true king, as Queen Elinor reminds John and the audience in an early aside. Her statement stands out like an axiom, a self-evident proposition coloring everything that follows. The last two acts dramatize the challenge from France, based in part upon Lewis's marriage to Blanch, John's widespread unpopularity, disaffection among the English nobility, and the use of naked force. The French are defeated, but John dies, executed as it were for his political sins but leaving the way open for a lawful successor.

MAIN CHARACTERS

The Bastard (Philip Faulconbridge)

Faulconbridge, Shakespeare's first major bastard, has been called "an astonishing break-away from his official self" (Tillyard, p. 229) and "the one first-class character in the play" (James Agate in *The Times* [London], November 1924, reviewing the Strand Fellowship of Players' production, quoted by Beaurline, p. 12). This character alone should indicate that Shakespeare conceived *The Troublesome Raigne*, for he is substantially the same figure in both plays.

The Bastard is certainly *King John*'s most memorable personality. The explanation may lie in his freedom from the constraints of history—of all the drama's figures he is the most fabricated, in but not of the action. He alone can truly choose, as he does in the decisive first scene when he opts to forego his patrimony. His reward is instant elevation, first to a knighthood, then promotion to the king's right-hand man, finally to supreme commander of his armies and England's de facto monarch. He grows; he prospers; he is the country's natural leader, the true descendant of Richard the Lionheart, whom he reincarnates in every particular. Tillyard calls him "one of Shakespeare's great versions of the regal type," citing John Masefield's view that he is a prototypical Prince Hal (Tillyard, p. 226).

Yet what sets Faulconbridge apart from the other characters is not only his success but also his capacity for introspection and philosophic generalization. He is the play's Chorus, or the nearest thing to it. His discourse on commodity, "the bias of the world" (2.1.574), is the only genuinely explicit overview we are given of *King John*'s moral universe and Tudor politics, at least as Shakespeare understood them. Like Ulysses on degree (*Troilus and Cressida*, 1.3.75–137), Faulconbridge delivers a speech that reverberates through all the historical tragedies (for example, *Macbeth*, *Hamlet*) and tragical histories (for example, *Richard II*, *Richard III*). We warm to him for seeing "how this world goes," as Lear expresses it (*King Lear*, 4.1.150–151), while yet declining to take part in its self-involved corruption. The Bastard understands full well the

> Sweet, sweet, sweet poison for the age's tooth,
> Which, though I will not practice to deceive,
> Yet, to avoid deceit, I mean to learn. (*King John*, 1.1.213–215)

While somewhat less than its hero—none of the characters in *King John* deserves that appellation—Faulconbridge is the drama's only idealist, the one man of principle who can be counted upon to do the right thing. Unsurprisingly, this trait is vectored through his use of language, a typical move expressing the fact that, as Auden notes, "Shakespeare's real interest is in the bastard's diction" (Arthur Kirsch, ed., *W. H. Auden: Lectures on Shakespeare* [Princeton: Princeton UP, 2000], p. 69). He sounds like a typical overreacher:

> Well, whiles I am a beggar, I will rail,
> And say there is no sin but to be rich;

> And being rich, my virtue then shall be
> To say there is no vice but beggary.
> Since kings break faith upon commodity,
> Gain, be my lord, for I will worship thee. (*King John*, 2.1.593–598)

Yet he declines to act as he says he will: he is, in the best sense, a unique Bastard. Auden adds that Faulconbridge's "type of speech, is serviceable for a cynic turning villain, like Iago, for example, or for an honest man in despair, like Timon." However, Shakespeare is merely exploring "how men of action *should* talk. . . . Out of this interest was to come the great development of his verse in the future" (Kirsch, pp. 69–70).

The Bastard's cynicism, it turns out, is in this context a sign of moral health rather than depravity, appropriate for a man in touch with the realities of his time. Resolutely and almost annoyingly neither a villain nor a hero, his final declaration of national pride and calls for unity vibrate with sincerity and earned authority. Shakespeare presents *King John* as a world without heroes, a desolate place where mutual support is England's last, best, and only hope.

Among the great studies of the Bastard's character is Harold Bloom's in *Shakespeare: The Invention of the Human*. Faulconbridge stands out, Bloom says, because he exemplifies our modern sense of psychic inner turmoil, of alternating hope and uncertainty accompanied by surges of optimism and doubt. Consequently, "No one in Shakespeare before Faulconbridge speaks with so inward a motion or with so subtly barbed an inflection" (Bloom, p. 55). The Bastard's inwardness is the quality that renders him a great exemplar of post-Shakespearean humanity, setting him on the same continuum as Othello and Shakespeare's other complex, internally directed figures. He has the self-conscious theatricality so distinctive of his creator, a "free artist of himself," as Bloom almost puts it, citing Hegel (ibid., p. 56). What Bloom seems to mean is that such figures convey a sense of inner life, of struggling to liberate themselves from the relentless imposition of the narratives in which they are trapped. Faulconbridge thus "shares Falstaff's and Hamlet's quality of being too large for the play he inhabits" (ibid., p. 51).

It is Faulconbridge's good-natured modesty—the fact that in the end he has no cutting edge—that renders him a lesser figure than Shakespeare's other great illegitimates, such as Edmund in *King Lear*. He also has no sex appeal, again unlike Edmund, despite his handsome, regal looks. *King John*'s Bastard is more a dry run than the true antihero (ruthless, ambitious, defeated) we secretly wish him to be. He is thus remembered but not admired.

Cardinal Pandulph

Faulconbridge's moral counterpart is the semifictional papal legate, Cardinal Pandulph, a classic Shakespearean Machiavillain of the first order. There is suggestive evidence that he may have been based on Thomas Arundel, Archbishop of Canterbury in the time of Henry IV, a notoriously bullying manipulator who when necessary invoked scripture to ensure compliance with his worldly will (Terry Jones, Robert Yeager, Terry Doran, Alan Fletcher, and Jeanette D'Or, *Who Murdered Chaucer?* [London: Methuen, 2003], *passim*). Both have much in common with the ruthless Cardinal Wolsey, whose political fall is the vivid subject of *Henry*

VIII, for as John E. Alvis notes, "The last of Shakespeare's English plays, *Henry VIII*, resolves a problem central to the first [in terms of English history], *King John*, and marks the appropriate culmination in the development implicit in the entire sequence. With Henry VIII the Christian church becomes formally subordinate to the English king" (Alvis and West, eds., *Shakespeare as Political Thinker* [Durham, NC: Carolina Academic P, 1981], 9–10).

While *King John* may be said to lack heroes, Pandulph is unquestionably its villain. In contrast to the Bastard he is unhealthily cynical and completely amoral, a smooth-tongued, dangerous manipulator entirely without scruple or principle save the interests of the Church. Nor are any of these remotely spiritual or to do with things even associated with the doctrines of his religion's founder. Pandulph's issues are power, control, and the aggrandizement of the pope's authority. He dispenses what might be called political indulgences—Heaven for those who comply with the will of Rome, Hell for those who don't.

Pandulph's curses are all instantly reversible, of course, and linked inexorably to the pursuit of temporal authority. He reminds one of Orwell's public orator who reverses direction in a single flowing movement. When Pandulph persuades the Dauphin to invade England ostensibly on Arthur's behalf, he shows himself to be the play's most cynical realist, the ultimate exemplification of commodity. Master of realpolitik centuries before Bismarck invented the term, he recognizes that as soon as the French land

> If that young Arthur be not gone already,
> Even at that news he dies; and then the hearts
> Of all his people shall revolt from him,
> And kiss the lips of unacquainted change,
> And pick strong matter of revolt and wrath
> Out of the bloody fingers' ends of John. (*King John*, 3.4.163–168)

The audience knows uncomfortably that he is right: it has just seen John command his henchman to assassinate the boy. To that extent Pandulph is the (im)moral center of the play, the force and intellect that confers a species of rationality or at least purpose upon evil. He is neither incomprehensible like Iago, nor irresponsible like Macbeth, but organizationally directed like no other villain in Shakespeare.

King John

It follows from the foregoing that John is simultaneously the play's most and least important character, its subject and its object, its strongest and its weakest player, a figure whose every triumph conceals a fresh defeat, a victim eliciting neither sympathy nor pity. His diplomatic victories turn into political disasters, for example, the marriage of Blanch to the Dauphin makes possible the Dauphin's claim to John's throne by virtue of his marriage to an English princess. John is the play's most important character because he is England's king, its least important because his reign turns out to be little more than a preparation for his successor. He is its eponymous subject yet simultaneously its tormented object, more acted upon than acting. Willing to do anything, he accomplishes nothing. He loses his Angevin empire trying to save it, canonizes Arthur without killing him, is compelled to surrender his crown in order to preserve it. He invades France only to have the favor returned with interest. The situation is redeemed not by his efforts but those of Faulconbridge, the betrayal of France's plans by Lord Melune, and a little luck (the loss of the French supply ships on the Goodwin Sands). His life is the negation of negation.

The best thing John does in the play—the high point of his reign—is ennoble Faulconbridge, and this is accomplished in 1.1. One expedient sellout after another follows, including the surrender of England's French possessions on his mother's disastrous advice and his craven (but in the end gratuitous) submission to Pandulph so as to avoid humiliating defeat.

John's lowest point is surely his reproach to Hubert for loyally carrying out his instructions to murder Arthur. John lacks even Pandulph's capacity for self-acknowledged evil, unable to accept the slightest responsibility for his opportunistic pursuit of tickling commodity, of which he is the play's most conspicuous representative. Yet this unmitigated disaster of a man and king finds—though he never knows it—a tiny morsel of immortality as one (though one only) of the Reformation's morning stars. Despite himself he is absolved by history.

Elinor and Constance

Finally, something must be said about the mothers in *King John*, for in many ways motherhood is the sharpest and most selfless emotion dramatized. Elinor and Constance are both Queen Mothers, Elinor de facto and Constance de jure. They look out fiercely for their children and are ruthless in their defense. Elinor gives up her life for her son, Constance her sanity. Some of the most tragicomic moments in the play portray the two women screaming abuse at one another, indistinguishable and in a typically Shakespearean way almost indissoluble:

Elinor: Who is it thou dost call usurper, France?

Constance: Let me make answer; thy usurping son.

Elinor: Out, insolent, thy bastard shall be king
That thou mayst be a queen, and check the world! (2.1.120–123)

But while Elinor fades, dying obscurely offstage, Constance becomes more prominent, first in her furious calls for France and Austria to make war on England in her son's interest (3.1.113–129), and then, when she realizes Arthur is doomed, may already be dead, weeping tragically for him in a scene that often steals the play:

I will not keep this form upon my head [*Tearing her hair*]
When there is such disorder in my wit.
O Lord, my boy, my Arthur, my fair son!
My life, my joy, my food, my all the world!
My widow-comfort, and my sorrows' cure! (*King John*, 3.4.101–105)

These lines carry, as Chambers puts it, "the authentic thrill" (E. K. Chambers, *Shakespeare, a Survey* [London: Sidgwick & Jackson, 1925], 98), exemplifying Shakespeare's supreme ability to personalize history by rendering it comprehensible in human terms. To that extent Constance is one of his great female characters.

DEVICES AND TECHNIQUES

King John's chief narrative device is contradiction, its main technique the counterpoising of contraries, scenic and thematic oppositions without which there would be no progression. The largest of these paradoxes is current reality, the Elizabethan present, rooted firmly in historic time. The play's serial conflicts are resolved in syntheses that themselves become conditional, the basis for fresh antitheses.

In 1.1 John's possession of the throne is the occasion for a war whose point is England's subjugation, that is, his removal. France's challenge—Arthur is no more than a stalking horse—seeks to replace a strong but illegal monarch with a weak but legal king, an adult with a child, an English ruler possessed of a French empire with an English empire controlled by France. The process is best exemplified in 2.1, when the rival armies confront each other before Angiers, an English-French town, each demanding the fealty and submission of its French-English inhabitants. The equivocating reply is that the burghers will give allegiance to the true king, whoever he may be, as proved by force. Elinor's axiom, that John is not king by right (1.1.40–43), is contradicted by a world that declares that "strong possession" (1.1.39) is the only right. John, who was initially seen to be wrong, is justified in the event. The two armies then engage and, as it were, mutually interpenetrate one another in uncertain victory/defeat and—at the instigation of the Bastard, whose suggestion itself seems simultaneously grave and satirical—in their decision to unite against the town and preserve it by destroying it. The idea reflects and comments upon John's later efforts to preserve his throne. Threats of destruction almost ludicrously transmogrify into the marriage of Blanch and the Dauphin, an act of peace and reconciliation. The territories for which a war was fought are now smilingly handed over as dowry. This union then becomes grounds for a renewal of the fighting. The equation war equals marriage equals war is a sequence of contumacious and almost insane logic: "Mad world, mad kings, mad composition!" as the Bastard remarks in his choral role (2.1.561).

The battle, when it moves to England, is also continually on and off as John's nobles first defect from him to support the Dauphin, then defect from the Dauphin and return to John. Arthur is both murdered and not murdered, alive when he is believed to be dead, dead when he is believed to be alive. John is king, then not king, then king again. He crowns himself repeatedly and yet never safely reigns. The equivocating Pandulph provokes and unprovokes, damns and absolves, uncrowns and crowns almost from scene to scene. The French invasion fails, but it also succeeds by helping to remove King John. It disunites England and then unifies it more powerfully than before. Faulconbridge becomes *pro tem* monarch, a sort of legitimate illegitimate, so that Henry III may take the throne permanently and bring the contradictions to a close.

King John's defining mode, as Deborah T. Curren-Aquino and Ralph Berry independently observe, is serial bewilderment, often expressed as a succession of interrogations (Curren-Aquino, p. 14; Ralph Berry, *The Shakespearean Metaphor: Studies in Language and Form* [London: Macmillan, 1978], 30–33). The tone is set at the outset, when John asks the younger Faulconbridge, completely puzzled, "Is that the elder, and art thou the heir?" (1.1.57). Later the betrayed Constance refuses to accept the news of Lewis's marriage to Blanch, pouring out her incredulity in a torrent of questions:

Gone to be married? Gone to swear a peace?
False blood to false blood join'd! Gone to be friends?
Shall Lewis have Blanch, and Blanch these provinces? . . .
What dost thou mean by shaking of thy head?
Why dost thou look so sadly on my son?
What means that hand upon that breast of thine?
Why holds thine eye that lamentable rheum,
Like a proud river peering o'er his bounds?
Be these sad signs confirmers of thy words? (3.1.1–24)

Dismayed queries and confusion are everywhere. The play's opening line is a question, "Now, say, Chatillion, what would France with us?" succeeded by "What follows if we disallow of this?" (1.1.1, 16), "What men are you?" (1.1.49), "What art thou?" (1.1.55), "Why, being younger born, / Doth he lay claim to thine inheritance?" (1.1.71–72), "What doth move you to claim your brother's land?" (1.1.91), and "What is thy name?" (1.1.157). Analysis of the first scene alone shows that John uses the interrogative 16 percent of the time, Elinor 14 percent, the Bastard 9 percent, his brother Robert 7 percent, and their mother, Lady Faulconbridge, who is on stage for only fifty-five lines, an astonishing 54 percent. In the play as a whole, John asks twenty-three questions, the Bastard twenty-two. (Joseph A. Porter provides these statistics and other numerical counts in "Fraternal Pragmatics: Speech Acts of John and the Bastard," in Curren-Aquino, p. 143.)

On hearing of the Dauphin's planned treachery, Salisbury responds, like Constance: "May this be possible? May this be true?" (5.4.21). Confronted by Pandulph's power play—betray John or face excommunication himself—Philip of France agonizes, then agonizes further at the cardinal's sophistical response:

King Philip: I am perplex'd, and know not what to say.

Pandulph: What canst thou say but will perplex thee more,
If thou stand excommunicate and cursed? (3.1.221–223)

At first Hubert doesn't quite understand the king's dark hints concerning Arthur's murder. Later, John tells a messenger, "Thou hast made me giddy / With these ill tidings" (4.2.131–132), adding to Faulconbridge, who has come with further news, "Bear with me, cousin, for I was amaz'd / Under the tide" (4.2.137–138). Arthur's mysterious death provokes, as Curren-Aquino expresses it, "a litany of *ifs*,"—

Bastard: If that it be the work of any hand.

Salisbury: If that it be the work of any hand? . . .

Bastard: If thou but frown on me . . .
If thou didst this deed of death . . .
If thou didst but consent (4.3.59–124)

—leading up to the Bastard's consummating exclamation: "I am amazed, methinks, and lose my way / Among the thorns and dangers of this world (4.3.140–141). Bafflement and confusion define a play that appropriately concludes on a note of doubtful certainty, the Bastard's final and most conditional "if"—"If England to itself do rest but true" (5.7.118). While invariably taken in its most positive way, a question lurks within.

THEMES AND MEANINGS

At issue in the play is the integrity and survival of England, its climax a political and emotional synthesis in many senses, including Henry III's accession—a boy-king like Arthur, but also John's son and only legitimate heir. Virtually unmentioned through the story, he appears almost miraculously at the moment of his father's passing, a kind of divine intervention, the future in the instant.

What we might call the drama's major premise and the theme of its first part is the Bastard's famous speech about "tickling commodity" (2.1.561–598), by which he means crude self-interest. It's what motivates John, Philip of France, Constance, Elinor, the citizens of Angiers, all the principal players except young Arthur and, of course, Faulconbridge. The action's minor premise, again spoken by the Bastard—the thesis/antithesis symmetry must be deliberate—is his declaration at the end of the need for his countrymen to abandon self-interest and self-regard, that is, commodity, and unite in the face of the collective foe. That way national salvation lies: "Come the three corners of the world in arms, / And we shall shock them" (5.7.116–117). The Bastard is transformed into a prophet—the reference to the Armada is unmistakable.

Faulconbridge's own modesty and refusal to seek the crown, which he might do given his royal lineage and the reality that at the play's end he is commander of a victorious army and the country's de facto ruler, is impressive and exemplifies his call for selfless unity. In many ways he is the most decent of all the major figures in Shakespeare's history plays. His principled refusal alone makes possible Henry III's peaceful accession and the drama's resolution.

Shakespeare's selections from Holinshed and other sources emphasize the analogies between John's reign and that of Elizabeth I. The youngest survivor among her siblings, denounced as a usurper and a bastard, in office by an act of will and testament, threatened with invasion by a Catholic power and excommunicated by the church, triumphant over both in battle, challenged by uprisings and disaffected nobles, morally responsible for the death in prison of her rival (Mary Stuart, queen of Scotland) and yet grimly hanging on—Elizabeth's career does indeed remarkably parallel John's, though it took a Shakespeare to perceive and develop the analogies. He did a similar thing with his next play, *Richard II*, as the queen herself famously noticed: "I am Richard II. Know ye not that?" (Chambers, *William Shakespeare*, 2.326–327).

Revealing Shakespeare's characteristically cynical hopefulness—despite everything, matters turn out for the best in this far-from-the-best of all possible worlds—the play both comments upon and instructs its present with the past while looking ahead, as the barren queen approaches her own end, to the succession of another monarch who had taken the throne as a very young child, James I.

It is often asserted that Shakespeare blunts the edge of *The Troublesome Raigne*'s anti-Catholicism, but this interpretation is an illusion based on his removal of the slapstick scenes of monastic vice. In many ways *King John* is a more profound because more seriously framed attack. Shakespeare's view is that there is nothing funny about the Church. In *King John* he concentrates on Catholicism's real power—the world-altering might of primitive belief. Pandulph brandishes salvation and damnation like blunt instruments, subtle as a sexton's spade about the mazard [head] (see *Hamlet*, 5.1.89–90). In his hands Hell is a shillelagh, an instrument of coercive policy, reminding our more secular age of dogma's force in an era when purgatory and damnation were not simply metaphors. Pandulph is genuinely frightening, the possessor of the play's real weapons of mass destruction: the power to provoke war or conclude a peace, to make and unmake kings, to excommunicate or readmit into the fold on the basis of nothing more than obedience or expedience.

The occasion for Pandulph's appearance is the historical argument over who was to head up the Church in John's England, that is, rule as Archbishop of Canterbury. After much squabbling between clergy and monarchy, the pope intervened and nominated Stephen Langton, a candidate unacceptable to John. In the play, as in actual history, the Church excommunicated the defiant king and forced France to declare war to enforce its will, or face the same dire fate. Even more dangerously, something Elizabeth I herself well knew, Pandulph promises not only absolution but sainthood to any of John's subjects who "takes away by any secret course / Thy hateful life" (*King John*, 3.1.178–179). He is thus in the end responsible for the murder of a king, the most heinous of all Elizabethan crimes.

The moment of Pandulph's greatest triumph occurs in 5.1 when John, believing himself to be on the verge of defeat by the French, yields completely to Rome in return for Pandulph's promise to avert the war. John hands over his crown and, kneeling, receives it back, a wordless image of iconic, medieval power. The moment is truly historic because, in effect, John pawns his kingdom to the pope, a promissory note presented for payment in full to successive English monarchs, including Henry VIII and Elizabeth I. In 1535 Pope Paul III demanded that the courts of Europe depose Henry, and immediately prior to Spain's 1588 offensive Pope Sixtus V issued a Bull reminding English Catholics and the world that—among other arguments justifying the Armada—King John had agreed "that none might be lawful kinge or Quene therof [that is, England], without the approbation and consent of the supreme Bishopp" (Sider, p. 214 and appendix). Philip II was merely his executor.

In a sense King John's successors had no alternative but to break with Rome. Who was to be master in England, pope or king? The answer drove directly into the heart of a Reformation still incomplete in Shakespeare's day. Its first front-line casualty, in the Tudor view, turned out to be the unattractive, at best equivocal figure of King John, martyr of circumstance yet hero of none. The oily Pandulph would have seemed to Elizabethan audiences both the face and force of history.

King John also explores the theme of legitimacy of inheritance and the rights inhering in possession. Its meaning appears to be that while possession may triumph in the short run, only legitimate inheritance can guarantee political stability. Conveniently for the Tudors, whose line began with Henry VII's deposing of Richard III, legitimacy is fairly quickly established. John is a usurper, but his son, Henry III, will reign legitimately. This same vision seems to prevail in the second Henriad as well. Henry IV's seizure of the crown from Richard II results in civil war, but Henry V unites England to triumph over France. Elizabeth, as granddaughter of Henry

VII, would therefore reign by "Our strong possession and our right for us" (1.1.39), by right as well as by might.

CRITICAL CONTROVERSIES

One major critical controversy concerning *King John* concerns its relation to the anonymous play *The Troublesome Raigne of John King of England*, as discussed in "Publication History" above.

Another issue concerns authorship of *The Troublesome Raigne*. The idea that *The Troublesome Raigne* might be a co-authored work is not new—indeed, the play's evident contradictions almost demand such a hypothesis. In 1725 Alexander Pope judged it to be a collaboration between Shakespeare and William Rowley; later F. G. Fleay suggested that Marlowe outlined it and Lodge, Greene, and Peele wrote the verse (Bullough, 4.4).

The point generally agreed is that Shakespeare cannot have been the versifier of *The Troublesome Raigne* in any important way since there is too little in common between its poetry and *King John*. Exceptions to this opinion include W. J. Courthope, who in the nineteenth century argued that Shakespeare was responsible for the whole thing ("On the Authority of Some of the Early Plays Assigned to Shakespeare and Their Relationship to the Development of His Genius," in *A History of English Poetry* [New York and London: Macmillan and Co., 1895–1910], vol. 4, Appendix), and more recently Eric Sams (*The Real Shakespeare*, 146–153).

The few minor echoes of Shakespeare that we do find in the text confirm the likelihood that he was indeed associated in some way with the writing of *The Troublesome Raigne*. These data are insufficient, however, to support the case that *The Troublesome Raigne* is some kind of early draft or "bad quarto" (corrupt version of *King John*), a critical category that in any event no longer has much currency. More decisively, its hallmarks are missing from the text, especially the coincidence of dialogue, whether mangled or not (see Kenneth Muir, "Source Problems in the Histories," *Shakespeare-Jahrbuch*, 96 [1960]: 60). But this now leaves open only two options: either Shakespeare stole the plot for *King John* from *The Troublesome Raigne*, or he was, early on, librettist for a more established playwright.

The second alternative is the more probable, especially because Shakespeare's later dependence on the anonymous work is of so different an order from his dazzling recreations of, for example, *King Leir* and *The Famous Victories of Henry the Fifth*. In those cases the originals are roughly appropriated and squeezed of their juice, the remainder contemptuously discarded like so much pulp and rind. *King John*, in contrast, is a straight remodeling job, updated and refurbished in the light of theatrical experience and perhaps with a different and more educated audience in mind. Shakespeare was frankly too good an historian, too self-conscious an analyst—too great a writer—to cravenly steal another's work (which is what "source-study" in the case of *The Troublesome Raigne* often amounts to).

These judgments are supported by Vickers's recent work identifying George Peele as the author of most of the *Raigne*'s verse ("*The Troublesome Raigne*, George Peele, and the date of *King John*"). Basing his analysis on the refined techniques of modern stylometrics and the research of earlier scholars, especially H. Dugdale Sykes, Rupert Taylor, and R. F. Hill, Vickers records literally dozens of word and phrase parallels between *The Troublesome Raigne* and Peele's dramas and poems (references are to C. T. Prouty, ed., *The Life and Works of George Peele*, 3 vols. [New Haven: Yale UP, 1970]). Among the most notable are:

> With moornefull tunes in stole of dismall hue (*The Arraygnment of Paris*, 610–611);
>
> And clad this Land in stole of dismall hieu [hue] (*The Troublesome Raigne*, I.5);
>
> My word is past, I am well agreede (Peele, *Edward I*, 1656);
>
> My word is past, receive your boone my Lords (*The Troublesome Raigne*, I.1567);
>
> Hang in the aire for fowles to feed upon (*Edward I*, 2066);
>
> And leave thy bodie to the fowles for food (*The Troublesome Raigne*, I.1056).

But, as Vickers ruefully notes, verse and line analogies are never decisive in resolving questions of authorial attribution, although without them a successful argument can never be made. He thus produces additional stylistic evidence showing the many ways Peele's literary manner closely resembles that of the author of *The Troublesome Raigne*. His discussion includes cognate preferences for the rhetorical device *ploké* (the repetition of a word with other words intervening, such as "Come, night, come" in *Romeo and Juliet*, 3.2.17) and other forms of symmetrical phrasing, a liking for the vocative followed by an imperative, excessive indulgence in multiple alliteration, and a strong tendency on the part of characters to self-address. Cumulatively these constitute Peele's technical profile and an unanswerable case for his contribution to *The Troublesome Raigne*.

Perhaps most persuasive is Vickers's compilation of data and statistics demonstrating the same inordinate preference for and use of alliteration on the part of Peele and the author of *The Troublesome Raigne*. He notes not only the coincidence of matching alliterative phrases—"mounting minde" (*The Battle of Alcazar*, 1320, *Edward I*, 177, *The Troublesome Raigne*, I.261), "damned deede," (*The Battle of Alcazar*, 852, *Edward I*, 2526, *The Troublesome Raigne*, I.1380, 1718, II.37)—but also both writers' distinctive predilection for alliterative word-pairs combining a verb and a noun, again often the same ones: for example, "to wreak wrongs" (*The Battle of Alcazar*, 306, 1302, *The Troublesome Raigne* I.1420).

The argument is then clinched by showing that Peele's liking for triple, quadruple, and even quintuple alliterative strings, frequently combining consonants— "Should shine discreet desire and lawless lust" (*Edward I*, 2517); "That they may march in number like sea sands" (*David and Bethsabe*, 1228)—appears also in *The Troublesome Raigne*: "Harmful and harsh, hells horror to be heard" (*The Troublesome Raigne*, I.345); "To sound the tromp that causeth hell triumph" (*The Troublesome Raigne*, I.1374).

Whether or not Peele was responsible for *The Troublesome Raigne*'s verse, it is clear that he could never have designed its plot. The story is frankly too coherent, too steady in its political focus and supported by an atypically cynical conception— but distinctively Shakespearean—of men, women, and their motives. Peele's amiable genius was anecdotal and episodic, "nondramatic," as even his loyal editors acknowledge, while "compared with the creations of Shakespeare and Marlowe, [his] characters seem to be mere sketches"(Frank S. Hook and John Yoklavich, eds., *The Dramatic Works of George Peele* [New Haven: Yale UP, 1961], 2.47–48). The plays that he both plotted and versified possess a "generalized chivalric-ethical colouring," as Vickers expresses it (*Shakespeare, Co-Author*, 177), wholly absent from *The Troublesome Raigne*. Peele's history plays in particular, such as *The Battle of Alcazar* (1589) and *Edward I* (1591), are "not history" at all in the traditional Elizabethan sense but "characteristically loose . . . the stuff of balladry" (Leonard R. N. Ashley, *George Peele* [New York: Twayne, 1970], 101, 111). Weak in concept and execution, they are "marked throughout by a shallowness of political and historical sense" (Hook and Yoklavich, 2.16). Like *The Old Wife's Tale* (1590) and *David and Bethsabe* (1587–1588), his work is generally—quoting from the miscellany of critical opinions cited by Vickers in support of his case for Peele's lifeless hand in *Titus Andronicus* 1.1—"discursive, haphazard, . . . repetitive and mechanical," an "incoherent succession of heterogeneous episodes" (*Shakespeare, Co-Author*, 458–459).

This is not the place to disparage Peele, nor is that my intention. He wrote successfully for his stage and audience and was, so far as we can tell, a reasonably popular dramatist—and he did work with Shakespeare. His narrative manner and stylistic habits, however, are simply not and never could be his co-author's, a more gifted and *engagé* poet who "never forgets that he is writing a history play depicting great political forces locked in deadly combat" (Hook and Yoklavich, 2.16). With the exception of the awkwardly interpolated monastic scenes, whose vulgarity and crude anti-Catholicism are typical of Peele (compare the Robin Hood sequences in *Edward I*), Shakespeare's is plainly the dramatic temperament controlling *The Troublesome Raigne*'s overall plot and thematic concerns. No other Elizabethan playwright, not even Marlowe, conceives, plans, and executes like the designer of *King John*, that is, of *The Troublesome Raigne*.

Someone other than he devised *The Troublesome Raigne*'s and its characters' illustrative behaviors, that is, prepared the play's narrative outline, the framework on which Peele hung the loose calfskin of his verse. But as Beaurline and many others have often observed, no dramatist of the time save Shakespeare—not Marlowe, Peele, Greene, Kyd, or Lyly—possessed "the combinative and structural powers" displayed by the author of *The Troublesome Raigne* (Beaurline, 197). This view is supported by Simmons, who claims similarly that "Of the known contemporary dramatists, only Shakespeare and Marlowe show the structural powers for handling such sprawling events from the chronicles" (J. L. Simmons, "Shakespeare's *King John* and its Source: Coherence, Pattern, and Vision," *Tulane Studies in English* 17 [1969]: 54). Actually, not even Marlowe could have done it: he was a good enough dramatist, but *The Troublesome Raigne* is not his style.

The Troublesome Raigne's narrative is so well conceived and executed that John Dover Wilson goes so far as to claim that it is "in some ways better constructed than *King John*. . . . Indeed, [Anonymous's] play possesses all the ingredients of historical drama except dramatic life" (Wilson, *King John*, pp. xix, xxxix). Tillyard concurs: "In construction *The Troublesome Raigne* is better balanced than *King John*. . . . Things happen evenly and in good proportion," though "its language is queer and fitful. . . . The masterly construction is quite at odds with the heterogeneous execution" (Tillyard, 215–216). He postulates that Shakespeare wrote an early version of the play, now lost, that Anonymous used as his source and Shakespeare consulted when he produced *King John* (Tillyard, 217).

As we have seen, however, no version of *King John* could have preceded *The Troublesome Raigne*. For Shakespeare to conceive and Peele to write this play would be neither anachronistic nor unrepresentative of the Elizabethan theater. It was indeed quite common for one writer to map out or design what was known as the Author's Plot, or detailed story, and for another, or even a series of others, to provide the actual verse. Somewhat less than a "treatment," in Hollywood parlance, the Author's Plot functioned as a kind of verbal storyboard or move-by-move visualization. Methods of work and contributions would surely have been as flexible and various as the projects and personalities involved. What we know for certain is that before anyone began composing lines and speeches, at least in a sustained kind of way, the basic narrative was assembled in detailed scenic outline together with a close understanding of the chief characters, the gist of their decisive speeches and revelations together with important exits, entrances, and key stage directions. The relationship was analogous to that between architect and builder, and may even have included drafts of important speeches, accounting for the apparently anachronistic Shakespearean lines and phrases in *The Troublesome Raigne*. Some of the play's speeches too have a distinctly Bardic ring, for example, John's dying lament:

> How have I livd but by another's losse?
> What have I lovd, but wrack of others weale?
> When have I vowd, and not infringd mine oath?
> Where have I done a deed deserving well?
> How, what, when and where have I bestowd a day
> That tended not to some notorious ill? (*The Troublesome Raigne*, II.1056–1061)

The value of supposing that Shakespeare was the principal devisor of *The Troublesome Raigne*'s Author's Plot (omitting the monastic scenes, as he later did himself) is that the hypothesis makes sense of all the facts, especially the way that in both plays England is the subtle hero of the action. Shakespeare alone among his contemporaries manages successfully and repeatedly to insinuate this dimension without intruding upon his story or its characters—Shakespeare alone, that is, and the anonymous author of *The Troublesome Raigne*. What we have is a kind of large-scale example of what Muriel St. Clare Byrne requires for "quality" verbal parallels in attribution studies: parallelism of both thought and format. The elimination of other candidates—Marlowe, Peele, Greene, Kyd, Lyly, and so forth—also satisfies her demand for "negative checks" (Muriel St. Clare Byrne, "Bibliographic Clues in Collaborate Plays," *Library*, 4th series 13 [1932]: 24).

The convergence with Shakespeare is indeed so singular that refusing to recognize his distinctive manner in *The Troublesome Raigne* verges on the perverse, a subset of Bardolatry. It is notable that scholars acknowledge the excellence of the play's plot when claiming that it follows *King John*, though when Shakespeare may be the debtor it is "brushed aside," as Honigmann puts it (p. xix), and metamorphosed into "a terrible play" (Chambers, *William Shakespeare*, 1.367). Bullough confusingly asserts in this context that while Shakespeare undoubtedly consulted "Holinshed, Foxe, etc. . . . he preferred to follow the unhistorical medley of *The Raigne* rather than make a new plot" (Bullough, p. 22 and n.).

Viewed thus, the play's algorithms become indecipherable. But if we allow Shakespeare's hand in both dramas we find, in addition to familiar characters, situations and political concerns, a double-layered process of composition for *King John* explaining all its apparent anomalies. Shakespeare researched and designed the plot in association with Peele around 1587 and perhaps contributed the odd phrase, line, or speech. Some years later, probably in 1594, he updated and revised his own work by way of an experiment, then put it aside and began to write *Richard II*.

PRODUCTION HISTORY

The first recorded performance of *King John* dates from 1737 at Covent Garden, London, though we may suppose earlier productions at Blackfriars some time between 1623 (when the text became available) and 1642 (when the theaters were shut down). Soon after its Covent Garden premiere the play seems to have become quite popular, with revivals every few years throughout the eighteenth century. L. A. Beaurline, who provides a detailed summary of the play's stage history, together with actors' names and roles, long quotes from contemporary reviews, and an exhaustive bibliography (Beaurline, 1–23), notes that for more than a hundred years *King John* "held the stage . . . and in some seasons (1760–61, 1766–67, and 1817–18) London theatergoers could compare rival productions. (There were North American tours and many indigenous productions too.)" (Beaurline, 3).

The most famous performances of *King John* were organized in the mid-nineteenth century by the actor-managers John Philip Kemble in 1823, and William Charles Macready in 1842 (following an American tour). In what was to become a defining production strategy, Kemble emphasized dramatic spectacle and historical accuracy in costumes. The gorgeous sets built and designed by J. R. Planché were greeted with roars of approval and repeated rounds of applause (J. R. Planché, *Recollections and Reflections*, 2 vols. [London: Tinsley Brothers, 1872], 1.56–57).

Macready, following suit, "advanced the antiquarian cause still further" with almost equally good-looking sets (Braunmuller, 85), and in addition gave John a depth of personality unmatched by any of Macready's predecessors or successors. He was so persuasive in conveying a man at war with himself that George Odell called his performance "an epoch-making event" (quoted by Curren-Aquino, p. 187), and for half a century afterward its recollection set a standard that even great actor-managers like Sir Herbert Tree felt unable to match. Indeed, trying to keep up with Macready and Kemble, both in staging and style, "became onerous" and "may have killed the play" in the late nineteenth and early twentieth centuries (Beaurline, 19). As Harold Child remarks, "Archaeology had settled itself in the theatre for nearly a century" (Wilson, p. lxxv).

King John continues to be revived periodically. Each time directors appear to find difficulty in finding the right mix of historical accuracy, symbolism, emotional realism, and psychological veracity. Modern directors, deeply influenced by Expressionism when it comes to political drama, tend to treat it as a play for thinking people in a quasi-Brechtian manner, deploying alienation almost as a marker of intellectuality. Such treatment seems invited by a play whose apparently conscious "alienations," as Virginia M. Vaughan observes, deliberately "remind the audience that it is watching a reenactment of history, an awareness that is reinforced by references to 'playing' in the text. The result is a dual perspective" (Virginia M. Vaughan, "*King John*: A Study in Subversion and Containment," in Curren-Aquino, 62).

Kingship in this politically self-conscious universe is thus for the kingly, just as in Bertolt Brecht's *Caucasian Chalk Circle* (1948) motherhood is for the motherly. Taken at face value, the play's concluding lines sound like patriotism triumphant, though, as already noted, the "if" renders the speech equivocal.

> This England never did, nor never shall,
> Lie at the proud foot of a conqueror,
> But when it first did help to wound itself.
> Now these her princes are come home again,
> Come the three corners of the world in arms,
> And we shall shock them. Nought shall make us rue,
> If England to itself do rest but true. (5.7.112–118)

But subtle equivocations are for critics in their studies, not audiences in wartime. For this reason *King John*'s most successful twentieth-century iterations, like the London Old Vic's productions in 1917 and 1941, have occurred during periods of national peril when calls for loyalty and unity sounded less cheap and manipulative than in the eras after Suez, Vietnam, and Iraq.

Perhaps because pageantry in the Kemble/Macready vein was felt to be exhausted, the 1957 Stratford production used lights rather than scenery to evoke mood and setting. The device succeeded only in emphasizing its own artsy tricks at the expense of both the play and players. The 1984 production by the British Broadcasting Company, still available on video, was similarly confused, part spectacle, part symbol, though excellent in neither. At Stratford and the Barbican, March 2001–February 2002, the Royal Shakespeare Company played *King John* as sparsely as possible, without visual glamor, on a black stage set only with a white wooden throne. The production was considered bleakly comic and performed, according to one reviewer, "with hollow, tub-thumping rhetoric" (http://www.albemarle-london.com/rsc-kingjohn.html). These effects seem deeply at odds with Shakespeare's darker purpose.

EXPLICATION OF KEY PASSAGES

1.1.40–43. "Your strong possession . . . shall hear." This important early speech, suggesting that John has in some way illicitly seized the throne, deliberately minimizes the fact that King Richard I designated John his successor and at his death required those present to swear fealty to him. (John T. Appleby, *John, King of England* [New York: Knopf, 1959], 77.) The parallel with Elizabeth I, who came to the throne thanks to her father's will, is obviously deliberate. Since she was also denounced as a bastard, the analogies with Faulconbridge, whose elevation follows immediately, confirms Shakespeare's intent to foreground the politically explosive issue of legitimate inheritance.

2.1.560–598. "Mad world . . . worship thee." This is the most famous speech in the play and one of two from it that resonate throughout Shakespeare's work. Taking as his starting point the cynical and unprincipled arrangement just concluded between Philip of France and John of England—that is, that accompanying the marriage of Blanch and Lewis England yields up its Angevin possessions and 30,000

Arnold Moss and Mildred Dunnock in a scene from *King John* at the American Shakespeare Festival Theatre, Stratford, CT, under the direction of John Houseman, 1956. Courtesy of Photofest.

marks while John gets to keep his crown unchallenged by Arthur—the Bastard laughs, "Mad world, mad kings, mad composition [that is, the peace agreement]!" (2.1.560). He then sketches out its ridiculous terms: "to stop Arthur's title in the whole," that is, Prince Arthur's claim upon the throne, "John . . . hath willingly departed with a part," that is, given up England's French possessions and transferred the town of Angiers to Arthur (2.1.562–563). France, however, has just as politically and swiftly forgotten its vaunted conscience, previously "buckled on" (5.1.564) in supposed principled support of Arthur's claim and for which it had even gone to war. The lesson the Bastard draws is that self-interest alone, "commodity" as he labels it, is "the bias of the world" (2.1.574), unbalancing its inherent disposition to justice. Left to itself, humanity "is peized well" (2.1.575), that is, in natural equilibrium, but the ruthless pursuit of self-interest pulls everything out of kilter. The image is that of the unevenly weighted bowling ball, curling off the straight. The Bastard then notes that he alone has not yielded to the siren song of selfishness but plans to do so in the future. Since kings themselves pursue nothing else, he too intends to worship "gain" (2.1.598). In fact, as we have seen, he does not. He is almost literally the only honest character in the play.

5.7.110–118. "O, let us pray . . . but true." Here is *King John*'s concluding declaration, spoken by the choric Faulconbridge and usually treated as its moral. Often associated with and anthologized alongside John of Gaunt's "scepter'd isle" speech (*Richard II*, 2.1.40–66), it is taken to be a patriotic paean to England, the country's military success and the importance of national unity. What is usually overlooked is the subtle grammatical function of the word "if" in the final line—victory is conditional and to that extent uncertain. As so often, Shakespeare plants a kind of semantic time bomb that goes off only after a period of reflection.

Annotated Bibliography

Beaurline, L. A., ed. *King John*. Cambridge: Cambridge UP, 1990. A scholarly edition taking the view that *The Troublesome Raigne of John King of England* is subsequent to *King John*.

Braunmuller, A. R., ed. *The Life and Death of King John*. Oxford: Clarendon P, 1989. A scholarly edition taking the view that *King John* is subsequent to *The Troublesome Raigne*.

Bullough, Geoffrey, ed. *Narrative and Dramatic Sources of Shakespeare*. 8 vols. Vol. 4, *Later English History Plays: "King John," "Henry IV," "Henry V," "Henry VIII."* London: Routledge & Kegan Paul; New York: Columbia UP, 1962. Contains the most readily accessible version of *The Troublesome Raigne of John King of England*, together with a useful review of the which-came-first debate. Note that the original text is not divided into acts and scenes. Bullough uses Through Line Numbers (TLN), that is lines 1–1740 (Part One) and lines 1–1196 (Part Two). When citing this edition, I prefix "I" (Part One) or "II" (Part Two) followed by the TLN.

Campbell, Lily B. *Shakespeare's "Histories": Mirrors of Elizabethan Policy*. San Marino, CA: The Huntington Library, 1947, 1965. Contains the fullest discussion of the analogies between the reign of Elizabeth I and that of King John as reflected in both *King John* and *The Troublesome Raigne*.

Curren-Aquino, Deborah T., ed. *"King John": New Perspectives*. London: Associated University Presses, 1989. A useful collection of essays ranging from source-study to gender issues, including a tabulated chronology of the play's performance history.

Holinshed, Raphael. *Holinshed's Chronicles of England, Scotland, and Ireland*. 6 vols. London: J. Johnson et al., 1807–1808. Indispensable for understanding what Shakespeare did and did not take from his principal source.

Honigmann, E.A.J., ed. *King John*. London: Methuen & Co., 1954. The most influential statement of the case for the chronological and creative priority of *King John* over *The Troublesome Raigne*.

Sider, J. W., ed. *The Troublesome Raigne of John, King of England*. New York: Garland, 1979. A useful review of all the editorial issues together with a well-edited text.

Thomas, Sidney. " 'Enter a Sheriffe': Shakespeare's *King John* and *The Troublesome Raigne*." *Shakespeare Quarterly* 37 (1986): 98–100. A good article establishing the chronological priority of *The Troublesome Raigne*. See also Thomas's " 'Enter a Sheriffe': A Shakespearean Ghost," *Shakespeare Quarterly* 38 (1987): 130, which responds to criticism of the earlier note.

Tillyard, E.M.W. *Shakespeare's History Plays*. London: Chatto & Windus, 1961. One of the first and most influential studies of Shakespeare's histories, taken as a group.

Vickers, Brian. "*The Troublesome Raigne*, George Peele, and the date of *King John*." In Brian Boyd, ed., *Words that Count: Early Modern Authorship: Essays in Honor of MacDonald P. Jackson*. Newark: U of Delaware P, 2004. Proves that Peele was responsible for the verse of *The Troublesome Raigne*.

Wilson, John Dover, ed. *King John*. Cambridge: Cambridge UP, 1936. A classic edition establishing the close relationship between Shakespeare's play and *The Troublesome Raigne*, with a wealth of insights and information in its notes.

Richard II

Nicholas Crawford

PLOT SUMMARY

1.1. The play begins as King Richard II prepares to arbitrate a dispute between Thomas Mowbray, Duke of Norfolk, and Henry Bullingbrook, Duke of Herford, as the latter has accused the former of treason. Richard asks Bullingbrook's father, John of Gaunt, whether Henry has a legitimate reason to charge Mowbray or is merely trying to settle an old score. Upon receiving assurances from Gaunt that Bullingbrook considers Mowbray a genuine danger to the throne, Richard instructs his attendants to call the dukes before him so that he may hear "The accuser and the accused freely speak" (1.1.17). Mowbray and Bullingbrook greet the king with standard flatteries, but the king remarks that only one of the two is sincere, since the other must be a traitor. Bullingbrook now accuses Mowbray to his face and asks permission to prove it with his sword. " 'Tis not the trial of a woman's war" (1.1.48), comes Mowbray's contemptuous retort, as he explains that mere words will never settle their argument, and that his own words are constrained by the king's presence. Formally challenging his rival to combat, Bullingbrook throws down his "gage" (probably a glove); Mowbray accepts the challenge.

Richard now asks for a detailed description of the charges, and Bullingbrook obliges. He claims that Mowbray stole and squandered state funds intended to pay soldiers, plotted and committed the Duke of Gloucester's murder, and has been the source of all treasonous activities for the past eighteen years. Richard assures Mowbray that he may speak freely in his own defense, that the king will remain completely fair and impartial despite close blood ties with Bullingbrook. Mowbray returns the charges of treason and falsehood back on Bullingbrook, and he reiterates both his and Bullingbrook's intention to settle their differences in combat. The king puts a stop to the accusations, instructing the two to "purge this choler without letting blood" (1.1.153). Mowbray protests: "My life thou shalt command, but not my shame" (1.1.166). Richard insists that "Rage must be withstood" (1.1.173). However, Bullingbrook echoes his defiance and vows to fight as well. Neither Bullingbrook nor Mowbray will be reconciled to a bloodless resolution. The frustrated king finally agrees to let their "swords and lances arbitrate" (1.1.200), and he schedules the combat for "Saint Lambert's day" (some time in August or September) at Coventry (1.199).

1.2. John of Gaunt converses with the Duchess of Gloucester, widow of the slain Duke of Gloucester referred to in the first scene. Gaunt declares that though he is deeply troubled by Gloucester's murder, he can do nothing about it because it must be regarded as "the will of heaven" (1.2.6). Gaunt implies here, for the first time in the play, that Gloucester (Thomas of Woodstock) was murdered by order of King Richard, a divinely ordained monarch whose actions must be equated to God's. The Duchess tries to convince Gaunt to avenge his brother's death, but Gaunt repeats that "God's substitute, / His deputy . . . / Hath caus'd his death" (1.2.37–39), and so she must complain not to him but to God. The Duchess then expresses her wish that Bullingbrook's spear "butcher Mowbray's breast!" (1.2.48), indicating that she also holds Mowbray responsible for her husband's death. This second scene furnishes the audience with a different perspective on the preceding action, as it leads us to believe that Mowbray killed Gloucester on Richard's orders and that in the play's first scene they kept this information concealed. Gaunt says he must go to Coventry to witness the combat.

1.3. At the Coventry lists (arena), the Lord Marshall and the Duke of Aumerle confer with each other to establish that Mowbray and Bullingbrook are armed and ready to fight. Trumpets sound and Richard enters with his entourage, which includes Gaunt, Bushy, Bagot, and Green. Once they are seated, Mowbray enters and Richard instructs the Lord Marshall to have Mowbray declare his purpose there. Mowbray states that he intends to defend his "loyalty and truth" (1.3.19) and "To prove him [Bullingbrook] . . . / A traitor to my God, my king, and me" (1.3.23–24). Trumpets sound again, and Bullingbrook enters in his armor. The same formalities that Mowbray underwent now continue with Bullingbrook. Richard wishes Bullingbrook well if his cause is just, but vows not to avenge him if he should lose and die. Bullingbrook expresses his confidence and asks his father for additional reassurance. Mowbray then proclaims his own righteousness and faith in a favorable outcome.

Richard wishes him well also and orders the trial by combat to begin. Two heralds read out the charges of treason that each has levied against the other, and the Lord Marshall instructs the combatants to begin. But no sooner have the trumpets sounded than Richard throws down his "warder" (baton), putting an immediate stop to the fight (1.3.118). He informs the would-be combatants that he does not want to disturb the peace or start blood feuds. Instead, he will banish Bullingbrook for ten years and Mowbray for life. He further forbids them from contacting each other or plotting together against the king.

Mowbray laments most of all the loss of his native tongue, English, characterizing the king's sentence as "speechless death" (1.3.172). Bullingbrook implores Mowbray to confess his treason now that his sentence has already been meted out. Continuing to deny any wrongdoing, Mowbray predicts that the king will learn what a traitor Bullingbrook is. Claiming that he is moved by John of Gaunt's "sad aspect" (1.3.209), Richard reduces Bullingbrook's banishment by four years. Gaunt thanks Richard for this kindness, but only halfheartedly. Predicting he will die anyway before his son is able to return, Gaunt notes that the king, although able to take away years, is powerless to bestow time upon his subjects. Richard reminds

Gaunt that he consented to his son's banishment. The old Duke of Lancaster acknowledges his agreement but now wishes he had been asked what he thought as a father, not as a judge. Richard reiterates his sentence and exits with his retinue. The Lord Marshall offers to accompany Bullingbrook to the English border. Gaunt attempts to cheer up his son by insisting that a positive attitude can make banishment less onerous, that he might think of it as travel for pleasure, or "Think not the King did banish thee, / But thou the King" (1.3.279–280). Bullingbrook, though, ever the realist, insists on facing facts but proclaims that his pride and identity as an Englishman will never leave him no matter where he goes.

1.4. Lord Aumerle tells Richard how he accompanied Bullingbrook to the highway, where they parted. Through jokes and puns, Aumerle expresses both his great contempt for Bullingbrook and his wish that Henry be banished even longer. Richard becomes reflective and reveals his fears of Bullingbrook's appeal to the masses. The king enumerates the instances when he observed Bullingbrook's popularity. Reminding Richard that the Duke of Herford is now gone, Green changes the topic to rebellion in Ireland and counsels action. Richard admits that funds are low because his extravagant life at court has depleted the coffers. He proposes generating new revenue by leasing already occupied land as a kind of taxation. Bushy then enters with news that John of Gaunt is gravely ill. Richard is delighted and hopes that Gaunt will die quickly so that the king might seize his assets and use them to finance the Irish wars. In this scene, we see Richard as fearful of Bullingbrook, unfair to his people, ungrateful for Gaunt's loyalty, and ruthlessly greedy. The cautious and fair-minded peacemaker of the beginning of the play begins to present himself as an indecisive flip-flopper, and then as a ruthless, self-serving but inept manipulator.

2.1. John of Gaunt is dying. He and York lament what they consider the decline of English monarchy evidenced by Richard's reign. Gaunt aches to tell Richard personally what he thinks of him and how low the king has brought the country. In the king's absence, however, Gaunt delivers what is surely the most famous paean to England ever written, with such famous lines as "This royal throne of kings, this sceptred isle, / This earth of majesty, this seat of Mars, / This other Eden, demi-paradise" (2.1.40–42), and "This blessed plot, this earth, this realm, this England" (2.1.50). In this same speech, Gaunt articulates his displeasure over Richard's practices, particularly the king's policy of leasing out the land "Like to a tenement or pelting farm" (2.1.60). When Richard does arrive at Lancaster's deathbed, the old duke reiterates his complaints, declaring to Richard, "Landlord of England art thou now, not king" (2.1.113). The king threatens to kill Gaunt for his impertinence; but the duke expires promptly from natural causes, whereupon Richard seizes his money and possessions to finance the Irish wars. York objects to Richard's arrogation of Gaunt's legacy, as such action, in effect, disinherits Bullingbrook, who still lives though banished. Richard replies simply, "Think what you will" (2.1.209). When the Earl of Northumberland and Lords Ross and Willoughby learn of Richard's action, however, they too are outraged, as they see their own fortunes endangered as well. Northumberland then informs the others that he has word that Bullingbrook is returning presently with an army. They are all ready to offer their backing to the returning Duke of Herford.

2.2. At Windsor castle, Bushy tries to console the confused queen, who grieves over recent events that augur threats to Richard's kingship. Green arrives with more bad news: Bullingbrook has arrived, and many of the nobility are supporting his cause. York enters, and we learn that Richard has gone to the Irish wars and that York is effectively in charge of confronting the crisis that Bullingbrook now represents. To add to York's woes, he is informed that Gloucester's widow has just died. Though unhappy with Richard for a number of reasons, York conveys his resolve to meet the invading army himself. His serious misgivings about the king include Richard's disinheriting of Bullingbrook and his part in Gloucester's death. Nevertheless, York believes in the divine right of kings and feels compelled to side with Richard. After York leaves, Bushy and Green confide in each other that, given Bullingbrook's popularity, they do not think that York or the king will have any chance of success against him.

2.3. Bullingbrook advances with his army. Northumberland reiterates his support and admiration for Bullingbrook, and Northumberland's son, Harry Percy, arrives on the scene with news that his uncle Worcester has gone to Ravenspurgh to wait for Bullingbrook's troops. Northumberland introduces his son Harry (also known as "Hotspur") to the Duke of Herford. Hotspur offers his services, and the two, who will become bitter enemies in *1 Henry IV*, declare their friendship. Ross and Willoughby now express their support and join these forces. Berkeley appears with an inquiry from York but is rebuffed when he addresses Bullingbrook as "Lord of Herford" (2.3.69). The banished duke replies, "My lord, my answer is to Lancaster, / And I am come to seek that name in England" (2.3.70–71). York himself arrives to upbraid Bullingbrook for traitorous actions. In the king's absence, York will assume his duties and stop Henry: "the King is left behind, / And in my loyal bosom lies his power" (2.3.97–98). But Bullingbrook pleads the injustice of his disinheritance to his uncle, who we know was already critical of Richard's action. York, exasperated by the overwhelming force of the army he faces and by his own divided loyalties, admits that he is too weak to stop Bullingbrook and so will "remain as neuter" (2.3.159). He then invites his nephew and his forces to spend the night at the castle if they so desire.

2.4. At a camp in Wales, the Earl of Salisbury implores a Welsh captain to wait with his troops a bit longer for Richard's return. But the captain, noting the many signs that suggest the king's demise, replies, " 'Tis thought the king is dead; we will not stay" (2.4.7). He leaves, and Salisbury admits to himself that Richard's fortunes have indeed turned.

3.1. At Bristol castle, Bullingbrook and his men have taken Bushy and Green prisoners. Bullingbrook orders the two be brought before him so that he may list their crimes before he has them executed. According to Bullingbrook, Bushy and Green turned the king against him, caused a rift between the king and queen, and took gross advantage of Herford's banishment. Bushy and Green are defiant. "More welcome is the stroke of death to me / Than Bullingbrook to England" (3.1.31–32), trumpets Bushy. They are then led away by Northumberland for beheading. Bullingbrook tells York to send warm regards to the queen.

3.2. Richard has just returned to the coast of Wales, where he appeals to the earth itself, asking its assistance in defeating his foes. The Bishop of Carlisle reassures the king that he is protected by heaven. In a long speech, Richard proceeds to work up his faith in the invincibility of his own divine election: "Not all the water in the rough rude sea / Can wash the balm off from an anointed king" (3.2.54–55). Salisbury arrives and informs Richard that the Welsh, thinking the king dead, have gone to join Bullingbrook. Richard despairs again but tries to bolster his confidence by remembering that he is king and should be powerful simply by virtue of that title: "Is not the king's name twenty thousand names?" (3.2.85). Entering with bad news, Scroop tells the assembly that Bushy and Green have been executed. A discouraged Richard implores his followers to "sit upon the ground / And tell sad stories of the death of kings" (3.2.155–156).

As his downfall seems imminent and he has not the power to resist it, Richard begins to wonder what it means to be a king. He fears that he may have just been allowed "a little scene, / To monarchize" (3.2.164–165), that he may be more like his subjects than he thought possible: "I live with bread like you, feel want, / Taste grief, need friends: subjected thus, / How can you say to me I am a king? (3.2.175–177). The Bishop of Carlisle tells Richard that he should not indulge his grief and fear, that wailing only strengthens his enemy. Richard tries to regain his confidence momentarily, but Scroop delivers the final disheartening blow when he informs the king that the Duke of York has joined Bullingbrook. The scene's last line is Richard's, and it sums up the direction the play is taking: "From Richard's night to Bullingbrook's fair day" (3.2.218).

3.3. Bullingbrook and his followers confer near Flint Castle, where Richard is staying. Bullingbrook orders Northumberland to approach the castle quietly and deliver what amounts to an ultimatum. If Richard will restore Bullingbrook's lands and repeal his banishment, then Bullingbrook will lay down his arms and swear his and his troops' allegiance to the king. If not, he will "lay the summer's dust with show'rs of blood / Rain'd from the wounds of slaughtered Englishmen" (3.3.43–44). Richard appears on the castle walls with Carlisle and other followers. York remains duly impressed with the spectacle of kingship, remarking, "Behold, his eye, / As bright as is the eagle's, lightens forth / Controlling majesty" (3.3.68–70). Richard warns Bullingbrook of his treason, claiming with his own bloody rhetoric that Herford has "come to open / The purple testament of bleeding war" (3.3.94).

Northumberland delivers Bullingbrook's demands, and Richard agrees to them. But no sooner has the king acquiesced than he regrets the apparent impotence of his concession. He demands of his audience, "What must the King do now? Must he submit? / The King shall do it. Must he be depos'd? / The King shall be contented" (3.3.143–145). Richard is then asked to descend to the base court to meet with his cousin Henry. Even to Richard, this trip down from the walls is immediately symbolic of his fall from power. "In the base court, come down? Down court! down king!" (3.3.182), exclaims Richard. Although Bullingbrook still purports to seek only restitution, Richard understands who wields the most power. He resignedly asks whether he must go to London, presumably to be officially deposed. Bullingbrook says yes.

3.4. In York's garden, the queen's attendants propose activities for her amusement and distraction in an effort to lift her from despair. Some gardeners arrive, and the women hide so as to eavesdrop on what the queen is sure will be commentary on the affairs of state. The queen proves to be right, as the gardeners discuss politics through horticultural metaphors. For example, speaking of Richard, the chief gardener allows, "Superfluous branches / We lop away, that bearing boughs may live; / Had he done so, himself had borne the crown" (3.4.63–65). The gardener goes on to say that Richard is already deposed. Emerging from her hiding place, the outraged queen reprimands him for his insolence. The gardener states that he is only repeating what is known and does not think ill of Richard or wish him harm. The queen exits, cursing his plants and wishing them never to grow. The gardener feels only sorrow for the queen.

4.1. Echoing Richard's role as judge in the play's opening scene, Bullingbrook must now arbitrate a similar set of opposing claims. Bagot accuses Lord Aumerle of responsibility in the killing of Gloucester. Fitzwater, Percy, and others side with Bagot, but Surrey backs Aumerle. Bullingbrook calls for peace and postpones any trial until he has had a chance to repeal Mowbray's banishment. But we soon learn from Carlisle that Mowbray (Norfolk) is already dead. York then arrives with the news that "plume-pluck'd Richard" is ready to yield his scepter (4.1.108). For the first time in the play, Bullingbrook is called by his subsequent title, as York exclaims, "And long live Henry, fourth of the name!" (4.1.112). The Bishop of Carlisle recoils in disgust at Bullingbrook's readiness to wear the crown: "My Lord of Herford here, whom you call king, / Is a foul traitor" (4.1.134–135). Then the bishop utters a line that previews subsequent action in the second tetralogy: "if you crown him, let me prophesy, / The blood of English shall manure the ground, / And future ages groan for this foul act" (4.1.136–138). The bishop is quickly placed under arrest, and the deposition is scheduled to proceed as planned. York ushers in Richard, and the transfer of the crown proceeds, with Richard ceremoniously handing it over to Bullingbrook.

For Richard's pride and for Bullingbrook's political stature it is essential that Richard "give" the crown rather than have Herford seem to take it forcibly. Richard recites, "With mine own tears I wash away my balm, / With mine own hand I give away my crown" (4.1.207–208). But just as Richard thinks the ceremony is complete, Northumberland hands him a list of crimes he is to read and to which he must confess. Richard refuses, comparing himself to Christ and Bullingbrook's followers to Pilate. He expresses his self-disgust for capitulating to their demands and asks for a mirror so that he might read his face instead: "the very book indeed / Where all my sins are writ" (4.1.274–275). Richard smashes the looking glass, imploring Bullingbrook to send him away. Henry obliges by having him escorted to the Tower. Before exiting himself, Henry announces that his coronation will be the following Wednesday. In his absence, the Abbot of Westminster and Aumerle agree to plot against the new king.

5.1. As Richard is being led to the Tower, the queen waits with her attendants to intercept him to say goodbye. When Richard arrives, she laments his condition. He tells her to go to a cloister in France and think of him in their happy days and not as he is now. She is disturbed that he seems humbled and not raging like a lion. He instructs her to preserve and relate his story. Northumberland and company come to inform the deposed king that Henry has decided to imprison him at Pomfret castle instead of the Tower and that the queen will be taken to France. Richard complains that he has been divorced twice, once from his crown and once from his wife. And just as Carlisle did earlier, he predicts strife and internecine wars, warning Northumberland that the crown's usurpers will in time turn against one another. The queen pleads that Richard be banished with her instead of imprisoned, but her request is quickly refused. Richard and the queen say a fond and tearful goodbye.

5.2. The Duke of York tells his wife of Richard's and Henry's procession through the streets of London, "Where rude misgoverned hands from windows' tops /

Threw dust and rubbish on King Richard's head" (5.2.5–6). By contrast, he describes Henry as "great Bullingbrook, / Mounted upon a hot and fiery steed" (5.2.6–7), massively popular and welcomed by crowds shouting, "God save [thee], Bullingbrook!" (5.1.11). York feels sorry for Richard but clearly acknowledges Henry as the new king: "To Bullingbrook are we sworn subject now" (5.2.38). Their son Aumerle arrives home. He is now known officially as Rutland, as he has been stripped of his ducal title. His father asks him how things are going in his studies at Oxford, but then notices part of a sealed document on his son and demands to read it. Aumerle refuses, but York insists, snatches it from him and reads the document. The paper details a plot to assassinate Henry at Oxford. York yells, "Villain, traitor, slave!" at his son and prepares to go directly to King Henry and report the treasonous plot (5.2.72). The Duchess pleads with York not to betray their son. She asks York if he is betraying his own flesh because he believes that Aumerle is actually illegitimate, a bastard child of another man. She reassures him that Aumerle is his own. York dismisses her appeal and leaves at once. The Duchess instructs her son to hurry to the king before York arrives and beg pardon before he has been accused. She vows to follow quickly and to plead for him as well.

5.3. Henry asks Percy and the lords in attendance about Henry's son Prince Hal. He alludes to Hal's dissolute behavior, his frequenting of taverns, and his "unrestrained loose companions" (5.3.7), but also to "some sparks of better hope, which elder years / May happily bring forth" (5.3.21–22). This is our first introduction to Hal, who does not appear in this play but becomes a central character for the remainder of the second tetralogy. At this point, Aumerle arrives and asks for a private conference with the king, which Henry grants. York interrupts their meeting and tells Henry that Aumerle is a traitor before Aumerle has had a chance to make his own confession. Henry praises York and damns his son. Now the Duchess arrives and pleads on Aumerle's behalf, as the action takes a somewhat comic turn. As Henry puts it, "Our scene is alt'red from a serious thing, / And now chang'd to 'The Beggar and the King'" (5.3.79–80). While his wife grovels, York insists that his own shame be erased and that his son be punished for treason. King Henry instead gives in to the Duchess's pleas and pardons Aumerle while vowing to kill the rest of the conspirators.

5.4. In this very brief scene, Sir Pierce Exton quotes the king to his servant as asking, "Have I no friend will rid me of this living fear?" (5.4.2). Exton interprets these words as a personal request to kill Richard, and he resolves to do just that to gain favor with King Henry.

5.5. Richard is alone in his cell at Pomfret castle, contemplating his lot. He attempts to use his imagination to create a world of thoughts to stand in for the populated world outside. He extends the metaphor of thoughts-as-people to imagine thoughts-as-actors who also inhabit each person. Thus Richard begins to dwell on the theatricality of life in general, and on the theatricality of the role of king in particular. He is astounded that he can be in life a king and then suddenly nothing. He hears music nearby, and this sets him thinking about time and the transitory nature of experience until he finally finds the notes altogether maddening.

A groom of the stable enters and tells the king that he wishes to pay his respects, as he used to tend to Richard's horse, Barbary. The Groom then relates how he witnessed Bullingbrook's coronation, and how Henry rode Richard's horse through the streets of London that day. Richard finds this fact particularly rankling and begins to curse the horse, but then realizes how ridiculous it is to do so. The Keeper then arrives with food, and the Groom leaves. Richard asks the Keeper to taste the food first, but he refuses, saying that Exton instructed him not to. Richard grows angry, curses Henry, and begins to beat the Keeper. Exton and his servants enter the cell in order to murder Richard, but the deposed king grabs an axe and manages to kill two of them before he is finally assassinated by Exton himself.

5.6. King Henry IV, York, and other lords enter. Northumberland, Fitzwater, and Percy report various executions they have carried out on Henry's behalf. They inform the new king that they have sent to London the heads of those killed. The Bishop of Carlisle, however, has been spared death and is present to receive his sentence of life imprisonment. Proudly displaying Richard's coffin, Exton and his attendants now enter. Henry's reaction, however, surprises Exton. The king says, "I thank thee not" and banishes the knight (5.6.34). While he admits to having wanted Richard dead, the new monarch proclaims his "soul is full of woe / That blood should sprinkle me to make me grow" (5.6.45–46), and as the play ends he vows to "make a voyage to the Holy Land, / To wash this blood off from my guilty hand" (5.6.49–50).

PUBLICATION HISTORY

Richard II was probably composed around 1595. A number of factors point to this as the most likely date of its writing, but perhaps the most compelling are stylistic. The metrical patterns, the numerous rhymes, the dearth of prose, and other such considerations prompt authorities to place *Richard II* with such plays as *Romeo and Juliet* and *A Midsummer Night's Dream*, dramas that the preponderance of scholars agree were written around 1594 or 1595. Another piece of evidence that helps fix the year at 1595 comes from a letter to Sir Robert Cecil from Sir Edward Hoby. Dated December 7, 1595, it appears to be an invitation to both dinner and a performance of *Richard II* at Hoby's residence. Given Cecil's prominence at court (he was Queen Elizabeth's lifelong chief advisor), it is likely that such a performance would be a play of topical interest; however, no one can say with certainty that Hoby is referring to Shakespeare's play in his letter. Finally, there is the matter of influence. *Richard II* is clearly indebted to a number of plays and histories whose publication or performance dates would have to be prior to Shakespeare's writing.

The first publication of *Richard II* was in quarto (Q1) in 1597. Before the First Folio was printed in 1623 (the first collection of Shakespeare's plays), four more quarto versions of *Richard II* were published: Q2 (1598), Q3 (1598), Q4 (1608), and Q5 (1615). Scholars generally believe that Q1 comes directly from Shakespeare's foul papers (documents in the playwright's own hand before being professionally copied by a scribe to produce a fair copy) and is therefore the most authoritative text of the play. However, Q1 lacks what is usually called the "deposition scene" (4.1), where Richard, the sitting monarch, actually relinquishes his crown. This scene may well have existed in the original performances of the play and then been censored in print due to its potential to be politically incendiary. Most modern editions use Q1 as the basic text of the play and add the deposition section from the First Folio's rendition of the play.

The historical relevance of *Richard II* to Elizabethan politics was substantial. In the monarchy of early modern England, where the ruler had tremendous and wide-ranging powers, the legitimacy of a claim to the throne was of obvious interest and importance to the populace. As it happened, Richard II was the last English king whose birthright to rule was unquestioned. Once Henry IV gained the throne, the idea of what made a monarch legitimate became a more complex and debatable topic. Elizabeth Tudor's claim, like the claim of every other English monarch after Richard II, was not universally recognized as valid.

A quite specific link, however, came to exist between Shakespeare's play and the political machinations of the day. In 1601, the ambitious Earl of Essex (Robert Devereaux) tried to stage a rebellion against Elizabeth I. His attempt failed, and he was put to death. The day before the abortive coup, however, Essex's followers paid the Lord Chamberlain's Men (Shakespeare's company) to perform what was probably Shakespeare's *Richard II*. The rebels apparently hoped the audience would see a connection between Essex and Bullingbrook and between Elizabeth and Richard II, viewing Essex as strong, competent, and popular, and Elizabeth as weak, ineffectual, and out of touch with her people. Further parallels between Richard and Elizabeth might be construed as well. Neither Richard II nor Elizabeth I produced an heir, and anxiety surrounding royal succession played a critical role in unsettling faith in the monarch's ability to serve the nation's future. Additionally, many felt that Elizabeth, like Richard, was unduly influenced by certain flattering courtiers, and that her tax policies, like Richard's, were grossly unfair. Essex and his men may also have believed that seeing a monarch deposed on stage would prepare the public to accept such an outcome on the real political stage. This is not to suggest that the play endorses Bullingbrook and damns Richard, only that Essex and his supporters must have felt that given the historical moment such parallels would work to their advantage. Even Elizabeth did not view the play itself as seditious, as she did not punish Shakespeare's company for the performance. However, the queen did recognize the connections the public might note or construct between her and Richard II. Her purported quip to William Lambarde in 1601, "I am Richard II. Know ye not that?" serves as but the most famous example of her sensitivity to the topic.

SOURCES FOR THE PLAY

Shakespeare drew from a variety of historical and literary sources to help him create *Richard II*. The histories that serve most prominently are Raphael Holinshed's *Chronicles of England, Scotland, and Ireland* (1587), Edward Hall's *Union of the Two Noble and Illustre Families of Lancaster and York* (1548), and Samuel Daniel's *The First Four Books of the Civil Wars between the Two Houses of Lancaster and York* (1595). Among the most likely literary sources, we can include the anonymous play *Woodstock* (not published until modern times), Christopher Marlowe's *Edward II* (published in 1594 but acted before that date), and *A Mirror for Magistrates* (1559), a pseudo-historical collection of monologues in verse by various poets assuming the voices of historical figures. Other possible contributions come from a number of French sources, including Jean Froissart's *Chronicles*, available at the time in translation, and Créton's *Histoire du Roy d'Angleterre Richard* (1399?).

Holinshed's *Chronicles* functions as Shakespeare's most important touchstone for the basic story, characters' names, particular events, and even the language of certain sections of the play. However, as with his other histories, Shakespeare adapts rather freely to suit his vision. These changes take many forms: the relative importance of characters and their representation, wholesale insertions and deletions, language, setting, and the combining, altering, or reordering of events for dramatic purposes. The aim behind such modifications may be illustrated by comparing how the two authors treat, for example, the moment when Richard gives up the crown. In Holinshed, Richard finally abdicates while imprisoned in the Tower. In Shakespeare's play, Richard's self-deposition before parliament acts as an emotional and dramatic high point.

Samuel Daniel's *The First Four Books of the Civil Wars between the Two Houses of Lancaster and York* also contains some events, ideas, and wording that link it to *Richard II*. In Daniel's view, history runs in cycles. Since it repeats itself, one can and should learn from the past. As *Richard II* and the whole second tetralogy reflect a distinct concern with these same issues, the influence of Daniel's work may not be limited to particular episodes.

The contribution of Edward Hall's *Union* does not lie in specific echoes one hears from Holinshed or even Daniel. Hall's influence is general rather than particular. His history reveals a much more theological and teleological point of view than Holinshed's, and this outlook manifests itself in *Richard II* when, for example, Carlisle predicts that generations of blood and strife will result from defying the monarch's divine right. The Christological imagery of kingship so prevalent in Richard's fall also serves to connect Shakespeare's play with Hall's vision of history. Shakespeare had used Hall when writing his first tetralogy, and so despite the absence of concrete, specific links to *Richard II*, Hall's account may be safely included as an influence on *Richard II* and, indeed, the whole second tetralogy.

Similarly, *A Mirror for Magistrates* was quite popular, was well known to Shakespeare, and contains "tragedies" of characters featured in the play, including Richard II himself, Mowbray, and Northumberland. The collection also links itself to the play through its absorption with the fall of kings and how they contemplate their own fortunes in relation to God's plan. Additionally, the scene in which Richard gazes into and then smashes a mirror may be a sly reference to this collection.

The crucial literary antecedents of *Richard II* are the anonymous play *Woodstock* and Christopher Marlowe's *Edward II*. *Woodstock*, from the early 1590s, treats many of the same events as *Richard II*, but as one might guess it gives greater prominence to the murder of Thomas of Woodstock, Duke of Gloucester, than does Shakespeare's play. Scholars have found numerous specific verbal similarities between the two plays, mostly limited to a few scenes and concentrated in particular lines. Other distinct though isolated parallels may be found in a few plot particulars and devices. For example, the first time either play shows Gloucester's widow, she is imploring Gaunt to avenge her husband's death. Music is heard shortly before Richard is killed in both plays. Some critics have even suggested that the character of Richard II in *Woodstock* helped Shakespeare imagine his own king.

Christopher Marlowe's *Edward II* also shares affinities with Shakespeare's play. Both plays feature an ineffectual, headstrong monarch at odds with his most revered counselors and corrupted by a flattering coterie upon which he dotes. The two plots show a number of resemblances, not the least of which is the pattern of corruption and dissolution leading to loss of the crown, imprisonment, and finally death at the hands of murderers. Similarly, both plays overlay this falling action of the king with the rising fortunes of his rival. There are many other points of confluence between these two dramas, but perhaps the most pertinent point to remember is that Christopher Marlowe, who had achieved great success with his *Tamburlaine* and *Doctor Faustus*, was the leading playwright of the day before Shakespeare eclipsed him. Shakespeare was undoubtedly intimately familiar with Marlowe's work in print and performance. Considering that *Richard II* was first published in 1597 and probably written in 1595, and that *Edward II* was published in 1594 and first performed in either 1591 or 1592, there is every reason to assume that Shakespeare was well acquainted with this play and that noted similarities are not coincidental.

STRUCTURE AND PLOTTING

Richard II's structure is chiastic, in that it tracks the fall of Richard and the corresponding rise of Bullingbrook. In this sense, Richard's fate is the familiar one of *de casibus* tragedy, wherein we witness the hero inevitably toppled from his exalted position. As in much tragedy, Richard is undone not simply by his opponent, Bullingbrook, but also by weaknesses that are paradoxically his strengths: his contemplative, poetic, and histrionic gifts, which complicate his perception and paralyze his actions. Although *Richard II*'s full title is sometimes listed as *The Tragedy of King Richard the Second*, modern scholars group it, as did the original producers of the First Folio in 1623, with the history plays and not with the tragedies.

History plays are often not as completely resolved or as unambiguously dark in their vision as are tragedies. The end of *Richard II* does not feel like the end of the story in the same way that, for example, the end of *King Lear* does, nor is the stage littered with the corpses of all the principals, as it is at the end of *Hamlet*. The title character has died, to be sure, but the other main character, Bullingbrook, lives on, and we wonder what will become of him and what will ensue during his reign. The Bishop of Carlisle predicts future conflict; King Henry talks of his son Hal and how he might turn out; and at the end of the play, Henry speaks of his plans to visit the Holy Land to expiate his sins. All of this may do more to prepare for the sequels than to enhance the present drama.

Neither Richard nor Bullingbrook is clearly heroic or villainous. The sense of a providential, predetermined course of events in Shakespearean history plays is countered not merely by the force of individual human will and action but also by societal dynamics that grind out their own agendas. The plot trajectory of *Richard II* may seem at first to follow the straight and tragic line of a king's fall, but the path is actually that of circular, or spiraling, history. We notice, for example, that at the beginning of the play King Richard presides over a dispute about whether Mowbray has engaged in treasonous behavior. Similarly, in the play's last act, King Henry presides over a dispute concerning Aumerle's treasonous behavior. Early in the play we learn that Richard has Gloucester's blood on his conscience. At the end of the play, it is Henry who is haunted by Richard's blood. Numerous such mirrorings, parallels, and loops can be found within the play and throughout the rest of the second tetralogy. Of course, these "repeated" scenes are not replications by any stretch, but are rather variations or echoes—reminders of how the past and the present intersect and influence one another.

How the present influences the story of the past becomes another central concern for Shakespeare throughout the history plays. *Richard II* begins with Mowbray and Bullingbrook rendering different accounts of the past. Their versions of events, and Richard's as well, are colored by their motives and their memories. The "true" and accurate version of, for example, Gloucester's death is something to which we are never privy. *Richard II*, and the Henry plays that will follow, thus comment not only on the problems of particular historical characters and events but also on the problems that pertain to formulating and thinking about history, the ways it is recorded and transmitted, and the ways in which we may try to interpret it.

A principal model of causality—or structure of the way things happen—that *Richard II* exploits as a metaphor is the natural cycle of plant growth, decay, and regeneration. Actions lead to or "grow" other events with a degree of predictability but not with complete inevitability. These actions are subject to the tending, or "gardening," of human intervention, which may be beneficial or detrimental and may have unintended consequences. This metaphor is made most clear in 3.4, where the gardeners liken England to a garden that Richard has failed to tend. Thus, when Richard disinherits and exiles Bullingbrook, he intends to remove the power of his wealth and position, and to nullify the duke's popularity by ensuring his absence. His actions, however, have the opposite effect. Bullingbrook becomes more popular still, as the other nobles identify with his plight. If the Duke of Herford can be stripped of his estate and disinherited, so can they. Moreover, by denying Bullingbrook's right to inheritance, Richard undermines the very system he wishes most to preserve. After all, Richard's right to the crown depends solely on his right to inherit his father's claim to it.

The play's structure allows us to appreciate Bullingbrook's complaint rather quickly, and then to witness Richard's protracted slide. By the end of the second scene of act 2, Richard has shown us his flattering entourage, his corruption, his incompetence, and his petulance. Gaunt has persuaded us that the nation's future is at stake, and Bullingbrook is already returning from banishment and is more popular than ever. York functions as a fulcrum for audience vacillation. We do not admire York, but we sympathize with his feeling that no good can come out of either Richard's staying in power or his removal. Although Bullingbrook is completely in control and behaving as if he is already king as early as the beginning of act 3, it is important for Henry's political approval that Richard be seen as abdicating of his own accord, not forcibly removed from power. Bullingbrook need only give Richard a little time to let the magic of anxiety and imagination undo him completely. Richard falls in love with his own fall, as he is transfixed by the specter of his own vulnerability. The confrontations between Richard and Bullingbrook in the third and fourth acts play out more like an elaborate verbal dance than a pugilistic face-off. Bullingbrook outmaneuvers his adversary until the king is cornered and finally bloodlessly checkmated; bloodletting can wait for a more opportune time. Bullingbrook understands that Richard's pathetic state must be underscored, and so he parades the deposed king for public humiliation before imprisoning him. But no sooner is Henry crowned than squabbles break out. Though events now echo those that occurred under Richard, they seem to have less dignity and gravity. No longer are we witness to a challenge of honor between two highly placed dukes, but rather to a domestic spat with comic overtones, as York and his wife bicker before Henry about their son's fate. A populist and contractual conception of kingship and rule seems to be replacing the notion of invincible divine election that Richard believes invests him with absolute individual power. The medieval world of divinely sanctioned kingship into which Richard was born is beginning to give way to a different cultural code, one that uneasily attempts to redefine an idea of monarchic legitimacy more responsive to the popular will, but one that in the play proves to be equally fraught with problems.

MAIN CHARACTERS

Richard II

Richard elicits complex and contradictory responses as the play progresses: weak, vain, callous, selfish, and self-absorbed on the one hand; sensitive, gifted, even tragic, on the other. Richard at the outset presents himself as a fair-minded, peace-loving monarch, calmly instructing Mowbray and Bullingbrook: "be rul'd by me, / Let's purge this choler without letting blood" (1.2.152–153). But he soon appears weak, duplicitous, indecisive, cowardly, and vindictive, capitulating to the dukes' insistence on fighting and then halting their combat in order to banish them both. Exiling both dukes seems either an arbitrary and outlandish exercise of royal prerogative or the cowardly action of someone who has something to fear and hide, or both. We soon learn that Richard was almost certainly responsible for Gloucester's death, something he did not disclose during the dispute between Mowbray and Bullingbrook. Displaying a cruel and callous disregard for his most sage adviser, John of Gaunt, Richard plots to raise money for his Irish wars by absconding with the nobleman's assets—which also represent Bullingbrook's inheritance—the moment Gaunt dies. Gaunt on his deathbed details to Richard the king's shortcomings and the grave harm he has done the nation, but to no avail. Over York's protestations, Richard immediately seizes Gaunt's money and belongings as soon as the duke expires. Richard is never more loathsome than during this scene, and he now absents himself for the rest of the act, leaving us with this sour impression.

The moment he returns, however, he begins to reveal his complexity and depth. His faith in his divine election is somehow touching, but it is so principally because Richard expresses it in beautiful, modulated, metaphoric verse. Though it may seem that nearly all of Shakespeare's characters speak wonderfully, Richard's language is exceptionally rich and musical. He is a master at shading meaning through elaborate metaphors and verbal ornamentation. Not only gifted in the arts of poetic language, Richard is able to let his imagination soar as no one else in the play can. But he prefers to reflect, analyze, and fantasize rather than act, and it is this characteristic that frustrates some of his closest allies. His penchant for introspection and self-dramatization prompts the exasperated Bishop of Carlisle to counsel him that "wise men ne'er sit and wail their woes, / But presently prevent the ways to wail" (3.2.178–179). Richard stages scenarios in his head, imagining himself the victim/star of his own drama, casting himself not only as a Christ-like martyr but also as an incipient literary legacy—"the lamentable tale of me" that he insists his wife preserve and disseminate (5.1.44). Richard's insistent fascination with his own plight and his intensely theatrical conception of it reveal him as part poet-king, part player-king: intelligent and possessed of potential for artistry but also somewhat pathetic and self-absorbed, self-pitying and self-indulgent.

As Richard is gradually stripped of his political power, however, his ability to gaze upon himself enables him to dispense with his illusions. In the process, he is humanized and made newly sympathetic. Whereas he initially thinks of himself as God's substitute, he ultimately gains a degree of dignity through his apprehension of his own humanity. He begins to view life and identity in theatrical terms, suspecting and fearing that his kingship was simply a role he had been assigned. The possibility of being deposed catalyzes for Richard a crisis of identity, a recognition of his own frail humanity, as seen in the following lines:

> For you have but mistook me all this while,
> I live with bread like you, feel want,
> Taste grief, need friends: subjected thus,
> How can you say to me I am a king? (3.2.174–177)

He cannot fathom how bearing the name of king does not ensure his remaining immutably king. He begins referring to himself as king in the third person, in a sense endorsing the medieval and Renaissance doctrine of the king's two bodies: one being the king's mortal human frame and the other the king as body politic. Richard, oddly defiant even as he acquiesces to his own deposition, exclaims, "God save the King! although I be not he, / And yet amen, if heaven do think him me" (4.1.174–175). And yet the thought of not being king leaves him with a sense of being nothing at all. "I must nothing be" (4.1.201), muses Richard as he relinquishes the crown to Bullingbrook. He must enact even his own deposition as a self-scripted performance in which he is both actor and spectator. "Now mark me how I will undo myself" (4.1.203), he proclaims, as he proceeds to narrate his self-erasing spectacle. But soon he calls for a mirror, as he must gaze upon himself even at his most humiliating moment so as to witness his own histrionics and their effect.

At the beginning of the play's final act, Richard, though still self-absorbed, seems less so, capable as he now is of expressing his love and devotion to his wife. Then, imprisoned at Pomfret castle, he reveals that his meditations have led him to try to accept existence without the trappings of kingship or any other symbolic apparatus. "Nor I, nor any man that but man is, / With nothing shall be pleas'd, till he be eas'd / With being nothing" (5.5.39–41). Though not completely successful in letting go of his role as king, he sees himself, and we see him as well, as more flesh and blood, less the abstracted egoist of earlier acts. Finally, when he has nearly made peace with his loss of kingship and seems also to have resigned himself to passive reflection, he takes decisive action and reasserts his claim to the crown. He kills two of his attackers and then proclaims himself king before his dying lines: "Exton, thy fierce hand / Hath with the King's blood stain'd the King's own land" (5.5.109–110).

Bullingbrook

Bullingbrook may at first appear to be simply Richard's natural dramatic foil, but upon closer examination we see that the two share certain talents that they display in dissimilar ways. Bullingbrook plays the pragmatist to Richard's poet, the sober realist to Richard's fantasist, the circumspect calculator to Richard's histrionic emoter, and the populist politician to Richard's elitist despot. In one sense, Bullingbrook, though not nearly as eloquent, shares with Richard a gift for language, but it is quite a different sort of language. If Richard is a lofty poet, then

Bullingbrook is a practical rhetorician. Where Richard waxes poetic, Bullingbrook speaks persuasively. Where Richard thinks only of his own self-expression, Bullingbrook thinks only of the effect his words will have on his listeners. Similarly, Richard wears his crown theatrically and wears his theatricality like a crown.

Bullingbrook, however, is an actor, too—perhaps a much better one than Richard because he never appears to be dissembling or engaging in stagy histrionics. We should not miss York's description of the London crowd's negative reaction to Richard and their positive reception of Henry. Having just witnessed Bullingbrook's triumphant ride, York compares it to an actor's entrance: "As in a theatre the eyes of men, / After a well-graced actor leaves the stage, / Are idly bent on him that enters next" (5.2.23–25). Bullingbrook plays the reluctant king and hides his manipulations behind a mask of simplicity and forthrightness. Though Bullingbrook presents himself and is viewed by most as honest and direct, his actions often outstrip his announced intentions. He claims to have come back to England only to regain his title and his lands, but soon everyone including a resentful Richard understands that shortly he will be king. Bullingbrook cleverly arranges circumstances and orchestrates allegiances so that he may gain power without appearing ever to have craved it.

Although Bullingbrook does not hesitate to exploit his superior position once he gains the upper hand, he slyly continues to manage people's perception of him. He summarily and illegally executes Bushy and Green, claiming in part that they have wronged not only the king but also the queen, to whom he then sends his "kind commends" (3.1.38). Where Richard is emotionally impulsive and given to panic and inaction, Bullingbrook is patient, coolly purposeful, and always in command of himself and his decisive actions. Finally, Richard's character conveys a sense of human tragedy because though we may feel contempt for him much of the time, we come to know the deposed king. Bullingbrook, in contrast, remains a cipher, a master poker player whose "real" identity and character we glimpse only indirectly and through prisms.

John of Gaunt

John of Gaunt, York, Northumberland, and the queen are characters who inhabit less crucial but nonetheless important roles. Gaunt is principally emblematic of tradition, honor, wisdom, and integrity, qualities that contrast sharply with Richard's impetuous and willful follies and that bolster his son's reputation among noblemen and the populace at large. His is the voice of experience stating that Richard is not behaving as an English king should. Because of his absolute belief in the divine right of kings, however, Gaunt is only willing to chastise the monarch verbally. He will not hear of opposing Richard militarily or defying his orders directly.

York

York, an elder duke like his brother John of Gaunt, possesses more of his nephew Richard's weakness than Gaunt's firm principles. He totters between his allegiance to divine right and his sense of common sense and justice. He strongly disagrees with Richard's decision to disinherit Bullingbrook but agrees to act in the king's place to oppose the offensive that Bullingbrook mounts upon his return. He criticizes Gaunt's son for presumption and treasonous behavior but just as quickly steps aside and resigns himself to Bullingbrook's ascension. Toward the end of the play, he proclaims himself fully the subject of Henry IV, ready even to turn in his own son for complicity in traitorous plots against the new king.

Northumberland

Northumberland gradually becomes Bullingbrook's chief ally and ultimately his main henchman. He readily follows all of Bullingbrook's commands to execute or imprison any who oppose them, and he remains completely unmoved by Richard's fate. What seems to be a natural alliance between these two noblemen will, in time, as Carlisle and Richard predict, crumble and turn to hostility. Northumberland's son, Henry Percy ("Hotspur"), will become the new king's chief threat in *1 Henry IV*, the next play of the second tetralogy.

The Queen

Until Richard bids her farewell on his way to prison, we never see the queen and him together. She appears in only two other scenes in the play, first with Bushy as she worries about Richard's problems (2.2) and then in the famous garden scene, where she hides behind some foliage to hear gardeners talking of her husband's downfall (3.4). Her concern about and devotion to Richard seem to be strong and utterly unshaken throughout the play, as do her sorrow, confusion, and disbelief at the ongoing events. The scarcity of women in *Richard II* and in the second tetralogy as a whole should not be taken to mean that the role of females and the feminine are of little importance. In fact their relative absence constitutes a major area of critical inquiry. The wreckage of Richard's marriage, for example, may appear a distant second to the demise of his kingship, but in the past decade such prominent feminist critics as Jean E. Howard and Phyllis Rackin have argued that since such English sovereigns as "Elizabeth and James repeatedly likened their relationships to England to that of a husband to his wife," Richard's recuperation of his family's kingship by virtue of a loving wife goes a long way to restoring and newly naturalizing the kingly patrimony he squandered as the country's king (*Engendering a Nation: A Feminist Account of Shakespeare's English Histories*, p. 159).

DEVICES AND TECHNIQUES

Ceremony, ritual, and courtly spectacle pervade the action of *Richard II*, and the language of the play matches the mood of such events in its formality and patterned musicality. The entire play is written in verse, a rarity in the Shakespearean canon, and it contains a high percentage of rhymed couplets. The balanced and ornamented utterances not only reflect the principal characters' high station and the gravity of events; they also echo the rigorous symmetry of the play's plot and its elemental imagery of sun, earth, fire, and water. Though speech is relentlessly structured, the poetic tone undergoes considerable variation depending upon the scene enacted, from the litigious parrying of Mowbray and Bullingbrook at the beginning of the play to the highly metaphoric whispering lyricism of Richard's self-studies, to Gaunt's gusty encomium to England in the second act.

Imagery in *Richard II* is abundant, complex, and carefully arranged. Calling attention only to some of the most prominent devices, we note that the chiastic plot, where Richard's fall coincides with Bullingbrook's rise, is underscored by various manifestations of seesaw imagery. The two buckets Richard speaks of as he abdicates function as the most blatant of these. Comparing the crown to a deep well and himself and Bullingbrook to the buckets, Richards imagines, "That bucket down and full of tears am I, / Drinking my griefs, whilst you mount up on high" (4.1.188–189). He reiterates this image of balances reversed when, just before being taken to the Tower, he exclaims to Bullingbrook's men, "Conveyers are you all, / That rise thus nimbly by a true king's fall" (4.1.317–318). Moreover, characters adumbrate the imagery of sun and earth, high and low, ascension and descent, and the reversal of these positions throughout the play. Richard compares his fall from kingship to the fall of Christ, and he complains that he must come down to the base court: "Down, down I come, like glist'ring Phaëton" (3.3.178). The lowering of the knee also becomes a recurring gesture, signaling anything from subservience to dissemblance, from Bullingbrook's disingenuous kneeling before York, when the latter has come to confront his army, to the Duchess of York's demeaning and almost comical supplication to Henry IV on behalf of her son's life. Related images include the throwing down from windows of "dust and rubbish on King Richard's head" (5.2.6), as York tells of events in London, and the throwing down of "gages" (or challenges)—first by Bullingbrook and Mowbray in the opening scene and then by others at the beginning of the fourth act.

Gardens and their tending operate as another imagistic cluster. In the celebrated garden scene, the state is likened to a garden, and lords and kings to gardeners who must grow and prune wisely, eliminating weeds and cultivating beneficial plants lest they themselves become noisome pests to the garden's health. When Carlisle warns that "the blood of English shall manure the ground" (4.1.137) as a result of Bullingbrook's usurpation, he echoes the trope of gardening and invests it with a historiographical edge. Events become like seeds that will grow into similar events, which will in turn propagate and generate a legacy of actions. The garden then becomes not only a metaphor for the current state but even a symbol of origins, as it alludes to its first form as Eden. But in its cycles of growth, decay, and regeneration, gardening imagery models both past and future events, history repeating itself, replicating evil deeds as well as good ones. The linking of kingship to gardening extends even to associating the royal office with the tangible land of England, as evidenced in Gaunt's "This blessed plot, this earth, this realm, this England" (2.1.50) and in Richard's embracing of the nation's soil upon his return from Ireland: "Dear earth, I do salute thee with my hand" (3.2.6). The greenness of the earth (not to mention such character names as Bushy and Green) is also counterpoised with the redness of blood that threatens to rain down "[u]pon the grassy carpet" (3.3.50) in a "crimson tempest" (3.3.46).

Finally, mirrors and mirroring play an indispensable role in the drama's imagistic dynamics. When Richard at his deposition gazes into the glass in order to "read" his face and then proceeds to smash the mirror to bits upon the ground, he enacts the symbolic fragmentation and destruction of his identity. Throughout the drama, Richard is concerned with the growing discrepancy between his image of himself as the reigning and rightful king and his refracted image as deposed irrelevancy. When he looks in the glass, does he see a king or someone playing the role of king? The mirror episode focuses a number of the play's thematic lenses, such as the difficulty in distinguishing between one's perception of oneself and the persona one projects, and the fine line between being and role-playing—in short, the distinction between perception and reality. Richard's gradual realization, or at least suspicion, that his identity is an elaborate construction is finally acknowledged for the first time when his image shatters into its constituent fragments.

The mirror's significance, though, extends beyond questions of subjectivity and perception, as mirroring and its distortions constitute one of the play's structural principles, with many scenes "mirroring" others imperfectly. Put another way, events are cyclical, and historical patterns repeated. Thus, the play begins with Richard II's presiding over a dispute between Mowbray and Bullingbrook. Richard's initial response is to tell the men to settle their differences peaceably. Once Henry is king, he presides over a dispute between Aumerle, Bagot, and others, and he counsels the same restraint. At the beginning of the play, Mowbray is accused of treason against Richard. When Henry is king, it is Aumerle who answers the charge of treason against the current king. At the beginning of the play, Richard appears to have Gloucester's blood on his hands, while at the play's close it is Henry who tries to come to terms with his responsibility for Richard's death. Many other instances of such "mirroring," both subtle and bold, can be found throughout the play.

THEMES AND MEANINGS

Monarchic legitimacy, the theatricality of kingship, the nature of language, and the way history is made, recorded, and understood—all figure as vital threads in the play's thematic weave. Moreover, these threads are so tightly knotted into one another as to be practically inseparable.

The play's focus on the question of what makes a monarch legitimate reflects a central concern in early modern England. The legitimacy of every monarch since Richard II, up to and including the reigning Elizabeth I, had been questioned by particular constituencies. Monarchic legitimacy, though obviously topical and of general interest, was a subject Shakespeare had to handle delicately because of its political volatility. The thematic question the play poses is whether a monarch's claim to the throne should rest solely in birthright, irrespective of ability or abuse of power, or whether popularity and competence should affect entitlement to this highest office. The Tudor claim in Elizabethan England could not be based solely on blood lineage that magically conferred heavenly approval upon the monarch. The first Tudor king, Henry VII, from whom Elizabeth I was descended, was the same Earl of Richmond who slew the "monster" Richard III at Bosworth Field. In the Tudor version of events, clearly the country was better off with the heroic Richmond than with the infamous Richard III, despite the fact that Richard had the stronger blood claim to the crown. It was in the interest of all royalty that some blood claim exist; otherwise, a purely populist monarchy would make anyone eligible. The competing claims of blood lineage versus popularity and competence signal, in part, the transition from a medieval conception of monarchy to an early modern one, in which some compromise between these two models is achieved. *Richard II* achieves a fine balance, as the play neither completely demonizes nor exalts either Richard or Bullingbrook. Both reveal significant faults and strengths. Similarly, depending upon the sector of society, Elizabeth I was a legitimate or illegitimate monarch due to her bloodline or because of her record as ruler.

Embedded in the play's representation of monarchy we find an abiding element of theatricality. The importance of performance and display in maintaining a sense of awe at the spectacle of kingship is underscored, but so is the difficulty in distinguishing between reality and representation, between a king who must play a role to maintain his image as king and a player-king, an actor who must project a convincing image of a king. When Richard appears on the high walls of Flint Castle, York remarks on the theatrical aspect of Richard's self-presentation: "Alack, alack for woe, / That any harm should stain so fair a show!"(3.3.70–71). As the play progresses, however, Richard begins to see himself as merely an actor of sorts: "Thus play I in one person many people" (5.5.31).

Similarly, the play examines the relationship between reality and the language that represents it. What, for example, does it mean to be called king? This is a question upon which Richard dwells incessantly: "The name of king?" (3.3.146); "I had forgot myself, am I not king?" (3.2.83); "I have no name, no title" (4.1.255). In *Romeo and Juliet*, possibly composed the same year as *Richard II*, Juliet will dwell on the power and impotence of names in much the same way: "What's in a name? That which we call a rose / By any other word would smell as sweet" (2.2.43–44). Richard at first thinks his words are almost God-like, anointed as he assumes he is by Heaven; his words should mystically enact what he says by the mere saying of them. Bullingbrook, in contrast, uses words as tools, carving out meanings to represent actions achieved through effort and will. For Richard, however, the realization that his pronouncements are no longer absolute but subject to negotiation, that they perhaps have no intrinsic authority, calls into question the finality and stability of words and their meaning in general. The play, in fact, begins with a contest of wills and arms—but also a contest of meaning. Bullingbrook accuses Mowbray of being a traitor, and Mowbray returns the indictment. What does it mean then to be a traitor? Traitor to what? To king? To country? Are they always the same thing? Bullingbrook becomes traitorous to his king, but is he true to his country for being so? Gaunt, whose great speech will soon follow, harbors apparently treasonous sentiments toward his king but expounds his faith not only in England but also in the office of the king. Toward the end of the play, Aumerle and others will be accused of treasonous, traitorous behavior, but this time the definition has been inverted: now to be a traitor means not to plot against Richard but against Bullingbrook, now king, now Henry IV.

The thematic strands of monarchic legitimacy and forms of representation crisscross within the broader cloth of history and its depiction. To write a history play is to transform the past into fiction, and to turn real events into theater. But doing so raises the question of the extent to which history is always fictionalized, interpreted, and recorded in an incomplete and partial manner. Additionally, the dramatic rendering of historical events in a play such as *Richard II* points up the way in which theatricality may actually contribute to the events themselves. The play concerns itself not only with the question of monarchic legitimacy but also with the dynamics of politics and history over time. The past looms over the play in the figure of murdered Gloucester and in Richard's past transgressions, just as the past will haunt Henry and Hal for the remainder of the *Henriad*. However, while *Richard II* treats actions and events as outgrowths of the past, it also highlights their capacity to engender, likening such events to seeds—as we have seen from the gardening imagery—that will grow into the history of the future, a drama to be played out over the course of the second tetralogy. We need not think that Shakespeare had the plots of the next three plays in mind when he wrote *Richard II*, only that he was already engaged in thinking about how to depict history, and that he was already prompting his audience to think about the meaning of history, how its recording came about, and how it influences the present. *Richard II* is, then, a play not only about the legitimacy of a particular king and his challenger but also about England's identity, its relation to its own history, and the role that both language and theater play in the formation and representation of the past.

CRITICAL CONTROVERSIES

One of the most enduring points of debate in *Richard II* criticism has been whether the play endorses or opposes the doctrine of the divine right of kings. Certainly the play criticizes Richard's behavior, but does it represent his dethronement and Bullingbrook's rise to power as a measured restorative to the state's health or as a wrongheaded solution with enduringly grim consequences? The question is more complicated than it may at first appear, and modern critics have approached it from multiple angles and have offered a wide variety of responses. In 1941, E.M.W. Tillyard, in his highly influential book, *Shakespeare's History Plays* (London: Chatto and Windus), claimed that the history plays subscribe to traditional Tudor ideology and a typically Elizabethan worldview, one that frowned upon disorder, disobedience to the monarch, and opposition of any kind to the providential model of kingship and history. The history plays following *Richard II* would then fulfill Carlisle's prophecy of coming strife, which would not be relieved until Henry Tudor killed Richard III at Bosworth Field, united the houses of Lancaster and York through marriage, became king, and thus "saved" England. Since Elizabeth I was a Tudor, this would be the view of history that she would want and that she would get, or so goes the theory.

Nearly all critics eventually came to disagree with some or all of Tillyard's claims, but the foundational nature of his contribution to further debate remains unquestioned. In the 1950s and 1960s, such critics as Norman Rabkin (*Shakespeare and the Common Understanding* [New York: Free Press, 1967]), A. P. Rossiter (*Angel with Horns* [London: Longmans, Green, 1961]), and Robert Ornstein (*A Kingdom for a Stage* [Cambridge, MA: Harvard UP, 1972]) demonstrated that *Richard II* presents a more complex and ambiguous vision of politics than Tillyard had acknowledged.

Subsequent criticism has been eager to apply reconfigured historicist, linguistic, poststructuralist, and performance approaches, as well as gender studies to the question of how the play represents royal legitimacy. Critics such as Graham Holderness (*Shakespeare's History* [Dublin: Gill and Macmillan, 1985]) and David Scott Kastan (see annotated bibliography) have argued, by very different means, and to differing degrees, that *Richard II* serves rather more to subvert royal authority than to endorse it. Such an apparently subversive spectacle is also sometimes viewed as providing an outlet for oppositional yet containable energy, whose release ultimately serves the interests of the monarchy. Scholars also explain how Shakespeare's history plays constitute a kind of historiography; how they comment on what history is and how it is made; how they dramatize the difficulty of fixing a single "true" version of events; how they interact with the stage of political events; and how the plays themselves participate in the construction of history.

History is, undeniably, recorded and transmitted through language, and the prominence of language as theme and of Richard's self-conscious speech have not been lost on critics from M. M. Mahood (*Shakespeare's Wordplay* [London: Methuen, 1957]) to more recent scholars, such as James L. Calderwood, Catherine Belsey, and others (see annotated bibliography). These writers ask, among other questions, to what degree the play is really about language and meaning. And how do these linguistic issues relate to questions of legitimacy and power? For example, do Richard's estrangement from his title and his disappointment that his words have ceased to be all-powerful function as evidence that he is king in name only and that the play shows divine anointment as a pathetic myth? Or should we take the ineffectuality of the king's eloquence instead as testimony to his tragic state? The answer to this last question lies partly in performance.

Critics have long debated what the "correct" or "proper" tone is for *Richard II*, because whether one sees the play on stage or in the mind's eye, the tone of the "production" contributes significantly to an understanding and interpretation of the drama and thus also bears on the play's attitude toward kingship. Not quite a tragedy, not simply a historical pageant, how should it be played or read? For many, the play requires a formal, ceremonial tone, one in keeping with the highly structured, embellished verse, the seriousness of the events, and the courtly setting. However, certain critics, notably Leonard Barkan ("The Theatrical Consistency of *Richard II*," *Shakespeare Quarterly* 29 [1978]: 5–19) and John Halverson (see annotated bibliography), have also found a disturbing comic tone in particular scenes, which they contend should alter our understanding of how the play works. If, for example, we see events toward the end of the play, such as the Aumerle conspiracy scene, as verging on the humorous, we may be prompted to view Bullingbrook's reign as indicative of a cheapened, degraded state. Such a response would lend credence to the view that the play disapproves of Richard's fall. Conversely, if we see events turning toward the absurd, we may come to the conclusion that the play endorses neither Richard's fall nor Bullingbrook's rise but rather comments on how events engender one another and outstrip individual control, making fools of everyone.

The way Richard controls and conducts himself reflects, in part, whether he possesses the ability to rule, but in the play it also contributes to a perception of his masculinity or femininity. Recently, such critics as Jean H. Howard and Phyllis Rackin (see annotated bibliography) have focused a good deal of attention on the neglected but profitable issue of gender in the play. Richard's sensitivity, his self-dramatization, his love of poetic expression, his talkativeness, his apparent weakness, all add to the "feminization" of his character. Although there are few women in *Richard II* and the rest of the second tetralogy, the role of femininity and the feminine have come to be seen as a crucial component of interpretive strategies. To appreciate the importance and complexity of, for example, portraying a male monarch as effeminate, all one needs to remember is that when *Richard II* was originally staged, a woman, Elizabeth I, was on the throne, and yet the society was strongly patriarchal. Similarly, if Bullingbrook is thought to have a legitimate claim to the throne, then that claim is based on popular approval and not genealogical descent. Such an idea of monarchy means that women are no longer able to ensure or harm the line of royal succession. In other words, the politics, power, and gender are inseparable in early modern culture and in the play.

PRODUCTION HISTORY

The Lord Chamberlain's Men may have first performed *Richard II* as early as 1595, and the company appears to have continued staging it even after making the Globe their home in 1599, as records testify to its performance there in 1601. Although *Richard II* was by no means the most successful play in Shakespeare's day, the King's Men continued to perform it after his death until at least 1631. In 1642, however, English theaters were closed due to pressure from Puritan reformers. When the playhouses reopened, *Richard II* languished in relative obscurity. When it was produced it was often hardly recognizable because of prescriptive adaptations and brutal cutting. In the eighteenth century, many found *Richard II* ill-suited to the neoclassical bias of the period. Later critics and theater professionals often thought that the play bored audiences with its lack of action, that its title character was distinctly un-heroic, and that it was more suitable for reading than acting.

In the nineteenth century *Richard II* enjoyed a revival. The English Romantics found in the character of Richard, and in the play's rich, allusive language, the kind of delicate and doomed sensibility that spoke to their aesthetic. The legendary actor Edmund Kean played the title role at London's Drury Lane in 1815, but it was his son Charles's production at the Princess Theatre in 1857 that registered the most successful staging the play had seen for centuries and would see for years to come. Both productions still veered widely from the original play, either by adding preachy moralizing, as did the script the elder Kean used, or by cutting so deeply that major elements of the drama were lost, as was the case in the younger Kean's version. The 1857 production, however, was attuned to the contemporary fashion for historical authenticity. It excelled at recreating the mood and spectacle of court life in the middle ages by using costly and elaborate sets, medieval music, and opulent costumes.

Sir Frank Benson first assayed the role at Stratford-upon-Avon in 1896. His portrayal of Richard was influential in the early part of the twentieth century, helping to captivate such redoubtable literary figures as W. B. Yeats and to cement Shakespeare's play in the permanent repertory of leading companies. Benson took few liberties with the text and gave a complex and subtly shaded interpretation of the title character.

John Gielgud's Richard II at London's Old Vic in 1929 represents the next landmark performance. This production returned the play to a more spare set than was customary at the time, recreating a style of staging closer to that of the original Elizabethan set. However, what truly distinguished this production was the actor's justifiably famous skill for speaking Shakespearean verse, for bringing out the subtle rhythms of the line, and for imbuing the verbal melodies with their proper proportion of emotional weight. Gielgud's performance struck an enviable balance between the rigors of the poetry and the affective life of the character, and so paved the way for great actors to vie routinely for the role of Richard. The list of Gielgud's successors reads like a who's who of British acting: Paul Scofield, Alec Guinness, Ian McKellen, Jeremy Irons, Derek Jacobi, and Ralph Fiennes, to name but a few.

Among the most notable of modern and contemporary stagings is John Barton's 1973 Royal Shakespeare Company production, in which the actors playing Bullingbrook and Richard switched roles from night to night. Hugely successful,

Sir John Gielgud as Richard II, circa 1935. © Getty Images.

this production took the symbolism of the mirror, already central to the play, as its directorial "concept" and then proceeded to heighten its implications. Rather than showing Richard and Bullingbrook as opposites, Barton elected to show them as, in a sense, an image and its inversion, one a king who thought he was divine and would suffer a fall to humanity, the other an ambitious man who would be king. The production united them as well in their commonality as "actors" in a political theater.

More venturesome interpretations have also been staged with some success. One example is Deborah Warner's casting of Fiona Shaw in the role of Richard for her National Theatre Production in 1995. Cross-gender casting in an Elizabethan drama should not be taken as outlandish in itself. Quite the contrary, as it was an absolute commonplace in Shakespeare's day because all the parts were played by men or boys. The provocative aspect of Warner's idea, however, lay in her vision of the king as a child at play, one whose sexual identity had not yet even been formed: an androgynous, capricious, and emotionally dependant creature lost in a strange political landscape, at once postmodern and premodern.

EXPLICATION OF KEY PASSAGES

1.2.9–36. "Finds brotherhood in thee . . . my Gloucester's death." Gloucester's widow, the Duchess, implores John of Gaunt to avenge her husband's death. Gaunt will reply that since it was God's "deputy anointed" (1.2.38) who was responsible (meaning that Richard rules by divine right), acting against Richard would be tantamount to acting against God. Although the story of Gloucester's murder is never clarified or resolved here or elsewhere in the play, this passage alludes to the crucial circumstances by which Richard came to power. It should remind us just how familial these conflicts are. When the Duchess reminds Gaunt that "Edward's seven sons, whereof thyself art one, / Were as seven vials of his sacred blood" (1.2.11–12), she counts on her auditor's familiarity with royal genealogy. King Edward III had seven sons, including John of Gaunt (Duke of Lancaster), Thomas of Woodstock (Duke of Gloucester, or "Gloucester"), Edmund of Langley (Duke of York, or "York"), and Edward the Black Prince, who was Richard II's father. Edward was the eldest, and so under the system known as primogeniture, whereby the eldest son holds the right of inheritance, Edward the Black Prince was to succeed Edward III and become Edward IV. The Black Prince, however, died before his father did, and so Richard, as his eldest son, became King Richard II upon Edward III's death. To better understand the actions and motivations of the characters over the course of the play it is helpful to remember that York, Gaunt, and Gloucester are brothers, that Richard is their nephew, and that Richard and Bullingbrook are first cousins. From this genealogy we cannot help but also remark how close all of these characters are themselves to the throne.

2.1.40–68. "This royal throne . . . my ensuing death." Gaunt sings the praises of England in this famous speech—its land, its history, its religion, its people, but most of all its feudal and martial traditions embodied in its line of exalted kings. Appointed an exceptionally Christian status, "This other Eden" (2.1.42), England is lauded too for its beauty and the natural protection afforded it as an island. The gist of Gaunt's rhetoric, however, is that Richard disgraces this chivalric and monarchic tradition and debases the nation through his behavior and his policies. Gaunt particularly objects to the king's practice of leasing out the land as a form of taxation. Gaunt's language likens Richard's laws to a kind of emasculation: "England, that was wont to conquer others, / Hath made a shameful conquest of itself" (2.1.65–66). But the gendering and relative passivity or aggressiveness assigned to England in this speech is complex. England is figured paradoxically as both feminine, "This nurse, this teeming womb of royal kings" (2.1.51), and masculine, warlike, "this seat of Mars" (2.1.41). Gaunt's speech is also a glittering display of rhetorical fireworks, highlighting as it does not only such poetic commonplaces as personification, alliteration, and metonymy, but also schemes of anaphora (same word or words to start each clause or line in a sequence), for example, lines 50–51, epizeuxis (repetition of same word with no intervening words), for example, line 57, and parison (lines of parallel construction), for example, lines 40–41.

3.2.144–177. "No matter where . . . I am a king?" Though Richard is still some distance from being deposed, he already seems to accept that he will not be able to play the role of king much longer. And it is his new view of kingship as theatrical that represents both a kind of recognition of himself as human rather than divine and a voiding of the only identity he has ever known. The poignancy of Richard's world, now "with a little pin" (3.2.169) pricked and destroyed, pulls against the contempt he generates by his defeatist, wallowing self-sympathy. Richard, though previously an often capricious and autocratic ruler, now moans for sympathy. He becomes fascinated, almost hypnotized, with the vision of his own fall. He yearns to dwell on other "sad stories of the death of kings" (3.2.156), eager to transform his reality into a literary, or perhaps theatrical, artifact and join the ranks of departed martyrs. In the meantime, while he lives, he sees that he will be "subjected thus" (3.2 176), beaten, made a subject instead of a king. But this "subject"(ivity) becomes for Richard a form of self-awareness. He sees his own theatricality, the realization that he has been merely playing the role of king, as evidence of his humanity: "I live with bread like you, feel want, / Taste grief, need friends" (3.2.175–176). These lines call to mind Shylock's famous plea in *The Merchant of Venice* that Jews be treated as human. But these lines also raise questions about the theatricality not only of kingship but also of life in general, and where the line between illusion and reality, between acting and being lies. The theater as a metaphor for the world (and vice versa) runs thematically throughout Shakespeare's work, as this trope enjoyed general currency in Renaissance England. After all, the theater most closely associated with Shakespeare and his company was itself named the Globe.

4.1.114–149. "Marry, God forbid! . . . cry against you 'woe!'" The Bishop of Carlisle's speech plays a central role in the drama and no doubt in its initial reception. Giving voice to the accepted ideological doctrine of not only the Middle Ages during which the play is set but also of Renaissance England, Carlisle takes a defiantly conservative stand just when everyone seems to accept that Bullingbrook will be king. Everything and everyone had an assigned place in the elaborate yet specific hierarchical order of the early modern cosmos, from the lowest beast to God in heaven. Carlisle reminds the assembled men that divine right and the king's authority are absolute, that whatever they may say or think, they are still mere subjects, and he asks, "What subject can give sentence on his king?" (4.1.121). The intractability of this cosmic order and the enormity of Bullingbrook's presumption in replacing the legitimate king constitute dramatic elements that a modern audience has more trouble appreciating than did an Elizabethan audience. Shakespeare's contemporaries probably needed no reminding that such a transfer of power was unprecedented and inherently highly dramatic.

But Carlisle's speech accomplishes much more than emphasizing the basic conflicts. This prelate's oration looks forward to the rest of the second tetralogy and backward to history, and it does so by elaborating on the trope of plant growth and decay already developed in the garden scene. Richard has been "planted many years" (4.1.127), and if Bullingbrook, "foul traitor" (4.1.135), is made king, then "the blood of English shall manure the ground" (4.1.137). Violence sprouts from violence, and its branches will ensnare "kin with kin, and kind with kind" (4.1.141) and plant new seeds of "Disorder, horror, fear, and mutiny" (4.1.142). Carlisle's comments preview the long strife to come between the houses of Lancaster and York, sometimes referred to as the Wars of the Roses, with the Lancastrians symbolized by a red rose and the Yorkists by a white one. "[I]f you raise this house against this house, / It will the woefullest division prove / That ever fell upon this cursed earth" (4.1.145–147). For the audience, this is of course already history, some but not all of which had already appeared in Shakespeare's first tetralogy of history plays. Carlisle's comments, then, prompt the audience to look back at history and previous performances and, more importantly, to look forward to the staging of the play's sequels.

Annotated Bibliography

Forker, Charles R. "Introduction." In *King Richard II*. London: The Arden Shakespeare, 2002. This introduction of 160-plus pages from a current scholarly edition of the play proves particularly useful for its authoritative and detailed discussion of historical, textual, and source issues.

Halverson, John. "The Lamentable Comedy of Richard II." *English Literary Renaissance* 24 (1994): 343–369. Halverson explores the play's comic possibilities, as have earlier critics, such as Leonard Barkan ("The Theatrical Consistency of *Richard II*," *Shakespeare Quarterly* 29 [1978]: 5–19) and Sheldon P. Zitner ("Aumerle's Conspiracy," *Studies in English Literature* 14 [1974]: 239–257).

Holderness, Graham, ed. *Shakespeare's History Plays: "Richard II" to "Henry V."* New York: St. Martin's P, 1992. Of particular interest in this collection are Catherine Belsey's "Making Histories," 103–120, which treats the play and its critical tradition in light of both Marxist and poststructuralist perspectives, and James L. Calderwood's "*Richard II*: Metadrama and the Fall of Speech," 121–135, which focuses on questions the play raises about linguistic and theatrical representation.

Howard, Jeanne, and Phyllis Rackin. "*Richard II*." In *Engendering a Nation: A Feminist Account of Shakespeare's English Histories*. London: Routledge, 1997. 137–159. This chapter illuminates the role of gender in the play, treating, for example, the gendering of emotions, the relative absence of women and their domestication, and connections between Richard's femininity and ideas of patrilineal authority.

Kastan, David Scott. "Proud Majesty Made a Subject: Shakespeare and the Spectacle of Rule." *Shakespeare Quarterly* 37.4 (1986): 459–475. Kastan argues that making the king into a subject on stage in front of a judging public functioned as a subversive rehearsal, helping to bring about a culture more ready to judge its monarch.

Newlin, Jeanne T. "*Richard II*": *Critical Essays*. New York: Garland, 1984. This collection gathers criticism from the period 1601–1976, including important nineteenth-century essays by Samuel Taylor Coleridge and Walter Pater, and excerpts from the influential work of E.M.W. Tillyard, E. H. Kantorowicz, and others.

Saccio, Peter. "*Richard II*: The Fall of the King." In *Shakespeare's English Kings: History, Chronicle, and Drama*. London: Oxford UP, 1977. 17–35. Saccio provides the most accessible and concise account of the historical Richard II, as well as comparisons between the history Shakespeare read and the history he represented in his plays.

Shewring, Margaret. *King Richard II*. Shakespeare in Performance Series. Manchester, Eng.: Manchester UP, 1996. The author discusses stage and screen performances of *Richard II* from the 1590s to the 1990s.

Henry IV, Parts 1 and 2

Rebecca Fletcher McNeer

PLOT SUMMARY

Henry IV, Part I

1.1. An air of both action and weariness opens this play. King Henry IV, having usurped the throne from his cousin and England's rightful king, Richard II, has little respite between the successful squelching of one rebellion and the hatching of another. Henry IV describes himself as "shaken" and "wan with care" (1.1.1). He longs to be free from "civil butchery" (1.1.13) in England and turn a united country toward a crusade. This plan must be delayed, though, because Edmund Mortimer, Henry's cousin and Richard II's designated heir, has been taken prisoner by the Welsh troops of rebel leader Owen Glendower. Not only that, but Westmerland fears "more . . . unwelcome news" (1.1.50) resulting from the battle of Humbleton between the forces of Archibald Douglas and Harry Percy ("Hotspur").

Sir Walter Blunt, who has traveled hastily from that battle is, however, able to recount the brave Hotspur's success, especially in taking prisoner the earls of Fife, Athol, Moray, Angus, and Menteith. Such good news is yet tinged with sadness, for the king wishes his own Harry, the Prince of Wales, would conduct himself more like Hotspur. Calling the son of the Earl of Northumberland "the theme of honor's tongue, / Amongst a grove the very straightest plant, / Who is sweet Fortune's minion and her pride" (1.1.82–84), King Henry sees only "riot and dishonor stain the brow" (1.1.85) of his own Harry. Before members of the court, King Henry praises Hotspur to the detriment of his son and heir by musing that perhaps "some night-tripping fairy" (1.1.87) had switched the babies in their cradles so that Northumberland's Hotspur is the true Plantagenet heir, and Henry IV's son really belongs to the Percy family. For all his glory in battle, however, Hotspur has refused to give up his noble prisoners for the king to ransom.

In this first scene, Shakespeare thus defines three of the themes this play will trace: rebellion, the contrast between Henry (or Harry) Percy and Prince Hal, and the strained relationship of King Henry IV with his eldest son.

1.2. From the serious business of the court, the play then moves to another setting to show the out-of-favor prince with his boon companion, Sir John Falstaff. Whereas at court there is a feeling of urgency, here the pace is much slower; the pastimes are much less weighty. Rather than making plans for crusades or the quashing of rebellion, the prince is drawn into a scheme for robbery at Gadshill in which an elaborate trick will be played on Falstaff. Yet, as his subsequent soliloquy indicates, neither his fellow revelers nor his father understands Hal or the motivation for his behavior.

1.3. Back at court Henry IV warns Northumberland, Worcester, and Hotspur that while he has been patient about "indignities" (1.3.2) suffered at their hands in the past, he will henceforth allow his kingly pride to assert itself. When Worcester answers that Henry IV's "greatness" is that "which our own hands / Have holp [helped] to make so portly" (1.3.12–13), the king banishes him from the court. Hotspur then defends his defiance of the king by recounting his disgust at the king's "perfumed" (1.3.36) messenger who, once the fighting was done, demanded Hotspur's prisoners for the king. Blunt defends Hotspur, yet when the king refuses to ransom Hotspur's brother-in-law, Mortimer (Hotspur being married to Mortimer's sister), Hotspur is incensed, calling Henry IV "unthankful" (1.3.136) for the aid of the Percy family in helping Henry to achieve the throne. Between Northumberland, Worcester, and Hotspur, a plan is hatched to ally themselves with the Archbishop of York and Glendower to get revenge for Henry IV's ingratitude and to take back the crown they believe they gave him.

2.1. The chamberlain at an inn confirms to Gadshill, a highway robber, that the following day a treasure of "three hundred marks" (2.1.55–56) will be in transit from Kent. Gadshill speaks of having help with the robbery from "other Troyans [Trojans, that is, riotous men] that thou dream'st not of, the which for sport sake are content to do the profession [of robbing] some grace" (2.1.69–71), alluding to Poins and the Prince of Wales.

2.2. Gadshill, as promised, carries through with the robbery of the king's men. According to plan, Prince Hal and Poins separate themselves from Falstaff and then, disguised, rob him of the money he has just stolen.

2.3. This mock robbery is balanced by the next scene of Hotspur at home, reading fulsome letters of support for the coming rebellion that, nevertheless, counsel caution. Though troubled in sleep with dreams of battle and aloof from his wife, Hotspur is consumed, disastrously, as it turns out, with what he believes are "a good plot, good friends, and full of expectation; an excellent plot, very good friends" (2.3.18–19).

2.4. The scene shifts again to the tavern in Eastcheap and Falstaff's exaggerated account of his robbery. This hilarity moves to play acting in which Prince Hal asks Falstaff to assume the role of Henry IV and "examine me upon the particulars of my life" (2.4.376–377), especially on the prince's pastimes and companions. They then reverse roles, with Hal playing the part of Henry IV and Falstaff that of the prince. The scene foreshadows the banishment of Falstaff at the end of *2 Henry IV,* when here Falstaff, advocating for himself, says "Banish plump Jack, and banish all the world" (2.4.479–480), and Hal, though speaking as his father, replies, "I do, I will" (2.4.481).

3.1. This scene shows the somewhat uneasy conspirators against Henry IV at home, staking out their spoils on a map of England. Glendower's claim of supernatural powers irritates Hotspur, who is unhappy with his allotted share of the divided country. Worcester warns Hotspur "to amend this fault" (3.1.178) of temper, and the rift is patched up.

3.2. Meanwhile, the king has a private audience with Prince Hal, whom he feels to be a "revengement and a scourge" (3.2.7) from God. Wisely, the prince refrains from making excuses, and Henry IV proceeds to give Hal a lesson in statecraft, comparing the style of Richard II to his own and warning Hal that Hotspur "hath more worthy interest to the state / Than thou the shadow of succession" (3.2.98–99). If Henry IV ascended the throne because he was a better man than Richard II, then Hotspur, as the better man now, has a better claim to the throne than Hal. Hal's response is to prophesy "the time will come / That I shall make this northern youth exchange / His glorious deeds for my indignities" (3.2.144–146).

3.3. The scene opens with Falstaff, Bardolph, and the Hostess, who is, as usual, asking Falstaff to pay her the money he owes her. She is also defending herself against the charge that Falstaff's pocket has been picked while he was in her tavern. Falstaff claims that he has lost "three or four bonds of forty pound a-piece, and a seal ring of my grandfather's" (3.3.101–103). Hal, now full of fire for the coming battle, goes to the tavern to give Falstaff the news that he has secured for him a charge of foot soldiers. Hal acknowledges being the thief and says that the only things in Falstaff's pockets were bills and a piece of candy. Hal also says that the money that Falstaff stole has been repaid. Falstaff is not happy with his command of "a charge of foot" (3.3.186), since, given his bulk, he does not like to march.

4.1. Encamped with Worcester and Douglas, Hotspur receives word from his father that, owing to the excuse of illness, the earl will not join his son for the upcoming battle. When Hotspur, who has heard as much of Hal as Hal has of him, asks of Sir Richard Vernon, newly arrived, if the "nimble-footed madcap Prince of Wales" (4.1.95) is about, Vernon's description is so full of praise for the prince that Hotspur cries, "No more, no more!" (4.1.111). Vernon also brings more bad news: Glendower will not be ready to join the rebels for two weeks, too late to help in the impending battle.

4.2. Bardolph and Falstaff are on their way to the battle with the soldiers Falstaff has secured, though by his own admission, he has "misus'd the king's press damnably" (4.2.12–13), taking bribes from the rich to exempt them from service and enlisting "the cankers of a calm world" (4.2.29–30). Joined by the Lord of Westmerland and the prince, Falstaff defends the poor quality of his soldiers by saying, "Tut, tut, good enough to toss, food for powder, food for powder; they'll fill a pit as well as better" (4.2.65–67).

4.3. The rebels are gathered, and Hotspur is so eager for battle that he wishes to sally forth that night. Sir Walter Blount presents the rebels with the king's generous overture for settlement, and Hotspur, showing more deliberation than he has in the past, promises a response.

4.4. The Archbishop of York, Richard Scroop, in conference with a member of his household, expresses his fears that, because the troops of so many allies have failed to come forth as promised, Hotspur will be outnumbered by the king's forces. Venturing off to write letters to his fellow rebels, the archbishop moves to ensure his safety should Hotspur fail.

5.1. Called to the king for a discussion of grievances, Worcester recounts old offenses, and reminds the king, "It was myself, my brother, and his son, / That brought you home, and boldly did outdare / The dangers of the time" (5.1.39–41). The king offers his grace and friendship to the rebels, if Hotspur will end his rebellion.

5.2. In a final act of duplicity among the rebels, Worcester, choosing not to trust the king, refuses to inform his nephew of the generous offer; instead, he tells Hotspur, "There is no seeming mercy in the king" (5.2.34). Queried by Hotspur about the Prince of Wales, Vernon gives another glowing report of the prince and a hint of things to come: "[L]et me tell the world, / If he outlive the envy of this day, / England did never owe so sweet a hope, / So much misconstrued in his wantonness" (5.2.65–68).

5.3–4. Battle is joined, and Falstaff's impressed soldiers are nearly all killed. A number of the king's trusted courtiers wear his own colors into battle, Sir Walter Blunt among them; he is killed by Douglas. Hal fights with valor, defending the king from Douglas and sustaining a wound before coming face-to-face with Harry Percy, whom the prince defeats. After killing Hotspur, the prince finds Falstaff, apparently dead. The old knight has, however, only feigned death to escape Douglas and, in Hal's brief absence, gets up. When Hal returns, Falstaff claims that he himself killed Percy. The prince agrees to support this lie.

5.5. The battle of Shrewsbury won, Vernon and Worcester are sentenced to die, and Hal sends his brother John of Lancaster to tell the prisoner Douglas he is "ransomless and free" (5.5.28), so valued was his courage and military prowess. Once again, a battle is won, but other enemies remain at large. The play ends with John of Lancaster and Westmerland leaving for York to intercept the Earl of Northumberland and the Archbishop of York, while the king and his son Harry head for Wales to meet with Glendower and the Earl of March, determined that "Rebellion in this land shall lose his sway" (5.5.41).

Henry IV, Part 2

Induction. This play is opened by the figure of Rumor "*painted full of tongues*" (s.d. before l. 1). Rumor tells of "King Harry's victory" (l. 23) at Shrewsbury, the death of Hotspur, and the putting down of the rebellion, then upbraids himself for telling the truth, when his job is to "noise abroad" (l. 29) the opposite.

1.1. Lord Bardolph (not to be confused with plain Bardolph, Falstaff's drinking buddy), who has evidently run across Rumor, reports to the Earl of Northumberland that his son has triumphed, that King Henry IV is gravely wounded, and that the Prince of Wales is dead. Almost immediately Travers, a servant of Northumberland, arrives with news to contradict that of Lord Bardolph. A soldier who has come from the battle tells Travers, "that rebellion had bad luck, / And that young Harry Percy's spur was cold" (1.1.41–42). Yet another servant arrives to resolve the contradiction, and in Morton's face Northumberland reads the truth. Worcester and Douglas have been taken prisoner, and Hotspur is dead. Northumberland, moreover, is in immediate danger because John of Lancaster and Westmerland have been sent to arrest him. Northumberland's initial grief is tempered by Morton's reminder that, given Hotspur's "forward spirit" (1.1.173), such an end was likely. The rebellion survives, however, through the efforts of the Archbishop of York.

1.2. In London, Falstaff, now accompanied by a page, is accosted by the Lord Chief Justice and his servant. These men, of similar age, represent polar opposites in the life of Prince Hal. The Lord Chief Justice, who knows of Falstaff's robbery at Gadshill but is willing to give him credit for action at Shrewsbury, accuses Falstaff of leading Prince Hal astray. However, through the Lord Chief Justice's intervention Falstaff and Hal are to be separated: Falstaff will accompany Prince John in their march northward. Falstaff then asks the Lord Chief Justice for a thousand pounds to equip himself for the expedition. The Lord Chief Justice replies, "Not a penny, not a penny" (1.2.225). After the Lord Chief Justice leaves, Falstaff complains of "this consumption of the purse," that is, lack of money (1.2.236–237) and dispatches his page with various letters, including one to a Mistress Ursula, to whom he has long promised marriage.

1.3. The rebels, now led by the archbishop; Thomas Mowbray, the Earl Marshal; and the lords Hastings and Bardolph, meet to consider the strength of their forces against Henry IV. They consider the likelihood of Northumberland's joining them, noting that Hotspur's efforts failed because he had "lin'd himself with hope, / Eating the air, and promise of supply" (1.3.27–28), that is, he counted on support that never materialized. Finally, however, the decision is made to proceed; their current strength is enough.

2.1. The hostess of the Boar's Head Inn has secured two officers, Fan and Snare, to arrest Sir John Falstaff for money owed. Falstaff, accompanied by his page and Bardolph, puts up a struggle, and the melee attracts the notice of the Lord Chief Justice, who has another opportunity to upbraid Falstaff. With an ensuing battle against the rebels looming, the Lord Chief Justice reminds Falstaff that he needs to take his soldiers to York, but Falstaff attempts to appease the hostess and makes plans to have supper with Doll Tearsheet at the Boar's Head that night.

2.2. The prince, with Poins, dissatisfied by the company he has been keeping and distressed by his father's great sickness, feels his reputation is such that to show his true feelings would be to invite a charge of hypocrisy. Poins devises another trick to show Falstaff "in his true colors" (2.2.170), and the prince will take part.

2.3. A family council is held at Northumberland's castle. In defense of his honor, Northumberland is planning to join the rebel forces. Lady Northumberland gives up trying to dissuade him, but Hotspur's widow, Lady Percy, uses a powerful argument to defeat Northumberland's intentions: he would not go to his son's defense, to whom he was more bound than to the rebels. While he wavers, Lady Northumberland suggests flight to Scotland, and Lady Percy says Northumberland can join the rebels after they have been tested. Persuaded at last, Northumberland opts for escape to Scotland.

2.4. Plans made earlier in the day are now brought to fruition at the Boar's Head Inn. Falstaff and Doll have their tête-à-tête interrupted by Falstaff's sergeant, Pistol, a miles gloriosus (braggart soldier) figure who, drunk and threatening Doll, must be roughly cast from the room. The prince and Poins then enter disguised as waiters and gain merriment from Falstaff's talk about them both to Doll. Upon Falstaff's recognizing them, the prince calls him to account for speaking of him so "vildly" (2.4.301), that is, vilely, creating an opportunity for Falstaff to make excuses, not unlike those he rendered for his conduct at the Gadshill robbery in *1 Henry IV*. The scene concludes abruptly when the king's messenger arrives looking for the prince and says that "a dozen captains" (2.4.358) have also been looking for Sir John Falstaff. All business now, the prince berates himself for playing when the rebellion is erupting "upon our bare unarmed heads" (2.4.365).

3.1. The ill and harassed king begins this act with a soliloquy on sleep and the awesome responsibility of power that renders him sleepless: "Uneasy lies the head that wears a crown" (3.1.31). The earls of Warwick and Surry enter to counsel briefly with the king, who muses on his former allies, now turned enemies, and how he came to the throne. Once more he says he longs to lead a crusade when "these inward wars" (3.1.107) are concluded.

3.2. In Gloucestershire, Falstaff reminisces in the company of old acquaintances, Justice Shallow and Justice Silence, and examines his pitiful recruits: Mouldy, Shadow, Wart, Feeble, and Bullcalf. The ablest of them buy their way out of service, while Feeble, a woman's tailor and the least likely of all to evince bravery, concludes that "a man can die but once, we owe God a death" (3.2.234–235).

4.1–2. The rebels, the archbishop, Mowbray, and Hastings, meet with Westmerland, the emissary of John, the Duke of Lancaster, prior to battle. They outline their grievances to Westmerland and are answered by the duke, who promises that "these griefs shall be with speed redress'd" (4.2.59). What he does not say, until the army of rebels is dispersed, is that, though the grievances will be taken care of, the rebels themselves will be arrested for treason.

4.3. Falstaff, late to the muster, is berated by John of Lancaster, who warns: "These tardy tricks of yours will, on my life, / One time or other break some gallows' back" (4.3.28–29). Left alone, Falstaff muses that Prince John is humorless because "he drinks no wine" (4.3.89). When the armies are dismissed, Falstaff resolves to return to Justice Shallow's house, where he hopes to borrow money from his old acquaintance.

4.4. At Westminster, where the king lies gravely ill in the Jerusalem Chamber, a prophecy that the king would die in Jerusalem will be fulfilled. He advises his sons Humphrey of Gloucester and Thomas of Clarence how best to deal with the Prince of Wales once he succeeds to the throne. The king worries that his heir's "headstrong riot hath no curb" (4.4.62), but Prince Hal's conduct is defended by Warwick. Westmerland and Harcourt arrive to tell the king the rebellion has been quashed.

4.5. King Henry IV collapses and is carried to a bed where his very stillness causes Prince Henry, now arrived, to think that the king has died. Speaking to the crown as the cause of his father's disease, the Prince of Wales takes it in due reverence and exits. King Henry IV awakens, finds the crown gone, and sternly upbraids the Prince of Wales for eagerness to reign and bring on a time when "apes of idleness" (4.5.122) will rule England. Prince Henry is stricken by his father's imputation, but the two are reconciled by the prince's protestations of loyalty and reform. The king gives his heir one last lesson in statecraft before dying: "Be it thy course to busy giddy minds / With foreign quarrels" (4.5.213–214). As Henry V, Hal will follow that advice, not the first or last ruler to do so.

5.1. Falstaff and Bardolph have returned to Gloucestershire and the house of Justice Shallow, who tells his servant, Davy, that he intends to treat his guest well, as "A friend i' th' court is better than a penny in purse" (5.1.30–31). Falstaff hopes to trade on his old friendship with Shallow first for financial gain, then with stories for the amusement of the prince.

5.2. The Lord Chief Justice arrives at Westminster to find King Henry IV dead and all the court anxious about the new king, Henry V. In particular, the Lord Chief Justice, who had earlier been called to reprimand the unruly prince, believes he has cause to fear. The anxiety of the court is readily apparent to Henry V when he appears: "You all look strangely on me" (5.2.63). Just as he has always privately proposed and said to his father, Henry V assures these assembled that he intends "To mock the expectation of the world" (5.2.126) and to demonstrate his true, regal abilities. The new king not only allays the fears of the Lord Chief Justice, he places him in an honored position of surrogate father, thus confirming his devotion to justice.

5.3. In Gloucestershire, with Justice Shallow, Justice Silence, their servant Davy, and Bardolph, Falstaff's revelry is interrupted by the arrival of Pistol with the news of Henry V's accession to the throne. Expecting preferment now that his "tender lambkin" (5.3.116) is king, Falstaff hastens to London, telling Pistol, "Let us take any man's horses, the laws of England are at my commandment. Blessed are they that have been my friends, and woe to my Lord Chief Justice!" (5.3.135–138).

5.4. This ominous scene shows Doll Tearsheet and Hostess Quickly being arrested, a sign of the new order.

5.5. During the coronation procession, Falstaff calls out familiarly to the new king, who denies him decisively and warns him: "Presume not that I am the thing I was" (5.5.56). If he will reform, Falstaff is promised advancement, but the days of tavern idleness and easy friendship are at an end. In the play's final lines, Prince John, in conversation with the Lord Chief Justice, commends the new king's conduct and hints at the prospect of a war against France, which will come to pass in *Henry V*.

Epilogue. The speaker says that the women in the audience have forgiven the performance, so the gentlemen should, too. More of Sir John Falstaff is promised in the next play, along with Katherine of France. Particular care is given, however, almost as a legal notice, to make clear that the fifteenth-century Protestant martyr Sir John Oldcastle is not to be mistaken for the riotous Sir John Falstaff, who originally in the play bore the name Oldcastle.

PUBLICATION HISTORY

Frank Kermode, in *The Age of Shakespeare* (New York: Modern Library, 2004), writes that the *Henry IV* plays date from 1597 to 1599, "just before and just after the move to the Globe," the theater to which *Henry V* refers specifically (91). Partly because of Shakespeare's topical references to impressed soldiers, Geoffrey Bullough, in *Narrative and Dramatic Sources of Shakespeare*, vol. 4 (London: Routledge, 1962), places *1 Henry IV* in late 1596 or early 1597 (156), dates that have led to conjecture concerning the cause and the timing for Shakespeare's revision of the play to change the name of Sir John Oldcastle to that of Falstaff (see "Critical Controversies," below). Bullough also notes that references to the subject of *Richard II* in *1 Henry IV* would indicate that Shakespeare turned to *1 Henry IV* soon after completing his study of the deposed Richard II. In part because the only quarto (Q) copy of *2 Henry IV* contains a vestigial reference to Oldcastle in a speech prefix someone neglected to expunge, Bullough proposes that *2 Henry IV* was written "immediately after" *Part 1* (156). Roslyn L. Knutson, in her article "Shakespeare's Repertory" (in *A Companion to Shakespeare*, ed. David Scott Kastan [Cambridge: Cambridge UP, 2002], 346–361), locates *1 Henry IV* in the repertory of Shakespeare's company, the Lord Chamberlain's Men and then the King's Men, in 1596–1597 and *2 Henry IV* in 1598–1599 (348).

No less difficult to trace precisely are the true texts of the plays, as noted by Thomas L. Berger and Jesse M. Lander in their article "Shakespeare in Print, 1593–1640" (in *A Companion to Shakespeare*, 395–413). They conclude that "perfect stability has never been achieved" (412). Part of the difficulty is, as G. Blakemore Evans writes in "Shakespeare's Text," in *The Riverside Shakespeare*, 2nd ed. (Boston: Houghton Mifflin, 1997), "no substantive manuscripts, either authorial or scribal, have survived for the main body of the Shakespeare canon" (56).

Five quarto editions of *1 Henry IV* were printed before John Heminge and Henry Condell, actors and shareholders of Shakespeare's company, the King's Men, put together the First Folio of Shakespeare's dramatic works in 1623. Of the first quarto published in 1598 (Q0), only one page, containing 1.2.210–2.2.111, survives. The second edition printed in the same year as Q0 has come to be known as Q1. Further editions were published in 1599 (Q2), 1604 (Q3), 1608 (Q4), 1613 (Q5), and 1622 (Q6); *1* and *2 Henry IV* were printed in the First Folio (F1), and a later quarto edition of *1 Henry IV* was published in 1639.

Not as popular as *1 Henry IV*, *2 Henry IV* had only one edition (Q) prior to inclusion in the First Folio and had, according to Evans, no separate printing during the seventeenth century. What is especially fascinating about this edition, however, is that it exists in two versions. Qa is missing 1.3, an omission that was not corrected until a number of copies had been sold. That issue was then canceled, and the missing portion was incorporated in Qb (Evans, 965). Speculation about the cause of the missing pages is unresolved but generally hinges on either "authorial afterthought" of Shakespeare (which would be an indication of his attention to revision) or an error caused by the enforced revision of the play to accommodate objections of Sir John Oldcastle's descendants (Evans, 965).

It would appear that present-day texts of both *1* and *2 Henry IV* evolved from "good" quartos because they are believed to have been printed from Shakespeare's foul papers or transcriptions thereof. Using the two handwritten segments of the play *Sir Thomas More* as a guide to Shakespeare's idiosyncratic spellings, scholars have fastened on the peculiar spelling of "scilens" for "silence" in that play and in the 1600 quarto of *2 Henry IV* as an indication of the play's having been printed from Shakespeare's foul papers, "where the name of Master Justice Silence is spelt eighteen times in this curious way" (Jackson, 169). Evans points out other instances from *2 Henry IV* that give "very strong" evidence to "foul papers" as a source for printing: 1. inconsistent references to characters, for example, Doll Tearsheet variously indicated as *Dol.*, *Dorothy*, *Teresh.* and *Whoore*; 2. stage directions for characters who do not appear; and 3. an instance of Falstaff's speech being indicated by the prefix *Old.* for Oldcastle, evidently one reference not caught and expunged (965).

An oddity of textual interest concerning the *Henry IV* plays is the Dering Manuscript, of which David Scott Kastan's account in the Introduction to the Arden Shakespeare edition of *1 Henry IV* (London: Thomson Learning, 2002) is the most thorough (1–131). Named for Sir Edward Dering (1548–1644), the document consists of fifty-five leaves, handwritten by a scribe, with unfinished notes in Dering's handwriting. Perhaps intended for a private performance (the names of friends and relatives assigned parts are on the back of one page) of which no record exists, the manuscript is a combination of the two parts of *Henry IV*, ending with Henry IV's death and the coronation of Henry V. According to Barbara Hodgdon (*The End*

Crowns All [Princeton: Princeton UP, 1991]), Falstaff's rejection scene in the Dering manuscript is reduced "to include only his approach to the new king, a warning from the Chief Justice, and most of Hal's last speech that concludes, in an emendation, looking forward to brave new deeds in France which history will record" (168). Discovered in the Dering estate library in 1844, the manuscript, now in the Folger Library, shows that Dering divided his play into acts and scenes, none of which is present in either of the quartos from which this manuscript is derived (Q5 [1613] for *1 Henry IV*, Q [1600] for *2 Henry IV*), omitted certain characters, reassigned a few speeches, revised and even added some speeches, provided a few additional stage directions, and in general seems to have intelligently prepared a conflated version of the two plays that is both coherent and possible to act.

An additional manuscript housed in the British Library notes twenty-four passages drawn from *1 Henry IV*, each fewer than nine lines, that seem to have been jotted down for inclusion in a commonplace book. While the Dering manuscript indicates a continuing interest in the dramatic power of Shakespeare, these handwritten copies of memorable lines from the play, according to Kastan, may be dated sometime between 1596 and 1603 and, as such, represent "the earliest-known manuscript extracts of any Shakespearean play" (352).

The popularity of Shakespeare's *Henry IV* plays reflects contemporary interest in the genre of history plays. Perhaps as many as three thousand such works were staged between 1588 and the closing of the theaters in 1642. Philip Henslowe's diary, which records plays performed at the Rose Theatre, which he managed, reveals that virtually every reign from 1066 to 1485 was dramatized by 1600 (see R. A. Smallwood, "Shakespeare's Use of History," in *The Cambridge Companion to Shakespeare Studies*, ed. Stanley Wells [Cambridge: Cambridge UP, 1986], 143–162).

SOURCES FOR THE PLAYS

The primary source for *1* and *2 Henry IV* is the second edition of Raphael Holinshed's *Chronicles* (1587), upon which Shakespeare relied for all his plays dealing with English history. He supplemented this work with other treatments of the period: Edward Hall's *The Union of the Two Noble and Illustre Famelies of Lancastre and York* (1548), John Stow's *The Chronicles of England* (1580), and Samuel Daniel's poem *The First Fowre Bookes of the Civile Wars* (1595). Historically, Henry Hotspur was more than twenty years older than Prince Hal, but Shakespeare probably got the idea from Daniel to make the two antagonists the same age. Daniel describes Hotspur as rash, a trait that Shakespeare develops in creating his character.

As he often does in his histories, Shakespeare compresses time. He conflates the various rebellions that plagued Henry IV's reign, and he reduces the destabilizing role that Owen Glendower played in leading uprisings against the king every summer for eight years. Shakespeare also deviates from his sources in suggesting that Henry IV's intention to lead a Crusade was long-standing, not, as Holinshed states, an idea that came to the king only in the last year of his reign. For obvious dramatic purposes Shakespeare enlarges the roles of minor historical figures such as Falstaff, Prince John, and even Lady Percy, whose name Shakespeare changes from Elianor to Kate.

In addition to relying on historical accounts, Shakespeare drew on the anonymous *Famous Victories of Henry the Fifth*. Though not published until 1598, it was staged earlier in the decade and was the property of Shakespeare's company, the Lord Chamberlain's Men. This play highlights the riotous youth of the future conqueror of France. The robbery in *1 Henry IV* (2.2), the tavern scenes in both parts of the play, and the reconciliations between Prince Hal and his father derive from this work.

Another literary source that Shakespeare probably used is *A Myrroure for Magistrates* (1559), a poetic examination of the fall of great figures from history. This poem devotes sections to Owen Glendower and Henry Percy, Earl of Northumberland (father of Harry Percy, also known as Hotspur). In this poem Glendower discusses the dispute between the Percys and Henry IV over the prisoners "the Percyes had tane in the feeld" (Bullough, p. 135) and the king's refusal to ransom Mortimer, the subsequent alliance between the Percys and Glendower, and the proposed division of the kingdom amongst Mortimer, Hotspur, and Glendower. The Earl of Northumberland mentions his illness just before the battle of Shrewsbury, an illness that is real in the poem but seems more equivocal in the play.

STRUCTURE AND PLOTTING

Questions regarding the structure of and relationship between *1 Henry IV* and *2 Henry IV* have sparked one of the more enduring controversies surrounding the plays. Chief among these questions is when Shakespeare conceived the plan for the second play. Whether *2 Henry IV* was planned from the beginning of Shakespeare's work on *Part One*, or whether *Part Two* was written because *Part One* became crowded with events or to capitalize on the popularity of *Part One* is a puzzle that has driven structural criticism of the plays since the eighteenth century.

Modern readers and audiences are accustomed to the idea of sequels. In the Elizabethan period, too, as Paul Dean points out in his study of two-part plays, "Forms of Time: Some Elizabethan Two-Part History Plays" (*Renaissance Studies* 4.1 [1990]: 410–430), the form was not so uncommon. By Dean's count, eleven two-part plays were performed in the period from 1578 to 1598, and eighteen two-part plays were performed in the next ten-year period. From 1597 to 1600, perhaps following the example of Shakespeare's *Henry IV* plays, ten two-part plays were written by Shakespeare's contemporaries for the stage at the Rose Theatre (Dean, p. 418). G. K. Hunter's "*Henry IV* and the Elizabethan Two-Part Play" (*Review of English Studies* 5 [1954]: 236–248)—in noting how both parts of *Henry IV* "are built up on parallel lines" (244)—refers to *Part One* and *Part Two* as a "diptych, in which repetition of shape and design focuses attention on what is common to the two parts" (237). Hunter's position is that unity between the two parts of the *Henry IV* plays is provided by the theme of the prince's education (245).

E.M.W. Tillyard's view of the two plays differs slightly in seeing *Part One* and *Part Two* as unified yet intended to show two separate facets of Prince Hal and his coming of age. *Part One*, with its comparison of Hal to Hotspur, culminating in Hal's vanquishing his rival at Shrewsbury, according to Tillyard, demonstrates Hal's trial in "chivalric virtues" (270). Similarly tested in *Part Two*, Hal must learn "civic virtues" in choosing between "disorder and misrule," as exemplified by his companions, and "Order" or "Justice" as embodied by the Lord Chief Justice (271). Till-yard calls attention to various "anticipations"—ideas, characters, or concepts mentioned in *Part One* but withheld from development and resolution until *Part Two* (270). One example is provided by numerous references to the Archbishop of York in *Part One*. The prelate's rebellion that comes to life in *Part Two* is anticipated in *1 Henry IV*. Sherman Hawkins ("*Henry IV*: The Structural Problem Revisited," *Shakespeare Quarterly* 33.3 [1982]: 278–301) calls the continuation of the character of the archbishop "fatal to the notion of *Part Two* as an unpremeditated addition" (281). Hawkins also cites Falstaff's repeated phrase "When thou art king" as alluding to some future time, to be realized in *Part Two*. Similarly, Hal's threat to banish Falstaff (*1 Henry IV*, 2.4.481) is taken to be indicative of Shakespeare's early plan to continue the prince's story beyond Shrewsbury and to show the final rejection, which occurs at the end of *2 Henry IV*.

The treatment of Prince Hal's reformations in both parts of *Henry IV* provides a point of structural quandary for many critics. The sticking point is Shakespeare's purpose in showing two such transformations. If the reconciliation with his father on the battlefield at Shrewsbury is genuine and complete, as it seems to be, the necessity of a second, unhistorical reconciliation in *Part Two* seems superfluous at best. Determined to see the plays as part of a unified plan, Hawkins draws on terminology of psychologist William James to label Hal's transformations as "lysis" (as opposed to crisis), meaning that it is gradual and continuing (300). Hawkins and H. Edward Cain ("Further Light on the Relation of *1* and *2 Henry IV*," *Shakespeare Quarterly* 3 [1952]: 21–38) are, however, on different sides of the question. Cain denies continuity: "what one finds is not a gradual development spread over ten acts, indicating how by stages 'The Prince Grows Up'; what one finds is not one but two distinct, abrupt, and marked changes, one in each play" (34). That in *Part Two* neither the prince nor his father, the king, acknowledges the previous reconciliation in *Part One* is also problematic for Cain (35).

For Harold Jenkins the twin reformations are problematic, as the second reformation would seem to negate the first (*The Structural Problem in Shakespeare's* "*Henry IV*" [London: Methuen, 1956]). Jenkins dismisses the prevailing idea that the plays "were planned either as a single drama or that *Part Two* was an 'unpremeditated sequel'" (12). His own theory is that Shakespeare originally intended to demonstrate Prince Hal's waywardness, his reform, and his glory at Shrewsbury in one play, but that late into the play Shakespeare "changed his mind" (16). *Part Two* exists, according to Jenkins, because Shakespeare discovered belatedly that he did not have room to contain all that he intended in *Part One*. Although the plays are judged to be complementary, Jenkins also sees them as being "independent and even incompatible" (21). This leads to Jenkins's famous, albeit bewildering, conclusion: "*Henry IV*, then, is both one play and two. *Part One* begins an action which it finds it has not scope for but which *Part Two* rounds off" (21).

With a slightly different slant, Robert Adger Law ("Structural Unity in the Two Parts of *Henry the Fourth*," *Studies in Philology* 24 [1927]: 223–242) also sees *2 Henry IV* as an entirely different play with a different purpose, written chiefly "in response to a public demand for more of Falstaff" (242). Accordingly, *2 Henry IV*, being concerned primarily with "the fortunes of Falstaff," reduces the roles of King Henry IV and Prince Hal while increasing the number of lines spoken by Falstaff (Law, 232, 230). The introduction of Hal, indeed, is postponed to act 2 (238); further, Law remarks that the prince is "remarkably passive until the very last act" (241), thus indicating Shakespeare's intent to present in 2 *Henry IV* a morality play-based battle between the Lord Chief Justice and Sir John Falstaff "for the soul of Prince Hal" (242).

Two other, more recent views of the structure of the *Henry IV* plays are of note. Giorgio Melchiori, in a publication of his Shakespeare lecture "The Corridors of History: Shakespeare the Re-Maker" (*Proceedings of the British Academy* 72 [1986]: 167–185), introduces a political motive to the composition, based on his theory of an "ur Henry," an earlier play written by Shakespeare after the pattern of *The Famous Victories of Henry the Fifth* (see "Sources for the Plays," above), presenting a stronger historical background and the precursor of Falstaff: Sir John Oldcastle, or Jockey (175–176). Melchiori believes this play was withdrawn during the brief period (July 1596 to March 1597) when Oldcastle's offended descendent William Brooke, Lord Cobham, was the Lord Chamberlain, the official in charge of certifying public entertainment. Realizing the potential of his subject, Shakespeare renamed Oldcastle and recast the play, expanding the tavern scenes and leaving the ending open. If the play were successful, a sequel could be written using the salient parts not treated in 1 *Henry IV*; if not, those episodes not treated could be carried over to the beginning acts of *Henry V* (177–179).

Finally, James C. Bulman's forward-looking essay "*Henry IV Parts 1 and 2*" (*The Cambridge Companion to Shakespeare's History Plays* [Cambridge: Cambridge UP, 2003], 158–176) finds *Part Two* "as much the obverse of *Part One* as its sequel" (167). Bulman claims that when viewed merely as the sequel to *Part One* and structurally patterned to mirror the original, *Part Two* suffers in comparison. In fact, however, *Part Two* marginalizes King Henry IV and Prince Hal through much of the play in order to cast "a wide net over England, gathering in social groups whose unwritten histories rival in importance, even supersede, the official history which concludes with Hal's accession" (167).

However imperfectly the plays compare, or whenever the dual consideration of Prince Hal, his companions, responsibilities, and historic place was conceived, the relationship of the two parts of *Henry IV* has engendered some of the most erudite and persuasive Shakespearean criticism ever written. Despite all the force and reason scholars' minds may bring to the question, however, Shakespeare's motivation and intent ultimately remain inscrutable.

Whether conceived together or not, the two parts of *Henry IV* show a similar internal structure, though in the first part this organizational principle is more effective or mechanical, depending on one's viewpoint. In this earlier play the worlds of the court, the tavern, and the rebels are neatly juxtaposed. In 1.1 the king and the Percys appear together. The next scene takes the audience to the tavern in Eastcheap, and 1.3 returns to the court for the final split between the former allies. The robbery occupies 2.1 and 2.2; in 2.3 the rebels, away from court now, plan to steal the entire country. The final scene of the second act returns to the tavern. Act 3 opens with the rebels, then moves to the court (3.2) and ends in Eastcheap (3.3).

With act 4 the three threads begin to come together as all move toward Shrewsbury. The act begins with the rebels again. When Falstaff and Bardolph appear in 4.2, they no longer are in London but rather heading north to confront the king's enemies. In 4.3 Hotspur and Blunt meet for the first time since 1.3. The fourth act ends with the Archbishop of York, whose rebellion will be treated in part 2. The battle scenes in act 5 tie together the characters from all three elements of the play. The final scene links the dead Percy and defeated rebels, Falstaff, and the world of the court.

While this same shifting focus occurs in 2 *Henry IV*, that play has a more leisurely (or bloated) feeling. The juxtapositions are less immediate and less obviously structured. The first two scenes are set in Eastcheap. The final scene of act 1 (1.3) shows the rebels, but act 2 is almost entirely devoted to the tavern world (2.1, 2.2, 2.4). Only the short 2.3 (sixty-eight lines) recalls the impending revolt. The world of the court is not introduced until 3.1. This scene is also short, barely a hundred lines. The next scene is set in a rural version of Eastcheap, the home of Justice Shallow. The rebellion is dispatched in the first three scenes of act 4; it is not the climactic event the battle of Shrewsbury was in the first part. This act ends with two scenes at court.

Only in the final act is there some of the same cross-cutting that characterizes part one. In 5.1 the play shows Falstaff with Justice Shallow. The next scene is set in London, where the new king shows his transformation. Hence, when Falstaff in 5.3 heads off for the coronation thinking that "the laws of England are at my commandment . . . and woe to my Lord Chief Justice" (5.3.136–138), the audience knows that he is about to suffer a rude shock. Back in London the new order is evident in the breaking up of the world of the tavern with the arrest of Mistress Quickly and Doll Tearsheet (5.4), and the play ends with Hal's coronation and Falstaff's long-expected but still jolting banishment.

Overall, part two lacks the focus of its predecessor, a central event that can unite the various strands of the plot. It seems that 2 *Henry IV* is marking time until Prince Hal becomes Henry V, so most of the scenes concern themselves with revelry. Given such a setting, Falstaff dominates this play more fully than he does 1 *Henry IV*, where Henry IV, Hotspur, the prince, and his friends from the tavern share the spotlight more evenly.

MAIN CHARACTERS

In his discussion of the two parts of *Henry IV* in *The Meaning of Shakespeare* (Chicago: U of Chicago P, 1951), Harold C. Goddard notes that "any one of three men may with reason be regarded as its central figure" and that "by stretching a point we might even find a fourth hero" (161). Referring to Henry IV, Prince Hal, Falstaff, and Hotspur, Goddard underscores the point that the *Henry IV* plays are crowded with complex characters who continue to inspire interest and commentary.

Henry IV

King Henry IV, father of Prince Hal, is a man of business with no time for leisure. His first words in 1 *Henry IV* reveal his character: "So shaken as we are, so wan with care, / Find we a time for frighted peace to pant" (1.1.1–2). He never finds that time to relax, to enjoy the fruits of gaining the throne from Richard II. He thereby serves as the antithesis of Falstaff, the pleasure principle in this play.

Henry IV gained the throne through Machiavellian maneuvering, and he retains it in the same way. At the battle of Shrewsbury, for example, he employs "counterfeits," or doubles, to confuse his enemies trying to kill him. The lessons he imparts to Hal smack of this same cunning. For example, he recounts his early strategy for gaining popularity: "By being seldom seen, I could not stir / But, like a comet, I was wondered at" (*1 Henry IV*, 3.2.46–47). As a means of tutoring his son, Henry IV recounts his next step:

And then I stole all courtesy from heaven,
And dress'd myself in such humility
That I did pluck allegiance from men's hearts,
Loud shouts and salutations from their mouths,
Even in the presence of the crowned King.
Thus did I keep my person fresh and new,
My presence, like a robe pontifical,
Ne'er seen but wond'red at, and so my state,
Seldom but sumptuous, show'd like a feast,
And wan [won] by rareness such solemnity. (*1 Henry IV*. 3.2.50–59)

In the way of statecraft, Henry IV has one last secret to share, though he waits until death is about to overtake him. The longing to mount a crusade to the Holy Lands that has pervaded Henry IV's exchanges with his courtiers has, he confesses, been a political ruse, calculated to keep his friends at court from looking "Too near unto my state" (*2 Henry IV*, 4.5.212). Accordingly, he tells Prince Hal, "Be it thy course to busy giddy minds / With foreign quarrels" (*2 Henry IV*, 4.5.213–214), advice his son appears to take to heart, as *2 Henry IV* ends with the rumor of plans to invade France and claim that country's throne. Regal, authoritative, and full of grace as he may be, Henry IV is also a political expert, a master of manipulation, and a man who, no matter how he came by the throne, is determined to keep it not only for himself but also for his heirs.

Prince Hal

Henry IV became king through his political skill, but his heir will come to the throne legitimately. For much of the *Henry IV* plays, though, the prince appears to his father (though not to the audience) to be a scapegrace. Early in *Part 1*, Henry IV laments the disparity between the soldierly reputation of Henry Percy (Hotspur) and that of Henry Plantagenet (Prince Hal) for "riot and dishonor" (1.1.84). Hotspur himself knows how strained is the relationship of Henry IV to his son, saying he would have Prince Hal "poisoned with a pot of ale, . . . [b]ut that I think his father loves him not" (*1 Henry IV*, 1.3.233, 231). This admiration of Hotspur, and the general sense of the king's disappointment in his own son, has not been lost on Prince Hal, whose play-acting in the tavern bespeaks the deeper wounds of continual comparison: "I am not yet of Percy's mind, the Hotspur of the North, he that kills me six on seven dozen Scots at a breakfast, washes his hands, and says to his wife, 'Fie upon this quiet life! I want work'" (*1 Henry IV*, 2.4.101–105).

If Henry IV had a better understanding of his son, the king might worry less. Hal has not only mastered the political lessons of his father; he shows more complexity, depth, and understanding. Contrary to his father's fears, Hal is always cautious. There is nothing venal or low about him. Though he clearly wishes to enjoy himself before the weight of the crown descends to him and commands all seriousness, Hal will not, for example, participate in the elaborate robbery at Gadshill: "Who? I rob? I a thief? Not I, by my faith" (*1 Henry IV*, 1.2.138). He goes along only to retrieve the money from the thieves and to have some fun at Falstaff's expense. Following the robbery and the unraveling of Falstaff's version of what happened, Hal declares, "The money shall be paid back again with advantage" (*1 Henry IV*, 2.4.547–548).

Though Henry IV thinks that Hal needs lessons in Machiavellian policy, Hal shows in his very first scene that he does not require such instruction. In his first soliloquy he explains his behavior in imagery and content that anticipates his father's instructions:

> I know you all, and will a while uphold
> The unyok'd humor of your idleness,
> Yet herein will I imitate the sun,
> Who doth permit the base contagious clouds
> To smother up his beauty from the world,
> That when he please again to be himself,
> Being wanted, he may be more wond'red at . . .
> I'll so offend, to make offense a skill,
> Redeeming time when men think least I will. (*1 Henry IV*, 1.2.195–217)

While he possesses his father's Machiavellian streak, he is, in addition, brave and chivalrous. He demonstrates these qualities in the battle of Shrewsbury. Whereas his father tries to hide himself through the use of counterfeits, Hal rejects subterfuge. When he encounters Hotspur, the latter says, "If I mistake not, thou art Henry Monmouth." Hal replies, "Thou speak'st as if I would deny my name" (*1 Henry IV*, 5.4.59–60). Hal fights bravely and successfully. After the battle he allows Falstaff to take credit for killing Hotspur, frees his brave adversary Douglas, and lets his younger brother Prince John give Douglas the good news.

Poised between extremes of Hotspur, who hazards all without regard for himself, and Falstaff, who will hazard nothing that does not benefit himself, Prince Hal represents what William B. Hunter Jr. ("Falstaff," *South Atlantic Quarterly* 50 [1951]: 86–95) calls the Aristotelian virtue of "the golden mean, the ideal pattern of action in the play . . . who is later to become the ideal king of England" (89). In *Shakespeare's History Plays* (1944 [New York: Penguin, 1991]), E.M.W. Tillyard likens Shakespeare's characterization of the prince to "the abstract Renaissance concept of the perfect ruler" (282–283). "Far from being a mere dissolute lout awaiting a miraculous transformation," Tillyard says of Prince Hal that "he is from the very first a commanding character, deliberate in act and in judgement, versed in every phase of human nature" (282). W. H. Auden (*Lectures of Shakespeare*, ed. Arthur Kirsch [Princeton: Princeton UP, 2000]) finds Hal "cold as a fish" (108), but Tillyard believes instead that the prince manifests *sprezzatura*, nonchalance, about his accomplishments and being given credit for them (283–284). It is enough, for example, that the prince knows he is the one who vanquishes Hotspur, so it matters little to him that Falstaff claims the honor (284–285). Sure of himself, confident, and balanced, Prince Hal need not court favor or acclaim; he is content to know that it will come. As Irving Ribner (*The English History Play in the Age of Shake-*

speare [London: Methuen, 1965]) notes, "For Prince Hal true honor has come to mean not reputation and glory, but the execution of his duty as a prince" (176).

Further, as Tillyard says, "Henry V was traditionally not only the perfect king but a king after the Englishman's heart; one who added the quality of good mixer to the specifically regal virtues" (304). Accordingly, this quality calls for balance in the characterization of Prince Hal in the *Henry IV* plays. It cannot have been Shakespeare's intent to show the prince-in-waiting as the complete wastrel Hal's most severe critics find him to be, for it would have been impossible, then, to rehabilitate him as the paragon he becomes in *Henry V*. At one point Henry IV may have wished to trade his son for Northumberland's, but Henry IV, like many a parent, consistently underestimates Hal, not realizing that the prince has not only learned his father's lessons, he has also taken his knowledge to the next level. As Auden has commented, Hal sees "the politics of the future, the politically new" (105).

Hotspur

As his nickname indicates, Hotspur, though an honorable man, is characterized by a fiery temperament. He is not a man in balance, deliberate in action, politic in speech, or given to the principle of thinking before acting. Hotspur's passion and reckless haste confine him to the manipulations and deceits of his so-called allies and lend luster to the character of Prince Hal. Shakespeare may pity but never rewards the man who acts without deliberation. Defined almost exclusively by his prowess in battle and his temperament, even in his sleep, according to his wife, Hotspur talks of "sallies and retires, of trenches, tents, / Of palisadoes [stakes set for defense], frontiers [ramparts], parapets, / Of basilisks [heavy artillery], of cannon, culverin [light artillery], / Of prisoners' ransom, and of soldiers slain, / And all the currents of a heady fight" (*1 Henry IV*, 2.3.51–55).

Of his fiery temperament, Lady Percy says, "A weasel hath not such a deal of spleen / As you are toss'd with" (*1 Henry IV*, 2.3.78–79). In a similar vein, Hotspur's uncle, the Earl of Worcester, characterizes the enforcing arm of the rebellion as "A hare-brain'd Hotspur, govern'd by a spleen" (*1 Henry IV*, 5.2.19). Dismissed by the king, Hotspur signals the extent of his recklessness when he not only vows that his prisoners will not be given over to the king but also threatens to return to Henry IV to tell him so.

A frightening specter on the battlefield, Hotspur proves amazingly naive about those who surround him. His love of honor wins admiration, though it seems excessive. Early in *1 Henry IV* he shows his true colors when he declares,

> By heaven, methinks it were an easy leap,
> To pluck bright honor from the pale-fac'd moon,
> Or dive into the bottom of the deep,
> Where fadom-line could never touch the ground,
> And pluck up drowned honor by the locks,
> So he that doth redeem her thence might wear
> Without corrival all her dignities. (1.3.201–207)

Yet as Auden has aptly noted, though "noble and respectable . . . Hotspur has no political sense" (105). Even when abandoned by his allies, Hotspur goes recklessly into battle against the king, shouting, "Doomsday is near, die all, die merrily!" (*1 Henry IV*, 4.1.134).

That Hotspur's character has engendered so much sympathy stems in part from his passion and highly defined sense of honor when juxtaposed with the selfish calculations of the other rebels or the king. Douglas calls Hotspur "the king of honor" (*1 Henry IV*, 4.1.10), and Hal, who has never doubted his ability to defeat this warrior paragon, accords Hotspur all due respect after having killed him in battle, calling him "great heart" and performs "fair rites of tenderness" by covering the dead man's face with the prince's own "favors" (*1 Henry IV*, 5.4.87, 98, 96). Arthur Colby Sprague (*Shakespeare's Histories* [London: Society for Theatre Research, 1964]) aptly describes Hotspur as a figure of romance, made real for us through his eccentricity" (56).

Falstaff

Few literary characters have excited as much interest, commentary, and partisanship as Falstaff. Every aspect of his character—his wit, his cowardice, his morality, his girth—has been scrutinized and argued with a fervency that belies his fictional character. In particular, as will be discussed in "Critical Controversies," below, the rejection of Falstaff by the newly crowned Henry V has prompted otherwise reasonable scholars to declare themselves as pro- or anti-Falstaff. Hugh Grady's "Falstaff: Subjectivity between the Carnival and the Aesthetic" (*Modern Language Review* 96.3 [2001]: 609–623) comment that Falstaff represents a "singular Shakespearean creation" (609) seems most apt.

Grady is among the critics, including John Dover Wilson, Elmer Edgar Stoll, and C. L. Barber, who see Falstaff as having been crafted from a variety of character types. Northrop Frye (*Northrop Frye on Shakespeare*, ed. Robert Sandler [New Haven: Yale UP, 1986]) lists these types as the miles gloriosus, or braggart soldier; the parasite, noted chiefly for his drinking, from Roman comedy; the victim of the comic trick; the Morality play character Vice; and the fool (74). To these, Grady adds the *picaro* and the Rabelaisian figure preoccupied with the body. C. L. Barber, in the working out of his critical theory in *Shakespeare's Festive Comedy* (Princeton: Princeton UP, 1959), sees Falstaff as a character representing holiday or misrule. Termed "perpetually interesting" (110) by Auden, Falstaff is, on the one hand, charming, witty, and full of life and fun—the quintessential boon companion. On the other hand, he is improvident, slothful, self-centered, irresponsible, a thief, a liar, and, quite possibly a coward. Seen in this latter guise, his substance as a man is derived solely from his girth, to which there are frequent references. Called "fat-kidney'd rascal," "fat-guts," and "Sir John Paunch," Falstaff "lards the lean earth as he walks along" (*1 Henry IV*, 2.2.5–6, 31, 66, 109). During the robbery at Gadshill, when he is advised to listen for horses with his ear to the ground, Falstaff responds: "Have you any levers to lift me up again, being down?" (*1 Henry IV*, 2.2.34–35).

Despite his great size and his age—"inclining to threescore" (*1 Henry IV*, 2.4.425)—the Falstaff of *Part 1*, his fortunes waxing, holds in balance his physical condition and his wit. In contrast, in *Part 2*, when Falstaff's activities have become more reprehensible, his fortunes are on the wane, and his physical health is similarly in decline.

Of himself, Falstaff remarks, "Thou seest I have more flesh than another man, and therefore more frailty" (*1 Henry IV*, 3.3.166–168). Embarking on a plan to fleece his old friend Justice Shallow and choosing a troop of soldiers based on who can least afford a bribe, Falstaff lives for the time when the man Pistol calls Falstaff's "tender lambkin" (*2 Henry IV*, 5.3.116) becomes king.

Hugh Grady sees Falstaff as "a comic colossus . . . Hal is unable to bestride" (623). More moderate, Irving Ribner, while agreeing that "Falstaff is one of Shakespeare's supreme achievements, perhaps the greatest comic figure in the world's literature," also sees this complex figure as "the device by which Shakespeare achieved the didactic ends of his history play" (171).

Rebels' Wives

Women are typically absent from, or marginalized in, the *Henry IV* plays. In a feminist study of Shakespeare's history plays (*Engendering a Nation: A Feminist Account of Shakespeare's English Histories*), Jean E. Howard and Phyllis Rackin note that "women are excluded from court and battlefield, but they play dominant roles in Eastcheap and Wales," which are perceived as "sexualized domains of idleness and play" (164). Only the rebels, for example, have wives who appear in the plays. Mortimer's wife seems to seduce him out of all concern for his role in the rebellion. (Because Richard II had named him as heir, he was the rebel's convenient candidate for king). He is more interested in learning Welsh than in pursuing his inheritance. Hotspur's wife, too, would detain him, if she could, or follow him, if he would allow it, but he will not even tell her his destination. All eager business, he tells her, "This is no world / To play with mammets [dolls] and to tilt with lips" (*1 Henry IV*, 2.3.91–92). Lady Northumberland resigns herself to whatever action her husband will take following the death of their son: "I have given over, I will speak no more; / Do what you will, your wisdom be your guide" (*2 Henry IV*, 2.3.5–6).

Mistress Quickly and Doll Tearsheet

These distracting or marginalized women are joined in the plays by the women to be found in the tavern at Eastcheap—Mistress Quickly and Doll Tearsheet—who participate "only on sexualized and criminalized terms" (Howard and Racklin, p. 180). As *2 Henry IV* draws to a close, Mistress Quickly and Doll Tearsheet are being roughly led off by officers because "There hath been a man or two kill'd about her" (5.4.6). Before this unsavory end, however, both women have provided much interest and humor in *2 Henry IV*. Doll Tearsheet actually has some tender moments with Falstaff, whose age she seems to ignore, saying, "I love thee better than I love e'er a scurvy young boy of them all" (*2 Henry IV*, 2.4.272–273). Of course, given her profession, she may simply be flattering her current customer. She asks several questions—about Falstaff's conduct, about the prince's character, and about Poins—that would seem to indicate a native intelligence. Still, gauging from the way she defends herself against Pistol's demands, she is quite capable of taking care of herself, if not downright dangerous: "Away you cutpurse rascal! you filthy bung [cutpurse], away! By this wine, I'll thrust my knife in your mouldy chaps, and you play the saucy cuttle [thief] with me" (2 *Henry IV*, 2.4.128–130). For a brief time, Falstaff seems more honest, less on guard, less full of bluster than he is anywhere else in the play when he is not sleeping.

Mistress Quickly, proprietor of the tavern frequented by Falstaff, the prince, and their circle, is much more consistent in her character than is Doll Tearsheet. Most often she is seen defending herself before the prince (1 *Henry IV*) or the Lord Chief Justice (2 *Henry IV*) regarding accusations or broken promises made by Falstaff. As is frequently the case with Shakespeare's comic characters, her language runs away with her: for example, using the word "conformities" when she means "infirmities" (2 *Henry IV*, 2.4.58), creating what James C. Bulman ("*Henry IV, Parts 1 and 2*," in *Cambridge Companion to Shakespeare's History Plays*, ed. Michael Hattaways [Cambridge: Cambridge UP, 2002], 158–176) calls "Quicklyisms" (170). Additionally, the defenses she presents are humorous, though she is unaware of the bawdy implications of the wordplay into which she is drawn, as in the exchange when Falstaff likens her to an otter because "she's neither fish nor flesh, a man knows not where to have her." The Hostess retorts, "Thou art an unjust man in saying so. Thou or any man knows where to have me, thou knave, thou!" (1 *Henry IV*, 3.3.125–130). As Bulman notes, "Her character is both defined and undone by her absurdly original speech" (170).

Married in 1 *Henry IV* to a man the prince asks after and compliments ("I love him well, he is an honest man" [1 *Henry IV*, 3.3.93]), in 2 *Henry IV* she is widowed and pressing for settlement of Falstaff's debt to her, "a debt which substitutes for his failure to honor his promise of marriage" (Bulman, p. 170). Falstaff not only appeases her, he is also able to extract yet another sum from her as a loan, in a pattern one senses has been the nature of their relationship for years. Still, she is, as the Lord Chief Justice observes, of an "easy-yielding spirit" (2 *Henry IV*, 2.1.115), so much so that, even facing the threat of pawning her plate and tapestries, this "poor widow of Eastcheap" (2 *Henry IV*, 2.1.70), as she styles herself, is moved to say of Falstaff she has never known "an honester and truer-hearted man" (2 *Henry IV*, 2.4.383–384).

John of Lancaster

Through Prince John, seen briefly in both parts of the *Henry IV* plays, Shakespeare is able to demonstrate that one man (one Lancaster) is not as good as another to be king. An ambitious, methodical, calculating, even cruel character, Prince John of Lancaster is not a man of contemplation or conscience: like his father, he is all business and cunning. Shakespeare contrasts the chivalric way in which Hal triumphs at Shrewsbury with the bloodless, deceitful manner in which Prince John lies to the rebels in 2 *Henry IV* and then arrests the leaders once the insurgents dismiss their armies. Falstaff's disquisition about Prince John's faults being due to his not drinking "sherris" (2 *Henry IV*, 4.3.86–125) is comic; however, it does point to another contrast with Prince Hal, whose time spent in the tavern in the easy, cordial company of others of widely varying social classes at least shows a humanity lacking in Prince John.

Poins

Edward Poins is a man of good family without a position; as a second son, Poins has no expectation of inheritance. He is the tireless deviser of schemes for himself and Prince Hal. Although, curiously enough, Prince Hal is never in the company of Falstaff alone, on two occasions he appears just with his confidant Poins. Trusting him slightly more than he does the others in the world of the tavern, Henry regards Poins as more like a friend than anyone else in the plays. Poins's friendship does not appear to be predicated on any hope he has for preferment when Hal becomes King. Hal seems more himself with Poins than with any other character in the plays except for the king himself.

Justice Shallow

Justice Shallow is, as R. L. Smallwood notes, "even unaware of which king he serves under, and one has the feeling he might never find out," but "it would scarcely alter the principles of his jurisprudence if he did" (157). Smallwood refers to Shallow's surroundings in Gloucestershire as almost "a golden world, where time and history can be kept at bay" (157). It may be that in Justice Shallow Shakespeare provides a contrast for Falstaff, whose portly roundness indicates a fullness of life, compared with the brittle thinness of the country justice, and with Prince Hal, for Shallow has no memories of his earlier days that are not related to his dissipation.

DEVICES AND TECHNIQUES

Regardless of when the two parts of *Henry IV* were written and their structural kinship, Shakespeare is careful to demonstrate connections between *1 Henry IV* and *2 Henry IV* through the application of two devices. First, he links the plays through a complex pattern of antitheses. Second, he uses repeated references to time, disease, and money.

Central to Shakespeare's method of writing is his practice of doubling. The contrasts within each play provide the means of defining and delineation wherein characters, settings, and actions reflect on each other. C. L. Barber, in his study *Shakespeare's Festive Comedy* observes that in the *Henry IV* plays, "Shakespeare's art has reached the point where he makes everything foil to everything else" (150).

To help complete this device, Shakespeare makes three important alterations to historical characters: Falstaff, Henry IV, and Hotspur. Supposing Falstaff to have been based originally, for whatever reason, on Sir John Oldcastle (see "Critical Controversies," below), Shakespeare changes the age of this character. Oldcastle died at the age of thirty-five, yet Shakespeare presents Falstaff as being much older. Indeed, as he confesses to Doll Tearsheet in a rare moment of depressed honesty in *2 Henry IV*, "I am old, I am old" (2.4.271). His age is taken to be such that, like Henry IV, nearing death, he should be considering the consequences of his life's conduct. Doll asks him, "[W]hen wilt thou leave fighting a' days and foining [thrusting, either in combat or sex] a' nights and begin to patch up thine old body for heaven?" (*2 Henry IV*, 2.4.231–233). As if the prospect is unsettling, Falstaff entreats her, "Peace, good

Doll, do not speak like a death's-head, do not bid me remember mine end" (*2 Henry IV*, 2.4.234–235).

As an older character, Falstaff is better able to serve as a contrast to Prince Hal's father, Henry IV. One is, for Hal, the father of whom he is the true heir, while the other is the false father. That Shakespeare intends the contrast is made clear in the deposition scene (*1 Henry IV*, 2.4; see "Explication of Key Passages," below).

In *2 Henry IV*, the incongruity of the old knight's youthful and irresponsible behavior is underscored by yet another counterpoint in the character of the venerable Lord Chief Justice, whose own behavior is shown to be more appropriate to his age than is that of the man he lectures in the streets. Falstaff claims youth in one encounter, but the realistic description of the Lord Chief Justice (as well as Falstaff's own earlier comments about his health) indicates the opposite:

> Do you set down your name in the scroll of youth, that are written down old with all the characters of age? Have you not a moist eye, a dry hand, a yellow cheek, a white beard, a decreasing leg, an increasing belly? Is not your voice broken, your wind short, your chin double, your wit single, and every part about you blasted with antiquity? and will you yet call yourself young? Fie, fie, fie, Sir John! (*2 Henry IV*, 1.2.178–186)

Hal will have to choose between these two men, as well as between Falstaff and his father, in navigating the course of his future.

Hotspur's age has been altered for a similar purpose. Although historically Harry Percy was more nearly the age of Henry IV, Shakespeare makes him of an age and generation to rival Prince Hal. The comparisons made by Henry IV between the two Harrys, and the competition between them, brings the character of each into sharper focus. To achieve the recognition of his father, Hal is well aware that he must vanquish his rival on the battlefield, the arena in which Hotspur has excelled and that defines him. Meeting Hotspur at Shrewsbury, though Hal greets him with full courtesy, he makes clear that it is no longer possible for both men to exist in the same sphere: "[T]hink not, Percy / To share with me in glory any more. / Two stars cannot keep their motion in one sphere, / Nor can one England brook a double reign / Of Harry Percy and the Prince of Wales" (*1 Henry IV*, 5.4.63–67).

The alteration of age for these two characters sets an overall contrast of youth versus age, according to W. H. Auden, whose commentary in *Lectures on Shakespeare* suggests many other examples of antithesis that inform the *Henry IV* plays: "sophisticated versus naive," "old order versus new order," and "private character versus public character" (102). To these may be added the contrast between court and tavern scenes.

Ironically, though young himself, and therefore supposed (wrongly) to be impressionable and malleable, Prince Hal is, in mind at least, far older than those around him would credit. Certainly in that respect he is, and will forever remain, more mature than Falstaff will ever be. While Falstaff may be knowledgeable to the point of cynicism with regard to the value of chivalry versus self-interest, compared with Prince Hal in the arena of politics he is innocent. Hotspur, too, is politically naive. His conduct is so guided by honor that he cannot fathom the possibility of treachery in others. Auden expands this antithesis of the naive and the sophisticated by ranging characters in the plays on the two sides. In addition to Falstaff and Hotspur, among the naive may be counted Blunt, Shallow, Silence, and the too-secure rebels of *2 Henry IV*: the Archbishop of York, Thomas Mowbray, and Lord Hastings; the sophisticated, according to Auden, include Henry IV and the Earl of Worcester, Prince John, and, as noted, the Prince of Wales (102).

The age of Shakespeare's Hotspur should place him on the side of youth and the new order, but in his alliances he belongs to what Auden has termed the old order. That is, Hotspur is found amongst the northern barons and their Welsh ally who would keep England in a feudal state carved up into small kingdoms for themselves rather than adhere to a strong central monarchy and a concept of national unity represented by Henry IV and his sons (Auden, 102). At the end of *2 Henry IV*, everyone of the old order has been swept away. The Lord Chief Justice, the figure of stability, is the man who remains, evenhanded throughout. The future of England, as Shakespeare makes clear, belongs to the younger generation of Lancastrians, chiefly to the newly crowned Henry V. This king, unlike his father, begins his reign without taint and without the disquieting, demanding, and divisive allegiances to the old order that brought Henry IV to the throne and plagued him ever after.

The antithesis Auden finds in the private and the public character is illustrated chiefly in Falstaff, Hal, and Henry IV. According to Auden, Falstaff is guilty of "counterfeiting a man of action" and is "exposed" as a fake, while Hal, "counterfeiting an anarchist bohemian is revealed not to be one" (103). Not named by Auden, Henry IV is another character whose outward life of certain majesty belies the unquiet mind that will not let him sleep, whose way to the throne was evidently less a matter of lucky circumstance than of ambition, and whose public desire to lead a crusade is privately confessed on his deathbed to have been intended to divert his subjects from scrutinizing the legitimacy of his reign.

The antithesis of the court and tavern scenes in *1 Henry IV* is demonstrated in pastimes, serious and frivolous, but chiefly through the imagery of time. At court and among the rebels, the emphasis is on the swift passage of time. The first scene of *1 Henry IV*, in fact, is replete with references to time's urgency. Between quelling one rebellion and facing another, Henry IV, for example, looks for "a time for frighted peace to pant / And breathe short-winded accents" (1.1.2–3). This desire for peace between civil wars is denied by Westmerland's news from Wales and Sir Walter Blunt's from the north. The king must act quickly; the world of the court offers no time for leisure.

While this scene moves briskly, through references to haste and speed, calling attention to the weighty matters of state with which the king must contend, the second scene of the play shows the Prince of Wales in the company of Falstaff, whose first question throws the play into another gear: "Now, Hal, what time of day is it, lad?" (*1 Henry IV*, 1.2.1). The prince's reply shows how disengaged from the dangers confronting Henry IV and the country Falstaff really is: "What a devil hast thou to do with the time of the day? unless hours were cups of sack, and minutes capons, and clocks the tongues of bawds, and dials the signs of leaping-houses [brothels], and the blessed sun himself a fair hot wench in flame-color'd taffata; I see no reason why thou shouldst be so superfluous to demand the time of the day" (1.2.6–12). Here the pace is leisurely, the pursuits those of self-indulgence, and the plans made for entertainment only.

The rebels being about serious business, their time, like that of Henry IV, is measured closely. In the third scene of act 1, the view of time shifts again. Worcester, for example, feels the current quarrel they have with the king "bids us speed, / To save our heads by raising of a head [army]" (1.3.283–284). Typically eager for action, Hotspur responds to these nascent plans of rebellion with the hope that time will pass quickly: "O, let the hours be short, / Till fields, and blows, and groans applaud our sport!" (1.3.301–302). From his home, once the rebels' plans are confirmed, Hotspur compounds the sense of urgency when he tells his wife, "I must leave you within these two hours" (1 Henry IV, 2.3.36). While the other rebels hold time in abeyance to listen to the daughter of Owen Glendower sing a Welsh song to her new husband, Mortimer, Hotspur's impatience is clear. He reminds his wife of his imminent departure, and Glendower notices that "hot Lord Percy is on fire to go" (1 Henry IV, 3.1.264). From the rebels' seat, the play shifts again, this time to the tavern and the high comedy of the Gadshill robbery. That the court and the rebels are serious, the prince and his companions frivolous, is shown in these antithetical scenes and measured by different senses of time.

Prominent as the multiple references to time are in 1 Henry IV, the time imagery in 2 Henry IV gives way to the passage of time, waiting, inactivity, and disease—time's companion. Falstaff's sense of time has not improved. He arrives so late to the scene at Gaultree Forest that the armies have already been dispersed, and he incurs the ire of Prince John, who upbraids him soundly: "When every thing is ended, then you come. / These tardy tricks of yours will, on my life, / One time or other break some gallows' back" (2 Henry IV, 4.3.27–29). Though Falstaff wants to live in a pastoral world where time has no meaning and one may remain forever young, Prince John reminds him that he is living in the real world, which is subject to time and mortality.

Having achieved glory and his father's high opinion at Shrewsbury, Hal in 2 Henry IV is forced into waiting and a period of inactivity, as he cannot achieve his apotheosis as king until his father dies. Engaged in halfhearted high jinks, once Peto brings news of some urgency regarding the rebellion, Prince Hal berates himself for idleness: "I feel me much to blame, / So idly to profane the precious time, / When tempest of commotion, like the south / Borne with black vapor, doth begin to melt / And drop upon our bare unarmed heads" (2 Henry IV, 2.4.361–365). Unlike Falstaff, Hal feels the passing of time and the need not to waste this commodity. His departure marks the last scene of the prince with Falstaff; next time they meet, Hal will have become Henry V.

The conclusion of the king's illness, resulting in death and Hal's ascension to the throne, seems long in coming. Throughout the play, images of illness and disease abound, physical disease on the one hand and political disease on the other. Henry IV's health is associated with that of his realm. Further, the illness of the king is counterbalanced by the illness of Falstaff, whose preoccupation with health is revealed in his first question in 2 Henry IV: "[W]hat says the doctor to my water [about my urine]?" (1.2.1–2). The rebel Lord Northumberland is said in the Induction to be "crafty sick" (2 Henry IV, Induction 37) and thus unable to go to his son Hotspur's aid at Shrewsbury. As Auden notes, in 2 Henry IV "the sickness of dissension in the body politic is counterpointed with various specific diseases" (103).

In conversation with Warwick about the newest rebellion for example, Henry IV asks him if he understands the danger of the time: "Then you perceive the body of our kingdom / How foul it is, what rank diseases grow, / And with what danger, near the heart of it" (2 Henry IV, 3.1.38–40). Warwick, though more positive in outlook, responds with the same imagery: "It is but as a body yet distempered, / Which to his former strength may be restored / With good advice and little medicine" (*2 Henry IV*, 3.1.41–43). Neither of them is quite the equal of the rebel Archbishop of York, however, when it comes to using disease to describe the state of England. As Christ's curate, the archbishop should be disposed to healing, but the medicine he offers is poisonous rebellion. To swell the numbers that follow the rebels, the archbishop reportedly "Derives from heaven his quarrel and his cause; / Tells them he doth bestride a bleeding land, / Gasping for life under great Bullingbrook" (*2 Henry IV*, 1.1.206–208). At Gaultree Forest, the archbishop warms to his theme when asked by Westmerland the reason for the rebellion: "[W]e are all diseas'd, / And with our surfeiting and wanton hours / Have brought ourselves into a burning fever, / And we must bleed for it (*2 Henry IV*, 4.1.54–57).

There is much prescribing in *2 Henry IV*. To dissuade the Lord Chief Justice from giving another lecture, Falstaff tries to change the subject to that of the Chief Justice's health: "Your lordship, though not clean past your youth, have yet some smack of an ague in you, . . . and I most humbly beseech your lordship to have a reverend care of your health" (*2 Henry IV*, 1.2.96–100). For the cold and ruthless Prince John of Lancaster, Falstaff would prescribe sack, without which "[t]here's never none of these demure boys come to any proof, for thin drink doth so overcool their blood . . . that they fall into a kind of male green-sickness" (*2 Henry IV*, 4.3.90–93).

For Falstaff's own disease of "not list'ning, the malady of not marking," the Lord Chief Justice declares a remedy: putting Falstaff in the stocks "would amend the attention of your ears, and I care not if I do become your physician" (*2 Henry IV*, 1.2.121–125). The real source of Falstaff's decline, however, in a literal as well as figurative sense, is improvidence: "I can get no remedy against this consumption of the purse; borrowing only lingers and lingers it out, but the disease is incurable" (*2 Henry IV*, 1.2.236–238).

The references to paying, "consumption of the purse," and "commodity" join to create another strong pattern of imagery in the *Henry IV* plays. Sandra K. Fischer's " 'He means to pay': Value and Metaphor in the Lancastrian Trilogy" (*Shakespeare Quarterly* 40.2 [1989]: 149–164), Nina Levine's "Extending Credit in the *Henry IV* Plays" (*Shakespeare Quarterly* 51.4 [2000]: 403–431), and Jesse M. Lander's " 'Crack'd Crowns' and 'Counterfeit Sovereigns': the Crisis of Value in *1 Henry IV*" (*Shakespeare Studies* 30 [2002]: 137–161)—all point out that the plays are rife with allusions to debt, contractual obligations, value, and coinage. Indeed, from the initial dispute of Henry IV with Hotspur over the ransom of prisoners in *1 Henry IV* to comments in the Epilogue of *2 Henry IV*, economic metaphors, comparisons, and considerations inform both plays. As Levine points out, "The language of credit and exchange is central to Shakespeare's staging of dynastic politics" (404).

Levine's persuasive argument traces the economic and commercial imagery in the *Henry IV* plays. The larger situations of the plays all tally with her insistence on the pervasive imagery of money and contracts. Henry IV, for example, arouses the enmity of the Percys in demanding Hotspur's prisoners, whom the Perceys are holding for ransom. Historically, according to Peter Saccio (*Shakespeare's English Kings*, 2nd ed. [Oxford: Oxford UP, 2000]), the Percys withheld the prisoners for money that Henry IV owed them for expenses. But what irks the Percys most in Henry IV's demands is the king's refusal to give them the recognition and gratitude they feel he owes them for helping him to depose Richard II and achieve the throne.

Similarly, the allegiance Hal owes his father and the honor paid to Hotspur that belongs to Hal are also at issue. Loyalty being a form of contract, the Percys not only fail to fulfill their contract with the king but also break that contract with Hotspur in failing to pay what is promised—troops to support the rebellion. On the battlefield at Shrewsbury, as Levine notes, "The reformed prince announces his newfound identity not as the god-like warrior feared by his enemies but as a man of credit, one who makes good on his promises and pays what he owes" (419–420). As proof, Levine cites Prince Hal's challenge to Douglas (1 Henry IV, 5.4.42–43): "It is the Prince of Wales that threatens thee, / Who never promiseth but he means to pay." Pay he does, first by opening "a line of credit" (Levine, p. 417) with the reader/observer in his first soliloquy. His vow to "pay the debt I never promised" and his plan of "Redeeming time when men think least I will" (1 Henry IV, 1.2.209, 217) lend credence to an understanding that his seemingly purposeless, wayward actions are not open-ended idleness. His credit, of course, depends on the surety of Hal's succeeding his father as king. This is the connection on which Falstaff is banking, his surest stock. To Falstaff, as Levine points out, the friendship of the Prince of Wales is, he says, "worth a million" (1 Henry IV, 3.3.137), against which he borrows a thousand pounds from Justice Shallow (Levine, p. 427).

Shakespeare is at pains to show that Prince Hal pays all his debts—the Gadshill money is repaid "with advantage" (1 Henry IV, 2.4.547–548). In a bawdy exchange with Falstaff, the prince insists that with Mistress Quickly "and elsewhere," that is, with other women, he has paid his way "so far as my coin would stretch, and where it would not, I have us'd my credit" (1 Henry IV, 1.2.54–56). Levine notes, "As one who pays his debts, the prince might appear to offer a counter example to Falstaff, and in many ways he does" (416). Falstaff's perpetual improvidence, his inability to keep money, his dishonest schemes to make more, his borrowing, and his promises of preferment are all a part of his characterization. Childlike in a way, Falstaff is venal in another. His first realization of the true nature of his relationship with Prince Hal comes with the knowledge that now he will have to pay his debt to Shallow because the new king will not. Levine says, "Henry V destroys Falstaff's credit by publicly refusing to acknowledge any debt to his former companion" (425). Even so, the new king will meet any honest obligation to "his wonted followers," as Prince John observes at the play's end. All "[s]hall . . . be very well provided for" (2 Henry IV, 5.5.98–99). As Levine observes, Hal

> redeems his name much as those in Shakespeare's audience did, by proving his ability to pay his debts and to honor contractual agreements. In casting himself as the divinely sanctioned ruler who disperses punishment but also as a man who pays his reckonings, the prince participates in a heterogeneous community bound together by the practices of everyday commerce. (420)

This idea of commerce carries over to the Epilogue of 2 Henry IV, which alludes to the debt of a former play that was "displeasing" (l. 2). Promising a better play to repay the audience for their "patience," the playwright hopes 2 Henry IV will have fulfilled the obligation to his "gentle creditors" (ll. 9, 12). If not, "as most debtors do," the playwright will "promise . . . infinitely" and beg for forgiveness (ll. 15–16). The play is thus rounded nicely, by Levine's reckoning, for in "conjoining playwright and audience in a relationship of credit" Shakespeare "supports the continuation of the theatrical production itself" (429).

THEMES AND MEANINGS

Themes of Shakespeare's plays are frequently less a measure of what is in the play than what each age needs to find in it. Opinions about the theme of the *Henry IV* plays run the gamut from E.M.W. Tillyard's World War II–era view of the two plays as an English epic to that of the twenty-first century opinion of Hugh Grady that the plays are a study in Machiavellian politics. The statement of Mark Van Doren in *Shakespeare* (New York: Holt, 1939) that "nothing is meaningless in *Henry IV*" (120) is certainly applicable to a discussion of the plays' themes.

Van Doren cautions against allowing the comedy of the *Henry IV* plays to obscure the history that is the chief interest. While Van Doren feels that the tavern and country scenes serve to expand the plays' scope and to provide realism, Lily B. Campbell, nearly thirty years later, in *Shakespeare's "Histories": Mirrors of Elizabethan Policy* (San Marino, CA: Huntington Library, 1968), echoes the emphasis on history, finding the plays' theme to be the rise and collapse of rebellion.

Campbell refers to "The Cult of Authority" in Franklin Le Van Baumer's study *The Early Tudor Theory of Kingship* (New Haven: Yale UP, 1940) to show how the fairly recently concluded Wars of the Roses and the persistent threat of foreign invasion led to the belief that rebellion was never excusable. According to Irving Ribner, in *The English History Play in the Age of Shakespeare* (London: Methuen, 1965), "No matter how great a tyrant might be, he remained the agent of God on earth, and only God had the power to depose him. Rebellion, no matter what the cause, was the worst of all possible sins" (154). Referring to contemporary Elizabethan accounts, Campbell demonstrates how in poems such as Samuel Daniel's *Civil Wars* and Hall's and Holinshed's chronicles, "Again and again Henry IV was used as a text for a lesson on rebellion" (218).

Even the actions of Prince John in subduing the rebellion in *2 Henry IV*, though it has "brought disillusion to many modern readers," nevertheless "would . . . have seemed quite orthodox to the Elizabethan audience" acculturated to the moral wickedness of rebellion (Campbell, p. 226). Henry IV, himself rebellious against Richard II, is punished in Shakespeare's plays by suffering through rebellions mounted against himself, as well as by his heir, whom he regards as unworthy of the throne of England and as God's vengeance on his disappointed father. Seen in this light, the plight of the battle-weary Henry IV at the beginning of *1 Henry IV* is an example of divine retribution.

The prince's conduct and companions figure prominently in the view of the plays' theme held by Irving Ribner, who states his theory that the "delineation of how an ideal king is educated comprises Shakespeare's most significant political purpose in *Henry IV*" (182). From the beginning of the plays, Ribner holds that Shakespeare demonstrates how the weighty concerns and office of the monarch isolates Henry IV from the company of men, and that, as king, he must take onto himself the responsibility of all men. In this halcyon time of waiting to assume the throne, Prince Hal is nonetheless aware, certainly from his father's example, that as king he will be called upon "to reject . . . many of the simple joys of living, the possibility of escape from care" (Ribner, p. 172). What Prince Hal is shown to learn in the *Henry IV* plays, though he appears idle, is "the art of government" (Ribner, p. 181). In *Part One* he is shown to have mastered the art of chivalric conduct in battle; in *Part Two*, in peace, he shows the proper inclination by choosing justice as his guide to behavior. As Ribner says, "Prince Hal is taught to be a soldier in *1 Henry IV* and a statesman in *2 Henry IV*" (168).

Ribner also notes the way in which Shakespeare adapts the folk story of the prodigal son who, after a riotous life, reforms and redeems himself before the eyes of his father and the world. By providing insight into Hal's motivations and offering the comments of various characters who see method in the prince's actions, Shakespeare transforms the prodigal's story in such a way that the reader/observer is never allowed to doubt the outcome.

In a similar approach, E.M.W. Tillyard (*Shakespeare's History Plays*) finds the *Henry IV* plays "built on the Morality pattern . . . but without the mental conflict" (274). In other words, like the central character in a morality play, Prince Hal must choose between responsible and derelict behavior, represented by Henry IV and Falstaff, respectively. He must elect the path to redemption as the true heir to the throne, or he must continue in the way of the wastrel. Any mental conflict over the choice is missing, both for Hal, who says in his first soliloquy that the choice has already been made (he is only waiting for the most propitious moment to make it known), and for the reader/observer, who has Hal's word as well as the historic record. Tillyard's view also indicates the central aspect of Hal's character to the theme of the *Henry IV* plays in holding that Shakespeare has at last created the prototype of the ideal king in Prince Hal, "The copy-book paragon of kingly virtue to balance Richard [III] the monstrous pattern of concentrated vice" (309).

For Tillyard, in fact, the theme of the *Henry IV* plays is nothing less than that of England itself. Because the characters, settings, and subjects in the plays touch all classes of England, from the palaces of the great and powerful to the taverns, and from the center of power in London to the country life of Gloucestershire, the *Henry IV* plays, according to Tillyard, show more of Elizabethan life as it was lived in Shakespeare's time than any other play he wrote (304). Lauding the plays, Tillyard finds in them "enough confidence in England to make the two parts Shakespeare's ripe expression of what he felt about his country" (308). If the quality that defines an epic is "breadth or variety" of life, Tillyard believes that the *Henry IV* plays qualify (300).

Although Northrop Frye finds Prince Hal manipulative and callous in his dealings with others, he, like Tillyard, also sees merit in the concept of Prince Hal as an ideal ruler and of the *Henry IV* plays as traversing the various social classes of the time. Reflecting on Prince Hal's activities and the company he keeps, Frye finds that Hal has "soaked himself in every social aspect of the kingdom he is going to rule. He is becoming the entire nation in individual form, which is symbolically what a king is" (*Northrop Frye on Shakespeare*, p. 78).

In contrast, Hugh Grady in "Falstaff: Subjectivity Between the Carnival and the Aesthetic" (*Modern Language Review* 96.3 [2001]: 609–623) takes a skeptical view of the England that triumphs in the *Henry IV* plays, finding the study of power and political character to be alarmingly modern, ethically bereft, and "specifically Machiavellian" (610). Grady finds the end result of Prince Hal's accession to the throne and his designs on a war with France, alluded to at the end of *2 Henry IV*, "the absorption of the playful and harmless Prince of Wales into a formidable Machiavellian politician responsible for the death of thousands" (613).

Whatever a modern reader/observer may make of it, given the political climate of Elizabethan England when Shakespeare wrote the plays, it is unlikely that Shakespeare's primary purpose was to write a treatise on political expediency. Frank Kermode's excellent brief overview of the period, *The Age of Shakespeare* (New York: Modern Library, 2004), notes the role of the Church and the Crown in fostering some "sense of nationality" through a "common ground" (43) amongst the English. Drawing as they do upon a shared past, Shakespeare's *Henry IV* plays would more nearly have conjured pride in the reign of Henry V, England's greatest monarch before Elizabeth I, than chagrin for a model of national shame.

In *A New Mimesis: Shakespeare and the Representation of Reality* (London: Methuen, 1983), A. D. Nuttall provides a mediating approach to the extremes of interpretation given the themes of the *Henry IV* plays. On the modern side, Nuttall names Prince Hal "a white Machiavel," forgiving him only in part for holding back on his plans for the future. Yet he expresses the view that, as Elizabethans would recognize, Prince Hal's methods might be excused since all his actions are directed, as the ideal ruler's would be, toward "the good end of stable government" (147).

CRITICAL CONTROVERSIES

Aside from the controversy emanating from the structure of the *Henry IV* plays, as discussed elsewhere (see "Structure and Plotting"), two other controversies relevant to the plays have captured the attention of Shakespearean scholars. Both involve the protean character of Sir John Falstaff. One attempts to trace the political and legal shift that made Sir John Oldcastle into Falstaff; the other is concerned with Falstaff's rejection at the end of 2 *Henry IV* by the newly crowned Henry V.

Peter Saccio (*Shakespeare's English Kings: History Chronicle, and Drama*, 2nd ed. [Oxford: Oxford UP, 2000]) succinctly gives two sources for Shakespeare's Sir John Falstaff: the unhistorical Sir John Falstaff of 1 *Henry VI*, who is made to run away from battle, and Sir John Oldcastle, relative, by marriage, to the powerful Brooke family (62). The reference to Falstaff in Shakespeare's earlier play has little bearing on the Falstaff of the *Henry IV* plays except, perhaps, as a source for Sir John's seeming cowardice in battle. In 1 *Henry VI*, when asked whether he would leave his commander, Talbot, Falstaff replies, "All the Talbots in the world, to save my life" (1 *Henry VI*, 3.2.108).

Although he was forced to change the character's name from Oldcastle to Falstaff, Shakespeare's originally naming the Falstaff character Oldcastle is fraught with significance of a political nature and has been the source of much interest, investigation, and conjecture. To a Protestant Elizabethan audience, Oldcastle was a martyr (Saccio, p. 71–72). Moreover, to the powerful Brooke family, descendants of Oldcastle's third wife, Oldcastle was not a man to be represented onstage by a comic buffoon whose alliance is more to Vice than to virtue. The question therefore arises as to Shakespeare's use of a well-known martyr's name for the character whose self-interest is renowned.

E.A.J. Honigmann's article "Sir John Oldcastle: Shakespeare's Martyr" (*Fanned and Winnowed Opinions: Shakespearean Essays Presented to Harold Jenkins*, ed. John W. Mahon and Thomas A. Pendleton [London: Methuen, 1987], 118–132) lists the

possibilities for this strange disconnect: (1) Shakespeare didn't think anyone would
be offended; (2) he thought there might be a problem but did not care; or (3) Shakespeare actually "wished to offend" (118). Honigmann does not give credence to Geoffrey Bullough's cautious theory in *Narrative and Dramatic Sources of Shakespeare*,
vol. 4 (London: Routledge, 1962) that Shakespeare simply lifted the name from the
Famous Victories of Henry the Fifth without making the connection. Indeed, he finds
it incredible that Shakespeare would have been unaware that the character of Sir
John Oldcastle in the *Henry IV* plays and that of the historical Oldcastle were so
dissimilar. Particularly because Raphael Holinshed, one of Shakespeare's sources,
notes the character of Oldcastle and because other contemporary accounts (Stow's
Chronicles and Foxe's *Acts and Monuments*) treat Oldcastle respectfully, Honigmann
believes that, with the "backing of powerful friends" (119), Shakespeare indeed intended to have a good joke by "metamorphosing the most renowned member of
the Cobham family, the Protestant martyr, into a penniless adventurer and buffoon" (120).

Further, Honigmann believes the powerful friends of Shakespeare to be Robert
Devereux, the Earl of Essex, as well as Shakespeare's patron, to whom *Venus and
Adonis* and *The Rape of Lucrece* were dedicated, the third Earl of Southampton, a
good friend of Essex, with whom he served on expeditions to Cadiz (1596) and the
Azores (1597). Both men were enemies of Henry Brooke, Lord Cobham (120). Given
that Essex was at the apex of his career and that Lord Cobham was seventy, it would
have seemed safe to help Essex and Southampton in their joke, particularly, as
Honigmann notes, if any part of *1 Henry IV* was written in the first half of 1596
(122). Unexpectedly, however, upon the death of the Lord Chamberlain, the patron
of Shakespeare's acting company, Lord Cobham was appointed to that position,
which he held only until his death in 1597, less than a year. Rather than offend the
official whose approval was necessary for the licensing of plays, Shakespeare could
have claimed that the use of the name Oldcastle was the result of a "misunder-
standing" (122–125) and redressed the error, as he does in the Epilogue of *2 Henry
IV*: "(for any thing I know) Falstaff shall die of a sweat, unless already 'a be kill'd
with your hard opinions; for Oldcastle died a martyr, and this is not the man" (ll.
29–32).

In linking Shakespeare to recusant Catholics, Giorgio Melichiori ("The Corridors of History: Shakespeare the Re-Maker," *Proceedings of the British Academy* 72
[1987]: 167–185) gives the opinion that Shakespeare intended the comic character he
makes of Oldcastle to be a negative if veiled reflection on Protestantism, "a contrast with his celebration by Foxe [John Foxe's *Acts and Monuments of Martyrs*] as
a Protestant proto-martyr" (174). Honigmann seems to agree that Shakespeare's
naming was not accidental and argues that Shakespeare intended to use a reformed
Oldcastle in *Henry IV* as "a pious fraud who pretends to be what the king commands [at the end of *2 Henry IV*], and who thus acquired his reputation as a Lol-
lard" (127). Hugh Grady's "Falstaff: Subjectivity Between the Carnival and the
Aesthetic" also sees the name and character of Oldcastle significant as a satire on
Puritanism, which loses its point of reference in the text when the name is changed
to Falstaff (614).

The other signal controversy of the *Henry IV* plays remains unresolved and a
subject of continuing debate. Indeed, concerning the exchange between the newly
crowned Henry V and Falstaff at the end of *2 Henry IV*, Edward Berry ("Twentieth

Century Shakespeare Criticism: The Histories," in *Cambridge Companion to Shakespeare Studies*, ed. Stanley Wells [Cambridge: Cambridge UP, 1986], 249–256) writes: "Every approach brought to bear on the histories, it seems, finds its severest test in this episode" (254). Robert Adger Law ("Structural Unity in the Two Parts of *Henry the Fourth*," *Studies in Philology* 24 [1927]: 223–242) finds that "this episode of the rejection of Falstaff has caused more dissension among critics than has any other part of the play" (236). That the scene is most frequently referred to as the rejection of Falstaff indicates the tenacity with which the viewpoint of Falstaff as a victim has taken hold.

"The Rejection of Falstaff" is, of course, the title of A. C. Bradley's famous essay in which he brings his formidable intellect and elegant prose to bear in an attempt to present Falstaff as "the most unfortunate of Shakespeare's famous characters" (*Oxford Lectures on Poetry* [London: Macmillan, 1919], 247). Bradley's case is interspersed with his rhetorical question, "What are our feelings during this scene?" (251), and implies throughout that the reader/observer's feeling toward Falstaff at the moment he is shunned and banished by the new king is a measure of not only the witness's own generosity of character and largeness of heart but also the degree of pleasure derived from scenes with Falstaff: "If we have not keenly enjoyed the Falstaff scenes of the two plays, if we regard Sir John chiefly as an old reprobate, not only a sensualist, a liar, and a coward, but a cruel and dangerous ruffian, I suppose we enjoy his discomfiture and consider that the King has behaved magnificently; otherwise, what one experiences is a good deal of pain and some resentment" (251).

Among the causes Bradley names for resentment is the public nature of the king's rupture with Falstaff, the subsequent arrest, the lecture Henry V gives his former companion, and even the fact that, when still only a prince, Hal had not made it clear to Falstaff that one day their paths would, of necessity, diverge sharply (253–254). Although Bradley identifies Falstaff as "the enemy of everything that would interfere with his ease, and therefore of anything serious, and especially of everything respectable and moral" (262), it is clear from his essay that he (Bradley) could never have banished Falstaff. That may be, Bradley surmises, because in Falstaff Shakespeare "overshot his mark" and in Falstaff "created so extraordinary a being, and fixed him so firmly on his intellectual throne, that when he sought to dethrone him he could not" (259).

In his essay, Bradley has mounted a personal defense that continues to have an effect. Yet, as Frank Kermode points out in *The Age of Shakespeare*, "Sentimentality has always been a nuisance in Shakespeare studies" (38). Kermode also finds the dismissal of Falstaff "disagreeably managed," but he notes that contemporary readers/observers are not used to the concept of morality in literature (93). Critics in the late twentieth and early twenty-first centuries who wish to fault Prince Hal for "priggery" (John Palmer, for example, in *Political Characters of Shakespeare* [London: Macmillan, 1948]) or for political duplicity, in fact, base their distaste for this chrysalis of the perfect king on his treatment of Falstaff. William B. Hunter Jr.'s essay "Falstaff"(*South Atlantic Quarterly* 50 [1951]: 86–95) establishes the controversial dichotomy at work in *Henry IV* in the Prince Hal/Falstaff relationship: "If he [Falstaff] is really an old scalawag with a heart of gold beating some feet beneath his rough hide, the Prince becomes . . . a heartless prig"; if the opposite is true, that "Falstaff is really evil, there is the opportunity for the moral rehabilitation of Prince Hal which Shakespeare seems to have intended" (86).

Two particular actions by Falstaff might have had more resonance with an Elizabethan audience than they have had with a modern one. Hunter makes the argument that Falstaff's misuse of his powers to raise troops and to raise funds for himself by accepting bribes from those who could afford to buy their way out of service would have caused the groundlings watching the play to regard Falstaff with skepticism. Hunter believes that many in the audience, no doubt subject to the evils of impressments themselves, "would not have looked upon Falstaff thereafter with any real affection" (87; see also Lily Campbell, *Shakespeare's "Histories": Mirrors of Elizabethan Policy*). Shakespeare would appear to indicate the character of Falstaff by tying him so decisively to one of the evils of the time that had garnered much in the way of public protest (Campbell, p. 251).

To Elizabethans, moreover, Falstaff's getting and spending would have been quite telling. Barbara Hodgdon notes in *Henry IV, Part Two* (Shakespeare in Performance Series [Manchester, Eng.: Manchester UP, 1993]) that the money he asks of the Lord Chief Justice (and is finally able to borrow from Justice Shallow) was "approximately half the average income of a noble or well-to-do member of the merchant bourgeoisie; the price of a short cloak and slops he has ordered from Master Dommelton would far exceed the wages of an artisan . . . or schoolmaster" (4–5).

Nina Levine's essay, "Extending Credit in the *Henry IV* Plays," also makes a point of Falstaff's excesses revealed in the bill that the Prince finds in Falstaff's pocket:

Item, a capon . . . . 2s. 2d.

Item, sauce . . . . 4d.

Item, sack, two gallons . . . . 5s. 8d.

Item, anchoves and sack after supper . . . 2s. 6d.

Item, bread . . . . ob. [half-penny] (*1 Henry IV*, 2.4.535–539)

Levine cites the *Acts of the Privy Council of England, AD 1596–1597* in noting that "Falstaff's appetite for luxury foodstuffs would, in fact, have bordered on the criminal in the dearth years of 1596–1597, when, under orders from the Privy Council, London citizens were instructed to curb their 'excessive dyet' and 'be contented with fewer dishes' so that the excesses could be distributed to the poor" (415).

In addition to these topical references to Falstaff's excesses, Shakespeare also seeds both *Henry IV* plays with indication of Falstaff's relationship to the prince. If the question raised by the court concerns the kind of monarch Prince Hal will become, there can be no question from the text as to the future Falstaff contemplates. Although it is always possible to read/hear Falstaff's comments as humorous banter, on several occasions the hint of a threat is implicit. In an exchange with the prince, for example, Falstaff asks, "Dost thou think I'll fear thee as I fear thy father? Nay, and I do, I pray God my girdle break" (*1 Henry IV*, 3.3.150–151). In another exchange, Falstaff says to Hal, "By the Lord, I'll be a traitor then, when thou art king" (*1 Henry IV*, 1.2.146–147).

Two other instances in *2 Henry IV* provide glaring examples of Falstaff's thinking. Both comments are made in gleeful anticipation of the power and privilege that will fall to him once he learns that Hal has come to the throne: "Master Robert Shallow, choose what office thou wilt in the land, 'tis thine. Pistol, I will double-charge thee with dignities" (*2 Henry IV*, 5.3.122–125). Falstaff then declares, "Let us take any man's horses, the laws of England are at my commandment. Blessed are they that have been my friends, and woe to my Lord Chief Justice!" (5.3.135–138).

In addition to Falstaff's own comments, it is remarkable to note as well that Prince Hal, who under all other circumstances is moderate, restrained, and courteous, is twice moved to violence by Falstaff's behavior. Hal withstands the blasts of his father's withering lectures without rebuttal, and in the heat of the battle he even greets his archenemy and nemesis, Harry Percy, as "A very valiant rebel" (*I Henry IV*, 5.4.62). Yet when in swordless pursuit of the enemy and therefore defenseless, Prince Hal asks Falstaff twice "I prithee lend me thy sword" (*I Henry IV*, 5.3.43–44 and 5.4.48–49) only to be handed a bottle of sack taken from Falstaff's pistol case, the prince loses control. In astonishment, he demands, "What, is it a time to jest and dally now?" (*I Henry IV*, 5.3.55) and, according to the stage direction, throws the bottle at Falstaff.

A second instance, apparently with a more dangerous result, is buried in the comic relation Mistress Quickly makes of the proposal she claims to have had from Falstaff: "Thou didst swear to me upon a parcel-gilt [partially gilt] goblet, sitting in my Dolphin chamber, at the round table by a sea-coal fire, upon Wednesday in Wheeson [Whitsun] week, when the Prince broke thy head for liking [likening] his father to a singing-man of Windsor, thou didst swear to me then, as I was washing thy wound, to marry me and make me my lady thy wife" (*2 Henry IV*, 2.1.86–92). A. R. Humphreys, editor of the Arden *King Henry IV, Part 2* (London: Thomson Learning, 2001), in appendix 3 of that work attempts to clarify the allusion to "a singing-man of Windsor." According to Humphreys, the reference has much intrigued scholars, and although a specific identity has not been established, it would appear to apply to a false-pretender (234). If Falstaff has, in fact, trespassed the bounds of his relationship to Prince Hal to the extent of casting aspersions on the legitimacy of Henry IV's reign to the king's own son, Hal has responded with uncharacteristic violence. That the prince and Falstaff are not seen in each other's company much in *2 Henry IV*, the one scene in which they are together being brief and lacking in true jollity, should scarcely be surprising then.

In addition to Prince Hal's soliloquy and the deposition scene (see "Explication of Key Passages" below), these examples are among the cautions Shakespeare takes care to place in his text. They provide an index to King Henry V's banishment of his former companion, if an excess of love for Falstaff does not cloud the vision.

PRODUCTION HISTORY

Records concerning the first performances of either of the *Henry IV* plays are not available. From the first known performances, however, the attention of playgoers was captured more by Hotspur and Falstaff than by either Henry IV or Prince Hal. Scott McMillin's *Henry IV, Part One* (Shakespeare in Performance [Manchester, Eng.: Manchester UP, 1991]) notes, in fact, that during the time of James I, "the two *Henry IV* plays were sometimes known as 'Falstaff, Parts One and Two'" (2), an emphasis not to be altered until the twentieth century.

David Scott Kastan's thorough commentary on the plays in performance in his Introduction to the Arden Shakespeare edition of *King Henry IV, Part I* (London: Thompson Learning, 2002) refers to a few performances of *1 Henry IV* in the early part of the seventeenth century (1–131). The play was called *Sir John Old Castell* in March 1600 when Lord Hunsdon had it performed for the Flemish ambassador, the title no doubt being in deference to the play's comic appeal (Kastan, p. 79). Subsequent performances in 1612–1613 as a part of festivities to celebrate the marriage of Princess Elizabeth to the Elector Palatine and for "new years night" at Whitehall in 1624–1625 again refer to *1 Henry IV* by alternative names, "the Hotspur" in the first instance and *The First Part of Sir John Falstaff* in the second. "Olde Castell" was performed at court on January 6, 1614, and "Ould Castell" on May 29, 1638. Even during the Commonwealth Interregnum, when theaters were officially closed, Falstaff aficionados were treated to selected scenes from the *Henry IV* plays in *The Bouncing Knight, or the Robbers Robbed*, a "playlet" subsequently published in 1662, with illustrations, as *The Wits, or Sport Upon Sport* (Kastan, p. 80–81).

McMillin notes that a list of actors who performed the parts of either Falstaff or Hotspur "includes almost every famous male performer in the history of the English theatre" (2). Barbara Hodgdon's companion volume on *Henry IV, Part Two* (Shakespeare in Performance [Manchester, Eng.: Manchester UP, 1993]) cites an argument that, from the beginning, the part of Falstaff was constructed around the actor most equal to performing it: William Kempe, the great comedic actor and a favorite of Elizabeth I (9). Subsequent productions drew on the talents of William Cartwright, Thomas Betterton, James Quin, Stephen and Charles Kemble, R. W. Elliston, Samuel Phelps, the American James Henry Hackett, John Henderson, and Herbert Beerbohm Tree, among others, all notable figures in the theater, for the roles of Hotspur or Falstaff. A decline in interest of the *Henry IV* plays at the end of the nineteenth century is, in fact, attributed to the death of the much-loved Henderson as Falstaff. According to accounts cited by Kastan, however, Stephen Kemble's stint as the knight, though innovative in some respects (Falstaff being found asleep at the beginning of 1.2, for example) and played without the need of false padding, nevertheless drew the ire of William Hazlitt, who wrote in an 1816 review: "We see no more reason why Mr. Stephen Kemble should play Falstaff, then why Louis XVIII is qualified to fill a throne, because he is fat, and belongs to a particular family" (quoted in Kastan, p. 86).

Although the *Henry IV* plays enjoyed a revival when theaters reopened in 1660 and continued to be popular (the diarist Samuel Pepys saw *1 Henry IV* twice), the plays were altered during this period and the nearly two centuries and a half that followed "to bring them into line with contemporary taste and expectation" (Kastan, p. 83). Scenes cut included the deposition scene from *1 Henry IV* (2.4.376–481) and the speeches of Northumberland in *2 Henry IV*; moreover, the role of the play's namesake was severely cut. The first American performance of *Henry IV* took place in 1761, and almost a hundred years later at least one person familiar with the printed version of the play was unhappy with the alterations to the text. Following a performance of James Hackett as Falstaff in 1863, Abraham Lincoln, a devotee of Shakespeare, asked why the deposition scene had been omitted. Hackett's reply, noted by John Hay, Lincoln's secretary of state, apparently reflects standard thinking: "It is admirable to read but ineffective on stage, that there is nothing sufficiently distinctive about the actor who plays Henry to make an imitation striking" (quoted in Kastan, p. 85).

Kastan notes the beginning of a shift in the plays' emphasis from the comic Falstaff to a consideration of history with the performances of William Macready as

Hotspur in productions from 1815 to 1847 (89). Covent Garden was the scene of an 1821 production of *2 Henry IV* that, in keeping with the aim of celebrating the accession of George IV to the throne, ended with a spectacular procession that, Hodgdon notes, "seems designed to overwhelm Falstaff with royal authority" (10). Spectacle was, in fact, becoming something of an end in itself, according to Kastan's description of Charles Kemble's 1824 production of *1 Henry IV* in Covent Garden. The playbill for the production emphasized the authenticity of the production: "Every character will appear in the precise Habit of the Period; the whole of the dresses being executed from undisputable authorities, viz. Monumental Effigies, Painted Glass, etc." (quoted in Kastan, p. 89). Arthur Colby Sprague, in *Shakespeare's Histories* (London: Society for the Theatre, 1964) refers to this excavation of period detail as "archaeology" and remarks that it was "carried to astonishing lengths" (5).

No doubt this attention to visual effects helped nudge the scruffy, portly Falstaff to the wings. Hodgdon notes that Hackett's 1841 production of *2 Henry IV* "rid the commonwealth of Falstaff *before* the accession scene" (10). In fact, Beerbohm Tree's 1891 performance as Falstaff was the last important production of *1 Henry IV* in the nineteenth century. Generally well-received, the performance came after the 1888 remark by Frank Marshall that *1 Henry IV* was "virtually dead to the stage" (quoted in Kastan, p. 90). Russell Jackson's article "Shakespeare on the Stage From 1660–1900" (in *Cambridge Companion to Shakespeare Studies*, 187–212) concludes a study of the vicissitudes experienced in the staging of the *Henry IV* plays during this period with the following direct judgment: "The history of Shakespearian production between 1660 and 1900 can seem to be an account of 240 years of lost labours, in which a succession of actors and managers wrenched the plays into a shape basically unsuited to their meaning—or to most of the meanings we might wish to release from them" (210).

Frantz Dingelstedt's presentation of a cycle of seven of Shakespeare's history plays in one week in Germany in 1864 to commemorate the playwright's birthday presages the treatment of the history plays throughout the twentieth century (Kastan, p. 92). Frank Benson's 1901 "Week of Kings" at Stratford's Shakespeare Memorial Theatre included *2 Henry IV*, along with *King John*, *Richard II*, *Henry V*, *2 Henry VI*, and *Richard III*. The selection of plays was repeated in the 1905–1906 Stratford season, though at that time the plays were not yet being presented chronologically or in sequence with each other (Hodgdon, p. 11). Both parts of *Henry IV* were staged in 1932 by Barry Jackson at the Birmingham Repertory Company and again in 1932 for the opening of the Memorial Theatre in Stratford on Shakespeare's birthday (Kastan, p. 93).

Thereafter, the publication of E.M.W. Tillyard's influential 1944 study *Shakespeare's History Plays* and a resurgence of national pride in the aftermath of the ravages of World War II had a profound effect on production in the mid-twentieth century, particularly in the Old Vic staging by Ralph Richardson, Laurence Olivier, and John Burrell as artistic directors. Richardson and Olivier, already well-established actors, were released from the Fleet Air Arm to perform another kind of service. According to Hodgdon, rehearsals began in a portion of the National Gallery from which art had been removed for safety, and, in fact, the bomb raids had not yet stopped. Among the first plays staged were Shakespeare's histories: *Richard III* in the 1944–1945 season and both parts of *Henry IV* in 1945–1946

(Hodgdon, pp. 15–16). These productions were especially notable because they made "clear that the British Theatre had not only survived the war, but had survived with what was arguably the best theatre company in the world performing what were arguably the best plays of the greatest dramatist in history. Some there were who thought Shakespeare had helped to defeat Germany" (Hodgdon, p. 17).

Under the direction of Anthony Quayle the second tetralogy from *Richard II* through *Henry V* was performed at Stratford-upon-Avon as part of the Festival of Britain celebrations in 1951. Actors carried over roles from one play to the other. The influence of Tillyard's interpretation of these history plays as creating an epic of which England was the subject was much in evidence: "Shakespeare was being used for nationalistic purposes" (McMillin, p. 36).

Quayle played Falstaff in the *Henry IV* plays, and Michael Redgrave played Hotspur in *1 Henry IV*. An as-yet unknown Richard Burton was hired by Quayle to play the part of Prince Hal and Henry V, "the longest Shakespearean role in its full extent across three plays" (McMillin, p. 38). In large part, this dramatic casting of the Welsh actor focused attention on the political rather than the comic aspects of the plays. In a true cycle format, Quayle's presentation, according to McMillin, became a "landmark": indeed, "later versions had to take the 1951 production as a standard to be challenged—it was that good. A better *orthodox* version would be hard to imagine" (50–51).

The 1960s brought Peter Hall's indictment of power to the Royal Shakespeare Company in what McMillin calls a Brecht-influenced production of the *Henry IV* plays in 1964. Hall's Prince Hal is able to win his combat with Hotspur at Shrewsbury only when Hotspur's sword gets stuck in a pig trough long enough to allow Hal (played by Ian Holm) to stab him with a dagger and push him into the swill. As McMillin notes, "Antiheroism can do no more with the Battle of Shrewsbury than dump Hotspur into a pig trough" (65). Kastan observes that in performances throughout the 1960s Hotspur's character and particular excellences on the battlefield were lost to an audience used to a different sort of warfare (96).

By 1975 the artistic directorship of the Royal Shakespeare Company had passed from Peter Hall to Terry Hands, who wished to put his own stamp on the company by distancing himself from the overtly political productions of the 1960s. The *Henry IV* plays, *Henry V*, and the *Merry Wives of Windsor* were offered as what Kastan calls a Falstaffiad, as opposed to the more familiar Henriad invoked to describe the *Henry IV* plays and *Henry V* (97). At the time, the Royal Shakespeare Company faced grave financial difficulties from which the success of this cycle of plays lifted it, the not entirely pleasing idea being that "The RSC had become ... accustomed to taking the *Henrys* as curtain-raisers for occasion of wealth and power" (McMillin, p. 86).

In a 1982 performance, both parts of *Henry IV* were directed by Trevor Nunn to herald the opening of the Barbican Theatre. Nunn's production was highlighted by the multilevel scaffolding used in his previous direction of *Nicholas Nickleby* (Kastan, p. 98). Having just come from dealing with Dickens, it is not surprising that Nunn was "interested in the play as portrait of a society divided along class and ideological lines" (ibid.).

No doubt trying to use the draw of Shakespeare in 1986, the new English Shakespeare Company chose *1 Henry IV*, directed by Michael Bogdanov, as its first offering. The strange production saw Hal attired as a kind of hitchhiker in jeans and

Brewster Mason as Falstaff (on ground) and Alan Howard as Hal (center) in *Henry IV, Part 2*, directed by Terry Hands. Royal Shakespeare Theatre, Stratford-upon-Avon, 1975. Courtesy of Photofest.

boots. Worse, this Hal wins his battle with Hotspur by stabbing his rival in the back (Kastan, p. 102). Finally, to commemorate the millennium, the Royal Shakespeare Company staged six of Shakespeare's history plays in 2000, in a program called *This England*, intended to show the playwright's own view of his country.

Two film versions of the plays require mention: Orson Welles's *Chimes at Midnight* (1966) and a version of the *Henry IV* plays sponsored by the British Broadcasting Company. Welles's film, a collation chiefly of the two parts of *Henry IV* was, in fact, based on his *Five Kings*, a play he presented in Boston in 1938. Welles draws his title from Justice Shallow's nostalgic remark to Falstaff about having in their younger days caroused long and late enough to have heard church bells toll the midnight hour (*2 Henry IV*, 3.2.214); his "film is a tragedy of a man who lives in a world of historical necessity that must repudiate him" (Kastan, p. 105). It has, according to McMillin, become "an underground classic" (105).

In 1979 a production by the British Broadcasting Company featured Anthony Quayle in a reprise of his role as Falstaff. Quayle's performance was deemed especially remarkable as he chose to speak his soliloquies directly to the television camera; as a result, "Falstaff transcends the barrier of time and confides in us" (McMillan, p. 100). Another striking feature of the production was Jon Finch's (as Henry IV) use of his gloved hands, twisting, wringing, and otherwise calling attention to them. The impression intended was of the king's illness, leprosy, but to viewers it may well have suggested implicit guilt, in the manner of Lady Macbeth, for his role in the deposition of Richard II.

EXPLICATION OF KEY PASSAGES

1 Henry IV, 1.2.195–217. "**I know you all . . . least I will.**" This soliloquy, spoken by Prince Hal after he has contracted with Poins to take part in an elaborate joke to be played on Falstaff, provides the first opportunity to gauge the personality and motivation of the prince. Previously, Hal has been shown in a negative fashion by his father who, in his son's absence, berates his heir to members of the court council, publicly voicing strong resentment of Hal's pastimes and seeming want of courage. Subsequently, Hal is seen in the company of the leviathan, lethargic Falstaff and others, whiling away the hours in idle conversation and plans for amusement. But in this speech Hal establishes the fact that the "madcap Prince of Wales" (*1 Henry IV*, 4.1.95) is a man who considers his actions closely and who, far from being one who lives exclusively in the present, has already gone a long way toward planning his future. It is a justification, a rationale for his current behavior.

Readers divide over this speech. One group declares the soliloquy to be Shakespeare's attempt to reassure the reader/observer with information about the true nature of the Prince as well as reasons for his conduct. The other group sees in this soliloquy a reprehensible calculation, a cold, self-serving, if not altogether wicked, duplicity. A. O. Nutall (*A New Mimesis: Shakespeare and the Representations of Reality* [London: Methuen, 1983]) represents the most extreme of these viewpoints in writing "the distance between Prince Hal and Iago [the archetype of a villainous character found in Shakespeare's *Othello*] is great but not, perhaps, unbridgeable" (146).

Hal's soliloquy, however, may be supposed less to be about the behavior of his companions ("I know you all") than about the projection of his own, and when he will show himself to be other than his enemies and his father have imagined. Unlike Iago, whose "seeming" is intended for the purposes of willful destruction, Prince Hal's will be of a positive nature. He knows what others think of him, but on the field at Shrewsbury he will prove himself worthy. The king may be astonished, Hotspur fatally surprised, but the reader/observer, having been privy to this soliloquy, cannot be.

1 Henry IV, 2.4.376–481. "**Do thou stand . . . I do, I will.**" The deposition scene conducted as playacting between Prince Hal and Falstaff presages many of the events that follow. It functions also as an indication of Prince Hal's knowledge of his father's opinion of him, Harry Percy's reputation, and the character of Falstaff. The game does not go well when Falstaff takes the part of Prince Hal's father at the instigation of the prince: "Dost thou speak like a king? Do thou stand for me, and I'll play my father" (2.4.433–434). Already Falstaff has been demoted from king to Prince of Wales.

Hal's words are harsh, as he begins, apparently talking about himself but also, in fact, about Falstaff: "The complaints I hear of thee are grievous" (2.4.442). Prince Hal, acting as his father, calls Falstaff (as his son) "ungracious boy," banishes him ("henceforth ne'er look on me" [ll. 445–446]), and warns him that his very soul is in jeopardy: "Thou are violently carried away from grace" (ll. 446–447).

Then, speaking as his father, and therefore, significantly, as king, which Prince Hal will become, he gives the unmistakable hint of Falstaff's future banishment. Speaking of "Falstaff, that old white-bearded Satan," (463), Prince Hal inquires: "Wherein is he good, but to taste sack and drink it? wherein neat and cleanly, but to carve a capon and eat it? wherein cunning, but in craft? wherein crafty, but in villainy? wherein villainous, but in all things? wherein worthy, but in nothing" (455–459). To Falstaff's response, "My lord, the man I know" (464), Hal, still acting as the king, speaks a parody of his words to Falstaff as the newly crowned Henry V, "I know thee not, old man" (*2 Henry IV*, 5.5.47), in saying, "I know thou dost" (465). When Falstaff as Prince Hal says to the pretend king, "[B]anish plump Jack, and banish all the world" (479–480), the prince replies, "I do, I will" (481). As king he will keep his word.

1 Henry IV, **5.1.128–141. " 'Tis not due yet . . . ends my catechism."** Falstaff's battlefield speech on honor seems to a modern audience a practical, realistic disquisition on the subject: "Can honor set a leg? No. Or an arm? No. Or take away the grief of a wound? No. Honor hath no skill in surgery then? No. What is honor? A word" (5.1.131–134). Northrop Frye, however, notes that "to many in the original audience this . . . must have seemed . . . about as funny a speech as ever spoken on a stage, because they accepted more of the idealism about honour, and for them the speech would probably have had a greater psychological release than for us" (*Northrop Frye on Shakespeare*, p. 74).

Frye refers to George Bernard Shaw's *Back to Methuselah*, where, in a futuristic setting, a statue has been erected to the memory of Falstaff, for "after a few experiences of warfare . . . it had been realized that cowardice was a major social virtue" and the townspeople wanted to recognize the first person to advocate such forward thinking (74). Frye believes a modern audience is much closer to Shaw's thinking than to that of the Elizabethans. When Falstaff encounters the body of Sir Walter Blunt and says, "There's honor for you!" (*1 Henry IV*, 5.3.32–33), in an indication of a culture shift that has generated real skepticism about warfare, a contemporary audience might agree.

2 Henry IV, **Induction.** A painted figure of Rumor, a seeming holdover from the allegorical medieval Morality plays, begins this work, "Stuffing the ears of men with false reports" (8) about the Battle of Shrewsbury. Rumor has, in fact, been active throughout *1 Henry IV*. The king hears stories about where and how the prince spends his time. Similarly, the prince knows the reputation of Hotspur, and Hotspur knows of Prince Hal's wild reputation and his troubled relationship with his father.

Here Rumor, behaving in character, reports false news about the outcome of the battle of Shrewsbury. Rumor's mendacity suggests yet again that the reports of Hal's prodigal behavior are equally untrue. The Induction also suggests how false surmises and misinformation will pervade this play, just as they have its predecessor.

2 Henry IV, **3.1.4–31. "How many thousand . . . wears a crown."** The weighty responsibility a monarch takes on is poignantly rendered in this troubled soliloquy by Henry IV. Sleep will not come to him, commanding and great though he is, yet it gives "repose / To the wet [sea boy]" (3.1.26–27). Thousands of his "poorest subjects" (3.1.4) are asleep, but that balm of "forgetfulness" (3.1.8) is denied him. Shakespeare here gives psychological depth to Holinshed's observation that Henry IV had trouble sleeping "for feare of strangling." The speech also shows what awaits Prince Hal and so justifies his choice of diversion and ease while he can seize them.

Annotated Bibliography

Bevington, David, ed. *Henry the Fourth, Parts I and II: Critical Essays*. New York: Garland, 1986. Essays on the plays ranging from 1744 to 1983, including criticism by Samuel Johnson, Maurice Morgann, and A. C. Bradley.

Bradley, A. C. "The Rejection of Falstaff." In *Oxford Lectures on Poetry*. London: Macmillan, 1919. 247–275. Provides an elegant appeal on behalf of Falstaff, the centerpiece of criticism that sees the old knight as the victim of a too-calculating prince.

Bullough, Geoffrey. *Narrative and Dramatic Sources of Shakespeare's Plays*. 8 vols. Vol. 4. London: Routledge, 1962. The section for each of the *Henry IV* plays begins with an extensive introductory essay followed by a reprinting of the sources cited. An excellent introduction to Shakespeare's transformative art.

Howard, Jean E., and Phyllis Rackin. *Engendering a Nation: A Feminist Account of Shakespeare's English History*. London: Routledge, 1997. Long viewed as having little to say about women, the history plays of Shakespeare have, in this volume, been provided an important new life.

Levine, Nina. "Extending Credit in the *Henry IV* Plays." *Shakespeare Quarterly* 51.4 (2000): 403–431. Lucid rendering of Shakespeare's economic and financial imagery in the plays, an example of the wealth to be retrieved by a close reading of Shakespeare.

Ribner, Irving. *The English History Play in the Age of Shakespeare*. Rev. ed. London: Methuen, 1965. Provides a solid overview of the plays, from the inception of the genre to its decline.

Saccio, Peter. *Shakespeare's English Kings: History, Chronicle, and Drama*. 2nd ed. Oxford: Oxford UP, 2000. The indispensable historical companion to the plays.

Shaaber, M. A. "The Unity of *Henry IV*." In *Joseph Quincy Adams Memorial Studies*. Ed. James G. McManaway, Giles E. Dawson, Edwin E. Willoughby. Washington, DC: Folger Shakespeare Library, 1948. 217–227. One of the many essays concerning the structure of the *Henry IV* plays, the viewpoint expressed here is of lesser import than the sensible, scholarly way in which it is presented; therefore, Shaaber is a good place to start an investigation of this continuing controversy.

Henry V

Sheryl A. Clouse

PLOT SUMMARY

Prologue. The play begins with the Chorus wishing for a "Muse of fire" to aid the acting troupe in presenting the mighty subject of the play (Prol. 1). He wonders how the actors on stage, the "flat unraised spirits" working on the "unworthy scaffold," can possibly show the great battles fought in "the vasty fields of France" (Prol. 9, 10, 12). The Chorus finds the answer in a metaphor that turns the insufficiency of the stage into a strength by comparing the power of the stage (aided by imagination) to the power of zero. The Chorus argues that since the "cipher" seems to be nothing but can "attest in little place a million," so one actor, who seems to be nothing, can be divided "into a thousand parts" with the help of the audience's imagination (Prol. 17, 16, 24). Insisting that it is the audience who must "piece out our imperfections with your thoughts" and make "imaginary puissance," the Chorus urges the audience members to become active participants in the play (Prol. 23, 25).

1.1. In Henry's castle, the Archbishop of Canterbury and the Bishop of Ely discuss a bill that is before parliament. The bill would transfer numerous parcels of church land to the king. As the clerics discuss whether or not the king will support the bill, they remark on the character of the king. The bishops praise Henry's miraculous transformation from a reckless youth (depicted in *1* and *2 Henry IV*) to the pious man he is now, asserting that "consideration" has "whipt th' offending Adam out of him" (1.1.29). They also describe Henry in secular terms, stating that he is a master of judgment, debate, war, logic, and politics. The archbishop states that he has offered the king a large sum of money to support the reclaiming of his "true titles," including "the crown and seat of France," but before he had heard the king's response to the offer they were interrupted by a French messenger (1.1.87, 88). The two men exit to hear the news the herald brings.

1.2. Like the previous scene, 1.2 is set in Henry's castle. King Henry and his entourage enter. When the archbishop arrives, Henry asks whether he "justly and religiously" can claim the crown of France (1.2.10). He warns the archbishop to be prudent and truthful in his response because his words may "awake our sleeping sword of war" and cause many deaths (1.2.22). The archbishop delivers a long and detailed speech declaring that the Salic Law, according to which inheritance cannot descend through the female line, does not bar Henry from being the lawful inheritor of France (see "Explication of Key Passages," below) because, says the archbishop, the Salic Law applies to Germany, not to France. Convinced of the justness of his claim, Henry now worries that a war in France will leave England open to attack from Scotland. The archbishop, Exeter, and Ely deny the validity of this threat, ultimately convincing the king that England will be safe.

The king now agrees to hear the French herald sent by the Dauphin (Prince) of France. The Dauphin, in response to Henry's claim to some French dukedoms, has sent a barrel of tennis balls and an insulting message that tells Henry that his reputation makes him better suited for playing games than ruling kingdoms. The jest enrages Henry, and he unleashes his verbal prowess. In a heated speech, the king turns the mockery of the tennis balls into a metaphor for his campaign against France and warns the Dauphin that the prince will regret his joke "when thousands weep more than did laugh at it" (1.2.296). Henry sends the herald back to France with his message and tells his lords to prepare for war.

2.Chorus. The Chorus again begins the act by invoking fire, but this time it is not a muse, but "all the youth of England" who are "on fire" as they prepare to follow Henry, "the mirror of all Christian Kings," to war (2.Chor.1, 6). The Chorus contrasts the English forces, filled with patriotic "Expectation," with the French, who "Shake in their fear" (2.Chor.8, 14). But not all Englishmen are "kind and natural," and three men—Cambridge, Scroop, and Grey—have conspired with France to kill the king in Southampton before he departs for France (2.Chor.19). The expectation of getting to see France is delayed, however, as the audience is left waiting for the king in Southampton.

2.1. The scene is not set in Southampton, as the Chorus stated, but in a London tavern (familiar from the *Henry IV* plays). Corporal Nym expresses his anger with Pistol because Mistress Quickly, "troth-plight" (engaged) to Nym, has married Ensign Pistol instead (2.1.19). Pistol and Quickly enter, and a humorous verbal brawl breaks out between Nym and Pistol. The fight threatens to become physical, but the two are stopped by Bardolph, who reminds them that they should "be friends" because they "must to France together" (2.1.102, 91). The argument continues until the Boy enters and announces that his master (Falstaff) is seriously ill. Quickly states that "the King has kill'd [Falstaff's] heart" (2.1.88), thus reminding the audience of Henry's rejection of his old companion: "I know thee not, old man" (*2 Henry IV*, 5.5.47). Once Quickly and the Boy leave to attend Falstaff, Nym and Pistol draw swords on each other. Bardolph now draws his as well and threatens to kill the first man who attacks. Nym and Pistol settle their dispute, which seems to be more about a gambling debt than Mistress Quickly. Quickly reenters to deliver the news that Falstaff's condition is grave and urges the men to go to their old friend.

2.2. The scene opens in Southampton with Exeter, Bedford, and Westmerland discussing the fact that though the king has discovered the traitors that the Chorus spoke of, he has done nothing to punish them. The king enters, accompanied by the traitors: Richard Earl of Cambridge, Lord Scroop of Marsham, and Grey of Northumberland. Henry asks Exeter to release a man from prison who, while drunk, spoke out against the king. The traitors try to convince the king to punish the man, arguing that if he is left unpunished his action will encourage more crimes against the king. The king frees the man anyway, saying that if "little faults" cannot be "wink'd at," then how will he react to well-thought-out "capital crimes" (2.2.54, 55, 56). He presents the traitors with what he says are their commissions (papers giving them governing powers in England while Henry is away in France) but are really indictments for their treachery. Learning that their plot has been discovered, the three plead for Henry's mercy, but he denies it, justifying the action by stating that he is following their own advice: "The mercy that was quick in us but late, / By your own counsel is suppress'd and kill'd" (2.2.79–80). Henry shows a personal and touchingly human side as he laments that the treachery of his "bedfellow" Scroop, who, Henry admits, "knewst the very bottom of [his] soul," is like "[a]nother fall of man" (2.2.8, 97, 142). The traitors confess, and Henry gives glory to God for revealing the plot as he orders their deaths. The king leaves for France, vowing, "No king of England, if not king of France!" (2.2.193).

2.3. In the tavern, Pistol, Nym, Bardolph, and the Boy prepare to leave for the war and say good-bye to Mistress Quickly. Pistol tells the men that they must mourn for the now dead Falstaff. Quickly delivers a touchingly poetic elegy that reminds the men and the audience of the humor and life Falstaff brought to the *Henry IV* plays. Pistol tells his wife to trust no man because "oaths are straws," and the men leave for the war (2.3.51).

2.4. In the French court, King Charles, the Dauphin, and several nobles discuss the impending threat of war. The Dauphin says that he believes Henry is a "vain, giddy, shallow, humorous youth" and that the invasion is nothing to take seriously, but the Constable warns the Dauphin that he is "too much mistaken in this king" (2.4.28, 30). Reminding the Dauphin of Henry's ancestors and the blood and humiliation they brought to France, the king urges his nobles to prepare for war.

A messenger (Exeter) arrives from the English king to assert Henry's claim to the throne of France and demand that Charles immediately relinquish the crown. Charles asks what will happen if he refuses, and Exeter explains that a bloody and warlike Henry "in fierce tempest" will create devastation as widows, orphans, and maidens weep for the men "swallowed in this controversy" (2.4.99, 109). Exeter then delivers a scornful message to the Dauphin, threatening to make France shake for the mockery of the tennis balls prank and declaring that the Dauphin will see first-hand what the English people have seen, Henry's glorious transformation. Charles says that in the morning he will have a response to Henry's claim.

3.Chorus. The Chorus urges the audience members to use their imaginations to see the preparations for war, the army sailing across the English Channel, and the siege of Harfleur. The Chorus orders them to "Suppose that [they] have seen," "play with [their] fancies," to "think," "[f]ollow, follow" and "grapple [their] minds" (3.Chrous.3, 7, 13, 17, 18). He informs the audience that the king of France offered his daughter and some small dukedoms to Henry in order to avoid the war, but Henry refused and the war has begun. With one last reminder to "eche [eke, stretch] out our performances with your mind," the Chorus departs, and the siege at Harfleur begins (3.Chor.35).

3.1. The scene is outside the wall of Harfleur. Henry delivers one of the most famous speeches in Shakespeare's canon, urging his soldiers to continue attacking the breach at all costs: "Once more unto the breach, dear friends, once more; / Or close the wall up with our English dead." (3.1.1–2). Henry, reminding the soldiers that their forefathers fought with nobility and success in France, charges his men to prove that "those whom you call'd fathers did beget you" by copying their warlike manners and success in taking this city (3.1.23). Henry also makes a more egalitarian appeal to the common soldiers by assuring them that their English breeding makes them strong soldiers and that there are none so low that they do not have "noble lustre" in their eyes (3.1.30). He ends his speech by rallying them to "Cry, 'God for Harry, England, and Saint George!'" as they surge again into battle (3.1.34).

3.2. Bardolph enters shouting, "On, on, on, on! To the breach, to the breach!" effectively parodying the grandeur of Henry's speech in the preceding scene (3.2.1). He is joined by Nym, Pistol, and the Boy, who state that they would rather live in safety than die in pursuit of fame. Fluellen (a Welsh captain) enters and physically beats the men into battle. The Boy is left on stage to deliver a soliloquy about the cowardliness and petty thieving of his comrades, all three of whom added together "could not be man to me" (3.2.30–31). He concludes that he must find a new master.

As the Boy exits, Fluellen returns and Captain Gower (an Englishman) enters. Fluellen complains to Gower that the mines are not laid properly, as described in Roman military precedent, and blames the Irish Captain, Macmorris, for the error. Captains Macmorris and Jamy (a Scot) enter. Fluellen challenges Macmorris to a debate about the disciplines of war, but Macmorris refuses to debate while "the trumpet calls us to the breach" (3.2.108–109). The men's anger rises until a parley (a trumpet signal) is sounded, and the men unite as they respond to the call.

3.3. King Henry stands before the gates of Harfleur to deliver a terrifying speech about the violence his soldiers will inflict on the townspeople if the town is not immediately surrendered. His speech threatens the citizens with images of "naked infants spitted upon pikes," "most reverend heads dash'd to the walls," and the "hot and forcing violation" of rape (3.3.38, 37, 21). The governor responds that the request he sent to the Dauphin for help has been denied, and he surrenders the town. Henry puts Exeter in charge of Harfleur and urges him to "use mercy to them all" (3.3.54). Since it is almost winter and his army is growing sick, Henry decides to retire to Calais.

3.4. At the French Court, Princess Katherine demands that her gentlewoman Alice teach her English. Her lesson begins with the English words for the parts of the body, starting with the hand. She learns the words for her body parts (hands, arm, elbow, nails, fingers, and so forth) but is shocked to learn that the words for foot and gown sound like vulgar French words.

3.5. In the French court, the king, Dauphin, and other nobles discuss the progress of the English. The French king gathers an immense army to fight Henry. Displaying their vanity and pride, the French nobles speculate about the fear the English will feel when seeing such a strong, healthy force. They predict that Henry will make a ransom request immediately and, in anticipation, send Montjoy (the herald) to hear the plea. As the nobles are sent into battle, the Dauphin is told he must stay with the king. (This is a textual inconsistency. In the Folio, the Dauphin is at the battle of Agincourt. In the Quarto, this inconsistency disappears, and the Dauphin never goes to the battle.)

3.6. In the countryside on the way to Calais, Fluellen tells Gower that the English, led by Exeter, have held the bridge (the bridge is over the river Ternoise, which the English must cross) and that one soldier, Pistol, was particularly brave in the battle. Pistol enters and asks Fluellen to speak to the king on behalf of Bardolph, who is to be put to death for stealing a pax (a small silver disk engraved with a picture of the crucifixion used to give blessings at communion) from a church. Fluellen refuses, stating that the thief should be hanged for stealing. Pistol curses Fluellen and leaves. Fluellen perceives, with Gower's help, that Pistol is a liar, not a valiant soldier. Henry arrives and learns that his soldiers control the bridge and that Bardolph is to be hanged for stealing. He endorses the execution: "We would have all such offenders so cut off" and orders that no one should take anything from the French without paying, and no French people are to be injured or abused (3.6.107–108). Montjoy arrives announcing the battle and telling Henry to name his ransom. Henry responds that his army is sick, depleted, and tired. He declares that he will not be ransomed. He tells Montjoy, "We would not seek a battle as we are, / Nor, as we are, we say we shall not shun it" (3.6.164–165). The herald leaves, and Henry orders his troops to camp for the night.

3.7. In the French camp, the nobles express their pride and vanity by competing with each other about who has the better accoutrements of war. The Dauphin praises his horse with such intensity that he states, "[M]y horse is my mistress" (3.7.44). The nobles are eager to get into battle and, assured of their victory, wait impatiently for the morning. They spend the time playing dice, wagering future English prisoners. The scene ends with the Duke of Orleans declaring that the each French soldier will have "a hundred Englishmen" by ten o'clock (3.7.157).

4.Chorus. It is the night before Agincourt. The Chorus asks the audience to imagine the universe filled with heavy darkness as he describes the sounds (horses, armorers, and whisperings) that float from camp to camp. Entering the French camp, he describes the arrogant pride of the soldiers there cursing the lazy night for being so slow in leaving. In the English camp, the Chorus describes the soldiers who "sit patiently and inly ruminate" with their "war-worn coats," looking like "horrid ghosts" (4.Chor.24, 26, 28). The English soldiers receive some comfort as "the royal captain" of the English army greets each of his soldiers with "a modest smile" and "a largess universal, like the sun" which melts away their cold fear (4.Chor.29, 33, 43). Each soldier receives "a little touch of Harry in the night" (4.Chor.47). Finally, the Chorus prepares the spectators to see the battle of Agincourt by reminding them that the theater cannot do justice to the scene and that they will have to imagine "true things by what their mock'ries be" (4.Chor.53).

4.1. It is almost morning in the English camp. King Henry asks Bedford, Gloucester, and Sir Thomas Erpingham to gather the nobles into his pavilion. Borrowing Erpingham's cloak, Henry leaves the nobles and wanders off alone to think. As he walks through the camp he meets a number of soldiers. He first sees Pistol who, not recognizing Henry, states his love for the king and his hatred for Fluellen. Next, the king listens as Fluellen tells Gower to speak softly to prevent the French from overhearing them. Henry notes that there "is care and valor" in Fluellen (4.1.84). Finally, Henry meets three common soldiers (Bates, Court, and Williams) who lament the approaching morning. The men and the disguised king discuss what responsibility the king has for the life and death of his subjects. The soldiers argue that the king is responsible for their souls because their duty to him outweighs their obligation to discover the justice of the fight. They argue that if the cause is not just, the king will pay a heavy reckoning on Judgment Day. Henry counters that the king is no more responsible for a soldier's death than a father is responsible for the death of a son killed while running an errand on which the father sent him. Henry further contends that war is God's way of punishing men for sins committed in their lives and that no king is responsible for such actions. Urging the soldiers to make a reckoning with God for their sins, Henry states that "every subject's duty is the King's, but every subject's soul is his own" (4.1.176–177). Henry and Williams get into an argument about the truthfulness of the king's refusal to be ransomed, and the two exchange gloves as a token of a quarrel that they vow to finish, if they live, after the battle.

Henry leaves the men and delivers a soliloquy about the burden of kingship. He bemoans the fact that kingship offers nothing in return for the heavy burden, except "ceremony" (4.1.239 and ff.). Noting the difference between the commoners' idea of kingship and the reality, Henry laments that all the trumpery of kings cannot "sleep so soundly as the wretched slave" (4.1.268). His soliloquy is briefly interrupted as Erpingham informs him that the nobles are waiting. Henry orders Erpingham away and finishes his soliloquy with a prayer. Asking God to "steel" his soldiers' hearts (4.1.289), he pleads with God not to take vengeance for his father's wrongdoing (usurping the crown and murdering Richard II). Gloucester enters and they leave for battle.

4.2. In the French camp the nobles are boasting as the sun rises. They anticipate an easy victory and are scornful that they must fight such a raggedy mob so their strength cannot be truly shown. The French imagine their future victims crying and state that the image of the French soldiers is enough to "suck away their souls" (4.2.17). Saying that the English "stay for death," the French line up for battle (4.2.56).

4.3. In the English camp, the lords await Henry's arrival. Westmerland reports that the French have 60,000 soldiers. Exeter states that the English are outnumbered five to one, "fearful odds," as Salisbury points out (4.3.5). Henry enters and delivers one of the most famous speeches in Shakespeare's canon and perhaps one of the most famous pieces of patriotic rhetoric in English. Turning the soldiers' weakness into glory, Henry asserts that he would not have one more man with them in the field, because "The fewer men, the greater share of honor" (4.3.22). Using an egalitarian rhetoric, Henry insists that there is a fellowship in war, and "he to-day that sheds his blood with me / Shall be my brother" (4.3.60–61). He not only inspires his men with the promise of kingly equality, but also with their ability to write themselves into history. Insisting that on this day from now on each of them will tell the tale of how he fought in this battle, Henry once more urges that there are enough men there to share this glory. The speech rises in pitch and excitement until Montjoy interrupts, having come one last time to ask Henry to negotiate his ransom. Henry says there will be no ransom "but these my joints" and tells Montjoy that though his army is tired and ill equipped, their "hearts are in the trim" (4.3.123, 115). Montjoy leaves, and as Henry sends his troops to battle he asserts that God will decide the victor.

4.4. Pistol enters the English camp with a French prisoner. The prisoner attempts to bargain for his life in French, but Pistol speaks only English and mistakes the words of death and fear for financial terms. The Boy enters and acts as a translator for the two men, helping the Frenchman secure his life, and helping Pistol to two hundred crowns' ransom. As Pistol leads his prisoner off, the Boy delivers a soliloquy about the cowardly nature of Pistol. He tells the audience that both Bardolph and Nym have been hanged for stealing and then leaves the stage to join the boys who are guarding the supplies at camp.

4.5. In the French camp, the nobles are stunned by the heavy casualties they have sustained. The Constable of France tells the Dauphin that all of their ranks are broken, and the Dauphin wonders if these are "the wretches that we play'd dice for" (4.5.8). The French consider retreat, but Orleans convinces them that there are still enough troops alive to take the English. Bourbon leads them back into the battle crying, "Let life be short, else shame will be too long!" (4.5.23).

4.6. On the English side, Henry tells his nobles that they have fought valiantly. Exeter relates the touching story of the deaths of Suffolk and York. When York saw Suffolk fall, York, already mortally wounded, went to him, kissed him, and cried that his own soul would accompany Suffolk's on the way to heaven. York then commended himself to the king, and died kissing the old man. Exeter begins to cry in telling the story, and Henry admits to tearing up as well, but an alarm sounds indicating that the French have regrouped on the battlefield. Henry orders the killing of the French prisoners and heads back into battle.

4.7. The scene opens with Fluellen's grieving that the French have broken the rules of warfare by killing the boys and looting the camp. Gower says that the king ordered the killing of the French prisoners in retribution for this action and praises the "gallant king" (4.7.10). Fluellen joins in praising Henry by comparing him to Alexander the Big (that is, Great), which, in Fluellen's accent, becomes "Alexander the Pig" (4.7.13). Furious at the murder of the boys, the king says that he "was not angry since [he] came to France / Until this instant" (4.7.55–56). Threatening the French soldiers on the hill and ordering the cutting of the prisoners' throats, Henry prepares to return to battle. Montjoy enters and asks permission to go through the field so that the French can recover the bodies of their dead. Noting that there are still French horses and men on the field, Henry admits that he is unsure who has won the day. Montjoy tells him, "The day is yours" (4.7.86). Henry thanks God for the victory. Fluellen lightens the scene by reminding Henry of his Welsh heritage. Henry assures Fluellen that on St. Davy's Day (March 1) he will wear a leek "for a memorable honor" (4.7.104). Henry orders the English and French heralds to count the dead.

Williams enters with the glove from the challenge he made with the disguised king on the eve of battle. Henry asks him why he wears the glove, and Williams answers that he promised a man to fight, if they lived. Fluellen says it is good that a man keep his word, no matter how great or small his enemy. Henry urges Williams to keep his promise to fight and sends him off to find Gower. Henry gives Fluellen the other glove, saying that it came from a French duke and that whoever recognizes it must be an enemy to England and should be arrested as a traitor. He then sends Fluellen after Gower. Henry quickly charges Warwick and Gloucester to follow the men to make sure there is "no harm between them" (4.7.182).

4.8. The scene opens with Williams's telling Gower that the king has called for him. Fluellen, faithfully following his orders, finds the two of them. Williams recognizes the glove and strikes Fluellen. Fluellen, remembering the king's story, charges Williams as a traitor. Gower demands an explanation from Fluellen. Warwick and Gloucester enter and ask what is going on. Fluellen claims that Williams is a traitor. Henry and Exeter appear. The king desires to know what is wrong, and after letting the men tell their stories, he reveals the trick he played on Fluellen. He also says that he is the one whom Williams challenged and demands that Williams explain his behavior. Williams states simply that Henry was not his royal self when they quarreled, so Williams is not accountable for his actions as they pertain to a king, only as they pertain to a normal man. Henry accepts his answer and rewards him by returning his glove after filling it with money.

The English herald enters with the count of the prisoners and dead. The French have suffered more than 10,000 casualties. The English lost only 25 men and have taken more than 1,500 prisoners. Henry exclaims that "God fought for us" (4.8.120) and orders the singing of *Non nobis* (Psalm 115) and *Te Deum*, songs of praise and thanksgiving to God.

5.Chorus. The Chorus describes Henry's triumphant return to England and the glory of his travel across the countryside and return to London. He depicts Henry's modesty and constant insistence on giving glory to God. The Chorus then elides five years and describes Henry's return to France.

5.1. In France, Gower asks Fluellen why he is still wearing his leek now that St. Davy's Day is past. Fluellen explains that he was assaulted by Pistol for wearing the leek and that he will wear it until he can repay Pistol for his abuse. Pistol enters and Fluellen repeatedly cudgels him and forces him to eat the leek. Fluellen gives Pistol some money for the injury caused, and Gower tells Pistol he should have more respect for things done in remembrance and honor of former valor. Fluellen and Gower exit. Pistol, in a soliloquy, reveals that his wife has died of a venereal disease. He says that he will return to England, where he will become a pickpocket and a thief, passing off the injuries he received from Fluellen as war wounds.

5.2. In the French court the French and English delegations meet to discuss peace. Burgundy, arbiter and facilitator of the meeting, describes how war has caused the garden of France to fester and overgrow to produce only rankness and soldierly natures. Henry says that peace must be bought by meeting his demands. The French king and some lords leave to discuss the terms of the peace treaty. Henry asks that he be left to speak with Katherine, his "capital demand" (5.2.96). Alice and Katherine remain, and Henry begins to woo Katherine across the language barrier. Henry tries conventional tricks, like telling her she is angelic, but Katherine notes "les langues des hommes sont pleines de tromperies" (the tongues of men are full of deceits; 5.2.115–116). Katherine asks if it is possible for her to love France's enemy, to which Henry responds that he loves France so much that he "will not part with a village of it" (5.2.174). The scene of courtship goes on until Katherine finally agrees that if her father wishes she will marry the English king. Henry responds that it will please her father and tries to kiss her, but she objects that it is not the fashion of France to kiss before they are wed. Henry states that they "are the makers of manners" (5.2.270–271), and he boldly kisses her just as the delegates return. The French king says that he has agreed to all the terms save one: he refuses to call Henry heir to the throne of France. Henry insists, and the French king is forced to give in to this demand as well. The scene ends as Henry orders the preparation of the wedding.

Epilogue. The Epilogue is written in sonnet form and begins by turning the audience's thoughts from the stage to the "bending author" of the play, stooped over from writing (Epil.2). Henry's life is still being celebrated; he is called "This star of England" (Epil.6). But the jubilation of the peace and his triumph in France are undercut by the Chorus, who warns that Henry's life will be short and that his son's rule will be as unhappy as Henry V's was happy. The play ends by reminding the audience of the popularity of the *Henry VI* plays and asking for a favorable judgment of this play.

PUBLICATION HISTORY

Henry V is one of the few Shakespearean plays that can be dated with a fair degree of accuracy. The Chorus in act 5 mentions "the general of our gracious Empress" returning "from Ireland . . . / Bringing rebellion broached on his sword" (5.Chor.30–32). Scholars commonly agree that this "general" is Robert Devereaux, the Earl of Essex, who left England for Ireland on March 27, 1599, to squelch Tyrone's rebellion. Essex returned on September 28, having failed in his mission. The patriotic fervor and optimism of the Chorus' lines reveal that the text was written after Essex's departure, but before his failure was known. Therefore, the most probable dates for production are in the early spring or summer of 1599.

As with any of Shakespeare's plays, there is no "true text" that comes to us directly from the author. It was common for actors, scribes, and even the playwright (or other playwrights) to alter a play as it was translated from the page to the stage and back again. The first published version of *Henry V* is a 1600 Quarto (known as Q1) edition titled *The Chronicle History of Henry the Fifth*. This Quarto was evidently a financial success, as it was reprinted in 1602 (Q2) and 1619 (Q3). These two reprintings, however, indicate only limited popularity, considering that other plays such as *I Henry IV* went through nine editions between 1598 and 1640. Because Q2 and Q3 were printed from Q1 with very few corrections, only Q1, known as "the Quarto," has any textual authority. In 1623, the First Folio (the first collected works of Shakespeare) printed the play as *The Life of Henry the Fifth*. Since 1623, editors have overwhelmingly preferred the Folio text, concluding that it is a later version of the play based on Shakespeare's foul papers (the author's original handwritten manuscript that was given to a professional scribe from which to produce a fair copy) that was never edited for performance.

The Quarto differs greatly from the Folio. The Quarto does not indicate scene or act divisions and eliminates the part of the Chorus. Scenes are often transposed, and scenes 1.1, 3.1, and 4.2 are omitted entirely. In addition, all of the major speeches are shortened, and the total number of lines is cut in half. The differences between the Folio and the Quarto have led editors to conclude that the Quarto is a memorial reconstruction of a text abridged for performance and produced with a reduced cast (it could be performed with as few as nine adults and two boys). These scholars believe that the text was probably produced from the memory of actors playing the parts of Exeter and Gower because the text in the sections where those actors appear most closely resembles that of the Folio. These ideas, coupled with the First Folio editors' insistence that the plays contained within it were Shakespeare's own versions and not "stolne, and surreptitious copies," have led to the Quarto version of *Henry V* being labeled a bad Quarto.

This easy distinction has, however, been challenged by scholars who maintain that the Quartos are a compelling area of interest. Stephen Gurr presents many arguments supporting the reinvestigation of the Quarto version of *Henry V*, including his contention that the 1600 Quarto of *Henry V* is probably the best surviving example of a Shakespeare play as it was performed by the company that bought it, not a reduced touring company as previous scholars have argued (see Gurr, *The First Quarto of Henry V* [Cambridge: Cambridge UP, 2000]).

Though editors continue to prefer the longer Folio version of the play, it does present some textual problems (potentially a byproduct of the provisional nature of the foul papers). Problems include imprecise speech prefixes, Pistol's reference to his wife as Doll Tearsheet instead of Nell Quickly (5.1.81), and the inconsistency between the French king's order that the Dauphin not join the army at Agincourt (3.5.66) and the Dauphin's presence there throughout act 4. Many editors choose to use emendations from the Quarto to alleviate some of these problems. For example, if the Quarto's text is followed, the Dauphin is removed from Agincourt and his speeches in act 4 are given to the Duke of Bourbon.

Written in 1599, *Henry V* is the culmination of Shakespeare's history plays, though historically and structurally it is the midpoint between the reigns treated in *King John* and *Henry VIII*. The defeat of the Spanish Armada in 1588 marked the apogee both for the power of England's queen and for the nation. Ten years later, the country was ripe for a play exploring again the nationalism and strength of the English people. By 1599, political unease was increasing. Elizabeth was aging, no heir to the throne was apparent, and the decades of relative internal peace in England were beginning to fade away as the Irish conflicts became more costly in terms of money and lives. Henry's transformation from recreant youth to powerful and unifying king was a tale that could unite the nation. While the concerns in the *Henry IV* plays were the rights and powers of a ruler, a major theme of *Henry V* is the creation of a nation. The play contains Shakespeare's only Irish character, Captain Macmorris. Macmorris and the captains from England, Wales, and Scotland find a way to bury the jealousies of regionalism and unify as an English "band of brothers" to fight a common enemy (4.3.60). The traitors are found out, the enemy is conquered, and the bickering is laid aside to help Henry and England achieve their greatest victory, but the play is not entirely positive about nationalism. The Epilogue reminds the audience that the victory and the king are short-lived. Act 5 violently reintroduces nationalistic quarreling over the Welsh leek; and the demonization of the French as "others," even as the realms are united, underscores the complicated issues involved with nationalism and patriotism.

SOURCES FOR THE PLAY

Originality of story was not the measure of great authorship during the Renaissance, and indeed most of Shakespeare's plays are based on other works. What makes Shakespeare great is not his ability to invent a story, but the way in which he shapes his subject matter, combines it with other materials, and uses language to investigate the ideas that he is exploring.

In writing *Henry V*, Shakespeare relied heavily on two sources. His primary source for the history, character, and even occasionally language was the second edition of Raphael Holinshed's *Chronicles of England, Scotland, and Ireland* (1587). Shakespeare uses Holinshed's *Chronicles* as the foundation for the actions, events, and the heroic description of Henry. Many of the terms that the Chorus uses to exalt Henry come directly from Holinshed's *Chronicles*. In addition, some of the modern difficulties with the play are a result of Shakespeare's remaining extremely close to his source. For example, in the Archbishop of Canterbury's speech on the

Salic Law (1.2.33–113), Shakespeare is so faithful to the original material that he seems merely to convert Holinshed's lengthy prose passage into blank verse. Henry's religious zeal and repeated appeals to God, his belief in the justness of his claim to the crown of France, and his conviction that the guilt for the war lies with the French for resisting that claim and not on him for pursuing it all come from the *Chronicles*. It should be noted that the *Chronicles* portrays Henry as an epic hero and that Holinshed certainly did not intend to disparage Henry's character.

Shakespeare usually treats the *Chronicles* in a much more nuanced way than in the above examples, picking and choosing which material from the sources to include so as to create greater drama and meaning. For example, the *Chronicles* details how the archbishop deliberately schemes to distract Henry from the parliamentary bill by encouraging him to attack France. Although Shakespeare presents the bill and the threat it imposes to the church, he treats the motives of the archbishop very casually compared to Holinshed. In the *Chronicles*, Henry's attack on Harfleur ends with rapine and murder, but in Shakespeare the mere threat of those horrors causes the city to surrender, and mercy is shown to all citizens. The expertise of the English archers and Henry's military acumen are painstakingly rendered in the *Chronicles*, while Shakespeare skips these English feats entirely, focusing solely on Henry's rhetorical power. In each of these cases, Shakespeare alters the *Chronicles* to create a better drama by clarifying and purifying Henry's motives, ignoring some of the brutal effects of war, and heightening the effect of Henry's eloquence.

Shakespeare's other primary source for *Henry V*, especially for the comic scenes, was the anonymous play *The Famous Victories of Henry the Fifth: Containing the Honourable Battel of Agin-court*. The surviving copy of *Famous Victories* is dated 1598, but the Stationers' Register has an entry for the play dated May 14, 1594. *Famous Victories* is the work of a novice playwright. Although the play lacks the poetry, characterization, and structure of Shakespeare's play, the author has a good sense for choosing dramatic scenes from source materials and a very good ear for humor. The play's humor is attested to by the fact that the greatest comedic actor of the times, Richard Tarleton, played the part of Dereck in that work.

Shakespeare took from *Famous Victories* many of the comedic moments of the play. Pistol's capture of the French soldier Le Fer is based on Dereck's capture of a French soldier. The French soldiers' dicing for English prisoners comes from *Victories*, as does the clumsy wooing of Katherine. Shakespeare also occasionally chose to follow *Famous Victories* in the ordering of events. In the *Chronicles*, the scene with the tennis balls happens before Henry's decision to go to war. Shakespeare chooses to follow *Famous Victories* in having the tennis balls arrive after Henry has resolved to invade France, thus removing any sense that the war is revenge for the joke. Like *Famous Victories*, Shakespeare's play retains King Charles as the ruler of France. Holinshed states that the French king was lunatic and France was governed by the Dauphin. By retaining the French king as a sane and competent ruler, Shakespeare magnifies Henry's greatness and achievement. The Dauphin's disdainful gift and dismissive message to Henry come from *Famous Victories*, but Shakespeare furthers the characterization by giving the Dauphin dialogue (the Dauphin does not speak in *Famous Victories*) that exposes his pride, vanity, and foppishness. Finally, Shakespeare copies *Victories* in omitting the five years between Agincourt and the Treaty of Troyes (1415–1420) to give the play a greater impetus.

Another notable source for *Henry V* is Edward Hall's *The Union of the Two Noble and Illustre Famelies of Lancaster and York* (1548). Hall provides an outline of the character of Henry, whom he celebrates as a just leader, warrior, and hero of England, calling his reign the "Victorious Acts of King Henry the Fifth." In addition to providing an outline of Henry as hero, Hall contributed to the archbishop's speech comparing England to a bee kingdom (1.2.183–220) and the Constable's speech describing the tired and worn English army before Agincourt (4.2.16–37). Other sources include Tacitus's *Annals* (trans. 1598), which provided the basis for Henry's visit with the common soldiers; John Lyly's *Euphues* (1580), also a source for the archbishop's discussion of the bee kingdom; and, finally, *A Brief Discourse of War* (1590), written by Welsh knight Sir Roger Williams, and Thomas Digges's *Stratioticos* (1579), the sources of Fluellen's military ideals.

The episodes that are original to Shakespeare increase the humanity of the play. The touching moment where Mistress Quickly discusses Falstaff's death (2.3.9–26), the comedy of Fluellen and his not so subtle ways of reminding Henry of his Welsh heritage (4.7.92–115), Henry's debate with the common soldiers (4.1.92–229; the germ of this conversation derives from Tacitus, but the vast majority of the debate is original to Shakespeare), and Henry's soliloquy on the night before the battle of Agincourt (4.1.230–284) are all Shakespeare's inventions. Shakespeare also had no literary source for the scene where Katherine receives her first English lesson from Alice (3.4). Shakespeare's inventions are the touching scenes that recognize the difficulty and joy in being a human.

STRUCTURE AND PLOTTING

A criticism often directed at *Henry V* is that it is less cohesive than Shakespeare's later plays because its structure is episodic (a succession of loosely connected incidents) rather than organically developed from the awareness and actions of the characters. This interpretation, however, fails to consider that the focus of *Henry V* is not on a man, though Henry is undoubtedly the hero, but on a nation. Thus, a character-driven structure and its concentration on the development of an individual would be incongruent with the play's emphasis. Other scholars, keeping the national focus in mind, have argued that the play is structured as an epic. Although the play is epic in its concern with the destiny of a nation and employs some epic conventions (such as invoking a muse), this view of the play's structure is limiting, too. While Shakespeare explores the heroic scope of the epic, he also compares the ideals of that heroism with the imperfect reality of human existence by reminding the audience that the king is also a man. A more useful way of thinking about the play's structure is to keep both of these concerns in mind. The play is epic in its treatment of the unification and triumph of the English nation, but that epic structure is balanced by the knowledge of the limits of human greatness.

The play follows a linear path that runs parallel to Henry's military incursion into France. Beginning with the decision to go to war, the play builds momentum as it proceeds on an upward trajectory that celebrates the nation's heroism and patriotism by depicting Henry's victories. This patriotic path culminates with the battle at Agincourt. Considered in this way, the play does suggest an epic, but the work creates a more complicated perspective by balancing this structure with the consideration of Henry's humanity. Shakespeare uses the other characters in the play to comment upon the idealized patriotic rhetoric of the crucial scenes. Comic interludes enhance and qualify Henry's greatness. Scenes and characters reflect on the play's themes and on each other through juxtaposition, constantly asking the audience to reconsider the action through new perspectives.

The Chorus that opens *Henry V* urges the spectators forward and creates momentum by telling them to cram years "[i]nto an hour-glass" (Prol.31). This momentum quickens as the play moves on, driving forward at an increasing speed. Act 1 shows Henry's decision to go to France and reveals the change in the king's character. The slow pace and detailed dialogue underscore the justness of Henry's claim. That justness of the war is complicated, however, in 1.1, where the archbishop reveals his self-interested motives for sending Henry to fight. Though these motives do not mean that Henry's claim is not just, they do ask the audience to consider the human motives in waging war.

Act 2 opens with the Chorus describing the "fire," "winged heels," and back and forth motion across the English Channel as England prepares for war, but the Chorus leaves us waiting on the shore to be transported to France, thus arousing the audience's expectation (2.Chor.1, 7). This speech is followed, though, not with the promised revelation of treachery and trip to France, but with Nym and Pistol's fighting over Mistress Quickly. This low comic scene reveals what men fight over, women, and shows that domestic disputes move these men in ways that the national dispute does not, despite what the Chorus promised in his introduction to the act. Act 2 continues to build in this balanced way, repeating and varying the themes and action developed in Henry's scenes. The moving speech Henry delivers to Scroop about the cost of his treachery reminds the audience of Henry's treachery in abandoning his old friends for his new.

Henry's "Once more unto the breach" (3.1.1) is paralleled and mocked by Bardolph's "On, on, on, on!" (3.2.1), and Henry's assertion that the soldiers should desire honor more than life, that they should "close the wall up with our English dead" (3.1.2) is satirized by the Boy's insistence he "would give all my fame for a pot of ale and safety" (3.2.13).

The play continues to build momentum as Henry moves through France toward the emotional and structural climax of the play, Agincourt. The Chorus reaches his poetic climax in his introduction to act 4, using imagery, sentence structure, and the sounds of words to create the anxious scene between the camps. His rhetoric is at its apex as he turns from the panorama of the scene to describe the "little touch of Harry in the night" and the soldiers who "[pluck] comfort from his looks" (4.Chor.47, 42). This heightened rhetoric describes a touching familiarity between the common soldiers and the king, and Henry appears, as Williams later states, "a common man" (4.8.51).

After building the audience's expectations and desires for four acts, the play finally arrives at the eve of England's great victory. But before the victory is gained, as every member of the audience knew it would be, Shakespeare introduces a touchingly human moment that questions the justice, righteousness, and costs of war. The structures collide to demonstrate that even under this best of kings, war still carries a price.

Act 5 has disappointed many readers. Despite the glorious description the Chorus elicits of Henry's return to England, the scenes that follow feel like a letdown. It is best to think of them as a denouement. The Epilogue undercuts the linear progression by bringing the action back into the circular motion of history. Here the Chorus speaks in deflating terms of real consequences for the first time. By reminding the audience that everything that Henry V won will be lost and that the baby who derives from the union of Katherine and Henry will, in fact, be the means of the separation of England and France, the Epilogue firmly places events in the circular pattern of conquest and loss.

MAIN CHARACTERS

Henry V

Though the play features a multitude of characters, it is Henry who dominates in the number of lines (more than double that of any other character), in presence, and in the role of director of the action. Henry evokes strong reactions from audiences, who view him either as a Machiavellian warmonger or as the ideal Christian king (see "Critical Controversies," below, for further discussion of this issue). However, almost everyone agrees that Henry is, first and foremost, an actor and rhetorical master. Henry's skill with language reveals both his knowledge of the many roles a king plays and his ability to manipulate scenes and people as necessary. He can turn himself into the bloody soldier at the gates of Harfleur, threatening to unleash "murther, spoil, and villainy" (3.3.32). He can inspire common soldiers to fight by telling them that they "shall be [his] brother" (4.3.62), and even win the Princess by speaking to her in "plain soldier" (5.2.149).

The strong presentation of Henry as an actor has led some critics to see him more as a type than as a character. They argue that Henry does not develop during the course of the play, but is instead a static figure presented in a series of roles: Henry as soldier, Henry as motivator, Henry as wooer, and so forth. This is, in fact, how Holinshed (Shakespeare's primary source—see "Sources for the Play") presents Henry, as the ideal monarch on display in different rhetorical situations. Shakespeare, however, creates a more complex picture by combining the portrait of Henry's greatness with glimpses into his human side.

As the play opens, the Chorus describes Henry as Mars (the god of war) holding in his hands the powers of "famine, sword, and fire" (Prol.7). When we meet Henry, however, he is not like Mars. Instead, he is calm and patient as he listens to the tediously long speech from the archbishop. This presentation of Henry is important because it enforces the idea that Henry has transformed himself from the passionate and impulsive youth of the *Henry IV* plays into a patient and careful king. The king is still human though, as we are shown when the Dauphin's tennis balls arrive. His reply to the insult is witty, measured, and passionate, revealing both a king aware that he is on public display and an indignant man who has been insulted.

As the play goes on, the complexity of Henry's character continues to develop. When the traitors are exposed in Southampton, Henry's speech and the punishment he orders are for the public treason against his public body and role; he speaks as the righteous king sanctioned by God. However, his touching address to Scroop reveals his personal feelings of pain, betrayal, and inability to trust anyone now that he has taken on the role of king. While the speech is moving, it also reminds the audience of Mistress Quickly's assertion that Falstaff died because Henry denied him, thus betraying the old man's trust and love and killing Falstaff's heart. The audience is pulled in two different directions. While audiences feel pity for Henry's personal pain, they also remember that he, too, on a personal though not on a political level, has committed the same crimes as the traitors.

The conflict between Henry the man and Henry the king reaches a climax on the eve of Agincourt in the debate with Williams and in Henry's soliloquy. Some see in this scene a ruthless politician whose rhetoric during the debate works to deny all responsibility for his soldiers' lives and for the consequences of waging war. As in the scene at Harfleur, where Henry blames the death and the horrors of war on the French for defending themselves and not on himself for invading France, Henry again manages to use his rhetorical ability to manipulate language and dodge responsibility for the human cost of war. However, the man behind the king is deeply affected by the conversation that begins as a display of Henry's formal rhetorical abilities, but ends with Henry's losing his self-control and promising to fight a common soldier. The conversation affects Henry, prompting him to investigate the nature of his rule and the responsibility of kingship in his only soliloquy of the play (4.1.230–284, 288–305), which immediately follows the conversation with Williams.

The soliloquy is often noted for its self-pitying tone, but the speech also reveals the very human toll that the pressures of kingship have taken on Henry. Henry shows that he is human and that all his "ceremony" cannot buy him one night's sleep, for he is, as he notes, the one who must "bear all" (4.1.239, 233). Despite the outward assuredness that he feels he must maintain to hearten the soldiers, his own human fears creep in. He begs God to not revenge Henry IV's wrongdoings on his soldiers, "Not to-day, O Lord, / O, not to-day" (4.1.292–293). This moment shows the unification of Henry the king and Henry the man as he begs that his family's personal wrongs not be paid for by his subjects, that his human problems not affect his kingship. It is only after the discourse with the common soldiers and coming to terms with his own human fears that Henry can unite humanity and patriotism in the famous "band of brothers" speech he delivers to the English army (see "Explication of Key Passages," below).

Act 5 shows Henry in a continued struggle to unite his public role and his humanity. The wooing of Katherine is unnecessary; she has been won in the war, but the attempt to win her love shows Henry's fusing the personal and the political by attempting to wed the political marriage with real affection.

The Chorus

The multitude of other characters all reflect importantly on Henry, and it is in relation to him that their characters are best understood. A few of the most important are the Chorus, Fluellen, Katherine of France, and the Boy from the London tavern. Though the Chorus as a device is treated in the next section, he also appears as a character in this play. His rhetorical abilities, aimed at controlling the emotions and judgments of the audience, rival Henry's. In this way, he works as a sort of dramatic foil echoing the effects of Henry's rule on his people by creating similar responses in the audience. As the people of England submit to Henry by allowing him to lead and shape their thoughts, they are given, in recompense, a united England and a glorious battle. Similarly, as the audience lets the Chorus shape its thoughts, it is given "a mirror of all Christian kings" and a brilliant story of hero-ism, unity, and patriotic fervor (2.Chor.6). If the people of England and the audi-ence do not permit the king or Chorus to "work [their] thoughts," then they are left only with manipulation, warmongering, and needless death (3.Chor.25).

Fluellen

Fluellen's character deserves special note, not just because he exists beyond the scenes with the other captains, but also because his is the second largest role in the play. Fluellen brings humor to many of the scenes and was so popular on the stage that his character inspired its own play, *The Half-Pay Officers*, by C. P. Molloy (1720). Audiences laugh at his antiquated idea of military strategy and his exagger-ated accent, but as the play develops, his loyalty and humor become endearing. Even his insistent reference to the king's Welsh background changes from an annoyance into a lovable idiosyncrasy. When Henry tricks Fluellen and causes him to be struck by Williams after Agincourt (4.8), the audience is stunned not only by Henry's use of this loyal man, but also by the secure knowledge that Fluellen would gladly take the blow for his countryman and king, insisting that "Your Grace doo's me as great honors as can be desir'd in the hearts of his subjects" (4.7.160–161).

The Boy

Another character the audience feels affection for is the Boy. Though Henry has no soliloquies in the play until act 4, the Boy often speaks in soliloquy, showing his self-confidence and insight, and creating a strong connection with the audience. Structurally, the Boy serves to distance the audience from the Eastcheap gang. The humor and tenderness of these characters throughout the *Henry IV* plays are now, as the Boy tells us, turned to sloth and thievery. He further states that all three men, Bardolph, Pistol, and Nym, "do not amount to a man" (3.2.31–32). The Boy also serves to remind us that war has real costs. It is for this Boy that the audience weeps when Fluellen reports the death of "the poys" (4.7.1).

Katherine

Women barely exist in this play, but their scenes, particularly Katherine's, com-ment upon the larger themes of the play with acuity. Katherine's English lesson (3.4) provides insight into her character and the power of Henry's threats. Katherine's self-dissection as she separates and Anglicizes her body parts follows Henry's bloody speech at Harfleur, where he threatens to hang bloody body parts from pikes and to rape and destroy with his soldiers' "bloody hand" (3.3.12). The aural repetition of images makes the audience realize that it is her body and ability to produce an heir to both crowns that will be conquered and won. Further, the conquering that seems innocent as Katherine learns the English names for her hand and foot alludes to Henry's potential to use rape and murder to get what he wants. Katherine's lan-guage lesson reveals her to be vulnerable to Henry's threat and valuable as a uni-fying commodity.

Women are, however, not entirely powerless. Queen Isabel insists that she "may do some good" (5.2.93) by joining the parties negotiating the peace treaty. Katherine, too, displays some of this French power in the wooing scene. She forces Henry to attempt to woo her in French, and Henry notes that it is easier for him to conquer all of France than to speak French in trying to win her affection (5.2.184–185).

DEVICES AND TECHNIQUES

The most obvious device employed by Shakespeare in *Henry V* is the Chorus. Though Shakespeare uses a chorus in a few other plays, this character usually disappears by act 2. Here, the Chorus appears throughout the play to fulfill several functions: to introduce the play and each ensuing act; to deliver the Epilogue; to inform the audience of historical events that have occurred during the lapses between acts; to set the scene for the audience, and to celebrate the king. The most important function, however, is to guide the audience members' theatrical experience.

The Chorus asks the audience to overcome the limits of the theater through creative imagination, which can turn one actor "into a thousand parts" and "make imaginary puissance" (troops) with the mind (Prol.24, 25). The Chorus does not apologize for the theater because Shakespeare felt that the stage would not and could not do what he wanted. Rather, the emphasis on the theatrical limitations raises the audience's awareness of the unfolding theatrical experience. As the Chorus asks the audience members to engage imaginatively with the drama, to "[p]lay with your fancies" (3.Chor.7), he creates what Pamela Mason calls a "theatrical contract" (177). The contract, built on acknowledging the limits of the theater, paradoxically serves to empower both the theater and the audience by creating a grander vision than would be possible on stage and by allowing the audience to move from spectator to active participant in the artistic creation. Thus, the audience becomes a part of the glory of Henry and of the play.

Shakespeare's use of the Chorus in *Henry V* is so extensive that the Chorus becomes a character. In fact, the two most powerful and poetic speakers in this play are Henry and the Chorus. The Chorus' poetry reaches its peak in act 4. Describing the scenes in the French and English camps as the armies prepare for battle, the Chorus weaves a masterful picture full of sensual details of the sights and sounds that cross the "poring dark" and fill "the night's dull ear" (4.Chor.2, 11). However, when he speaks the Epilogue, the Chorus leaves behind his characteristic blank verse and turns instead to the highly structured sonnet. This change in his poetry signals a change in his vision. Before, the Chorus' poetry was expansive, enlarging the theater, the audience's imaginations, and the scope of the play. Now, the expansiveness of the Chorus is constrained into sonnet form, and his vision is reduced from seeing all of England and France to focusing on the author's "all-unable pen" and the "story" of a "[s]mall time" (Epil.1, 2, 5). It is with this collapsing motion that the Chorus deflates the nationalistic fervor of Henry V and his victory by reminding the audience that the victory was fleeting, that "This star of England" soon fades and his heir makes "England bleed" (Epil.6, 12).

Though both Henry and the Chorus use powerful poetry to excite emotions and actions, this play does not develop a prevailing image cluster that arises as the play's dominant image, as the garden of England imagery does, for instance, in *Richard II*. This absence perhaps derives from the king's abilities as an actor to utilize the imagery most appropriate for individual circumstances. Thus, in battle Henry employs the imagery of animals. Seeing his men tire, he demands that they "imitate the action of the tiger" and later sees them as "greyhounds in the slips" (3.1.6, 31). At Agincourt, he likens himself to "the lion's skin" with the lion still in it (4.3.93). Pistol picks up on the animal imagery in calling Nym an "Iceland dog," "egregious dog," and "hound of Crete" (2.1.41, 46, 73). Fluellen uses this canine imagery as well, pushing the men to the breach and calling them "dogs" (3.2.20). Battle also inspires Henry to use the imagery of dismembered body parts, particularly hands. His threat to Harfleur is full of hands, the "bloody hand," the "foul hand," and the "hand / Of hot and forcing violation" threatening rape and murder (3.3.12, 34, 20–21).

At other times, Henry's imagery is more innocent. His speech to Scroop is full of religious terms, and Scroop's treason is likened to "[a]nother fall of man" (2.2.142). Henry's wooing announces it will leave aside the language of love and speak as "plain king" and "plain soldier" with "plain and uncoin'd constancy" (5.2.124, 149, 153–154), thereby eschewing all imagery.

The Chorus invokes the visual imagination of the audience with allusions to fire. The Chorus uses fire in the opening lines of two of his speeches, invoking "a Muse of fire" (Prol.1) in the prologue and describing how the "youth of England are on fire" (2.Chor.1) in act 2. This burning desire to join the action is matched in act 3 with the burning of Henry himself as he is described by the Chorus as Phoebus, the sun god, (recalling the Prince's assertion that he will "imitate the sun" (1 Henry IV, 1.2.197). Act 4 is full of "watchful fires" and "fire answer[ing] fire" as the armies prepare for battle, so recalling the fire of devotion from act 2 (4.Chor.23, 8). By act 5, the images of fire are removed from battle and are now placed in the audience's mind as the "quick forge and working-house of thought" (5.Chor.23). Caroline Spurgeon has also noted that the "swift and soaring movement" of the Chorus' imagery suggests birds (*Shakespeare's Imagery and What It Tells Us* [Cambridge: Cambridge UP, 1935], 243). The references to "winged heels" (2.Chor.7), "imagin'd wing" (3.Chor.1), and the adding of "[m]ore feathers to our wings" (1.2.307) create an uplifting feeling that both heightens the audience's imagination and quickens the pace of the play.

THEMES AND MEANINGS

Henry V, more than any other play in Shakespeare's canon, examines the nature of war. It is through this primary theme of war that the secondary themes of nationalism and kingship are explored. The play investigates war's ability to create heroes, a unified nation, and a great king, but balances these themes with the horrors and loss that war also generates. The complexity of the play's structure and the multitude of perspectives that Shakespeare creates produce a variety of responses to this theme. Act 1 questions the reasons for waging war. The scene between the bishops presents the idea that war can be waged for selfish reasons, while Henry's repeated request to know whether he can "with right and conscience" claim the French crown (1.2.96) reveals his wish for war to be waged only when the cause is just. Act 2 continues to expand on the idea that not all are going to war for heroic reasons. Though Henry argues his claim is just and the fight is about honor, for Bardolph, Pistol, and Nym the war is merely a chance to profit (rather like the archbishop's motive).

In act 3, the heroism and the bloody costs of war are revealed more fully. The passion of Henry's speech before Harfleur reveals his compelling leadership and heroic charisma that carry the play and the soldiers on to the victory at Agincourt. The heroic king is revealed in his passionate words to the troops, but the need for the troops to go "once more" (3.1.1) to the breach shows that they have, to this point, failed. The gruesome vision of a wall of "our English dead" (3.1.2) exposes the cost at which heroism is bought. Thus, in one speech both the heroic spirit and the barbarism of war are revealed. The frightful images of war continue as Henry threatens the citizens of Harfleur with a gruesome series of hyperboles. The vivid images of infants on pikes and bloody hands murdering old men create a terrifying vision of the reality of war. Yet it is Henry's rhetorical abilities that allow him to overtake the town by simply delivering these verbal threats. The grisly images save the soldiers and the townspeople from the gruesome violence of the actions described.

Act 4 again presents the cost of war in human lives. Though the king warns the bishop in the first act that his words may cause "many now in health" to "drop their blood" (1.2.18, 19), it is here that the audience and the king emotionally experience death. The deeply moving elegiac description of the deaths of York and Suffolk develops the idea of a heroic death. Dying in the camaraderie of battle, they provide a touching picture of the ideals of soldierly loyalty. Their valiant deaths are immediately followed, however, by death of another kind: the death of the Boy. The senselessness of the loss of this young and innocent life is deeply felt. Shakespeare enhances the audience's connection to the Boy through a series of soliloquies, so that when Fluellen reports his, and indeed all the boys', death, the audience's sense of loss is enormous. The English corpses filling the breach are now characters who have names and whose deaths are keenly felt.

Kingship is investigated in a similarly complex way, focusing on the theatricality of being (playing the lifelong part of) the king. The play forces the audience constantly to reconsider the distinctions between the king and the man, the soldier and the ruler, the reality and the fiction. As the play opens, the bishops describe Henry's miraculous change from fanciful and carefree youth to pious and considerate king. For the audience of the time, familiar with the *Henry IV* plays, this transformation is not miraculous, but a device contrived by Henry so that his "reformation, glitt'ring o'er [his] fault, / Shall show more goodly and attract more eyes" (*1 Henry IV*, 1.2.213–214). Thus, the theatrical fiction Henry devised is, to the bishops, proof of the reality of his kingship. As the play continues, Henry's heroism is increased by his verbal and performative abilities. The importance of performance is realized in scenes such as the threat to Harfleur. As discussed above, the ferocity of Henry's words reveals his soldierly side and shines a heroic light on the leader and king. Yet the audience is aware of the fiction on which the heroic speech is built. The soldiers did not take the town when he inspired them to attack "once more," and Henry's retreat to rhetoric reveals that his soldiers are still unable to achieve victory. Thus, the performance Henry delivers is, in essence, a bluff.

Dramatizing Henry's failure to take the town after the breach speech is not meant to show the powerlessness of his words to inspire his soldiers, but rather to emphasize that his rhetoric is more powerful than his army as words take the town that arms could not. Henry's bluff wins the day, but the moment also reveals that Harfleur surrenders because the town believed a fiction to be a reality. Curiously, this play about war and a great English victory never shows a battle scene, though Shakespeare does so in other works. Language, not English archery, defeats the French.

This play does not focus, as Shakespeare's other history plays tend to do, on who should be king, but instead explores the making of a nation. National harmony is invoked by the archbishop's beehive metaphor in act 1, where "happy England" is to be achieved by everyone's working in the "divers functions" given by God (1.2.214, 184). The four professional fighters, Captains Jamy, Gower, Macmorris, and Fluellen, serve Henry with loyalty and love, but they also represent the characteristic nationalities of the people who constitute England. The soldiers reveal that they, like England, are a band of people held tenuously together by the strength of their ruler. Although small nationalistic spats arise, these problems never grow into major differences or physical confrontations, but instead are laid aside to create a united England and to fight against a common enemy. There is, however, the potential for real violence. The argument at Harfleur between Macmorris and Fluellen reveals the real potential of civil war (a civil war with the Irish was threatening to erupt in 1599 when the play was written). The petty differences of the captains are quickly set aside, however, when the men hear an alarm and return to the field united against a common enemy, France. Thus the captains represent both Henry's ability to unite England and the differences within the nation. It is only after the battle with France has ceased that the internal regional conflicts result in physical violence. After the war, Fluellen is struck twice, first by Williams (arranged by Henry) and then by Pistol. Though his valiant loyalty in the war was valued, the ending of the war allows this lovable character to be abused.

CRITICAL CONTROVERSIES

Criticism of *Henry V* has focused on the character of the title character. Romantic critics, often confusing the historical Henry V with Shakespeare's creation, were dissatisfied with what they viewed as Henry's Machiavellian warmongering. William Hazlitt concludes that Shakespeare "labors hard to apologize for the actions of the king" but succeeds only so far as to create "an amiable monster" (*Characters of Shakespeare's Plays* [London: Taylor & Hessey, 1818], 125, 127). After the publication of E.M.W. Tillyard's *Shakespeare's History Plays* (London: Chatto & Windus, 1941), critical concern shifted. Concentrating on how the play fit into the larger structure of the second tetralogy (the plays *Richard II*, *1 Henry IV*, *2 Henry IV*, and *Henry V*) and the Tudor ideology that Tillyard outlined, these critics focused on how Henry is, as the Chorus proclaims, the "star of England" and "the mirror of all Christian kings" (Epil.6, 2.Chor.6). Tillyard himself saw Henry as "the residue of [Shakespeare's] obligation" to create "a *hero* King" as counterpart to Richard III (304; emphasis mine).

Since then, opinion has remained deeply divided between these two versions of Henry. Is Henry an admirable king who brings greatness to himself and his country through heroic words and deeds? Or is he a self-interested jingoist who manipulates others and refuses to take responsibility for his actions and decisions? Some, like John Middleton Murry, find in Henry the "ideal of kingship" (*Shakespeare* [London: J. Cape, 1936], 150). Others see in the dramatic structure and Henry's rhetorical prowess a "princely power that originates in fraud" (Stephen Greenblatt, *Shakespearean Negotiations: The Circulation of Social Energy in Renaissance England* [Berkeley: U of California P, 1988], 65).

These opposing views are mirrored in the structure of the play. While the Chorus constantly presents Henry in what John Russell Brown called a "hero-centered pageant narrative" (introduction to *Henry V* [New York: Penguin, 1965, 1988], xxv), the play also presents the bloody reality of war and the often self-interested motivations of the people involved (see "Structure and Plotting"). In "Rabbits, Ducks, and Henry V" Norman Rabkin describes how the play forces this polarized response. Rabkin argues that the work is like the classic gestalt drawing of a "rare beast" (280) that can be seen as either a rabbit or a duck, depending on how you view the image. Although it is easy to discover both images, Machiavellian politician and ideal king, you can see only one image at a time. Rabkin celebrates this balance, arguing that the "ultimate power" of the play lies in its ability to create both sides with equal effectiveness and warning that although both readings are persuasive, choosing only one is "reductive, requiring that we exclude too much to hold it" (294).

The play's apparent focus on war's ability to unite a nation, to destroy lives, to create heroes, or to reveal ruthless Machiavels changes as contemporary taste does. The modern view of Henry as national hero reached its apex with the 1944 film version (based on a 1937 theatrical production) directed by Laurence Olivier that celebrated the unity and power of England under a mighty monarch at a time when the allied forces were planning their D-Day landings in France. After Vietnam, the Falklands war, and the wars in Iraq, the world has grown increasingly suspicious of war, politics, and the political leaders. Late-twentieth- and early-twenty-first-century interpretations of *Henry V* have reflected that altered zeitgeist. These reassessments include such titles as *Henry V, War Criminal?: and Other Shakespeare Puzzles*, by John Sutherland and Cedric Watts, with an introduction by Stephen Orgel [Oxford: Oxford UP, 2000] and R. A. Foakes's *Shakespeare and Violence* [Cambridge: Cambridge UP, 2003].

The concern with war and violence reflected in these titles, however, does not eliminate the debate over the play's message. Jonathan Dollimore and Alan Sinfield regard Henry as a representation of the Tudor attempt to control the civil unrest that forever threatens to erupt into violence. The ultimate exclusion of the subversive elements, they argue, undermines Tudor legitimacy and power ("History and Ideology: The Instance of *Henry V*," in *Alternative Shakespeares*, ed. John Drakakis [London: Methuen, 1985], 206–227). Conversely, Stephen Greenblatt argues that civil unrest is subversive and must be contained, but the ultimate marginalization and exclusion of the subversive elements are, for him, a part of the dominant ideology's structure of power. Because discordant elements are allowed to exist in a space that is sanctioned within the power of the monarchy, they are not really threatening (*Shakespearean Negotiations*).

It is worth noting that most of these critical controversies never arise when one is watching a production of the play. The pace, grandeur, and forward momentum of the action keep the audience from asking the questions that have troubled scholars. In production, it is clear that the characters believe in their cause, and that the play requires the audience, like the English nation, to be swept up in the charisma and power of Henry.

PRODUCTION HISTORY

Plays about the reign of Henry V were being staged in the 1590s. Philip Henslowe's diary records thirteen performances of a new play, "*harey the v*," between November 1595 and July 1596. His 1598 diary also inventories props for *"Harye the v.,"* and the Stationers' Register lists the anonymous play *The Famous Victories of Henry the Fifth: Containing the Honourable Battel of Agin-court* on May 14, 1594 (see "Sources for the Play" for discussion of this play as a source for Shakespeare). In addition, Thomas Nashe's *Pierce Penniless* (1592) mentions a scene that does not exist in any of the surviving Henry plays. So Shakespeare's *Henry V* must have been one of at least three plays on this subject. Scholars believe that the play was probably written in 1598–1599 and perhaps performed for the first time to celebrate the opening of the Globe in mid-1599 (see "Publication History" for dating the play). According to the 1600 quarto it had been played "sundry times," attesting to the work's initial popularity. However, other than a single 1605 revival for court, there is no evidence of a major revival of Shakespeare's play until 1738.

During the beginning of eighteenth century, the play was quite popular as a source for other productions. Fluellen and Pistol star in Charles Molloy's *The Half-Pay Officers* (1720). *King Henry the Fifth or The Conquest of France by the English* (1721), by Aaron Hill, is also loosely based on Shakespeare's production. Hill's play, however, takes great liberties with the story line. Cutting the battle and tavern scenes, Hill recreates Katherine as the heroine of the play and features Harriet, a woman Henry seduces and abandons, and who eventually commits suicide. Though this is not Shakespeare's play, it is an interesting record of the tastes of the times. The association between the play and politics has been present since the first productions, and revivals of the play tend to occur at times of war and national crisis. During the latter half of the eighteenth century, the wars with France and the ensuing Francophobia excited renewed interest in the play. During the Seven Years War (1756–1763), Covent Garden had a production of *Henry V* every season. John Philip Kemble, the leading actor of the times, played Henry sixteen times between 1789 and 1792. These productions tended to cut the play in order to glorify Henry's heroism and the national unity he creates, resulting in a text that closely resembles the quarto of 1600.

Every major nineteenth century producer staged *Henry V*. William Macready's 1839 production is famous for Clarkson Stanfield's use of dioramas (painted cloths mounted on a pair of rollers). Dioramas were created for Agincourt, the king's reentry into London, and for representing the back-and-forth movement across the English Channel. Macready also reinstated the part of the Chorus, stressing in the playbill that the production was a "dramatic history." The focus on the visual spectacle continued well into the Victorian age. Charles Kean in 1859 stressed the pageantry and spectacle of the play by moving the battle scene onstage, filling the stage with people, guns, smoke, and noise. Despite the spectacular nature of Kean's production, the most popular of the Victorian revivals was Charles Calvert's. In 1872 Calvert returned Katherine's English lessons to the text (though he placed the scene directly before the wooing scene), and the New York and touring versions of this production featured George Ringold's riding in on a white horse named Crispin. The emphasis on spectacle continued into early twentieth century with Frank Benson's legendary pole-vault in full armor onto the walls of Harfleur (1897–1916).

During World War I the play was very popular, and it remained in production during the 1920s and 1930s. Response to the play during World War II was largely shaped by Laurence Olivier's 1937 Old Vic production (translated to the screen in 1944). This larger than life portrayal embodied the patriotism of the English people.

Productions since Olivier's have either followed its portrayal of the heroic king (as the 1975 Hand/Howard version, Royal Shakespeare Company) or reacted strongly against it (as the 1989 Michael Bogdanov production, English Shakespeare Company).

Notable twentieth-century productions include the 1964 Peter Hall version (Royal Shakespeare Company), performed in battle uniforms against a backdrop of war footage, and Adrian Noble's 1984–1985 (Royal Shakespeare Company) staging with its rain besieging troops marching in France. Noble featured Kenneth Branagh as a king who drops to his knees, cries as he prays, and falls off a ladder at Harfleur. Michael Bognadov (English Shakespeare Company, 1989) popularized producing the history plays in sequence. Starting with *Richard II* and running through *Henry V* (he later added the *Henry VI* plays and *Richard III*), this interpretation focused on the development of the king and the loss of the Eastcheap tavern humor. Michael Pennington starred as a sensitive, mature, and exhausted antiwar king in this post Falklands production.

There are two influential film versions of *Henry V*: the 1944 Olivier production and the 1989 movie starring Kenneth Branagh. Dedicated to the Royal Air Force, Olivier's World War II production displays a powerful wartime sentiment by celebrating the theatricality and patriotism of Henry. The movie starts by looking at a play, *Henry V*, being performed on stage at the Globe. As the movie proceeds, Olivier creates a more and more mimetic vision, moving from the stylized acting of the Globe, to pictorial settings for act 1 and the French Court, and finally to a real landscape for the battle of Agincourt. The movie focuses on the play's artful construction, and it is undeniably visually stunning. Using bright colors and a rousing musical score by William Walton, the film created a public interest in Shakespeare while maintaining its artistic appeal.

Olivier's king is heroic and charismatic. By cutting almost half of the play (1700 lines), Olivier emphasized the heroic nature of Henry. He eliminated the bishops' discussion of the parliamentary bill to confiscate church lands, the incident with the three traitors, Henry's ruthless threats to Harfleur, his approval of Bardolph's hanging, his admission of his father's fault in taking the crown, and, of course, the order to kill the French prisoners. Usually placing Henry in the center of a large group of people, this film portrays a valiant leader. The famous "band of brothers" speech begins as Henry steps onto a cart, making it his stage. As the speech builds to its climax, the camera moves slowly back from its tight focus on the king to show an increasingly large group of people gathered around Henry. By the end of the shot, the vast number of people surrounding the king is stunning.

Kenneth Branagh's 1989 film responds to the artistic statement made by Olivier. His movie is darker, using dingy, earthy colors. Branagh's film was not made during a time when the country pulled together under a war effort, but rather in a climate that had become suspicious of war. Using some of Olivier's devices, like the cart and the long shot for the "band of brothers" speech, Branagh creates a heroic king but balances that figure with a more personal, emotional man. Critics often turn to the scene after the battle at Agincourt as emblematic of Branagh's artistic statement. After the bodies are counted, Henry finds and carries the body of the dead Boy as the strains of *Non nobis* (a song, based on Psalm 115, that gives thanks to God) reach their crescendo. Carrying the Boy's body through the mud to the cart epitomizes the internal dynamic of Branagh's king. Whereas Olivier's film featured long shots with Henry surrounded by groups of men, Branagh emphasizes the in-

Henry V (Kenneth Branagh, center) rouses his tired and ailing troops for battle against France in Branagh's 1989 film *Henry V*. Courtesy of Photofest.

ternal nature of the king by using closer shots focusing on Henry's eyes. The emotional pull of Branagh's play is shown by Derek Jacobi's Chorus, who moves from stepping over cameras and opening doors in the beginning, to ducking into trenches and displaying true sadness in the Epilogue as he relates Henry VI's future loss of France and England.

As king, Branagh presents a multifaceted man. He includes flashbacks to make Falstaff's loss more touching by revealing the warmth the king's former companion brought to the scenes, but he also reveals the cool and calculating Henry. The fire in his eyes as he responds to the tennis balls jest is chilling. The bloodlust looks and feels absolutely real as he threatens Harfleur, but his relief after the town surrenders is revealed as he half closes his eyes. The movie is ultimately ambivalent about war, showing a victory that is sanctioned by God, yet still allowing viewers to feel the loss of the dead Boy Branagh carries across the field.

EXPLICATION OF KEY PASSAGES

Prologue. "O for a muse . . . our play." The Chorus opens the play by evoking an epic scope that is simultaneously both restrictive and expansive. He asks for "A kingdom for a stage, princes to act, / And monarchs to behold the swelling scene!" (ll. 3–4). The objects of the sentence move into increasingly restrictive groups (anyone in the audience can be in the kingdom, only a few can be princes, and only one the monarch), but they also expand across the hierarchy of social class from pauper to king. At the same time, these two lines create an outwardly moving gaze of the theater by moving the focus from the "stage," to the actor, and finally to the viewer who will "behold." Properly prepared for the power the theater can invoke, the audience is now reminded that the stage is "unworthy" and the actors are "ciphers" and "flat unraised spirits" since they can never alone recapture the grandeur of Henry's reign or show the splendor of troops marching into battle at Agincourt (Prol. 10, 17, 9). The Chorus continues to balance the expansiveness of imagination with the restrictive appearance of the implements of acting. The name Agincourt arouses the patriotic feelings of the audience and creates a desire to see this battle. But to get to that victory, the audience members will have to invoke their imaginations, collaborating with the performers, to make up for the deficit in the theater. The Chorus apologizes for breaking the unity of time and collapsing into this one play events that occurred between 1414 and 1420. He ends by asking the audience to hear and judge the play kindly. In the Renaissance, the word "kind" carries multiple meanings, indicating nice or generous, but also type (human kind) and kin or family. The Chorus asks the audience to judge the play as English, as the "kind" of men they are, as well as kindly (nicely).

1.2.33–113. "Then hear me, . . . cold for action." The Archbishop of Canterbury discusses whether the king can "with right and conscience" claim the throne of France (1.2.96). This scene is important because it provides the audience with the justification for Henry's war. The speech follows the clergymen's discussion, where they revealed possible ulterior motives for the war, but the detail, length, and structure of the speech create a strong sense that Henry's claim is just. Each audience must decide for itself whether or not the war is justified. The argument is that the French have stated that the Salic Law bars Henry from inheriting France because the Salic land cannot be inherited through female lines: "'In terram Salicam mulieres ne succedant,' / 'No woman shall succeed in Salique land'" (1.2.38–39). The archbishop argues that the Salic Law does not bar Henry's claim because the Salic land is not France, but the land between the rivers Sala and Elbe, that is, Germany. He also explains that the French king has himself inherited through female lines and that Henry's claim (through his great-great-grandmother Queen Isabella, Edward II's French wife) is stronger than that of the French king. Thus Henry is the rightful king of France. He finishes by asserting that the Bible itself, in the Book of Numbers 27:8, states that inheritance can "[d]escend unto a daughter" (1.2.100).

The speech can be taken as a clear justification for Henry's claim. It may also be read as a confusing pleading. The welter of names and dates is confusing even when read slowly. Heard, the speech is even harder to follow. At the conclusion of the argument, even Henry V seems uncertain what to make of the presentation and asks again whether his claim is just.

The archbishop's address now shifts from detailed legal argument to patriotism, and Ely, Exeter, and Westmerland second this appeal. Henry's claim now rests on the wars waged by Henry V's ancestors, and Edward the Black Prince's victory at Crécy (1346) becomes the precedent for Henry V's invasion. Legality (whether questionable or not the viewer must decide), patriotism, and finally bribery (1.2.132–135) combine to drive Henry to pursue his claim.

3.4. Until recently, the scene with Katherine and Alice was seen as comic relief that provided a break from the imagery and violence of the Harfleur threat that precedes it. Katherine's butchering of the English language offers a funny alternative to the actual butchery of war. "Sin" instead of "chin," "nick" rather than "neck" (3.4.36) serve as amusing malapropisms, as amusing, and as innocent, as Fluellen's Welsh accent.

The scene is, however, structurally significant, providing a new perspective on the events just witnessed. Henry describes himself as "a soldier" (3.3.5), as he does later in his 5.2. wooing, when he threatens the citizens of Harfleur with the "bloody hand" that will move over the "fresh fair virgins" with "hot and forcing violation" (3.3.12, 14, 21). Katherine's language lesson, presumably required by England's invasion, begins with her hand and proceeds to anatomize her body by Anglicizing it. The scene ends with the realization that the Englishing of her body ultimately ends in a sexual way with a bilingual sexual pun ("de foot, le count," 3.4.59). Supporters of a positive reading of the play argue that the threats to Harfleur are merely rhetoric and that the rhetoric is strong enough to enable the king to avoid physical violence. Rhetoric, however, in Katherine's scene, symbolically turns a virginal French body into a sexualized English colony.

4.3.18–67. "What's he . . . upon St. Crispin's Day." Westmerland, learning how outnumbered the English army is, longs for "one ten thousand" of the men idling back home in England (4.3.17). Henry overhears him and uses the occasion to speak to his men, this time leaving behind the imperatives of Harfleur in favor of a personal address focused on "we" and revealing his desires as an "I." Insisting that he would not wish one more man from England, Henry argues that if the troops in France are to die, they are enough to do the "country loss," but if they live, "The fewer men, the greater share of honor" (4.3.21, 22). Presenting honor as a product (one the king himself covets) that can be bought in battle sets up an egalitarian vision that allows any man to attain what the king desires. By repeating (with slight variation) the phrase "not one man more" (4.3.23, 30, 32) until the climactic "Oh, do not wish one more!" of line 33, the king shows that his desire for this honor is real, thus inspiring his men to share with him as equals. To enforce the idea that the men will buy honor, Henry offers a vision of the future. Focusing the men's imaginations (as the Chorus has focused that of the audience), Henry anticipates a future version of the battle, a version that each man can write himself into. He describes how on the eve of St. Crispian's Day (October 25, the date of the battle of Agincourt) the men will have a feast and will brag to their neighbors, showing their battle scars as badges of courage and pride. They will talk about "Harry the King" and the other nobles who fought alongside them as equals (4.3.53). The use of the familiar "Harry" asserts that the men are equals if they stay and fight, equal even to the king himself, "From this day to the ending of the world" (4.3.58). Henry continues to build the idea that battle will create equality as he concludes by repeating his key images of honor, bravery, equality, and strength in fewness:

> We few, we happy few, we band of brothers;
> For he to-day that sheds his blood with me
> Shall be my brother; be he ne'er so vile,
> This day shall gentle his condition. (4.3.60–63)

The vision of the soldiers' recounting the battle "with advantages" (4.3.50), that is, with exaggerated accounts of their actions, offers a bit of humor in a tense situation. It also implies that the soldiers will survive to tell those stories and so glosses over the immediate danger that might dismay the English.

After the battle, the rhetoric of brotherhood is left behind. Henry reads out the English dead: "Edward the Duke of York, the Earl of Suffolk, / Sir Richard Ketly, Davy Gam, esquire; / None else of name" (4.8.103–105). The list is hierarchical, not egalitarian, and the common soldiers are not even named, and are certainly not treated as the king's brothers. The speech is a magnificent lie that is the pinnacle of the play. In *Henry V* the Battle of Agincourt is not shown. Words, not arms, triumph. Harfleur surrenders to a speech, and after Henry's address to his troops in 4.3 the French have no chance. As the greatest wielder of the English language knew, the word is mightier than the sword.

Annotated Bibliography

Greenblatt, Stephen. "Invisible Bullets." In *Shakespearean Negotiations: The Circulation of Social Energy in Renaissance England*. Berkeley: U of California P, 1988. 21–65. Greenblatt investigates the connection between monarchical power and theater with particular emphasis on the transformation of Hal from profligate to king.

Mason, Pamela. "*Henry V*: 'the quick forge and working house of thought.'" In *The Cambridge Companion to Shakespeare's History Plays*. Ed. Michael Hattaway. Cambridge: Cambridge UP, 2002. Mason provides an excellent discussion of the importance of the Chorus and of Katherine.

Rabkin, Norman. "Rabbits, Ducks, and Henry V." *Shakespeare Quarterly* 28.3 (1977): 279–297. Rabkin investigates the opposing critical views of Henry as ideal king or as Machiavellian ruler. He maintains that though it is possible to see both interpretations, they are ultimately irreconcilable.

Saccio, Peter. "*Henry V*: The King Victorious." In *Shakespeare's English Kings: History, Chronicle, and Drama*. London: Oxford UP, 1977, 2000. 65–89. Saccio presents a close examination of the historical Henry V and Shakespeare's *Henry V*, noting where the drama is consistent with, partially consistent with, or entirely different from the historical king.

Smith, Emma. *King Henry V*. Shakespeare in Production Series. Cambridge: Cambridge UP, 2002. Smith provides an elaborately detailed account of *Henry V* in production, including a table listing all known major productions.

Taylor, David. "Introduction." In *Henry V*. The Oxford Shakespeare. Oxford: Oxford UP, 1982. This introduction, though a bit old, is still one of the most detailed and concise looks at the important themes, structures, and arguments in the play.

Henry VIII

Yashdip S. Bains

PLOT SUMMARY

Prologue. The speaker assures the spectators that they will watch a play "weighty" and "serious" (l. 2), "full of state and woe" (l. 3). He states that the "To make that only true we now intend" (l. 21), that is, to present what really happened. The line puns on the play's subtitle (or perhaps its original title), *All Is True*.

1.1. The Duke of Norfolk describes to the Duke of Buckingham and Lord Aburgavenny the colorful meeting in France between Henry VIII and the French king, organized by Cardinal Wolsey. This meeting place, in the Vale of Andren, in Picardy, was known as the Field of the Cloth of Gold because of its sumptuous display of wealth. The meeting occurred in June 1520. Buckingham expresses surprise at Wolsey's exercise of power. The three lords continue their exchange and regret that the peace with France has already broken down. When Wolsey joins them, Wolsey and Buckingham look at each other disdainfully. The cardinal speaks to his secretary about an imminent interview with Buckingham's surveyor and leaves. He lets Buckingham know that the duke will be humiliated soon. Buckingham discloses to Norfolk his plan to reveal to Henry VIII that Wolsey is accepting bribes from the Holy Roman Emperor Charles to prevent an Anglo-French alliance. Brandon and other officials arrest Buckingham for high treason.

1.2. King Henry, Cardinal Wolsey, and courtiers enter. According to the stage directions, Henry is leaning on Wolsey's shoulder, thus providing visual evidence of the king's dependence on his Lord Chancellor. Queen Katherine is ushered in by the Duke of Norfolk. She denounces Wolsey's special taxes. The king does not know about them, voids the order, and pardons their defaulters. Wolsey whispers to his secretary to give him credit for the change. The queen also protests that the charges made against Buckingham by his surveyor are wrong, but the king still upholds his indictment for high treason.

1.3. While on the way to attend a dinner at the cardinal's palace, York Place, in Westminster, the Lord Chamberlain, Lord Sands, and Sir Thomas Lovell declare their disapproval of French fashions. They also note Wolsey's generosity.

1.4. Henry VIII and his party disguise themselves as shepherds and enter Wolsey's dinner. They choose partners and dance. The King's partner is Anne Bullen; he unmasks and leads her into the banquet.

2.1. Two gentlemen express their sympathy for Buckingham, who has been condemned to death. Buckingham appears and proclaims his innocence. He forgives those who have brought about his downfall. After Buckingham leaves, the gentlemen reveal that the cardinal or someone else close to the king has prompted Henry to launch divorce proceedings against Katherine, to be taken up in front of Cardinal Campeius, who has just arrived from Rome. Katherine had married Henry's older brother, Arthur, in 1501. When Arthur died in 1508, Henry received a papal dispensation to marry his sister-in-law. In 1527 Henry began to have misgivings about his union as being incestuous.

2.2. The Lord Chamberlain enters reading aloud a letter stating that Wolsey has taken some of the lord's horses. Norfolk and the Duke of Suffolk enter and speak against the cardinal's plots. The thoughtful king sends Norfolk and Suffolk away; he receives Campeius and Wolsey and speaks to Wolsey's secretary, Stephen Gardiner. Campeius implies that Wolsey envied his former secretary so much that he caused the man's death. Wolsey replies, "He was a fool— / For he would needs be virtuous" (2.2.131–132). Gardiner will prove more malleable. The king sends Gardiner to tell the queen that her case will be debated at Blackfriars, where the play itself was staged.

2.3. Anne Bullen speaks sympathetically with an Old Lady about the queen's difficulties. The Old Lady suggests that Anne may be exhibiting a bit of hypocrisy, since the king has elevated her to be Marchioness of Pembroke. The Old Lady says that Anne will be queen, but Anne claims to lack ambition and to feel sorry for Katherine.

2.4. In the very room where Katherine's case was heard on June 18, 1529, Shakespeare reenacts the divorce proceedings against Katherine. The queen argues with dignity for the legality of her marriage and for her life as a loyal wife. She refuses to accept the authority of a court on which Wolsey sits as judge; she submits a petition to the pope and leaves. The king gives an account of his concerns about the legality of his marriage to Katherine on account of the question of the legitimacy of his children. Katherine's marriage to his older brother has pricked the king's conscience and made him disturbed over the taint of incest. But he also announces that he will obey its verdict if the court delivers in her favor. Acting evasively, Campeius postpones the proceedings. The king places his hopes in his adviser, Thomas Cranmer, and says that he distrusts the cardinals and the "tricks of Rome" (2.4.238).

3.1. As if at work among her women, Katherine listens to a song. Wolsey and Campeius advise her strongly to agree to a divorce. Furiously protesting that they use English instead of Latin, the queen sticks to her position with courage, but gradually she sinks into grief.

3.2. Norfolk, Suffolk, Lord Surrey, and the Lord Chamberlain have consolidated their position against the cardinal. The king has seen the letter in which the cardinal advised the pope to disallow the divorce. With Cranmer's approval, Henry VIII has married Anne Bullen. The Lords are delighted when an unhappy Wolsey is called before the king, who has accidentally come across an inventory of the cardinal's personal property. The king commends Wolsey's service with sarcasm and withdraws. He leaves behind for Wolsey's perusal a list of holdings and his letter to the pope. The Lords come back to demand that Wolsey hand over the seal of authority into their hands; they order him to stay in Asher House under arrest, and state that the king has confiscated all his property. Standing alone, Wolsey bids good-bye to his glory, and Thomas Cromwell shares his grief with him. Cromwell gives him the news that Sir Thomas More has become the new chancellor, Cranmer the Archbishop of Canterbury, and Anne Bullen the new queen. Moved to tears by Cromwell's loyalty and sympathy, the disgraced Wolsey calls upon him to fling away ambition and to serve his king uprightly.

4.1. Two gentlemen describe the order of the coronation of Anne Bullen. A third gentleman gives details of the coronation itself and speaks of the discord between Cranmer and Gardiner, now Bishop of Winchester.

4.2. Queen Katherine, sick in bed, learns of Wolsey's death from Griffith, her usher, who lauds his good qualities and is sure that he repented his sins. Katherine responds by saying that Wolsey was an ambitious and corrupt priest. She falls asleep and has a vision of six personages in white robes who hold a garland over her head. Griffith and Patience, her woman, feel she is about to die. Capuchius, ambassador from her nephew Holy Roman Emperor Charles V, visits her. Katherine gives him a letter for the king requesting him to take good care of her daughter, Mary Tudor, and breathes her last.

5.1. Lovell tells Gardiner that Anne Bullen is in labor; Gardiner wishes that Anne, Cranmer, and Cromwell were dead. Gardiner has brought charges of heresy against Cranmer, who will be interrogated the next day. Meeting privately with Cranmer, the king cautions him about the plots of his enemies and gives him a ring as a mark of his protection. The Old Lady tells Henry that Anne has delivered a child. Henry hopes it is a boy. She replies that "'tis a girl / Promises boys hereafter" (5.1.165–166).

5.2. The Council insult Cranmer by having him wait outside the council chamber. Aware of this behavior, Dr. Butts has placed the king at a window above so that he can secretly watch the meeting. Gardiner and his faction accuse Cranmer of being a heretic. Cromwell comes to Cranmer's defense, but the council still want to send him to the Tower. Gardiner and his friends feel uncomfortable when Cranmer produces the king's ring. The king enters and reproaches Gardiner for his cruel nature; he forces the council to respect Cranmer and compels Gardiner to embrace Cranmer. He also shows his support for Cranmer by requesting him to be his daughter's godfather.

5.3. A porter and his man try in vain to keep under control the mob rushing to watch the state christening, and the Lord Chamberlain abuses the two men.

5.4. During the grand and colorful ceremony of Princess Elizabeth's baptism, Cranmer prophesies that the years of her and her successor's reigns will be golden ages.

Epilogue. This brief sonnet (though in rhymed couplets) states that the play will not please those who have come to sleep, since the trumpets will have awakened them. Those who came to hear abuse of the mercantile class will also be disappointed. Only good women will like the play, because "such a one we showed 'em" (l. 11). Whether that "one" is the Catholic Queen Katherine or the Protestant Anne Bullen the epilogue does not say, though Katherine has the bigger part. The epilogue concludes that if the good women applaud the play, the "best men" will, too (l. 13).

PUBLICATION HISTORY

The Famous History of the Life of King Henry the Eighth appeared for the first time in the Folio in 1623 as the last of the items in the second section, the histories. Most editors consider it to be a carefully edited text that is generally free of errors. The Folio provides act and scene divisions and contains elaborate stage directions for scenes of pageantry. Although assigned by the Folio editors exclusively to Shakespeare, most editors since the middle of the nineteenth century have speculated that John Fletcher may have composed some of its scenes. James Spedding raised questions about authorship in 1850 on account of his feeling about the inconsistency of style and incoherence of design. Spedding assigned Shakespeare 1.1–1.2, 2.3–4, 3.2.1–203, and 5.1 ("Who Wrote Shakespeare's *Henry VIII,*" *The Gentleman's Magazine* n.s. 34 [August 1850]: 115–123). Samuel Hickson arrived at a similar conclusion on his own the same year. Scholars differ in their assignment of scenes to Shakespeare and Fletcher. Hickson divided the play in this way:

Prologue	Fletcher
1.1 and 2	Shakespeare
1.3 and 4	Fletcher
2.1 and 2	Fletcher
2.3 and 4	Shakespeare
3.1	Fletcher
3.2.1–203	Shakespeare
3.2.204–459	Fletcher
4.1 and 2	Fletcher
5.1	Shakespeare
5.2, 3, 4	Fletcher
Epilogue	Fletcher

Questions of authorship cannot be determined on the basis of internal or stylistic evidence alone; hence it would be difficult to resolve the problem clearly. The stylistic tests based on peculiarities of syntax, vocabulary, spelling or orthography cannot be anything but inconclusive. Perhaps it is safer to defer to the authority of the First Folio and to accept Shakespeare's exclusive authorship of the play.

The Globe Theatre burned down on June 29, 1613, during a performance of a play about King Henry VIII. According to Sir Henry Wotton's account of the fire, it was a new play, entitled *All Is True*:

The King's players had a new play, called All is true, representing some principal pieces of the reign of Henry VIII, which was set forth with many extraordinary circumstances of Pomp and Majesty, even to the matting of the stage; the Knights of the Order, with their Georges and garters, the Guards with their embroidered coats, and the like: sufficient in truth within a while to make greatness very familiar, if not ridiculous. Now, King Henry making a masque at the Cardinal Wolsey's house, and certain chambers being shot off at his entry, some of the paper, or other stuff, wherewith one of them was stopped, did light on the thatch, where being thought first but an idle smoke, and their eyes more attentive to the show, it kindled inwardly, and ran round like a train, consuming within less than an hour the whole house to the very grounds. (quoted in McMullan, p. 59)

This play is probably *Henry VIII*, and one may infer from Wotton's comments that a new play on the stage in June may have been written during the first six months of 1613.

Foakes has suggested persuasively, if not supported by evidence, that Shakespeare may have created the play for a royal wedding: "It was an appropriate time for him to do so, when the great protestant wedding of Princess Elizabeth [daughter of James I and Anne of Denmark] to Prince Frederick [the Elector Palatine] was taking place, and recalling for many, with some nostalgia, the days of Queen Elizabeth" (xliv). The festivities before the marriage included performances of twenty plays in three months, eight of which were Shakespeare's. It seems most likely that *Henry VIII* would make a suitable piece for a celebration or a coronation (it was staged in 1727 and 1953 for the coronations of George II and Elizabeth II, respectively). This would make clear the use of masques and pageants, which were popular in the early seventeenth century, especially to celebrate marriages (see, for example, *The Tempest*, 4.1).

SOURCES FOR THE PLAY

Shakespeare's primary source for the play seems to be the third volume of Raphael Holinshed's *Chronicles of England, Scotland and Ireland*, published in 1587. Shakespeare also relied on Foxe's *Acts and Monuments* (1597) for the details about Thomas Cranmer in act 5. Some of the language can be traced back to Edward Halle's narration about Henry VIII, and some of it in Wolsey's farewell speeches may be derived from John Speed's *The History of Great Britain* (1611).

Playwrights create new versions of past history through the process of selection, omission, and addition, which determine the distinctive features of the new work. Shakespeare modified and altered historical events to create his own version of history instead of being limited by his sources. "Not only did Shakespeare transfer material from one time and person to another," says R. A. Foakes, "he also amalgamated stories from different sources, or took a phrase or an idea from a source not otherwise followed in the particular context" (xxxvi). Shakespeare also altered chronology to convey a strong idea of an unbroken sequence of events in his plot. He moved the date of Buckingham's trial in 1521 closer to Henry's acquaintance with Anne during a masque at Wolsey's house; Anne had not been at the masque. Shakespeare lets Henry and Anne's marriage take place before Wolsey's fall 1529; the actual date of marriage is 1532. Queen Katherine died in 1536, but in Shakespeare she is dead before Elizabeth's birth in 1533.

Shakespeare arranged dates and events to create a unified pattern of his interpretation of history. His deliberate alterations conform to his presentation of events in such a way as to reinforce the authority of James I as the rightful successor of his Protestant ancestors—Henry VIII and Queen Elizabeth.

STRUCTURE AND PLOTTING

John Heminge and Henry Condell divided Shakespeare's works into three genres: comedies, histories, and tragedies. Thus they went beyond the traditional classification of comedy and tragedy and presented histories as a new type that had been recently taken up by dramatists like Christopher Marlowe and further developed by Shakespeare. History, for Shakespeare, was not understandable through the medieval providential view of human life that begins with Creation and ends with Judgment, thus providing a beginning and an end to human affairs. The Elizabethan world order was not a continuation of the medieval one. Shakespeare discovered "the Tudor myth" in chroniclers like Hall and imposed it on his history plays, but his focus was the roots of disorder, disunity, and disharmony in the national narrative. He composed *Henry VIII* as a triumph of peace and prosperity over war and hardship.

Shakespeare adopts a secular view of time that does not end with Judgment. Unlike the writers of the mystery plays, which deal with events like Creation and Fall as examples of God's intervention, Shakespeare examines history as a sequence of interactions of human beings within the framework of secular time. David Kastan explains the shift:

> [Shakespeare's] vision is historical rather than historicist, confined to the continuum of human time. Though the orthodox schema of Tudor history does find occasional voice in the mouths of individual characters, the over-all dramatic articulation of the history plays more persuasively argues that we see them as firmly oriented in the world of time with no supra-historical perspective to redeem the post-lapsarian experience they portray. (269)

But *Henry VIII* differs from the earlier history plays in one respect. Since it belongs to the playwright's late period, it looks forward to the rule of forgiveness and reconciliation under Elizabeth I and her successor.

What unifies the structure of *Henry VIII* are the joys and sorrows of the king who watches over and determines the fortunes of the Duke of Buckingham, Cardinal Wolsey, Queen Katherine, and Anne Bullen. By the end of the play, Henry VIII has gained much self-knowledge, so that he begins to rule with confidence. In this parade of awe-inspiring figures, Shakespeare is focusing on a sequence of sensational conflicts and trials and the attempts of individuals to make decisions that shape their present and future. The most prominent players in politics are Henry VIII and Cardinal Wolsey. The king wins; the cardinal loses. Each individual follows and is limited by his or her own perspective, and Shakespeare lets each character have his (or her) say. This structure allows Shakespeare to say, *All Is True*. He presents each episode from multiple perspectives. The spectacle of the Field of the Cloth of Gold in France, organized by Wolsey, is impressive, but it did not achieve the desired political results and cost too much money. Buckingham and Norfolk criticize the cardinal severely, and Wolsey interrupts them and fixes his eye on Buckingham. The duke hopes to speak to the king about the "cunning Cardinal," but Wolsey outsmarts him. However, the accusations against Wolsey foreshadow Wolsey's fall later.

Time tells everything, and time never stops. It establishes Buckingham's innocence and confirms Cardinal Wolsey's treacheries. The king is neither a saint nor a villain; he is one of the figures engaged in a power struggle with domestic and foreign enemies. Wolsey weeps at the downturn in his fortune. Anne celebrates her coronation. Queen Katherine sleeps and witnesses a vision of glory in heaven. Gardiner, the Bishop of Winchester, emulates Wolsey's hideous schemes and plots against Cranmer. The king decides to defend Cranmer and gives him a ring. When he is in heaven, King Henry "shall desire / To see what this child does," and praise his Maker (5.4.67–68). James I, Elizabeth's successor, is secure on his throne, and there is peace and plenty in the foreseeable future.

Shakespeare orders the events in accordance with a controlling and unifying plan. The king's inaction at Buckingham's trial is balanced against his intervention in that of Thomas Cranmer's at the end. Queen Anne's terrestrial coronation is balanced against Queen Katherine's spiritual coronation. None of Shakespeare's earlier history plays had concentrated so sharply on the sheer splendor of the royalty that watches and presides over the fates of Buckingham, Queen Katherine, Cardinal Wolsey, and Thomas Cranmer. Richard II and other kings were fighting civil wars and disorder and struggling for their lives. Whereas their lives end in death and disgrace, Henry VIII's marches toward a triumphant climax. Its structure confirms that *Henry VIII* is a study in the nation's achievement of peace and stability.

MAIN CHARACTERS

Henry VIII

The parade of characters on stage includes some of the grand figures of British history—Henry VIII, the Duke of Buckingham, Queen Katherine, Anne Bullen, Cardinal Wolsey, Thomas Cranmer, and Princess Elizabeth. Shakespeare's Henry VIII gains self-knowledge and exercises authority over his kingdom by the end of the play. Each public meeting or trial has given him insights about himself and the persons around him. Sitting in clear view of the people on his throne of state, he confronts enormous political and private challenges that strain and test his abilities. His political and personal affairs intermingle and lead to the break with Rome and the creation of the Church of England with himself as its head. His handling of public grievances over excessive taxation reveals his empathy with the people. The king is neither a Machiavellian nor an agent of God's providence; an astute politician, he grows in stature in the course of the play and acts in his country's best interest.

The king's agony over his divorce and his unwillingness to live with his marriage win him sympathy. It is not easy for him to annul his marriage with Katherine, as he confesses to Wolsey:

> O my lord,
> Would it not grieve an able man to leave
> So sweet a bedfellow? But conscience, conscience!
> O, 'tis a tender place, and I must leave her. (2.2.140–143)

A little later, he admits to Wolsey that Katherine is "noble born; / And like her true nobility she has / Carried herself towards me" (2.4.142–144). During the negotiations for a marriage of Henry's daughter Mary and the Duke of Orleans, the Bishop of Bayonne raised questions about Mary's legitimacy, explains Henry VIII:

> This respite shook
> The bosom of my conscience, enter'd me,

Yea, with a spitting power, and made to tremble
The reign of my breast, which forc'd such way,
That many maz'd considerings did throng
And press'd in with this caution. (2.4.182–187)

The king gets angry with the cardinals when he realizes that they are ignoring the urgency of his dilemma:

I may perceive
These Cardinals trifle with me; I abhor
This dilatory sloth and tricks of Rome. (2.4.236–238)

This moment crystallizes the king's earnestness about divorce and his decision to break with Rome.

The king leans heavily on Wolsey, but as he observes the cardinal's machinations and arrogance and pride he begins to see through the tyrannical use of power and accumulation of wealth. Henry comes upon a list of Wolsey's properties and questions him slyly about all the favors Henry and his father have done for the cardinal. After hearing Wolsey's professions of loyalty, Henry surprises him and puts the papers on the table:

Take notice, lords, he has a loyal breast,
For you have seen him open't. Read o'er this,
And after, this, and then to breakfast with
What appetite you have. (3.2.200–203)

Henry exits, frowning upon the cardinal; the nobles throng after him, smiling and whispering.

By the time the plot against Thomas Cranmer, Archbishop of Canterbury, begins to mature under Stephen Gardiner, the Bishop of Winchester, Henry has acquired full control over himself and his kingdom. He protects Cranmer from his accusers. He stands hidden at a window above and watches how his council humiliates Cranmer. He intervenes in Cranmer's behalf and reprimands his council: "I had thought I had had men of some understanding / And wisdom of my Council; but I find none" (5.2.170–171). Some of the councillors act against Cranmer out of malice, and the king will never give them a chance to do harm "while I live" (5.2.182). Henry VIII proves himself to be a strong monarch when he modestly thanks the archbishop for the prophecy about Queen Elizabeth's reign: "Thou hast made me now a man!" (5.4.64).

Buckingham

The Duke of Buckingham is a powerful nobleman in England and fully aware of the cardinal's machinations and manipulations, so that he calls him a "holy fox, / Or wolf, or both" (1.1.158–159). But Wolsey beats him in the political game and gets him arrested for high treason by using the duke's surveyor as a witness against him. When Katherine speaks in favor of the duke, the king assures her that Buckingham "is become as black / As if besmear'd in hell" (1.2.123–124). During his trial, the duke spoke sometime "in choler, ill, and hasty," but generally he "show'd a most noble patience," according to the First Gentleman (2.1.34, 36). The Second Gentleman calls him "the mirror of all courtesy" (2.1.53), and the First Gentleman speaks of him as a "noble ruin'd man" (2.1.54). A prominent participant in the country's politics, Buckingham exhibits immense patience, humility, and charity in his final words, but he also strikes a realistic note about being careful about the treacherous behavior of friends (2.1.124–131). He dies forgiving everyone and wishing his king a long life. At this point in the play the king is too inexperienced to see through the cardinal's designs and save Buckingham.

Queen Katherine

Queen Katherine has been divorced, but Shakespeare gives her fair treatment throughout the play. Shakespeare created a scene in which she opposes excessive taxation and holds Cardinal Wolsey responsible for it. She reminds her husband that Wolsey's action has tarnished his name. Her next appearance is at her trial. Katherine approaches the king and speaks about her precarious position:

> I am a most poor woman, and a stranger,
> Born out of your dominions; having here
> No judge indifferent, nor no more assurance
> Of equal friendship and proceeding. (2.4.15–18)

She would like her trial postponed until she has consulted her friends in Spain, but she has no success. She believes that Wolsey is her enemy who has "blown this coal betwixt my lord and me" (2.4.79). She leaves the court after nobly defending herself.

Shakespeare moves the audience in her favor when he shows Katherine asking her maid to sing a song:

> In sweet music is such art,
> Killing care and grief of heart
> Fall asleep, or hearing, die. (3.1.12–14)

When she receives Cardinals Wolsey and Campeius, she stands firm in her position and tells them how hypocritical they are in their advice. A little later, Griffith, her Gentleman Usher, informs her that Wolsey has died. She asks Griffith for somber music and slips into deep sleep. Katherine has a heavenly vision of six personages clad in white robes. Shakespeare treats Katherine with great sympathy and lets her earn the distinction of being the only Catholic character given a heavenly vision. Henry has no complaint against her. She wakes up and still remembers what she saw:

> They promis'd me eternal happiness,
> And brought me garlands, Griffith, which I feel
> I am not worthy yet to wear. (4.2.90–92)

She instructs her maids to scatter "maiden flowers" over her body and to bury her like a queen:

> When I am dead, good wench,
> Let me be us'd with honor; strew me over
> With maiden flowers, that all the world may know
> I was a chaste wife to my grave. Embalm me,
> Then lay me forth. Although unqueen'd, yet like
> A queen, and daughter of a king, inter me. (4.2.167–172)

Katherine has lost her husband, but she has gained God's kingdom. She remains sympathetic and noble throughout. A champion of the people against excessive taxation, an opponent of tyrannical and hypocritical actions by Wolsey and others, and a defender of her marriage and loyalty to Henry VIII, Katherine, a Roman Catholic, has nothing in her past to cast a shadow on her dignity. Her condemnation of Wolsey's behavior is a foreshadowing of Protestant critiques of the Catholic Church, and she is a reformer pitted against a corrupt Wolsey.

Anne Bullen

Shakespeare did not delineate Anne Bullen in much detail beyond the essentials of her part in Henry's struggle with divorce, her coronation, and Elizabeth's christening. She is seen in a sexual situation in Wolsey's grand banquet sitting next to Lord Sandys, who kisses her. The king chooses her as his companion during the masked dance: "The fairest hand I ever touch'd! O Beauty, / Till now I never knew thee! (1.4.75–76).

When he learns that she is Anne Bullen, one of Queen Katherine's women, the king names her "a dainty one" (1.4.94) and proceeds to kiss her. Anne feels immense sympathy for Katherine, who has been such an exemplary "lady that no tongue could ever / Pronounce dishonor of her" (2.3.3–4). When Anne declares that she prefers "to be lowly born" and "would not be a queen" (2.3.19, 24), the Old Lady reproaches her for hypocrisy. The Old Lady tells her plainly that she herself would "venture maidenhood for't, and so would you" (2.3.25). The Lord Chamberlain brings word that the king has bestowed on Anne the title of Marchioness of Pembroke and a thousand pounds a year. But Anne is still conscientious about her duties as Katherine's woman and worries that the queen "is comfortless, and we forgetful / In our long absence" (2.3.105–106). Is Anne sincere? Or is she, as the old Lady says, a hypocrite? Anne does not appear again except during her coronation, a scene in which she says nothing. She is absent from the christening because the child is brought in by the Duchess of Norfolk, Elizabeth's godmother.

Cardinal Wolsey

Cardinal Wolsey is proud, arrogant, and ambitious. Abusing his position as Henry's Chancellor, he oppresses people and considers himself more powerful than the king. He aspires to be the pope. He has amassed immense wealth. His brief description in a stage direction in the opening scene fixes his image in the mind of the spectator: "Cardinal Wolsey, the purse borne before him, certain of the Guard, and two Secretaries with papers" (s.d. after 1.1.114). Wolsey and Buckingham exchange glances, "both full of disdain" (ibid.). He plots against Buckingham, and the nobility hate him passionately. When Katherine brings up the charge of excessive taxation, he offers a slippery and deceptive defense against criticism:

> If I am
> Traduc'd by ignorant tongues, which neither know
> My faculties nor person, yet will be
> The chronicles of my doing, let me say
> 'Tis but the fate of place, and the rough brake
> That virtue must go through. (1.2.71–76)

Then he instructs his secretary to "let it be nois'd / That through our intercession this revokement / And pardon comes" (1.2.105–107). Norfolk unmasks Wolsey's character: "How holily he works in all his business! / And with what zeal!" (2.2.23–24). For Shakespeare, Wolsey is corrupt and hypocritical. When Henry gives him the paper to read, the cardinal regrets only his "negligence" or fatal error and not his accumulation of wealth:

> This paper has undone me. 'Tis th'accompt
> Of all that world of wealth I have drawn together
> For mine own ends (indeed to gain the popedom
> And fee my friends in Rome). O negligence!
> Fit for a fool to fall by. What cross devil
> Made me put this main secret in the packet
> I sent the King? Is there no way to cure this? (3.2.210–216)

Now Wolsey recognizes his fall and still shows no remorse for his actions. He shows no sense of regret:

> I have touch'd the highest point of all my greatness,
> And, from that full meridian of my glory,
> I haste now to my setting. I shall fall
> Like a bright exhalation in the evening,
> And no man can see me more. (3.2.223–227)

By saying that he is falling like a meteor, Wolsey is figuratively alluding to Lucifer's fall from heaven. He also laments that the public would not notice his falling star in the evening.

Instead of reviewing his policy of overreaching and conspiring even against the king, Wolsey ponders "the state of man" (3.2.352) and speaks in vague generalities that indicate his lack of self-knowledge. Through misleading imagery, he perceives himself as one of the "little wanton boys" who is at the mercy of "a rude stream:"

> I have ventur'd,
> Like little wanton boys that swim on bladders,
> This many summers in a sea of glory,
> But far beyond my depth. My high-blown pride
> At length broke under me, and now has left me,

Weary and old with service, to the mercy
Of a rude stream that must for ever hide me.
Vain pomp and glory of this world, I hate ye! (3.2.358–365)

Wolsey invokes Lucifer: "when he falls, he falls like Lucifer" (3.2.371). These words from a cardinal confirmed the opinions and fears of the Protestants about the mendacious mores of the Catholic Church.

Yet in the end he says, "I know myself now" (3.2.378). He urges Cromwell to abandon ambition, to "Love thyself last" (3.2.443), to be honest, to serve the king well. In Griffith's words, "he died fearing God" (4.2.68). In 4.2 Katherine presents the case against Wolsey, describing him as ambitious, deceitful, and cruel. Griffith then defends him. The play thus offers two perspectives, and all is true.

Thomas Cranmer

Thomas Cranmer is the moral and theological opposite of Wolsey. King Henry gives him the assignment to collect opinions about his divorce, and he does it efficiently, as reported by Suffolk:

He is return'd in his opinions, which
Have satisfied the King for his divorce,
Together with all famous colleges
Almost in Christendom. (3.2.64–67)

The king saves him when Gardiner and others are plotting against him and accuse him of spreading heresies in the realm (5.2.50–54). Cranmer gets the honor to preside over the christening ceremony and delivers his prophesy about the future of England under Queen Elizabeth and James I. This oracle of comfort pleases Henry VIII the most, and Shakespeare has completed his narration of the restoration of peace, order, and prosperity in the kingdom.

DEVICES AND TECHNIQUES

Shakespeare has filled the play with grand spectacles, exciting trials, and a heavenly vision in an epic structure. The Prologue promises a series of episodes "That bear a weighty and a serious brow, / Sad, high, and working [moving, emotional], full of state and woe" (ll. 2–3). The "noble scenes" (l. 4) will bring tears to the eyes of the spectators. The "great" ones of the country (l. 27) will be "follow'd with the general throng and sweat / Of thousand friends" (ll. 28–29). The play offers twelve grand entrances that exhibit the wealth and glitter of Henry's court. On display are the seal, the cross, the crown, and other marks of secular and religious authority. The cast includes several bishops, lords and ladies, scribes, officers, guards, and other attendants. Queen Katherine has a heavenly vision. These scenes underline the prosperity and accomplishments of the Tudors. Shakespeare uses a popular form of early seventeenth-century entertainment to capture the glamor and glitter of the monarchy. The iconography of these scenes enabled Shakespeare to impress upon the audience the climax of the panorama of his history plays from King John to James I.

The trials are another popular device used most effectively in this play. These confrontations are sensational and highly charged. They give Buckingham, Wolsey, and Katherine a chance to examine their lives and make their peace in different ways. Katherine's is probably the most affecting, because Shakespeare has portrayed her with sympathy and made her just and upright in her dealings. Her vision lets the audience see that she deserves to be rewarded for her virtue and will receive her remuneration in heaven. Buckingham also gets sympathy and tears from the public as a victim of the machinations of Cardinal Wolsey. He wishes to be remembered as loyal to Henry. Cardinal Wolsey, on the other hand, tries to exonerate himself by implying that he is the wretched man that hung on princes' favors and fell like Lucifer. The king proves himself to be in full control when he gives his ring to Cranmer and condemns the counselors for their lies and corruption.

Many of the events in *Henry VIII* are reported and not shown on stage. Shakespeare recreates them with the precision of his language. Norfolk is quite enchanting when he describes the "view of earthly glory" (1.1.13–38) that Buckingham and Aburgavenny had missed in France. The Two Gentlemen give an account of the coronation. By having Griffith relating Wolsey's death scene to Queen Katherine (4.2.11–68), Shakespeare is contrasting the lives of the two, for one will go to heaven and the other's case is not so sure.

Another device Shakespeare has used here and in other plays is music and dance: "Drum and trumpet. Chambers discharged" (s.d. after 1.4.49); "Trumpets, sennet [fanfare], and cornets" (s.d. before 2.4.1). The most emotionally affecting use of music occurs when Queen Katherine and her women are at work in 3.1. The queen says, "Take thy lute, wench, my soul grows sad with troubles" (3.1.1). The maid sings "Orpheus with his lute made trees" to soothe her spirits. Sad and solemn music introduces the queen's vision in 4.2, and the music continues after the six personages clad in white robes have vanished. Trumpets are sounded at the christening ceremony.

Though Aristotle listed music as fifth and spectacle as the sixth and hence least important of the elements of drama, Shakespeare recognizes their importance in pleasing audiences. Moreover, kingship is all about spectacle, the signs of majesty. Buckingham observes that before his trial he was Lord High Constable of England and a duke. After his condemnation he is merely Edward Bohun. Music and spectacle confirm, perhaps even confer, royal legitimacy and hence have thematic significance.

THEMES AND MEANINGS

Shakespeare's primary concerns in *Henry VIII* lie in the uses and abuses of power in relation to justice, injustice, conscience, and truth, and not so much the legitimacy of the monarch's authority that he had explored in the history plays covering the reigns from King John to Richard III. Henry VIII as an ideal ruler can correct his own mistakes and restore integrity to the throne. Shakespeare handles sensitively the problems of justice and injustice under Henry VIII. Does the king act justly in different trials? Could he have saved Buckingham? Did he treat Katherine justly? Some of his nobility had wondered if it was really his conscience that bothered him or if it was his meeting with Anne Bullen that cemented his resolve for divorce. Shakespeare lets the matter rest there. Henry took a while to grasp the extent of Wolsey's crimes, but he acted quickly once he understood them. When Cranmer is in trouble, even Henry VIII admits that justice does not always go with truth. The king counsels his archbishop that "not ever / The justice and the truth o' th' question carries / The due o' th' verdict with it" (5.1.129–131). But he assures Cranmer that Gardiner and other counselors "shall no more prevail than we give way to" (5.1.143).

Shakespeare brings up the theme of conscience or a person's awareness of right and wrong in moral law as a guide to his or her actions instead of the authority of the Church and its priests. He underlines how individuals vary in their appeals to it. Buckingham rightly swears by his conscience that he is loyal to the king. When the Lord Chamberlain suggests that the king's "marriage with his brother's wife / Has crept too near his conscience," the Duke of Suffolk replies, "No, his conscience / Has crept too near another lady" (2.2.16–18). The king has a "wounded conscience" (2.2.74). He does not want to divorce Queen Katherine but he is troubled by "conscience, conscience" (2.2.142). Drifting to and fro in the "wild sea of my conscience," the king sought "to rectify my conscience" (2.4.201, 204). After his fall, Wolsey makes the dubious claim that he has acquired a "still and quiet conscience" (3.2.380); he wishes that the new Lord Chancellor, Sir Thomas More, would "do justice / For truth's sake and his conscience" (3.2.396–397), something he himself did not do. Thomas Cranmer has detested the disturbers of public peace "in his private conscience and place" (5.2.75). Shakespeare is saying that a person's sense of right or wrong is not an abstraction; it is tied up with the social, religious, and political contexts in which he or she is making a decision. The king, for example, is justified in saying that he became aware of his marriage problem when the French raised questions about Mary's legitimacy as his daughter. He cannot be accused of falsifying the reasons for his action.

Yet the relativity of truth and the rightness of one's choices in personal and political matters depending on the specific perspective of an individual is another concern of Shakespeare's in the play, as the work's alternate title indicates. The Surveyor takes an oath: "I'll speak only truth" (1.2.177), but he tells only lies. As Buckingham complains, these are the liars "That never knew what truth meant" (2.1.105). The first rumors about Henry and Anne Bullen are a slander, but they turn out to be "a truth" (2.1.154). Katherine points out that Wolsey is not "a friend to truth" (2.4.84) because "truth loves open dealing" (3.1.339). Wolsey swears that he has served the king faithfully as will appear "When the King knows my truth" (3.2.302). Ironically, the king at this point does know, and Wolsey's false dealings cause his downfall. In spite of his lying, Wolsey advises Cromwell that his goals should "be thy country's, / Thy God's, and truth's" (3.2.447–448). Archbishop Cranmer prophesies that "Truth shall nurse" Queen Elizabeth I (5.4.28) and that "Peace, plenty, love, truth, terror" (5.4.47) will prevail in the kingdom. All may be true, but the truth embodied in the king and country triumphs at the end.

Before Cranmer can assert that the good he stands on is his "truth and honesty" (5.1.122), Henry VIII has stressed the Archbishop's dependence on royal authority: "Thy truth and thy integrity is rooted / In us, thy friend" (5.1.114–115). In his treatment of conscience and truth, Shakespeare is describing what men do, as Francis Bacon has put it: "We are much beholden to Machiavelli and other writers of that class, who openly and unfeignedly declare or describe what men do, and not what they ought to do" (*De Augmentis, Works*, ed. James Spedding, 15 vols. [Boston: Taggard and

Thompson, 1860–1864], 9: 211). Buckingham's truth is not enough to save him, and Cranmer's might not be without the help of the king. The play thus questions not only what is true but also what is the value of that truth when it lacks power.

CRITICAL CONTROVERSIES

The questions about the authorship of *Henry VIII* have contributed to doubts about its effectiveness. Written late in Shakespeare's career, perhaps after he had retired to Stratford, it is debatable whether it should be treated as a one of the romances or as a sequel to earlier histories. Irving Ribner dismisses it as deficient in its underlying philosophy: "The weakness of *Henry VIII* results from its failure to embody an over-all consistent philosophical scheme such as makes cohesive unities out of all of Shakespeare's earlier histories, including *King John*" (*The English History Play in the Age of Shakespeare* [Princeton: Princeton UP, 1957], 290). Several scholars have expressed dissatisfaction with Shakespeare's reading of history. Howard Felperin complains that Shakespeare's "golden age represents not creation out of nothing but the distortion of something, a gilded age passed off as a golden, and as such is hardly more than glorified propaganda." Felperin (*Shakespearean Romance* [Princeton: Princeton UP, 1972], 209) adds,

> Shakespeare's exclusion of the nastier aspects of a reign littered with corpses and haunted by ghosts, his all too orthodox whitewashing of Henry himself, and that wishful prophecy of glory under James I simply will not abide our questions—questions that the history form fairly demands that we ask.

G. K. Hunter characterizes the play as "a series of brilliant rhetorical moments linked together without being attached to an overriding purpose" (*English Drama 1586–1642: The Age of Shakespeare* [Oxford: Clarendon P, 1997], 268). Some critics object that the characters are weak and not fully developed. They find that play is morally ambiguous in its portrayal of Queen Katherine. There is too much reliance upon rhetoric and declamation, and some of the speeches are too general and detached from the speakers. Samuel Johnson in 1765 declared that the play remained popular because of its spectacle. He felt that "the genius of Shakespeare comes in and out with Catherine. Every other part may be easily conceived, and easily written" (*Johnson on Shakespeare*, ed. Arthur Sherbo [New Haven: Yale UP, 1968], 657).

G. Wilson Knight was one of the first to answer these objections. For him, the play has an epic rather than a dramatic structure. Whereas the earlier history plays

> were moralistic, on the pattern of medieval stories of the falls of princes, [*Henry VIII* is] eminently Elizabethan. Effects are deliberately got by juxtaposition, as when Buckingham's execution follows Wolsey's feast and the death of Katharine the coronation of Anne. We attend diversely two views of human existence; the tragic and religious as opposed by the warm, sex-impelled, blood; the eternities of death as against the glow and thrill of incarnate life, of creation. These two themes meet in the person of the King. (306)

"In Henry," Knight proposes, "we have a strength of life, a social sanity and commonsense, set against the profundities of tragedy and overruling the subtleties of religious disquisition" (314).

Looking at *Henry VIII* as one of Shakespeare's romances, Foakes emphasizes some of its similarities with them. Like Prospero, the king has the duty "to control, to intervene in events involving others, to act as an agent or an organizer for most of the play, and this aspect of him, as high-priest, beneficent controller, should appear most strongly at the end of the play and after the fall of Wolsey" (lxiii). Placing *Henry VIII* in the last year of Shakespeare's professional life, Foakes considers it "as the last innovation of a mind forever exploring; and if the history of its supposed deficiencies can be forgotten, then the conception of the play may be allowed its full originality, as a felicitous new solution to problems posed by the nature of the material with which Shakespeare's last plays deal" (lxiv).

Jay L. Halio finds that "the play is fascinating in its own right" (25). He points out "how the various episodes relate to each other and build to a climax at the end" (26). Halio stresses the coherence of the play's political message about the use and abuse of power and Henry's emergence as a strong monarch who can hold the country together the way Queen Elizabeth I did and the way James I is doing. The peaceful ascendancy of James I assured the country's future. Henry VIII is a model for James I, because, according to Halio, Henry "has become a successful and powerful king, and in the context that Shakespeare presents, that is something" (38). The playwright has modified and molded the events of Henry's reign into a tribute to James I, "though Shakespeare like some others in his audience and among his colleagues will not live to see it completely unfold" (38).

Some critics have seen the play as dealing with political truths of the Jacobean age: for example, Frances A. Yates, *Shakespeare's Last Plays: A New Approach* (London: Routledge and Kegan Paul, 1975); W. M. Baillie, "*Henry VIII*: A Jacobean History," (*Shakespeare Studies* 12 [1979]: 247–266). Others have focused on more philosophical aspects. Among these latter are Alexander Leggett, "*Henry VIII* and the Ideal England" (*Shakespeare Survey* 38 [1985]: 131–143), and T. McBride, "*Henry VIII* as Machiavellian Romance" (*JEGP* 76 [1977]: 26–39). Lee Bliss, "The Wheel of Fortune and the Maiden Phoenix in Shakespeare's *Henry VIII* (*ELH* 42 [1975]: 1–25); E. I. Berry, "*Henry VIII* and the Dynamics of Spectacle" (*Shakespeare Studies* 12 [1979]: 229–246); and F. V. Cespedes, "'We are one in fortunes': The Sense of History in *Henry VIII*" (*ELH* 45 [1978]: 413–438) also discuss the nature of truth and ambiguity in the play.

PRODUCTION HISTORY

During a performance of *Henry VIII* the Globe burnt down on June 29, 1613; a new Globe was built and opened a year later. The next known production of *Henry VIII* did not come about until July 1628. It had been "bespoken of purpose" by George Villiers, Duke of Buckingham, who attended a performance prior to his own assassination that year. He "stayd till ye Duke of Buckingham was beheaded, & then departed" (quoted in Foakes, lxiv). There are no records of any other revival until after the Restoration.

Henry VIII was assigned to Sir William Davenant as one of a collection of Shakespeare plays that he was entitled to produce at Lincoln's Inn Fields. John Downes comments on a performance he saw in December 1663:

This play, by Order of Sir William Davenant, was all new Cloath'd in proper Habits: the King's was new, all the Lords, the Cardinals, the Bishops, the Doctors, Proctors,

> Lawyers, Tip-staves, new Scenes: The part of the King was so right and justly done by Mr. Betterton, he being Instructed in it by Sir William, who had it from Old Mr. Lowen, that had his Instructions from Mr. Shakespear himself, that I dare and will aver, none can, or will come near him in this Age, in the performance of that part: Mr. Harris's performance of Cardinal Wolsey, was little Inferior to that, he doing it with such just State, Port and Mein, that I dare affirm, none hitherto has Equall'd him.

Downes praises the high production values of Davenant's company: "Every part by the great Care of Sir William, being exactly perform'd; it being all new Cloath'd and new Scenes; it continu'd Acting 15 Days together with general applause" (*Roscius Anglicanus*, ed. Judith Milhous and Robert D. Hume [London: Society for Theatre Research, 1987], 55–56). The play continued to be produced frequently in the eighteenth and early nineteenth century even if the audiences watched only truncated or altered versions. Muriel St. Clare Byrne classifies it as "perhaps the most viciously and unintelligently cut play in the whole canon" ("A Stratford Production: *Henry VIII*," *Theatre Survey* 3 [1950]: 120).

Famous actors like Thomas Betterton and James Quin played the role of Henry VIII. Colley Cibber mounted a lavish production at Drury Lane in 1727 to mark the coronation of George II. Charles Macklin and David Garrick included it in their repertories. Mary Porter from 1722 to 1733 and Hannah Pritchard from 1744 to 1761 excelled in the role of Queen Katherine. Thomas Davies stated that Mrs. Porter's "manner was elevated to the rank of the great person she represented":

> Her kneeling to the King was the effect of majesty in distress and humbled royalty; it was indeed highly affecting; the suppression of her tears when she reproached the Cardinal, bespoke a tumultuous conflict in her mind, before she burst into the manifestation of indignity, she felt in being obliged to answer so unworthy an interrogator. (*Dramatic Miscellannies*, 3 vols. [1784], 1.385)

Mrs. Pitchard's queen "has been much approved, and especially in the scene of the trial. She certainly was in behaviour easy, and in speaking natural and familiar; but the situation of the character required more force in utterance and dignity in action" (ibid.).

After Garrick's retirement from the stage in 1776, Kemble was a leading figure whose acting, according to Alan Downer, was "neoclassical in its accent on dignity, on carefully planned and minimal action, on rhetorical speech, on claptraps and addresses to the audience" ("Nature to Advantage Dressed: Eighteenth Century Acting," *PMLA* 58 [1943]: 1021). Kemble won praise for a revival in 1788 in which he played Wolsey against his sister, Sarah Siddons, as Katherine. According to Hugh Richmond, Siddons "achieved for Katherine far more than parity of interest with Henry VIII and Wolsey. In the course of defining her own role in the play she required of her fellow actors a shift in performance style towards the less 'macho' mode of interpreting Henry which remains identifiable in many twentieth-century production of the play such as Benthall's (1958)" (42).

From the 1850s to World War I, Charles Kean, Henry Irving, and Herbert Beerbohm Tree produced *Henry VIII* in a manner of extravagant opulence that had not been known before and would not be attempted afterwards. They spent lavishly on realistic sets and costumes. In 1855 Kean attempted "that scrupulous adherence to historical truth in costume, architecture, and the multiplied details of action, which modern taste demands." This was "a vivid resurrection of persons, places and events." It "was by far the most ambitious presentation as to splendour of background and pageantry of action that had ever been attempted, and considerable trouble was taken that the scenery might be historically correct." The finality was "a spectacular scene of pageantry in the church of the Grey Friars, restoring as far as it was possible to conceive, the interior appearance of the edifice at the time" (Cumberland Clark, *A Study of Shakespeare's Henry VIII* [London: Mitre P, 1938], 217–218).

Henry Irving developed further the spectacular effects to which Kean had devoted much of his energy. Welcoming the challenge to surpass others in gorgeous costumes, pageantry, and procession, Irving's was "the greatest in its own line to the time of its appearance" (George C. D. Odell, *Shakespeare from Betterton to Irving*, 2 vols. [New York: Charles Scribner's, 1920], 2.444). *Dramatic Notes* describes some of the spectacular effects:

> Scene I shows us the interior of the Palace at Bridewell, where Buckingham is the only one who will not doff his hat to the proud Cardinal, on his arrival with his almost kingly retinue. In Scene II we have the arrest of Buckingham; and Scene III is the Council Chamber of the Palace, where are seated bluff King Hal and Katharine, in all the pomp of state. "A Hall in York Palace" (Scene V) is the representation of a superb banquet given by Wolsey. (quoted in Odell, 2.444)

The most sensationally spectacular scene created by Irvings's designers is "a genuine reproduction of old London, 'A Street in Westminster,' with its three-storied wooden-beamed houses, at every casement of which are citizens and their wives and daughters" (Odell, 2.445). In awe of a spectacle of this magnitude, audiences seemed to pay little attention to the words.

Incredible as it may seem, Herbert Beerbohm Tree surpassed Irving in the dimensions of a spectacle. Tree's revival of *Henry VIII* in September 1910 in London and then in the United States in 1916 "was a revelation of old-time splendour in theatrical mounting, and still lives in memory as perhaps the most gorgeous thing ever attempted in that line of staging. It was so regarded in London" (Odell, 2.464). The East Anglian *Daily Times* (3 September 1910) underlines the excesses in scenery and costumes:

> Red-brown brick wall, the green and scarlet and gold and grey of the nobles' dress, the slow plain-song chant, the white-robed choir, sable-clad monks, and the resplendent crimson-gowned Cardinal, all this merges and blends into a glorious harmony, which needs no words to make it intelligible.

The London *Times* (2 September 1910) captures the sensual quality of the production.

> To see this King and the saucy little Anne in the revels of Wolsey's Palace is a flagrantly sensual experience. The sheer animalism of the King! Henry leers, kisses, smacks his lips. Anne ogles and frisks. The general company executes a Bacchanalian dance. It is a triumph of flesh and the devil. Immediately there follows the greatest possible contrast, the solemn tenderness of Buckingham's farewell on his way to death.

The paper concluded: "You are chastened and ashamed of your delight in the preceding orgy."

Arthur Bourchier represented Henry VIII in all the physical details so that he looked every inch a king:

> His make-up is nothing short of marvellous. The beard is only the beginning of it. The whole character seems to be there before he has said "Ha!" embodied in solid flesh, a mass of arrogant strength, of keen, remorseless, selfishness and self-confidence, of cunning, of knowledge, of mastery of men, of ready hypocrisy, and immense practical ability, of unbridled lust and invincible determination, all cloaked with a brisk and "bluff" geniality of the "faux bonhomme." (London *Daily Chronicle*, 2 September 1910)

One commendable result of Tree's expenses was that "he . . . made Shakespeare popular" (*Sporting Life*, 26 January 1911). However, no producer tried to emulate the spectacular excesses of Kean, Irving, and Tree after them. Shakespeareans have little regard for these extravaganzas because they cut and mutilated the text of *Henry VIII*.

Tyrone Guthrie revived the play three times: in 1933 at Sadler's Wells with Charles Laughton as Henry; in 1949 at Stratford-upon-Avon; and in 1953 at the Old Vic Theatre for the coronation of Queen Elizabeth II. His 1949 revival "had a pivotal role in restoring the play's waning popularity after the abandonment of the florid historicism epitomised by the productions of Beerbohm Tree" (Richmond, 75). Byrne gives a full account of Guthrie's interpretation, starting with his decision to select the Old Lady, Ann Bullen's friend (played by Wynne Clark), for delivering the Prologue. This proved to be "a sound device to associate its serious and pertinent comment with the theme of the Tudor succession which is responsible for the whole structure of the play." Clark was "a perfect Holbein portrait to look at, and she seized her twofold opportunity firmly; the quality of life in her, the persuasive zest of her way of speaking and the authenticity of her appearance, all struck the dominant note of the entire production." The stress put on the "truth" of the play, "our chosen truth, came over with full force as she drew us straight into a novel intimacy, speaking from the extreme front forestage (left)" (121). The spectators got engaged with the motives and intentions of Wolsey and the nobility and the king's disputes with the Catholic Church over his divorce.

Harold Hobson (London *Sunday Times*, 27 July 1949) provides a vivid picture of the challenging aspect of the production which would have surprised Shakespeare:

> Mr. Guthrie has come along to give Henry VIII a kick in the pants. The kick is well-aimed and neatly delivered, and it propels the play along at a rattling pace, even if it loses dignity in the process. There is always something happening to titillate the eye or the ear, and most of it would have been as fresh to Shakespeare as it was to the first-night audience. Whilst Cranmer delivers his grandiose address in honour of the infant Princess Elizabeth, the Duchess of Norfolk explodes in a mighty sneeze. In the scene where the scriveners take down Queen Katherine's plea for leniency, priests scribbling away on their parchment are rolled about the floor like bowls by careless courtiers.

Guthrie's unusual decisions made some of the spectators uncomfortable, but still they preferred his focus on a new reading of the text. Guthrie may not have satisfied everyone. Still, his production "unquestionably restored vitality, viability and

(Left to right) Walter Hampden as Cardinal Wolsey, Victor Jory as Henry VIII, and Eva Le Gallienne as Katherine of Aragón in the American Repertory Theatre's production of *Henry VIII*, which ran from November 6, 1946 to February 21, 1947. Courtesy of Photofest.

plausibility to a misunderstood script, thus ensuring that any future productions of it would not be vitiated by the prejudice based on the assumption that it was a dull, forced, incoherent production of a divided authorship" (Richmond, 89).

When Trevor Nunn took up the play at the Royal Shakespeare Company again in 1969, he gave it an openly political twist, as Richmond explains: "We were invited to see a more consciously political interpretation of the script than was customary: the costly evolution of a political despotism dangerously dependent on the personal character of the monarch" (93). Donald Sinden's Henry VIII was weighed down by the enormity of events he was immersed in, as Harold Hobson (London *Sunday Times*, 12 October 1969) describes it:

> This Henry threads his path through the play as if haunted by the murders he has not yet committed, his spirit wasted by the consciousness of years of lechery he as yet knows nothing of, the magnificent and aggressive Holbein body contradicted by the dead soul within. After the gorgeous apparel of the celebrants of the infant Elizabeth's christening, when everyone else for the last time has left the stage, Mr. Sinden's Henry also departs, but as he leaves he half turns, and momentarily gazes at the audience. His face is very strange; it is blanched and weary, and it seems in some inexplicable way to be questioning the future, questioning it with fatigue and apprehension.

In Hobson's words, "Mr. Sinden's Henry is capable of both crime and poetry as the bluff king Hal of tradition could never be."

Peggy Ashcroft played Queen Katherine sensitively and intelligently, and, as Trevor Nunn recalls "had become obsessed with Katherine of Aragon to the point where she brought into rehearsals every kind of defence of the character" (Richmond, 98). The reviewer of the London *Financial Times* (10 October 1969) extolled the production for turning Katherine into someone the audiences sympathize with so sincerely.

In 1979, Kevin Billington prepared the television production for the British Broadcasting Company in which, following Henry Irving and Herbert Beerbohm Tree's stress on verisimilitude, there was "a sustained insistence on authenticity of visual impressions and on vocal naturalism" (Richmond, 109). They shot it on location at Leeds Castle, Penshurst Place, and Hever Castle, all of which were connected with Henry VIII. John Stride played the King, with Claire Bloom as Queen Katherine and Timothy West as Cardinal Wolsey. Alan Shallcross describes how, working on the production, he realized that "each scene had a dynamic that I had simply not remembered from the theatre," because, "while traditional staging has exaggerated scenic effects to the disadvantage of the ultimate private and personal issues towards which the play progresses, television can correct the imbalance by its concentration on the individual's inward condition" (Richmond, 119). The company effectively used "the close-up, often in harmony with the play's consistent sense of covert political manipulations going on behind elaborate public facades" (Richmond, 113). Claire Bloom gave the most naturalistic performance which displays her closeness with the king in the early scenes: "The casual affection of her holding hands with Henry while enthroned, or of discreetly touching his knee to convey a point, registers her affection and concern with the greatest delicacy in ways almost impossible to communicate on the stage." This Katherine "emerges as the spokeswoman for purely private values in a society excessively concerned with public policy and political advantage" (Richmond, 117).

In 1983, Howard Davies directed Richard Griffiths, Gemma Jones, and John Thaw in the roles of Henry VIII, Queen Katherine, and Cardinal Wolsey, respectively in a highly controversial production. This production sought "to expose to view the duplicities and evasions usually cloaked in performance by mellifluence and magniloquence" (Philip Brockbank, *Times Literary Supplement*, 24 June 1983). Hence it "is very much a modern play, dealing with taxes, unemployment and social divisions," wrote the Birmingham *Post* reviewer (15 June 1983). Davies presented "a lively contemporary synthesis of almost all the positive elements in the precedents, through a production which was both genuinely modern in its stress on political ruthlessness yet also achieved a remarkable documentary fidelity to some of the most vivid surviving visual impression of Henry's historical court" (Richmond, 124).

Gregory Doran mounted *Henry VIII* at the Royal Shakespeare Company's Swan Theatre (Stratford-upon-Avon) in November of 1996. According to Robert Smallwood, Doran juxtaposed the "gaudy power shows with the everyday world of intrigue and jostling for position around the King":

> In contrast to the golden shows, the costumes in other scenes were mostly in subdued colours, greys, blacks, dark greens, a world in which the crimson robe and biretta of Ian Hogg's Wolsey, his podgy features and peering little eyes interrupting the silken sleekness, shone out like a beacon. (*Shakespeare Survey* 51 [1998]: 239–240)

Jane Lapotaire's Queen Katherine "spoke with a slight Spanish accent, which marked her off as the 'stranger' which she so often feels herself to be, and moved through the play with the sort of commanding dignity which made her frequent references to herself as a 'poor weak woman' seem more than usually ironic" (Smallwood, 240). Paul Jesson's "Henry, round-faced, crew-cut, ebullient, was an admirably enigmatic creation—and a triumph for the costume department, which managed to make him seem half as wide again across the shoulders as anyone else on stage (or in Tudor England)" (Smallwood, 241). Still, "for all the role's casual self-esteem and bullying self-assertion, for all the unthinking, unquestioning acceptance of absolute power, Jesson never allowed us the easy route to outright dislike of the man, for he, like the rest, was seen to be driven by the dictates of the power game, by the inexorable requirement that he beget an heir to continue the dynasty of which he is but the temporary representative" (ibid.).

These recent productions of *Henry VIII* prove that it need not be a slow-moving sequence of spectacle and pageantry. Like many of Shakespeare's plays, it goes far beyond offering a mere piece of propaganda for the Tudor monarchy or an unsophisticated delineation of characters. No director can exhaust its themes and meanings in a single performance.

EXPLICATION OF KEY PASSAGES

2.1.100–136. "Nay, Sir Nicholas, . . . forgive me." A victim of Cardinal Wolsey's plots and the false testimony of his own surveyor, the Duke of Buckingham has been convicted of high treason by his peers. He bears the verdict with most noble patience. People still love and dote on "bounteous Buckingham" (2.1.52). Sir Nicholas Vaux is ready to convey him to the Tower of London on a barge furnished with everything appropriate for his rank. In his last address, Buckingham delivers an account of his loyalty and accuses his enemies of disloyalty.

He rejects Sir Nicholas Vaux's offer of an elaborate conveyance, claiming that his conviction has stripped him of his titles and left him a plain subject. He speaks of his father's loyalty to Henry VII, father of Henry VIII, and of his own fealty to the current king. Buckingham's father was betrayed by a servant, as so is he. Buckingham warns his listeners against false friends, asks for the prayers of those present, and concludes with the hope that when people want a sad story, they will tell of his fall.

Buckingham's fall foreshadows Katherine's, and Henry's inaction here reveals that he has not understood Wolsey's treachery. Shakespeare wins sympathy for the duke to highlight Wolsey's evil nature.

2.4.13–64; 74–84; 105–121. "Sir, I desire you . . . judg'd by him." In these three speeches Katherine presents her case to her judges and to the audience. She is more successful in winning the sympathy of the latter than the former. Shakespeare draws many of the details of this section from Raphael Holinshed's *Chronicles* (1587).

She begins by noting that she is a foreigner facing a hostile court. Yet she states that she has been a good wife to Henry for more than twenty years. As to the legitimacy of the marriage, Katherine observes that Henry VIII's father, Henry VII, and her father, King Ferdinand of Spain (of Ferdinand and Isabella fame) were regarded as wise men, and they approved the match. She asks in her first speech that she be allowed to consult her friends in Spain.

Wolsey denies this request, and Katherine addresses him. Calling him the one who has "blown this coal betwixt my lord and me" (2.4.79), she rejects him as her judge. Wolsey denies that he is her enemy, but she again criticizes him. He pretends to humility, she says, but his "heart / Is cramm'd with arrogancy, spleen, and pride" (2.4.110). Rejecting the jurisdiction of the court, she appeals to Rome.

For a Protestant audience, such a request for papal intervention would have seemed disloyal. Yet Katherine clearly is right in saying that she cannot get a fair trial from Wolsey, and Wolsey is far less sympathetic than the queen. Even audiences who understood that Henry's marriage to Anne Bullen will lead to the golden age of Elizabeth will recognize that Katherine is a good person caught in a bad situation.

2.4.156–210. "My Lord Cardinal . . . first mov'd you." Queen Katherine leaves the court in protest over the proceedings against her. The king still acknowledges that no man can claim to have a better wife than his. Cardinal Wolsey is nervous and confides in the king that he has done nothing prejudicial against her. The king assures the cardinal of his trust in him and explains what has moved him to seek an annulment. When Henry was trying to arrange a marriage between his daughter Mary Tudor and the Duke of Orleance, future king of France, the Bishop of Bayonne, then the ambassador from France, raised the question of Mary's legitimacy because Henry had married his own brother's wife.

Henry then began to question the validity of his marriage to Katherine. He noted that their male children died in miscarriages or shortly after birth. Worried about England's future without a male heir, he wanted to "rectify my conscience" (2.4.204) to determine whether his marriage to Katherine was incestuous or not. Hence he appealed to the Bishop of Lincoln and then the Archbishop of Canterbury.

What really motivates Henry? Is it conscience? Does he think that for England's sake he needs a male heir and that Katherine can't provide a son? Does he want to divorce Katherine so he will be free to marry Anne Bullen? Henry's speeches address the first two of these questions. The scene just before the trial addresses the third, as the Old Lady recognizes that Henry wants Anne, and that Anne would "venture maidenhead" to be queen (2.4.25). Shakespeare allows Henry all three motives. The king is not a lustful villain, but he is not a disinterested ruler, either.

3.2.428–457. "Cromwell, I did not . . . to mine enemies." Henry VIII has discovered how much wealth Cardinal Wolsey has accumulated in his effort to gain the papal crown by bribing his friends at the Vatican. The king orders him to surrender the seal and strips him of authority. Since Wolsey is charged with asserting papal jurisdiction in England, thus preempting royal authority, he is subject to the writ of praemunire, under which the crown confiscates all his property and lands. Cromwell, servant to Wolsey, comforts and consoles him at this dark moment and weeps. Wolsey cannot keep from crying, too. Recognizing that he is doomed to death and oblivion (Henry VIII would rename Cardinal College, Oxford, as Christ Church and efface the cardinal's arms at Hampton Court), Wolsey asks that Cromwell keep Wolsey's memory alive by saying that the cardinal taught him how to act. Wolsey's lesson is Christian: he tells Cromwell to shun ambition, "Love thyself last" (3.2.442), be charitable to his enemies, be just, and serve his country, God, and truth.

Even such proceedings do not guarantee success, as the audience has seen in the cases of Katherine and Buckingham. But if Cromwell falls as an honest man, at least he will do so as "a blessed martyr" (3.2.449). Wolsey, who had not behaved as he instructs Cromwell, compares his fall to that of Lucifer. Wolsey concludes here with the sentiment Holinshed attributes to him: "Had I but serv'd my God with half the zeal / I serv'd my king, He would not in mine age / Have left me naked to mine enemies" (3.2.445–447). Abandoning any hope but in heaven, he exits. The next time the audience hears about him, he is dead.

Does Wolsey achieve self-knowledge and repentance in the end? The advice he gives Cromwell is sound Renaissance doctrine for the servant of the prince, and Wolsey recognizes that he has not behaved as he should have. Yet his final words indicate that he thought that while he was not serving God, he was serving Henry. The play shows that in fact Wolsey was always serving himself, even at the expense of the king. As the conversation about Wolsey between Katherine and Griffith in 4.2 demonstrates, the cardinal remains enigmatic.

5.4.14–55. "Let me speak, . . . and bless heaven." Henry VIII's daughter Elizabeth is about to be christened. The king and the nobility have gathered for the festive occasion. The king kisses the child, and Cranmer, Archbishop of Canterbury, delivers the sermon. There is no ambiguity here. Elizabeth will be as wise and virtuous as the Queen of Sheba. "Truth shall nurse her, / Holy and heavenly thoughts still counsel her" (5.4.28–29). She will be victorious over her enemies; Shakespeare's audience would think immediately of the defeat of the Spanish Armada in 1588. Hers will be a golden age, an age of "merrie olde England," where the Biblical vision of each man sitting under his own vine will be fulfilled.

Cranmer compares Elizabeth to the phoenix, which reproduces asexually by dying in a fire from which a young and more beautiful phoenix emerges. So Elizabeth will have no children, but her successor, James I, will inherit from her "Peace, plenty, love, truth, terror" (5.4.47). He will be a great king and "make new nations" (5.4.52), that is, the first permanent British settlement in the New World, Jamestown.

One would like to think that Shakespeare and not Fletcher penned this panegyric to the Elizabethan age, the age that made Shakespeare and that he in turn helped make glorious. It rings with that same love of England as John of Gaunt's speech in *Richard II*, 2.1.40ff ("This royal throne of kings, . . ."), and it offers a nostalgic and not altogether false synopsis of the reign that inaugurated the first British empire, that gave the world the plays of Shakespeare, Christopher Marlowe, and Ben Jonson, the poetry of Edmund Spenser and Sir Philip Sidney, the music of William Byrd and Thomas Tallis. It seems only right that this English Renaissance should be celebrated by one of its greatest products.

Annotated Bibliography

Bliss, Lee. "The Wheel of Fortune and the Maiden Phoenix in Shakespeare's *King Henry the Eighth*." *ELH* 42 (1975): 1–25. Henry VIII "is both the center of court power within the play and the focal point for a dramatic structure distinguished by constant and alarming shifts in its perspective on character and action. With a clear view of the way in which the play builds its disturbing effects, perhaps the final prophecy will seem less a retreat into fantasy (or obsequious flattery) than a significant, dramatically appropriate discontinuity" (3).

Cox, John D. "*Henry VIII* and the Masque." *ELH* 45 (1978): 390–409. Argues that in this play Shakespeare uses the conventions of the court masque for public drama.

Foakes, R. A., ed. *King Henry VIII*. The Arden Shakespeare. London: Methuen, 1964. Contains a full introduction and appendices (on the burning of the Globe Theatre and on the play's sources), stage history, and exhaustive textual criticism and annotations.

Halio, Jay L., ed. *King Henry VIII, or All Is True*. The Oxford Shakespeare. Oxford: Oxford UP, 1999. Provides modern-spelling text, commentary, and notes; introduction discusses the date of composition, sources, performances, and changing critical perspectives on the play.

Hunt, Maurice. "Shakespeare's *King Henry VIII* and the Triumph of the Word." *English Studies* 75 (1994): 225–245. *Henry VIII* and late romances reveal Shakespeare's stress on the redemptive function of speech: in most of *Henry VIII*, Shakespeare uses language to show decline and loss. However, Hunt argues that Cranmer's prophecy in the fifth act redeems the play and converts it from tragedy to a triumphant working out of a providential plan.

Knight, G. Wilson. "*Henry VIII* and the Poetry of Conversion." In *The Crown of Life*. London: Methuen, 1948. 256–336. Knight examines the authorship controversy to argue for Shakespeare's sole claim and the relationship of *Henry VIII* to his earlier plays; he proposes that the play draws on the ideas and skills that Shakespeare had developed in creating plays like *Macbeth*, *Timon of Athens*, and *Pericles*. In Cranmer's final prophecy, Shakespeare defines the English spirit.

McMullan, Gordon, ed. *King Henry VIII*. The Arden Shakespeare. London: Thomson Learning, 2000. Provides an introduction to the context of Britain's history and culture, discusses the play's stage performances, and includes detailed notes and commentary on the text and a survey of critical approaches.

Richmond, Hugh M. *Shakespeare in Performance: King Henry VIII*. Manchester, Eng.: Manchester UP, 1994. A comparative study of six productions: Beerbohm Tree (1910), Tyrone Guthrie (1949), Trevor Nunn (1969), Kevin Billington (1978), Howard Davis (1983), and Paul Shepard (1990). Richmond defends Shakespeare's authorship of the play and argues against the notion that the work shows any decline in Shakespere's powers.

Slights, Camille Wells. "The Politics of Conscience in *All Is True* (or *Henry VIII*)." *Shakespeare Survey* 43 (1991): 59–68. This play "embodies the sardonic but compassionate perception that to follow one's conscience—that is, to act according to one's personal understanding of moral law while attending to particular circumstance and probable consequence—is the only way to live at peace with oneself, but may also incur and inflict suffering" (68).